Richard Furman

Life and Legacy

Richard Furman

Life and Legacy

by
James A. Rogers

MERCER

ISBN 0-86554-151-5

All books published by Mercer University Press are produced on
acid-free paper that exceeds the minimum standards set by the
National Historical Publications and Records Commission.

Library of Congress Cataloging in Publication Data
Rogers, James A. (James Alton), 1905–
Richard Furman: life and legacy
Bibliography: p. 315.
Includes index.
1. Furman, Richard, 1755–1825. 2. Baptists—
United States—Clergy—Biography. I. Title.
BX6495.F85R64   1985   286'.1'0924 [B]   84-27248
ISBN 0-86554-151-5 (alk. paper)

Contents

Dedication

To the memory of Alester Garden Furman, Jr., great-great-grandson of Richard Furman, whose interest inspired this work and who in his person, and as businessman, industrialist, educator, community leader, churchman, and benefactor, faithfully interpreted for his time the heritage of his revered ancestor.

According to the grace of God which is given to me, as a wise master builder, I have laid the foundation, and another buildeth thereon; but let every man take heed how he buildeth thereupon.

1 Corinthians 3:10

Author's Note

In quotations from correspondence between Richard Furman and members of his family or his contemporaries, capitalization, spelling, and punctuation remain as they appear in the original letters unless, in the case of punctuation, a change is necessary for clarity.

Abbreviations in the footnotes are listed below.

SCBHS South Carolina Baptist Historical Society Collection

SCHM South Carolina Historical Magazine

JCC Journal of the Constitutional Convention of South Carolina

ACKNOWLEDGMENTS

Richard Furman was an early shaper of American educational and religious life. The best-known part of his legacy is Furman University, the institution in Greenville, South Carolina, that bears his name. His contributions, however, cannot be limited to a single institution. Seldom is there encompassed within one person so varied an involvement as during the seventy years of Furman's lifetime when America was in the making. Self-education, war, political and religious liberty, secular and religious education, denominational structuring and leadership, domestic and foreign missions, preaching and pastoral ministering, plantation management, parenthood, the duties of citizenship—all involved him in a life as fruitful as it was busy. Though Furman died in 1825, until now no attempt has been made to draw available source material together in a full-length biography.

The genesis of this work was in the mind of Alester Garden Furman, Jr., great-great-grandson of Richard Furman. As one of his many benefactions to Furman University, he wished to see the story of his forebear recorded more thoroughly than in existing references. To that end, prior to his death in December 1981, he placed the financial resources for such a work with the administration of Furman University. Associated with and supportive of him in this objective from the beginning has been his son, Alester Garden Furman III. Never has a more pleasant relationship existed between author and benefactors.

Because many factors went into his development, Furman cannot be separated from either the secular or the religious events of his times. Beginning with his conversion, religion was his element. In it he lived, thought, moved, and worked. But he did not view or experience religion in isolation. He understood the connection between political and religious liberty, and the importance of education to an effective ministry and enlightened society. As a leader among early American Baptists, he was a principal figure in laying foundations in education, missions, and denominational structure that are surviving influences in twentieth-century America.

In his personal life, he reflected the gravity of his Puritan heritage and the piety, in the best meaning of that term, typical of early American religious leaders. Remarkable habits of self-motivation, intellectual curiosity, gentleness of spirit, and human compassion were personal characteristics.

The treatment of his life has been done, in part, chronologically, and, in part, topically. Chronology seemed the better approach up to the years of his long Charleston pastorate. From that point, major events of American Baptist history in which Furman was involved as a strong leader and wise counselor emerge for topical treatment.

Many people have been helpful in the production of this work, and to them I owe a great debt of gratitude. Among them I would like to thank:

The *Furmans*, father and son, mentioned earlier, for their never-failing encouragement during the years of research, writing, and publishing.

Dr. John E. Johns, president of Furman University, and *Dr. Frank Bonner*, past vice-president and provost of Furman, both of whom attended the original conference to discuss the project and whose interest and support have been ever present.

Wayne Weaver, vice-president for financial affairs at Furman University, who has gone beyond the call of duty, both personally and officially, in making every way easy and adequate.

Dr. A. V. Huff, professor of history at Furman University, *Dr. Glen Clayton*, curator of the Baptist Historical Collection at Furman, and *Loulie Latimer Owens*, knowledgeable South Carolina Baptist author-historian, for critically reading the manuscript and making valuable suggestions concerning content and style. In addition, Dr. Clayton, as curator of the historical collection, cheerfully made available every resource at his command.

Ronald F. Deering, director, and *Paul M. Debusman*, reference librarian, James P. Boyce Library, Southern Baptist Theological Seminary, whose help in obtaining source material from their library was generously given.

David Yeidberg, curator, and *Mrs. Annette D. Steiner*, Special Collections Division, Gelman Library, George Washington University, who were especially helpful in supplying Luther Rice material, including his journal.

Dr. Robert A. Baker, author and church historian at Southwestern Baptist Theological Seminary, who in person, by correspondence, and through his published works has been a valuable resource person.

Dr. Walter B. Shurden, now of Mercer University, for time graciously given in his office at Southern Baptist Theological Seminary discussing Richard Furman.

The *library staff at Francis Marion College*, where the writing was done, and especially *J. Mitchell Reames*, for being exceptionally generous and cooperative in helping to bring together resource materials.

Dr. Joe Stukes, chairman of the history department of Francis Marion College and delightful companion and research assistant while traveling in England to the home of the English Firmin ancestors of the American Furmans.

Captain and Mrs. Richard Anderson, of historic Borough House, Stateburg, South Carolina, who made available a treasure trove of cartography, with supporting archival documentation, for identifying the Furman lands in the High Hills of Santee.

To *librarians and library assistants* at Wake Forest University, Duke University, University of North Carolina (Southern Historical Collection), University of South Carolina (Caroliniana Library), Brown University, Library of Congress, National Archives, United States Senate Library, South Carolina Archives, College of Charleston, Lutheran Theological Seminary (South Carolina), Southern Baptist Historical Commission, American Baptist Historical Society, South Carolina Historical Society, New England Historic Genealogical Society, Sumter County Historical Society, Guildhall Library (London), British Museum, and British Public Record Office.

Sue Butler Mills, typist-secretary and research assistant, who patiently and efficiently endured during most of the years that went into this work.

Virginia Allen Permenter and *Key White*, who rendered efficient and appreciated service in typing the several drafts of the manuscript, and *Dolores J. Miller* for invaluable service in preparing the index.

The *staff of Mercer University Press* for their high degree of professionalism in the publication of this work.

To these and others whose names may be inadvertently omitted goes the sincere appreciation of the author.

James A. Rogers
Florence, South Carolina

A Furman Album

Photo 1. High Hills Baptist Church, one of the earliest Baptist churches in the South Carolina backcountry, ordained Richard Furman in 1774. He was pastor here until 1787 when he accepted a call to become pastor of the First Baptist Church of Charleston.

Photo 2. This obelisk on the grounds of the High Hills Baptist Church memorializes John M. Roberts, an early beneficiary of the educational fund originated by Richard Furman to help young ministers obtain an education. Roberts was one of the first two students sent by Furman to Rhode Island College, now Brown University. Upon completion of his studies, Roberts returned to South Carolina, where he became pastor of the High Hills church and founder of Roberts Academy.

Photo 3. The First Baptist Church of Charleston built during the latter years of Richard Furman's pastorate. The architect of this Greek Revival structure was Robert Mills, designer of the Washington Monument.

Photo 4. This pulpit robe worn by Richard Furman during his Charleston pastorate is on display in the South Carolina Baptist Historical Collection in the James B. Duke Library at Furman University.

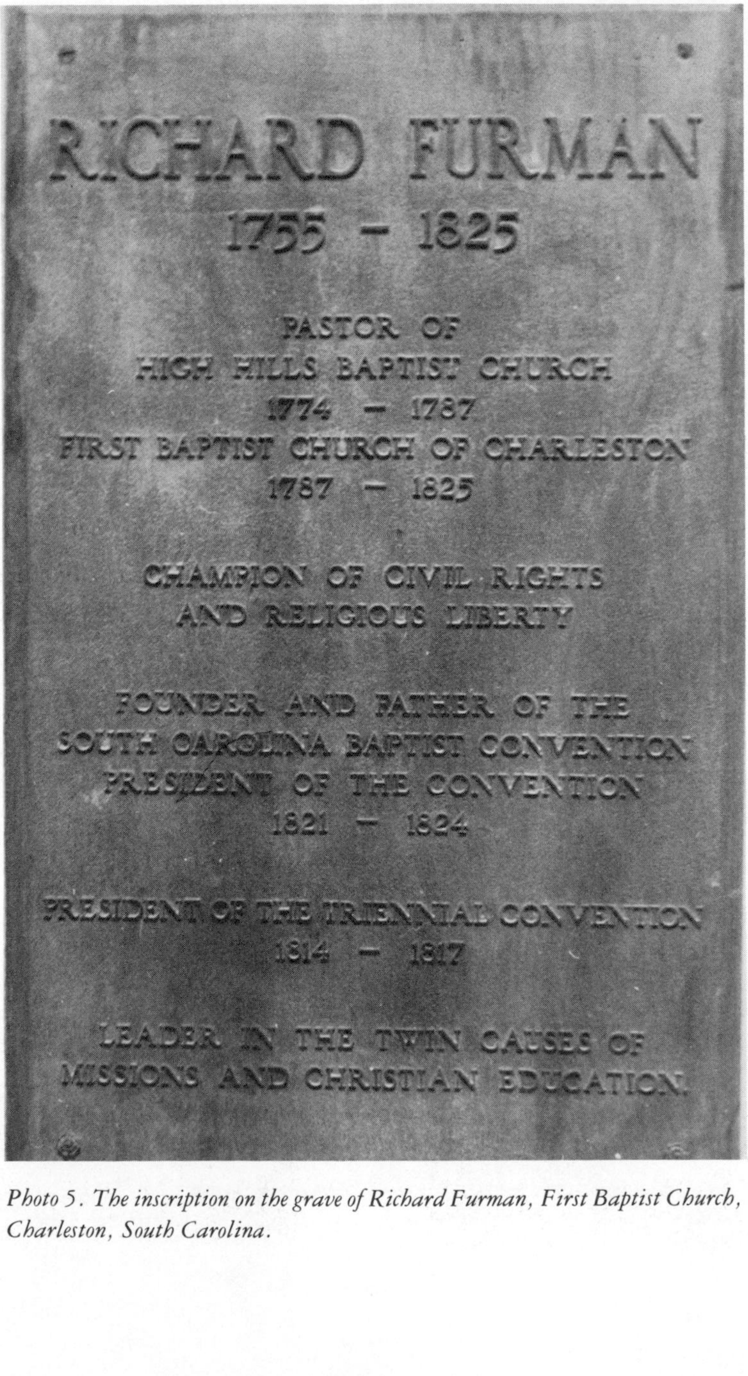

Photo 5. *The inscription on the grave of Richard Furman, First Baptist Church, Charleston, South Carolina.*

Richard Furman: Life and Legacy

Alester Garden Furman

James C. Furman

Richard Furman

Alester G. Furman III

Alester G. Furman, Jr.

Photos 6–10. Beginning with Richard Furman, four generations of his descendants have helped develop Furman University. James C. Furman was its first president (1858–1879). Alester Garden Furman, a great-grandson, was a member of the Board of Trustees and its secretary (1902–1936). Furman's great-great-grandson, Alester G. Furman, Jr., was a member of the board (1943–1953 and 1955–1959) and chairman of the board (1950–1953 and 1955–1959). Furman's great-great-great-grandson, Alester G. Furman III, was a board member (1967–1970, 1972–1976, and 1978–1982), and chairman of the board (1981–1982).

Photo 11. Begun one year following the death of Richard Furman, Furman Academy and Theological Institution was originally located at Edgefield, South Carolina. This stone pyramid marks the site of the academy that would later become Furman University.

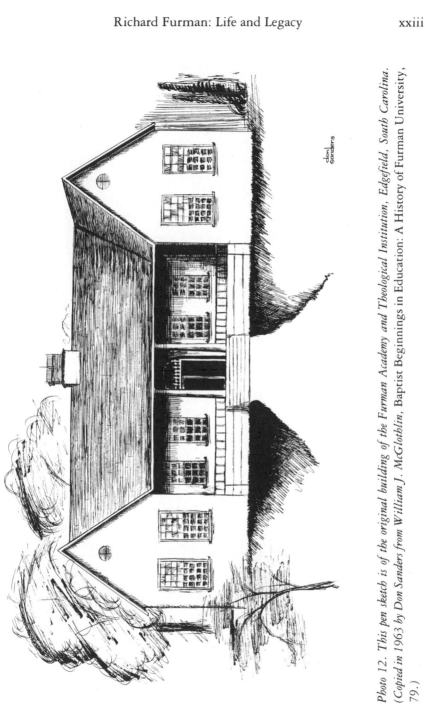

Photo 12. This pen sketch is of the original building of the Furman Academy and Theological Institution, Edgefield, South Carolina. (Copied in 1963 by Don Sanders from William J. McGlothlin, Baptist Beginnings in Education: A History of Furman University, 79.)

Photo 13. This site in Sumter County, near the High Hills Baptist Church, was the second location of the institution that would become Furman University. Roberts Academy, founded by John M. Roberts, was also near this site.

Photo 14. Standing beside the granite marker identifying the Fairfield location of the Furman Institution is Alester G. Furman, great-grandson of Richard Furman.

Photos 15 and 16. The two remaining buildings of Furman Institution in Fairfield County. Above, the classroom building; below, the faculty residence.

Photo 17. Rear view of Richard Furman Hall on the old Furman campus in Greenville, South Carolina. Completed in 1854, this Renaissance-style building, with its impressive Florentine bell tower, was the first permanent structure erected on the original Greenville campus. A replica of this tower was built on the new campus and preserves the memory of this building that became known as "Old Main" in early Furman history.

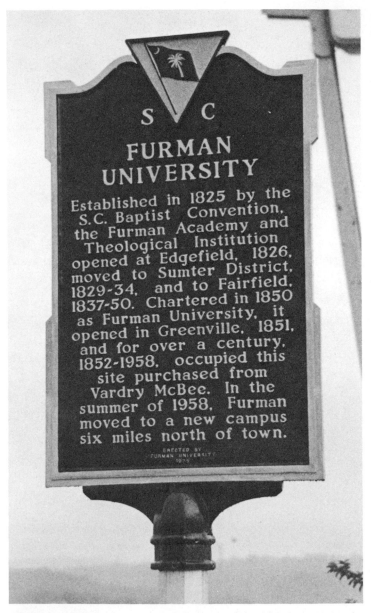

Photo 18. All that remains to identify the site of the old Furman University campus in downtown Greenville is this historical marker.

Photo 19. Entrance gate on the new Furman University campus north of Greenville.

James A. Rogers

Photo 20. McAlister Auditorium on the Furman campus.

Photo 21. The "Old College," one of two two-room classroom buildings used in 1852 while Richard Furman Hall was being constructed, was moved from the original Greenville campus and placed near the Bell Tower on the present-day campus.

Photo 22. The Bell Tower on the new campus, an exact replica of the bell tower of Richard Furman Hall on the original Greenville campus, stands on a small peninsula jutting into the lake. This dominant symbol of the university was a gift from the five great-great-grandchildren of Richard Furman—Alester G. Furman, Jr., Eleanor Furman Hudgens, Rebecca Furman Bailey, Constance Furman Westbrook, and Lucy Furman Arnold—to memorialize their father, Alester G. Furman. Together with the Old College, the Bell Tower symbolizes the struggles the university withstood to achieve the national eminence it enjoys today.

CHAPTER 1

Parentage and Boyhood

The Isle of Wight lies like a jeweled pendant off the southern coast of England. Its history dates back to the misty past of the English beginnings when Romans, Saxons, Angles, Danes, and Normans stormed across the channel from Europe. On the island's north coast, fronting the English mainland, is the port town of Cowes, the island's principal gateway to the sea. There in late March 1630, a fleet of four ships—the *Arbella*, the *Talbot*, the *Ambrose*, and the *Jewel*—awaited favorable winds to begin the voyage to New England. Across The Solent and upriver at Southampton lay seven other vessels, part of the same fleet anchored at Cowes and destined for the same voyage. Among them was the *Mayflower*, believed to be the same Mayflower of the Plymouth Pilgrims.[1] Together with those lying at Cowes, they formed the largest fleet yet to sail for the New World.

Since only the *Arbella* and her escort were ready for sailing, they formed a fleet for immediate departure. The remaining vessels at

---

[1]John Winthrop, *Winthrop's Journal*, "History of New England," 1630-1649 (New York: Barnes and Noble, 1966) 1:24n.

Southampton followed within days. The great Puritan exodus of the 1630s led by John Winthrop thus began. Two months later, on 8 June, after a stormy Atlantic crossing, the *Arbella* came in sight of Mount Desert on the Maine coast. An offshore wind blew in "so pleasant a sweet air as did much to refresh us, and there came smell of a small garden."[2] As the ship felt her way down the coast, Marblehead came into view, and on 12 June, with colors flying and sails swelling to a westerly breeze, she moved along the main channel between Baker's Island and Little Misery. In the shelter of Plum Cove she dropped anchor for the first time since sailing from Wight.

Among the *Arbella*'s passengers was John Firmin, son of Josias Firmin, a tanner of Nayland,[3] Suffolk County, in southeastern England. The Firmins had been numerous in Suffolk at least as early as the late fifteenth century. As a family, they were of the yeoman class, mostly farmers and landowners; however, some were merchants in Suffolk towns like Ipswich and Sudbury.[4] In the Puritan Massachusetts Bay Colony founded by John Winthrop, John, the emigrant Firmin, would be one of the founders of Watertown.[5]

Four generations later, in direct line of descent from John Firmin, Wood Furman, the son of Josias and Sarah Wood Furman, was born on 13 October 1712 at Newton, Long Island. After a brief mercantile ca-

---

[2]*Winthrop's Journal*, 1:47.

[3]Today, Nayland remains substantially as it was when Josias Firmin had his tanning business there. The River Stour, a small stream, flows lazily along its edge. St. Catherine's, the church in which the Furmans worshiped, dates back to Norman times and is near the heart of the village. Along the central street, a row of half-timbered houses, with sagging overhang, dates far back into English history. Older residents point to the traditional location of a one-time tanning business "around the corner."

[4]The Firmin name is still a familiar one around Sudbury. A check made by the author of the area telephone directory in the spring of 1982 showed thirty-one listings of residents who spelled their name "Firmin" and forty-seven who spelled it "Firman." Only one of the Firmins lives in Sudbury proper; the others live in the larger Sudbury area.

[5]Three hundred years later, a monument was erected in the center of Watertown memorializing its founders. Mounted on top is a bronze statue of Richard Saltonstall who came with Winthrop aboard the *Arbella*. Engraved on the shaft in alphabetical order are the names of the city's founders. John Firmin is listed among them.

reer in New York, Wood settled in Esopus, a frontier place (now
Kingston) up the Hudson River from New York.[6] His move to Esopus
followed ancestral migrations that led from Watertown to Long Island,
and thence to Hopewell, New Jersey. Wood spent the early years of his
life on his father's farm and acquired an elementary education.[7] But more
important to his education than the school was his father's small library
where he spent many hours in self-education.[8] Wood's mother, Sarah
Wood, was a granddaughter of Jonathan Wright, a soldier under Oliver
Cromwell.[9] Through her marriage the Puritan heritage of two families
was merged.

Richard Furman was born to Wood and Rachel Furman on 9 October 1755. Two other children had preceded him—a son, Josiah, and
a daughter, Sarah. Within less than a year after Richard's birth, the
family moved to a frontier settlement in South Carolina. What ac-
counted for this move cannot be established for certain, but early in the
1730s, Robert Johnson, the royal governor of South Carolina, made an
attractive offer of land grants to entice settlers into the state's interior.
The offer focused upon two features of a single plan: first, to push back
the frontier from the settled regions along the coast and, second, thus
to create a buffer against troublesome Indian marauders.

Johnson's plan called for eleven townships of 20,000 acres each along
major streams, the acreage to be divided into tracts of 50 acres for each
individual settled therein. One of the eleven lay along the Wateree
River, which flows south by southeast through the middle region of

---

[6]In the meantime, the grandfather of Wood Furman had been the first to change
the spelling of the family name from Firmin to Furman. We find no better reason for
the change than that given by Alfred Antoine Furman and Philip Howard Furman in
their *Memoirs of the Firmin-Furman Family in America*, bound copy, South Carolina
Baptist Historical Society Collection (hereinafter cited as SCBHS), James B. Duke
Library, Furman University, 30. They conclude that it originated from careless pron-
ounciation, or perhaps better still, spelling, and that writing "then not being a general accomplishment," the name appears "in dozens of different dresses, and sometimes
more than one style" for the same individual, as for instance, Firymn, Fermin, Firmin.

[7]Ibid., 45.

[8]Ibid.

[9]Ibid., 37.

South Carolina. East of the Wateree Valley, a line of hills rises to splendid eminence, forming what is known as the High Hills of Santee. Through them an old Indian path, the Catawba Path, connected the Catawba settlements to the north (Fredericksburg township) with Williamsburg township to the south. At convenient places, the path swung off to cross the Santee River and form a link between Charleston and the upper South Carolina backcountry.

In the summer of 1755 the attraction of these hills with their salubrious climate and promising land prospects lured Wood Furman and his son, Josiah, to South Carolina, where Wood obtained a land grant of 250 acres in the valley of the Wateree.[10] The following spring his wife, with their daughter, Sarah, and infant son, Richard, followed by sea. Upon landing in Charleston, they took the old Indian path, by that time a public road, and proceeded into the High Hills to what the family believed would be a permanent residence.[11]

It was a fertile land well suited to cotton, corn, wheat, indigo, and rice. Then, however, it was an untamed and largely unsettled land. The influx of settlers from North Carolina and Virginia soon to populate the backcountry had scarcely begun. Northward in Fredericksburg township, Joseph Kershaw had not yet built his store at a place that would become Camden. Westward toward mountain foothills, warlike Cher-

---

[10]By precept, 18 November 1755, certified 10 February 1756, South Carolina Archives, Sumter County.

[11]Some accounts say that the first move of the Wood Furmans to South Carolina was not to the High Hills but to St. Thomas Parish near Charleston. See, for instance, Hugh Charles Haynsworth, *Haynsworth-Furman and Allied Families* (Sumter SC: Osteen Publishing Co., 1942) 121, and Furman and Furman, *Memoirs of the Firmin-Furman Family in America*, 46. Harvey Tolliver Cook, however, in *Biography of Richard Furman* (Greenville SC: Baptist Courier Job Press, 1913) 2, says that Wood Furman had procured "on the border of the Wateree, an extensive tract of valuable land, to which he took his family, intending it for their future abode; but after a short residence settled on the sea coast." Since the biographical sketch in Cook's book is the work of one of Richard Furman's children, probably Wood or Susan, the information would undoubtedly have been obtained from Richard Furman, who would know it firsthand from his father. On this assumption, it seems clear that the first move was to the High Hills.

okees confronted frontier settlements with a fierce resentment that would lead to a bloody war against white encroachment upon their tribal lands.

The Furman land was in St. Mark's Parish, which was created by an act of the General Assembly in 1757. From the parish's itinerant rector, the Reverend Charles Woodmason, have come vivid accounts of backcountry life.[12] Woodmason's allegiance to the Church of England rendered him strongly biased against all religious dissenters, but his description of primitive and lawless conditions in St. Mark's is supported by the rise of the Regulators in the 1760s. In the absence of backcountry courts and the widespread prevalence of lawlessness, vigilantes called Regulators took the law into their own hands and were especially active in St. Mark's. In 1769 when the Assembly passed the Circuit Court Act to establish courts in the backcountry, Jeremiah Dargan, a Baptist preacher from North Carolina, preached in the High Hills and described the region as "a wild, wild place, a wicked, wicked, neighborhood" where preaching served "no purpose except provoking them to outrage."[13]

Wishing to rear his young family in a more hospitable environment, Wood Furman soon moved to the more cultivated society of the region around Charleston, settling first in St. Thomas Parish between the Cooper and Wando rivers. Among communicants of the St. Thomas parish church was Richard Beresford, a wealthy and influential citizen of the province. In his will, Beresford bequeathed the annual profits of his estate to the vestry of St. Thomas Parish, in trust, until his son, then eight years of age, reached the age of twenty-one. By the terms of the will, one-third of the annual estate profits were directed to the parish vestry for the support of one or more schoolmasters. The other two-thirds was designated "for the support, maintenance, tuition, and education of the poor of the said parish as shall be sent there to school."

---

[12]Charles Woodmason, *The Carolina Backcountry on the Eve of the Revolution; the Journal and Other Writings of Charles Woodmason, Anglican Itinerant*, ed. Richard J. Hooker (Chapel Hill: University of North Carolina Press, 1953).

[13]Quoted in Anne King Gregorie, *History of Sumter County* (Sumter SC: Library Board of Sumter County, 1954) 30, and Leah Townsend, *History of South Carolina Baptists, 1670-1805* (Florence SC: The Florence Printing Company, 1935) 150.

The fund became known as the Beresford Bounty, and the school it supported was named the Beresford Bounty School.[14]

When Wood Furman moved into St. Thomas Parish, he became schoolmaster for the school. The subjects taught were prescribed by the Beresford will. They included "reading, writing and casting accounts, Learning of Several Languages, Mathematics, or other Liberal learning, and Education, as the Vestry shall direct."[15] Rules and Orders agreed upon by the Vestry required that "the master shall bring the children to church every Lord's day when there is public worship, and shall teach them to behave themselves with all Reverence while they are in the House of God, and to join in the Public Service of the church, for which purpose they are to be furnished with Bibles and Common Prayer Books as soon as they can use them"; and further, "the master shall use prayers morning and evening in the school, and teach the children to pray, and to use Grace before and after meals."[16]

Schoolmaster Furman was far removed from the Puritan legacy of his emigrant ancestor, but in Beresford Bounty School it was a legacy that served him well. In a report to the Society for the Propagation of the Gospel on 10 May 1763, the Reverend Alexander Garden, Jr., then rector of the parish, stated that "the Free School in this Parish, founded by the late Richard Beresford, is flourishing under the care of the Vestry."[17]

---

[14]Frederick Dalcho, *An Historical Account of the Protestant Episcopal Church of South Carolina, from the First Settlement of the Province to the War of the Revolution* (Charleston: E. Thayer Theological Book, 1820) 236; David Ramsay, *History of South Carolina from Its First Settlement in 1670 to the year 1808* (Charleston: Walker, Evans and Cogswell, 1858) 2:198. See also Robert F. Clute, *The Annals and Parish Register of St. Thomas and St. Denis Parish in South Carolina from 1680 to 1884* (Charleston: Walker, Evans and Cogswell, 1884) 12. Richard Beresford died in 1721 when his son was eight years of age. When his son reached twenty-one and the final payment of the estate was made to the vestry it totalled £6500 (Clute, ibid., 12-13). The principal sum of the Bounty remains intact today.

[15]Dalcho, *Historical Account of the Protestant Episcopal Church*, 286.

[16]Ibid., 292-93.

[17]H. T. Cook, *Biography of Richard Furman*, 2, says that the school was located "near the brick church in St. Thomas Parish." This would identify it as the parish church, "now called the Brick Church, about three miles from Cainhoy," says Clute, 11.

Furman's schoolmaster career in St. Thomas continued for about five years.[18] He then moved to the lower part of the parish onto Daniel's Island and engaged in agriculture. Like upper St. Thomas Parish, the island lay between the Wando and the Cooper rivers but was separated from the upper parish by tidal creeks. The Furman family lived on the island during relatively serene years, with little to suggest the darkening clouds that would turn the place into a war theater and nearby Charleston into a conquered city.

Richard Furman was about six years of age when the Furman family moved to Daniel's Island. It was a short move, with only marshland and tidal creeks separating the island from the upper portion of St. Thomas Parish. Beyond the Cooper River and within eyeshot of the new Furman home was Charleston, then in a great age of ocean commerce. Between November and March, following the hurricane season, as many as one hundred vessels of all kinds—ships, brigantines, snows, schooners, sloops—could be seen riding at anchor. Eighty-five vessels in the harbor on 5 January 1767 were noted by the *Royal Gazette* and termed "fewer than usual." Charleston owed her place in the sun to the sailing ships. As long as they continued, the city was on the main Atlantic highway connecting principal domestic and foreign ports and transporting goods to and from England and her colonies. The inhabitants were a people of diverse history and culture. They were English, French, German, Irish, Scottish, Scotch-Irish, Antiguan, Jamaican, Barbadian, Bermudan, Granadan; and from their mixing of blood and ideas ultimately came a new culture.[19] Among them were names like Rutledge, Pinckney, Middleton, Gadsden, Manigault, Laurens, Lucas, Brewton, Lynch, Huger, Leigh, Moultrie—most of them early generation representatives of families who were influential shapers of South Carolina and early American history. Years later, Richard Furman would come to know them well—some of them intimately.

Rising high above the housetops, gleaming white in the sun, was the noble spire of St. Michael's Church, just completed after eleven years of building. North of Broad Street, which dissected the peninsula, the

---

[18]H. T. Cook, *Biography*, 2.

[19]George C. Rogers, Jr., *Charleston in the Age of the Pinckneys* (Norman: University of Oklahoma Press, 1969) 1-7.

spire of St. Philip's, dating back to 1711, graced the Charleston skyline as seen from Daniel's Island. The dominant religion of the city and the province was Anglican, and the Furmans with their membership in the parish of St. Thomas and their home in clear view of the Anglican spires rising out of Charleston were not unreminded of their faith.

Almost within the shadow of St. Michael's, the Reverend Oliver Hart was pastor of the first Baptist church in the South. A native of Pennsylvania, he came to Charleston in 1749; his arrival was considered to be a providential response to a letter from the Charleston church to the Philadelphia Baptist Association inquiring "if there were any minister sound in Faith" who might be prevailed upon to come to Charleston and accept a call from the congregation.[20] On the day of Hart's unannounced arrival, Charleston was mourning the death of the Reverend Isaac Chanler, a greatly beloved minister and pastor of the Ashley River Baptist Church. For months he had been assisting the pastorless Charleston church "once a fortnight."[21]

Within eyeshot of Charleston, Richard Furman spent boyhood years engaged in the chores of his father's Daniel's Island land and in studies, illustrating a precocious intellectual potential. Poetry, history, and travels early became favorite subjects. He read Homer's *Iliad* with such insatiable delight that by the age of eleven he had memorized most of the first book of that epic poem, and other selected parts. During part of a day when his parents were away on a visit, he memorized Alexander Pope's *Messiah*. The *Spectator*, coming in with the sailing ships from England, gave him pleasure, as did the works of John Milton and Jonathan Swift.[22]

His versatile father instructed him in theoretical and practical trigonometry, as applied to surveying,[23] a profession pursued by several

---

[20]W. W. H. Davis, *History of the Hart Family of Warminister, Bucks County, Pa.*, typescript of chapter concerning the Oliver Hart Family of South Carolina, Caroliniana Library, University of South Carolina, Columbia.

[21]H. A. Tupper, ed., *Two Centuries of the First Baptist Church of Charleston, 1683-1883* (Baltimore: R. H. Woodward and Co., 1889) 101.

[22]H. T. Cook, *Biography*, 2-3.

[23]Wood Furman was one of the advertised teachers for the Charleston area during

generations of Furmans before him. Charleston's educational and cultural climate drew him like a magnet. He was especially attracted to the home of a Charleston merchant, a Mr. Stocker, where one described as "an English lady of refined education" took special interest in him and stimulated him in the pursuit of classical knowledge.[24] In Charleston, too, he became acquainted with Dr. Hezekiah Smith, an eminent minister of Massachusetts then collecting funds for Rhode Island College.[25] His growth in mind and body during these years was so "un-

---

the mid-eighteenth century. In the 6 October 1758 issue of the *South Carolina Gazette*, he advertised his services as a teacher of "arithmetic, geometry, plain and spherical geometry, surveying, navigation, accounting." Cited in Hennig Cohen, *The South Carolina Gazette, 1732-1775* (Columbia: University of South Carolina Press, 1952) 34.

[24]H. T. Cook, *Biography*, 3, refers to the Stocker family and the "English lady" without identifying her. According to Cook, young Furman was "an occasional visitant" in the Stocker home where an English lady "took considerable pains to cultivate his taste." One may reasonably conclude that she was the one who instilled in him an appreciation for English and Greek classics, which led him to memorize large portions of these works. A Charleston book merchant, Charles Stevens Stocker (*South Carolina Gazette*, 7 January 1765) lived in St. Michael's Parish and was married to Mary Bedon, daughter of Henry Bedon. His death in 1771, and hers in 1786, place them in Charleston during the years when the Furmans lived on Daniel's Island (*South Carolina Historical and Genealogical Magazine*, 17:48; 19:180; 31:164; 36:103). The "English lady of refined education" referred to in Cook's account was probably Mary Stocker or some other lady living with the Stocker family. The manner of Cook's reference permits either conclusion.

[25]Townsend, *History of South Carolina Baptists*, 86n; H. A. Tupper, *Two Centuries of the First Baptist Church of Charleston, 1683-1883*, 127. Hezekiah Smith, born in April 1737, was a native of Hempstead, Long Island. In 1756 he was baptized into the fellowship of the Morristown, New Jersey, church by John Gano, who would become one of the most distinguished ministers of his time and a warm friend of Richard Furman. He was graduated from Princeton in September 1762, and soon thereafter he started south on an evangelistic tour, preaching in all the colonies as he traveled. For some time he made Charleston his headquarters where he became a member of the Charleston Baptist Church and there was ordained to the ministry in September 1763. He later returned to New England and for forty-six years was pastor of the Baptist church in Haverhill, Massachusetts. He took the deepest interest in Rhode Island College and, on one occasion, spent eight months in the South, especially in South Carolina, without compensation, raising funds for its equipment. (Albert H. Newman, *A History of the Baptist Churches in the United States* [Philadelphia: American Baptist Publication Society, 1915] 259-60).

commonly rapid" that before he had reached his sixteenth year, his stature had the appearance of a man and his mind was developed beyond that common to his age level.[26]

His interest in religion became evident early. From the Bible, his first textbook, he learned to read.[27] His Church of England father would not have neglected the spiritual needs of his children while attending to those of his pupils at Beresford Bounty School. Besides, there was the daily reminder that religion is part of one's personal and historical experience, symbolized by the towering spires of St. Philip's and St. Michael's beyond the Cooper. There, too, was his ancestral Puritan background that had evolved through generations of Furmans as a heritage. But whatever religious impressions were his as a growing boy on Daniel's Island, it remained for the next move of Wood Furman to establish the course that would carry his son to distinction among early American religious leaders.

---

[26]H. T. Cook, *Biography*, 3.

[27]Ibid., 2.

CHAPTER 2

Conversion and Early Ministry

Wood Furman's final move was made in 1770 when he and his family returned to his land in the High Hills of Santee. More than ten years had passed since he had gone to St. Thomas Parish, and many things had changed. The Cherokee War of 1760-1761, a bitter struggle of horror and destruction, had ended the Indian menace and set the stage for all the land east of the mountains to be ceded to South Carolina by the Cherokees in a treaty of 1777.

The volatile and frequently violent period of the South Carolina Regulators had ended with the passage of the Circuit Court Act of 1769. For the first time in the history of the colony it would no longer be necessary to make the long trip to Charleston in search of justice. Prospective courthouses at Ninety-Six, Orangeburg, Camden, and Long Bluff (now Society Hill) promised a stabilizing influence in frontier society agreeable to the flow of new immigrants into the South Carolina interior. They came up from the coast country, but more important to their bearing upon the early life of Richard Furman, they came down from northern colonies as far away as New England. They streamed in on horseback and wagon, driving their stock before them, bringing their crude possessions. With such tools as they had, they erected log cabins along the rivers and streams of the middle and upcountry. They were a simple folk, generally unlettered, but imbued with the spirit of the pioneer.

In American colonial history, this large movement of the population is associated with a great religious awakening occasioned by the preaching of Jonathan Edwards and George Whitefield. For a generation, New England ministers had observed with growing concern the evidence of diminishing piety. In 1734, under the power of Edwards's preaching, Northampton youth, contrary to their usual religious apathy, responded with such emotional fervor that revival fires spread throughout the community. Hundreds crowded the church, and similar outpourings spread to neighboring towns. Many saw in Edwards the catalyst that had sparked the awakening.[1] However, the phenomenon came to a halt in 1735 when, during a time of many conversions, Edwards's uncle by marriage despaired so deeply over the state of his soul that he committed suicide. Some saw this tragedy as an indication that God had withdrawn his favor. By 1736 the revival fervor had subsided.

The calm was not long-lived, however. Word began to circulate about a young English evangelist named George Whitefield, whose success in England and in the American southern and middle colonies had been attended by extraordinary results. In 1740 Whitefield traveled to New England and became the real instrument of revival that reached throughout the colonies. As conversions mounted, many came to believe that God had selected that time for a special outpouring of the Spirit, perhaps the last before the millenium.[2]

Emotional excesses stirred by Whitefield's preaching so offended the sensibilities of fashionable New England Congregationalists that they rejected his followers as "Separates" from the Congregational church, and the Separate movement that has influenced American Baptist history until the present day had its beginning. Contemporarily, two new terms—New Lights and Old Lights—came into common usage, with

---

[1]Edward M. Griffin, *Jonathan Edwards* (Minneapolis: University of Minnesota Press, 1971) 8.

[2]Ibid., 9.

New Lights despairing of the religion of Old Lights as "soulless and formal" and no longer having "the light of scriptural inspiration."[3]

Baptist churches in New England absorbed many of the Separates. Others moved south, swelling the roll of Baptist churches as they came.[4] After 1750 the Carolina frontier experienced a rising population due to a steady inflow of Separate settlers from Pennsylvania and North Carolina—most of them German, Dutch, Scotch-Irish, and dissenting English. With them came religious sects at such variance with the Church of England that in 1770 Lieutenant Governor Bull of South Carolina observed, " . . . our toleration comprehends every denomination of Christians except the Roman Catholics, and these are subdivided ad infinitum in the back parts, as illiterate or wild imagination can interpret the scripture."[5]

Among those making their way into South Carolina, Separate Baptists were the most numerous. Preceding them was a remarkable project in North Carolina under the leadership of Shubal Stearns. A native of Massachusetts, Stearns joined the Separates under the influence of Whitefield's preaching. He became a Baptist in 1751, and during the same year, he was ordained at Tolland, Connecticut. After a brief stay there, he left New England in 1754 and migrated to Virginia where he met his brother-in-law, Daniel Marshall, also a Separate, who had just returned from a mission among the Indians. Joining company, they settled in Virginia near Winchester. Unfortunately, they found Virginia an inhospitable and persecuting place for Separate Baptists,[6] so they proceeded southward into North Carolina and established residence at Sandy Creek in Guilford County. There they built a meetinghouse and formed a church of sixteen members.[7] Within seventeen years

---

[3]Joe M. King, *A History of South Carolina Baptists* (Columbia: General Board of the South Carolina Baptist Convention, 1964) 69.

[4]Loulie Latimer Owens, *Saints of Clay* (Columbia: R. L. Bryan and Co., 1971) 40.

[5]Quoted in King, *A History of South Carolina Baptists*, 69, from Records of the Province of South Carolina; Sainsbury Transcripts from the British Public Record Office (MS, Historical Commission of South Carolina, 32:370-71).

[6]William L. Lumpkin, *Baptist Foundations in the South* (Nashville: Broadman Press, 1961) 29.

[7]David Benedict, *A General History of the Baptist Denomination in America and Other Parts of the World* (Boston: Manning and Loring, 1813) 2:29.

the fruit of their work included forty-two new churches and one hundred and twenty-five ministers. The church at Sandy Creek so influenced Baptist history that David Benedict has called it "the mother of all Separate Baptists."[8]

The first movement of Separate Baptists into South Carolina came about 1759 or 1760 when Philip Mulkey, a convert of Shubal Stearns, led a group of thirteen to Broad River in South Carolina, where they established a church whose members soon increased to more than a hundred.[9] Two years later, the original body moved to a tract of land lying between Fairforest Creek and Tyger River. With their members closely settled along neighborhood creeks, they became a center of Separate Baptist missionary activity that "spread their principles far and wide."[10] From Mulkey's church at Fairforest, numerous branches

---

[8]Ibid., 42.

[9]Townsend, *History of South Carolina Baptists*, 125-26.

[10]Ibid., 126. Mulkey's conversion and work in South Carolina are related by Morgan Edwards in his *Materials Toward a History of the Baptists in the Provinces of Maryland, Virginia, North Carolina, South Carolina, Georgia*, 1772 (Bound MS, SCBHS, Furman University). In that account Mulkey's own narrative of his conversion is recorded. It was typical of the emotional experience that was a mark of Separate Baptists. When Richard Furman read Edwards's manuscript in 1795, he appended the following note to the account about Mulkey: "Oh! Lamentable. This Philip Mulkey whose experiences are related above, be the instrument for converting a number of souls; has been now for a course of years practicing crimes and enormities of which humanity shudders." In his own account of Mulkey's ministry, written in 1772, Edwards says, "Mr. Mulkey's acquirements entitle him to no higher degree than that of an English scholar; neither is there anything extraordinary in his natural endowments, except a very sweet voice, and a smiling aspect; that voice he manages in such a manner as to make soft impressions on the heart and fetch tears in a mechanical way. Mr. Garrick is said to have learned a solemn pronunciation of the interjection of 'O' from Dr. Pordice; but, if I mistake not, both might learn from Mulkey to spin that sound and mix it with awe, distress, solicitude, and other affections. His success has been such a hazzard [sic] being exalted above measure in his own esteem, and in the esteem of his converts; but a thorn was put in his flesh about four years ago which will keep him humble while he lives, and teach his votaries that he is but a man." In J. D. Bailey, *Reverends Philip Mulkey and James Fowler* (Cowpens SC, 1924) and quoted in Townsend, *History of South Carolina Baptists,* 125n., the following reference is made to Mulkey's apostasy: " . . . the last known ministerial service performed by him was as one of the presbytery constituting Cheraw Hill Church in 1782: excommunicated in 1790 and the churches warned against him for adultry [sic], perfidy and falsehood long continued in."

emerged in surrounding areas of South Carolina and into North Carolina.

In the South Carolina Congarees, a fork formed by the Congaree and Wateree rivers before they converge to form the Santee, Mulkey's preaching resulted in the establishment of the Congaree church. Among "early converts and constituents" of this church was Joseph Reese.[11] In 1745, at the age of nine,[12] Reese, a native of Pennsylvania, moved with his parents to South Carolina, where they settled in the Congarees. His conversion from the Anglican faith in 1760 created a stir among both Anglicans and Separates, and more still when he was baptized and began preaching as an unordained Separate Baptist minister. Ordination was delayed until 1768 when ordination ceremonies were conducted by Oliver Hart and Evan Pugh. By then Reese had established himself so well in the ministry that the Congaree church called him as pastor.[13]

By then residents of the Lowcountry were beginning to build homes in the elevated and healthy climate of the High Hills. Among first white settlers, about a third were from the South Carolina coastal country.[14] So numerous were those of Anglican persuasion that Episcopalians petitioned the Assembly for assistance in building a chapel of ease in St. Mark's, declaring that their district was "a very populous and growing settlement crowded with people."[15] Settlers moving in from the Lowcountry also brought with them Baptist influence from Charleston and the Charleston Baptist Association. Charleston Baptists were Regulars, modified Calvinists holding the doctrine of election. They traced their spiritual heritage to New England dissenters whose struggle for religious freedom was an American extension of their English antecedents. They were also known as Particular Baptists, as distinguished from General Baptists who rejected election in favor of universal redemption. The religious experience of the Separates was simple and direct, void of liturgical form and ceremony, and appealing to the primitive instincts of a frontier society.

---

[11]Townsend, *History of South Carolina Baptists*, 143; Benedict, *A General History of the Baptist Denomination*, 2:364.

[12]Benedict, *A General History of the Baptist Denomination*, 2:364.

[13]Ibid., 364-65.

[14]Gregorie, *History of Sumter County*, 15.

[15]Ibid., 31.

Both state authorities and Regular Baptists regarded Separates with suspicion. When the Reverend Shubal Stearns sought the assistance of the pastor of the Welsh Neck Baptist Church in ordaining Daniel Marshall, a Separate zealot, he was not only refused but refused with scorn. The Welsh Neck pastor[16] said that "he held no fellowship with the Stearns party, and he believed them to be a disorderly set, suffering women to pray in public, and permitting every ignorant man to preach that chose, they encourage noise and confusion in their meetings."[17]

It was a fortuitous circumstance that brought about the meeting of Regulars and Separates in the High Hills. The Separates needed the stabilizing influence of Lowcountry Regulars, their emphasis upon an educated ministry, and their more rational approach to worship. The Regulars needed the evangelistic enthusiasm of the Separates to inspire a more urgent mission concern. When the two eventually merged, the resulting Baptists bore the better marks of both.[18]

When the Furman family returned to the High Hills, they found the settlement "destitute of the regular means of grace, but favored with the occasional ministry" of this same Joseph Reese of the Congaree church. Reese had been coming from the Congaree to hold three-day open-air meetings near the site of a meetinghouse then under construction on a four-acre tract of land given by Dr. Joseph Howard,[19] a neigh-

---

[16]Probably Nicholas Bedgegood; Benedict, *A General History of the Baptist Denomination*, 2:39n.

[17]Albert H. Newman, *A History of the Baptist Churches in the United States*, 294; Benedict, *A General History of the Baptist Denomination*, 2:39; Townsend, *History of South Carolina Baptists*, 125.

[18]In his biography of Richard Furman, 65, H. T. Cook calls the High Hills "a place where two civilizations met." Joe M. King, *A History of South Carolina Baptists*, says of Furman, "In him coastal and back country religion were effectively fused." In a similar vein, the *Encyclopedia of Southern Baptists* (Nashville: Broadman Press, 1958) 1:518, says, "The union of the enduring qualities of the Regular and Separate Baptists in Furman made him the arch-proto-type of the prevailing norm of the Southern Baptists of the 20th Century."

[19]The deed of Dr. Howard's gift of land reads, in part: "For and in consideration of the great Want of an House and Place of Public worship, and seeing that sundry of the Inhabitants have subscribed Sums of Money toward building a Meeting House

borhood physician converted under Reese's preaching. Intended for ecumenical worship, "for any Protestant preacher to preach in," the church "almost immediately" became Baptist.[20] The meetinghouse was completed in 1770, but frequently the crowds came in such large numbers as to overflow the building. On such occasions, they assembled in the adjoining valley where the different elevations formed a natural amphitheater well suited for such services.[21] The High Hills church was "gathered" as a congregation in 1770 and two years later, 4 January 1772, constituted as a church.

A more important consequence of Reese's preaching was the conversion of Richard Furman to the Separate Baptist faith from the Church of England.[22] The Furmans had been back in the High Hills about two

---

for any Protestant religious Preacher to Preach in and for the great Desire I have and do bear toward so laudable an Undertaking's being Carried on and finished, I so by these presents give unto John Wheeler, Thomas Woodward, John Perry, and William Reese, including myself as being one of the Managers chosen before the Subscribers, Four Acres of Land, at the Place nominated, and on which the House is raised . . . the said House to be free for any Protestant religious Denomination to Preach in . . . " (H. T. Cook, *Biography of Richard Furman*, 66; Townsend, *History of South Carolina Baptists*, 150-51n). Morgan Edwards gives the date 4 January 1772 for the constitution of the church (Edwards MS, 61). A current tradition says that the Howard gift of land was located on the King's Highway (State Highway 261) near the point where Fish Road originally intersected. (Fish Road is an old roadway from Ketchall to Sumter's landing on the Wateree River.) The tradition is based on information obtained from Colclough E. Sanders, a lifelong resident of the area, who heard it from his mother, Mattie Jackson Sanders, born 4 June 1893. She, in turn, had heard it through her ancestors, who had passed it down from generation to generation. The present church, east of the King's Highway, also known as the Camden Road, is on a tract granted 6 October 1803 by General Sumter to the Reverend John M. Roberts and his successors in office. The tract is described as "a lot of land . . . near Stateburg whereon the old Meeting House now stands" (Sumter County Clerk of Court, Deeds AA, 297; cited in Townsend, *History of South Carolina Baptists*, 154 and note). This description raises serious questions concerning the Sanders tradition, since it locates the present church on the land where "the old Meeting House stands," thus suggesting that the Sumter land given to the church may have been the same land granted by Dr. Howard.

[20]Townsend, *History of South Carolina Baptists*, 150.

[21]Unsigned MS, Furman Papers, SCBHS.

[22]Gregorie, *History of Sumter County*, 15.

months when they learned that Reese would come again for one of his preaching missions. He arrived the following Saturday, and that night Richard Furman went to the meeting place[23] and saw and heard Reese for the first time. He would thereafter refer to him as his "spiritual father."[24]

It was typical of the intellectual character of Richard Furman that he did not respond to Joseph Reese's preaching with the sudden outburst of emotion typical of Separate revivals. On the night Furman heard Reese for the first time, thirteen persons went forward for baptism.[25] This was Furman's initial exposure to the Reese style of evangelism and his first experience at a Separate revival. The scene inspired his interest and deepened the religious impressions he had felt since childhood. It also focused attention upon the fundamental Separate doctrine that conversion is a scriptural precondition for baptism. In his Anglican upbringing, Furman had accepted pedobaptism[26] as biblical, but now for the first time he began to question that assumption seriously. Reese had preached baptism for believers with such earnestness and eloquence that Furman resolved to make the mode of baptism a subject of "serious inquiry."[27] With the Bible before him during long periods of quiet study, he sought for what he could believe to be the mind of God. Larger questions than baptism claimed his attention—the justice of God, the universality of redemptive grace, justification by faith alone, and the whole democratic process of the Separate cause. In theology and ecclesiology, the Separates were far removed from Furman's religious rearing.

Some months later, Reese came again to the High Hills and Furman went to the meeting to present himself as a candidate for baptism. One who chronicled this event in Furman's life notes that once at the church he became so overwhelmed by a "sense of guilt and unworthiness" that, being unable to control his feelings, he removed himself from the assembly and sought a secluded place where he underwent a renewed

---

[23]Unsigned MS, Furman Papers, SCBHS.

[24]Ibid.

[25]Ibid.

[26]Ibid.

[27]Ibid.

struggle to be assured of the correctness of his course.[28] Following that solitary vigil he returned to the church and "related what he believed to have been effected by divine grace in his heart."[29] Among those listening was his mother. She, too, had become so deeply impressed by Reese's sermons, and especially by the manifest concern of her son,[30] that she experienced the same constraining influence as he. That night the little church nestled in the High Hills found a place in Baptist history when Richard Furman became a Baptist by conviction. Before Joseph Reese returned to his church in the Congarees, he had baptized both Furman and his mother in a little baptistry fed by a spring flowing from the valley hillside hard by the church.

Like Paul after his Damascus experience, the young convert then chose retirement for a season to strengthen his faith through Bible study, prayer, and private meditation. The natural surroundings of his home in the valley inspired the meditative mood. Looking east, the hills that rose in a series of eminences paralleling the Wateree River were splendidly verdant in spring and summer and riotously colored when autumn worked its miracles among the hardwoods. Beyond the Wateree, another line of hills, shrouded in a bluish haze, ranged northward along the river and paled away into the distant horizon. In the solitude of his thoughts, the world without and the world within enforced the validity of his faith.

Withdrawal, however, was only preparatory. The evangelical zeal of the Separates had laid hold upon him. Undeterred by his youth, he soon abandoned retirement to share his experience with family, neighbors, friends, and his "father's servants."[31]

----

[28]Ibid.; H. T. Cook, *Biography*, 5.

[29]Unsigned MS, Furman Papers, SCBHS.

[30]Ibid.

[31]Ibid., 6. This is the first reference in source material that documents the ownership of slaves by Wood Furman. A. S. Salley, cited in Haynsworth, *Haynsworth-Furman and Allied Families*, 37, says that land grants were based on fifty acres for each slave owned. Wood Furman's 250-acre land grant in 1756 thus suggests that he owned at least five slaves at that time. By the time of the first U.S. census in 1790, the High Hills region of Claremont County, now Sumter, was populated by many inhabitants who were large slaveowners. See *Heads of Families, First Census of the United States, 1790, South Carolina* (Baltimore: Genealogical Publishing Co., 1966), South Carolina Heritage Series No. 6.

How Wood Furman reacted to this change in his family's religious affiliation is left chiefly to conjecture. His Anglican connection, with its liturgy and tradition, and his own Puritan heritage made him less responsive to preaching by the Separates than his impressionable son. There is a family tradition that the elder Furman had designed a law career for Richard[32] and that paternal concern, lest he be swayed by juvenile religious emotion, led to frequent father-son discussions on the subject. Wood Furman was cautious, conservative, and too Episcopalian in his thinking not to be concerned by what had happened in the life of his youngest son.

While the High Hills church remained a branch of the Congaree with no regular pastor, Reese frequently came across the Wateree to conduct services. On such occasions, Furman customarily arose to "exercise his gifts" or "exhort," to the general satisfaction of his listeners. This was his earliest preaching experience.

In 1772 there were but twenty Baptist churches in South Carolina, including the Separates, sixteen ordained ministers, and twenty-one licensed preachers.[33] Roads were little more than trails, travel was difficult, streams were many, and bridges and ferries were few.[34] But to the young convert, the opportunity for preaching and "gathering" churches so pressed upon him that neither the difficulties of travel nor the ridicule of youthful peers in the High Hills community dampened or discouraged his evangelistic zeal.[35] He traveled eastward toward the Pee Dee and southward toward the Santee—preaching, evangelizing, and baptizing. Sometimes accompanying him was Timothy Dargan,[36] an older man of the Congaree church and one of the revered men in early South Carolina Baptist history.

---

[32]H. T. Cook, *Biography*, 7.

[33]Edwards MS, SCBHS.

[34]A petition to the General Assembly in 1778 for incorporation of a "seminary of learning" in the High Hills takes note of other societies formed for that purpose in other parts of the state, but it points out that accessibility of these to the High Hills was blocked "by the swamps and rivers that lie between" (MS, Caroliniana Library, University of South Carolina, Columbia).

[35]H. T. Cook, *Biography*, 68.

[36]Ibid., 2.

Amid travels and the dutiful discharge of home chores normal to family living on a frontier plantation, Furman continued his habits of study. The Bible was his principal textbook, but his enquiring mind encompassed broader fields of learning. He studied history, philosophy, literature, language, rhetoric, and theology. From his friendship with Dr. Joseph Howard he derived an interest in medical science. With Howard's assistance he became so proficient in anatomy and related subjects that in later years he acted as a surrogate physician when doctors were too few to meet the need for patient care during recurring epidemics of smallpox and yellow fever. From his father he learned surveying and its corollary subjects, mathematics and trigonometry.

In January 1772 when the congregation at High Hills was constituted as a church independent of Congaree, Richard Furman, his mother, Rachel, and Dr. Howard, the church's benefactor, were among its charter members. Furman was still unordained, but upon the invitation of the church he agreed to preach regularly.[37] Two years later, in May 1774, the Reverend Evan Pugh came from his Cashaway church on the Pee Dee, and the Reverend Joseph Reese came from his church beyond the Wateree. At the meetinghouse in the Hills they conducted services formally ordaining Richard Furman into the Baptist ministry. Six months later, the church invited him to become its pastor, and he accepted.[38]

Furman's ordination followed a "big meeting" that began at the High Hills in December 1773 and continued into 1774. On 27 December Oliver Hart came up from his church in Charleston to attend the meeting.[39] News of Separate revivalism in the backcountry had come to Hart's attention early, along with word of the promising work of Richard Furman. Going to the High Hills was an opportunity to witness what he had heard, and to have a close-up experience with the Separates. What Hart saw was a scene typical of religious gatherings in the backcountry. The High Hills church was the only one of any denomi-

---

[37]Townsend, *History of South Carolina Baptists*, 153.

[38]Ibid., 152; Edwards MS, 62.

[39]*Extracts from the Diary of the Rev. Oliver Hart, from A.D. 1740 to A.D. 1780, with Introductory Letter from William G. Whilden*, published in *Yearbook, City of Charleston, S.C., 1896* (Charleston: Lucas and Richardson, 1896) 386.

nation in that general area,[40] and when the Separates held a revival they filled the roads with people eager to hear the Word or excited by the prospect of a festive occasion.

The winter winds blew cold in the High Hills, but when Hart arrived on 31 December the weather of that mid-winter day proved no deterrent to the "big meeting." Farmsteaders had come with their families from miles around, reminiscent of earlier meetings when Joseph Reese had so deeply stirred the settlers and made a Separate Baptist of Richard Furman. On the day of his arrival Hart preached, and did so again on Sunday morning, 2 January. Among his most earnest listeners was Richard Furman. In the afternoon Furman followed with a sermon of his own. That night, "by desire of the Rev. Mr. Reese, and the Church, Hart administered the Lord's Supper." By Hart's own account, "it was a time of refreshing for the People of the Lord."[41] Hart and Furman had never met before. Hart was then fifty-one years of age and Furman not yet nineteen. The broad generation gap notwithstanding, this was the beginning of an enduring friendship for both.

An early convert of Furman following his ordination was his sister, Sarah. On 10 March 1774 she had been married to Henry Haynsworth, one of nine children of Richard and Elizabeth Haynsworth. The Haynsworths had obtained a 350-acre grant of land east of the High Hills in 1756, but family tradition holds that they had already settled on a grant obtained more than ten years earlier.[42] On deeds to which his name is attached, Henry Haynsworth is referred to as "Planter," an Old South

---

[40]It should be noted, however, that the present Church of the Holy Cross at Stateburg originated in 1770 as a chapel of ease for St. Mark's Parish (Gregorie, *History of Sumter County*, 31) and that as early as 1759, Presbyterians had erected a log meetinghouse on the Black River that would become Salem Black River Presbyterian Church (George Howe, *History of the Presbyterian Church in South Carolina* [Columbia: Duffie and Chapman, 1870] 1:327). While St. Mark's chapel of ease, only later to be constituted as a church, was within close proximity of the High Hills Baptist Church, Salem Black River was some distance removed and outside the High Hills.

[41]Hart's Diary, 86. The reference is evidently to Joseph Reese.

[42]The tradition is based on wording in the 1756 grant, which describes the 350 acres as bounded "part on said Haynsworth's land and part on Mr. Osborn's land." The Haynsworth home place was located on land now occupied by Shaw Air Force Base, therefore, eastward across the High Hills from the Furman land in Wateree Valley (Haynsworth, *Haynsworth-Furman and Allied Families*, 37, 39).

term applied to the owner of one or more plantations and numerous slaves.[43]

In November following the marriage of Henry Haynsworth and Sarah Furman, the Haynsworth and Furman families became more closely bound by another marriage. On the twentieth day of that month, Richard Furman, then nineteen, married Elizabeth Haynsworth, also nineteen, Henry Haynsworth's sister. Furman referred to her affectionately as Betsy. What is known of her portrays her as a gentle person whose loyalty to her husband never faltered. Their married life spanned the war years and resulted in the birth of four children: a son, who died at birth in August 1775; a daughter, Rachel, born 16 March 1777; a second son, Wood, born 12 July 1779; and a third son, Richard II, who lived only sixteen months after his birth in July 1783.[44]

Richard and Elizabeth began their married life on land on or near Wood Furman's plantation.[45] The Haynsworth and Furman lands were separated by about six miles and were connected by a road that ran generally east to west over the High Hills and through what would become Stateburg. The marriage of sister and brother to brother and sister brought the two families together in ties of genuine affection.[46] But marriage did not make a Baptist of Elizabeth. Unlike her sister-in-law, Sarah, she remained true to her Anglican upbringing. Considering the "uncommonly serious" manner in which young Furman took his conversion, it is unlikely, however, that she escaped being the object of his persuasion. She took seriously the duties of wife and mother and perhaps considered this to be her part in the ministerial career of her husband.

---

[43]Ibid., 38.

[44]Ibid., 123.

[45]Robert Mills's *Atlas of South Carolina* (a new facsimile edition of the original 1825 edition; Columbia: Lucy Hampton Bostick and Fant H. Thornley, 1938), shows "R Furman" owning a home place on or near the original 250 acres granted to his father in 1756. In a letter to his father, written in 1782 while a refugee in North Carolina during the war, Richard Furman speaks with anticipation of returning to the High Hills and "living near you once more."

[46]This is apparent from family correspondence between the High Hills and Charleston after Furman moved to that city in 1787.

These early years of Furman's ministry saw him engaged in pastoral duties for the High Hills congregation and ranging widely in missionary evangelism on both sides of the Wateree River. His style of preaching was described as animated, but without the emotionalism of Separate Baptist preachers.[47] The qualities ascribed to him, intellectual power combined with gentle manner and benevolent spirit, were those that would carry into the floodtide years of his ministry. But circumstances were evolving that would temporarily interrupt his pastoral ministry and cast him in the role of a champion of political and religious liberty.

---

[47]H. T. Cook, *Biography*, 8.

CHAPTER 3

Patriot of the Revolution

When Oliver Hart left Charleston on 27 December 1773 to attend the "big meeting" at the High Hills, he left a city seething with excitement over the British imposition of a tax on tea. The same month far to the north, New Englanders had staged the Boston Tea Party in defiance of British policy. On 1 December, the arrival in Charleston of 257 chests of tea, consigned by the East India Company to Charleston merchants to be sold on commission, had raised the issue to such public notice that a mass meeting was held on 3 January at the Exchange Building and a resolution adopted against importing or buying any tea taxed to raise revenue in America.

This marked the beginning of a series of events that would find South Carolina joined in a continental association of colonies to resist British violation of American rights. Before the end of the year, Thomas Lynch, Christopher Gadsden, Edward Rutledge, Henry Middleton, and John Rutledge had represented South Carolina in the First Continental Congress. By successive stages of extra-legal provincial organization, the state abandoned its loyalty to Great Britain and inaugurated representative self-government under its own constitution. In his diary of 26

March, Oliver Hart wrote, "South Carolina broke off the British yoke and established a new form of Government upon a free and generous Plan, and Rulers being chosen from among ourselves. May we never again be enslaved!"[1]

The second session of the First Provincial Congress convened in June 1775 following news that the opening guns of revolution had been fired at Lexington and Concord, Massachusetts, in April. Hasty action was taken to organize defensive military organizations, procure arms and equipment for the troops, issue paper money to finance military expenses, and elect unit commanders. Also adopted was a test oath termed the "Association."[2] Signers of the agreement pledged to defend the colonial cause against Great Britain by arms if necessary. Before its adjournment, the Congress called for an election of delegates from every district and parish to meet that autumn in the Second Provincial Congress. A Council of Safety was authorized to exercise broad executive powers in matters of defense and finance.

The Congress further provided that copies of the Association oath be printed "on the largest paper that can be procured," to be signed by

---

[1] Diary of Oliver Hart, 1740-1780, MS in the South Caroliniana Library, 135, quoted in *Extracts from the Journals of the Provincial Congresses of South Carolina, 1775-1776*, ed. William Edwin Hemphill and Wylma Anne Wates (Columbia: South Carolina Archives Department, 1960) xviii.

[2] The Association oath read as follows: "The actual commencement of hostilities against this continent, by the British troops, in the bloody scene on the 19th of April last, near Boston—the increase of arbitrary impositions from a wicked and despotic ministry—and the dread of insurrections in the colonies—are causes sufficient to drive an oppressed people to the use of arms; We, therefore, the subscribers, inhabitants of South Carolina, holding ourselves bound, by that most sacred of all obligations, the duty of citizens toward an injured country, all thoroughly convinced, that, under our present distressed circumstances, we shall be justified before God and Man, in resisting force for force; DO UNITE ourselves, under every tie of religion and of honour, and associate, as a band in her defence, against every foe: Hereby solemnly engaging that, whenever our Continental or Provincial Councils shall decree it necessary, we will go forth, and be ready to sacrifice our lives and fortunes to secure her freedom and safety. This obligation to continue in full force until a reconciliation shall take place between Great-Britain and America, upon constitutional principles—an Event which we most ardently desire. And we will hold all those persons inimical to the liberty of the colonies, who shall refuse to subscribe this association" (Hemphill and Wates, *Extracts from the Journals of the Provincial Congresses of South Carolina, 1775-1776*, 36).

its own members, and that deputies for each parish or district be furnished with two copies each to obtain signatures from the inhabitants they represented. Failure to sign was considered evidence of being opposed to the cause of independence.

The Furman home district east of the Wateree had ten representatives in the First Provincial Congress. The ones best known to history were Colonel Richard Richardson, later a general, of lower St. Mark's Parish, senior officer of the state militia; Joseph Kershaw, merchant and founder of Camden; William Richardson of Bloom Hill Plantation in the sand hills at the entrance to the High Hills; Matthew Singleton, owner of Melrose Plantation, now a part of Poinsett State Park; and Thomas Sumter, then a country squire operating a store near the Nelson Ferry crossing of the Santee River.

Since Joseph Kershaw traveled the road to Camden that led through the High Hills on his return from the Provincial Congress, he probably circulated the Association oath through the Furman neighborhood. For the entire district east of the Wateree, 101 persons signed. Among them were Wood Furman and his son-in-law, Henry Haynsworth.[3]

Richard Furman's name does not appear on the Association oath, but his support of the Revolution became one of the distinguishing marks of his career. In 1775, just one year into his pastorate at the High Hills, he sought support among backcountry settlements for the new government and for the constitution created by the provincial congresses. The mere isolation of these regions prevented their feeling British wrongs as did coast dwellers or planters in constant contact with the more restrictive laws. Furthermore, deep-seated resentment at the long delay in granting courts and representation, for which the backcountry men held the coastal planters and merchants more responsible than the king, and resentment at the disdain with which the backwoodsmen were often treated, were a poor preface for an invitation to join in war against the king. Particularly disturbing was the situation among Scotch-Irish settlers in that large part of the backcountry between the Broad and Saluda rivers. As accustomed to fighting for their political opinions as were the English in the Lowcountry, they were led by men of influence and intelligence, like Robert and Patrick Cunningham, whose family had

---

[3]Haynsworth, *Haynsworth-Furman and Allied Families*, 40.

struggled for religious liberty in Scotland before migrating to Virginia in 1769. The Cunninghams represented "the virtues as well as the better-known cruelty of the Tories."[4]

Faced with the threat of revolutionary dissidents, the Council of Safety, headed by Henry Laurens, appointed William Henry Drayton and the Reverend William Tennent, pastor of the Independent or Congregational church in Charleston, to go to the frontier to encourage loyalty among the settlers for the American cause. Both were members of the Council of Safety. Four days later, Laurens addressed a letter to Oliver Hart asking him to join Tennent and Drayton on the backcountry mission. Hart accepted the assignment and set out on the journey on 31 July 1775. His diary records their purpose as "to reconcile a number of the inhabitants, who are disaffected to Government."

Furman received no official appointment as did Drayton, Tennent, and Hart, but he addressed himself to the same cause. During wide-swinging preaching missions between the Congaree and Wateree rivers on the west and the Pee Dee on the east, he listened with growing concern and alarm to the prevalence and depth of Tory sentiment. Charles Woodmason, rector of St. Mark's Parish, had warned in 1771 that backcountry settlers would prefer the protection of Parliament rather "than be subject to a junto in Charleston."[5] At Camden, Furman was not allowed to preach in the courthouse when the sheriff learned that he was not a clergyman of the Church of England.[6] He then preached in the open air, and so effectively that "the principal resident of the place, by whose instigation, it was believed, the sheriff acted [,] was seen after the sermon showing the preacher marked attention."[7]

Among the Scotch-Irish between the Broad and Saluda, a body of Tories was formed during the summer of 1775 led by Thomas Fletch-

---

[4]D. D. Wallace, *South Carolina: A Short History, 1522-1948* (Columbia: University of South Carolina Press, 1961) 264.

[5]William M. Dabney and Marion Dargan, *William Henry Drayton and the American Revolution* (Albuquerque: University of New Mexico Press, 1962) 90.

[6]Thomas J. Kirkland and Robert M. Kennedy, *Historic Camden* (Columbia: The State Company, 1926) 2:277, taken from a sketch of Camden Baptist Church by T. E. Goodale.

[7]Ibid.

all, colonel of the militia and a man of considerable influence. The Provincial Congress had named Fletchall to a committee to obtain signatures among his people for the Association oath; but when the Council of Safety heard that his support for the patriot cause was wavering, Henry Laurens, council president, wrote a letter on 14 July asking him to declare where he stood in the dispute between the colonies and the Crown. In his reply, Fletchall declared the reports false, said that he had mustered his troops, ordered the Association oath read to each company, and noted that no one had signed it and that he could not compel them to do so. Instead, he added, the people of his section had drawn up an association of their own and adopted a resolution declaring that

> . . .upon mature deliberation it is our opinions . . . that our Sovereign Lord the King George the Third of Great Britain, etc., has not acted inconsistent with and subversive of the principles of the constitutions of the British empire, at least at present; that we have no authority sufficient or testimony authenticated to convince thereof to such a degree as to forfeit his right to our allegiance as formerly.[8]

As a frontiersman himself, and a young minister of dissenting faith who had traveled and preached among them, Furman could address the dissidents as "Friends, Brethren, and Fellow-Subjects." His lengthy letter to the Broad River-Saluda Scotch-Irish, written in November from the High Hills of Santee, was a strong defense of the action of the Continental Congress and the South Carolina Provincial Congress. For a young man just twenty years of age, it illustrated how well informed he was on issues stirring the public mind. Signed "A Loyal Subject," it portrayed himself and the colony not as favoring separation from England but as wanting correction of grievances against the Mother Country.[9]

Civil war was already threatening the backcountry with the arrest of Robert Cunningham and a retaliatory seizure of public ammunition by his brother Patrick in October and November 1775. The fear among backwoodsmen was that the Council of Safety was sending ammunition

---

[8]*Collections of the South Carolina Historical Society*, 1858, 2:72-73.

[9]See Appendix A for full text of Furman's letter.

to the Cherokee Indians to attack the British Loyalists. A three-day battle occurred near Ninety-Six, 19 to 21 November, in which the first
blood of the Revolution in South Carolina was shed. As a reinforcement
contingent under the command of Colonel (later General) Richard
Richardson was en route to Ninety-Six, a copy of Furman's letter fell
into his hands. He was so impressed with its contents that he had copies
made and distributed in advance of his army.[10]

Furman's visits to Tory settlements were seldom without danger to
his personal safety. An instance is recorded when the chief men of a Tory
encampment toward which he was moving determined to deliver him
to the British. Unaware of any danger, upon his arrival Furman defended the American cause with such force and logic that his listeners
suspected they were mistaken and abandoned their opposition.[11]

The year 1776 was ushered in against this backdrop of the mount-
ing tension of 1775. On 4 July, the Continental Congress adopted the
Declaration of Independence. Soon thereafter Furman took the oath of
allegiance administered by General Richardson at the head of his bri-
gade. With the die thus cast and the state threatened with invasion,
Furman marched off to Charleston with a volunteer company commanded by his brother, Captain Josiah Furman, prepared for military
duty. But President John Rutledge advised him to return to the backcountry, declaring that his influence there as a minister and supporter
of independence would be more valuable than as a soldier in uniform.[12]

Furman's activities during the following several years are not easily
traced. His only surviving letter prior to the end of the war is dated
November 1782. Compounding the silence, the High Hills church book
prior to 1875 was burned that year in the house of Deacon C. C. Jackson.[13] What is known is that he broadened his acquaintance with other

---

[10]H. T. Cook, *Biography*, 51. This is an apparent addition to the letter made by
an unknown person.

[11]Ibid. Cook says that Hart was present with Furman on this occasion, but he was
probably in error since nowhere in Hart's diary does he say that Furman was with him
on any of his backcountry travels.

[12]Ibid.; H. T. Cook, *Biography*, 11.

[13]Townsend, *History of South Carolina Baptists*, 154n.

ministers, advocated the cause of civil and religious liberty, attended to his pastoral duties, assisted in the organization of new churches, and began rearing a family. To him and his wife Elizabeth a son was born in August 1775, but the child died at birth. There followed a daughter on 16 March 1777, and a son on 12 July 1779.[14] With parental loyalty they named them Rachel and Wood, in honor of his parents.

In Furman's travels during this period, he was accompanied by Timothy Dargan, a convert of Joseph Reese who would later become the first pastor of Ebenezer Baptist Church on Jeffrey's Creek, which was constituted in January 1778. For its constitution, the Reverend Evan Pugh, pastor of the Cashaway Church[15] and itinerant minister throughout the Pee Dee, was assisted by Furman.

Among ministers with whom he broadened his acquaintance was the Reverend John Gano, a native of New Jersey who engaged in extensive missionary journeys into the South during a long pastoral and itinerant ministry. Furman's first acquaintance with Gano came when he accompanied him into Georgia and gained early impressions of his knowledge of the Scripture and his eloquence, evangelical zeal, and personal devotion.[16] On this trip Furman also met for the first time the Reverend Daniel Marshall, father of the Reverend Abraham Marshall, and the Reverend Edmund Botsford, then a resident of Georgia. Botsford would later become pastor of Welsh Neck Baptist Church and the church at Georgetown, in that order. Between Furman and Botsford developed a warm friendship that lasted a lifetime.

He also met Joseph Cook whose ordination into the ministry was conducted by Furman at the High Hills church on 27 April 1776, assisted by Hart.[17] Cook was a native of Bath, England, who was converted under the preaching of George Whitefield and admitted at nineteen years of age into the college of Lady Huntingdon at Trevecka,

---

[14]Haynsworth, *Haynsworth-Furman and Allied Families*, 123.

[15]Townsend, *History of South Carolina Baptists*, 106.

[16]H. T. Cook, *Biography*, 10.

[17]Hart Diary, Manuscript Division, William R. Perkins Library, Duke University, with introduction by Loulie Latimer Owens, 392.

in Brecknockshire, South Wales.[18] In 1774 he came to America under the sponsorship of Lady Huntingdon. Ostensibly an Episcopalian, he became strongly impressed with Baptist views respecting believers' baptism. Upon his marriage to a young lady of Baptist parents, who resided at Dorchester about eighteen miles from Charleston, he settled there and preached to a mixed congregation of Episcopalians, Baptists, and Independents.

Cook was at the High Hills church in April 1776 for a discussion by dissenting ministers on religious liberty. He remained until the next Sabbath, since it was the season to administer the Lord's Supper. As was the custom, worship services were held on the two preceding days. On Saturday he was invited to preach, but before the service began, he took Hart and Furman aside to tell of his belief concerning baptism. On the following day he was baptized, and a few days later Hart and Furman ordained him into the Baptist ministry.[19] Soon thereafter, he became pastor of the Euhaw Baptist Church, one of the four original churches comprising the Charleston Baptist Association. He preached there without interruption until war conditions along the coast caused him to move to an interior part of the country. At war's end he returned to Euhaw and labored with much success.[20]

---

[18]Lady Huntingdon and her husband, the Earl of Huntingdon, were both descendants of ancient monarchs. An early childhood experience laid hold on her conscience and developed in her a serious mind that turned her thoughts to religion. Accustomed to walking in royal circles, she found no pleasure in their way of life but sought by good deeds to "establish her own righteousness." During this time of English history, England was being shaken by zealous preachers given the name Methodists, among them the Wesleys and George Whitefield. Converted under their preaching was her husband's sister, Lady Margaret Hastings, who testified to the joy she had experienced as a consequence. It was a joy that Lady Huntingdon had never felt. Soon thereafter, she was stricken with a serious illness and considered sending for Bishop Benson of Gloucester, who had been her husband's tutor. But recalling the words of Lady Margaret, she experienced a similar conversion herself. Recovering from her illness, she dedicated herself to Christian works—among them the establishment of schools for the training of ministers, some of whom, including Joseph Cook, were sent to America under her sponsorship. John Rippon, *The Baptist Annual Register of the State of Religion among Different Denominations of Good Men at Home and Abroad*, 4 vols. (London: Dilly, Button, and Thomas, 1790-1802) 4:684-86, James P. Boyce Library, Southern Baptist Theological Seminary, Louisville, Kentucky.

[19]Benedict, *A General History of the Baptist Denomination*, 2:280-86.

[20]Ibid., 286.

Another who came with Cook from England under Lady Huntingdon's sponsorship was Lewis Richards. For a while he suppressed his convictions and worked in an Episcopal parish as a candidate for the rectorship. He later united with the Baptist church at the High Hills of Santee and was baptized by Furman. For many years he was the distinguished pastor of the Baptist church in Baltimore, Maryland.[21]

Furman's acquaintance and correspondence with ministers would in time extend up and down the Eastern seaboard and to prominent English ministers. But as a young minister during the early years of his High Hills pastorate when Baptist churches were few and ordained Baptist preachers were fewer,[22] his ministerial associates were limited.

RELIGIOUS LIBERTY

The 27 April 1776 meeting of dissenters, mentioned earlier, is one of the more important events in South Carolina religious history. Though a provision of state government permitted religious tolerance for all sects, the constitution recognized and legally supported through taxation the Church of England as the established church. For religious dissenters, especially Baptists, this was a grievous infringement upon religious liberty.

At a Welsh Neck church meeting, the Reverend Elhanan Winchester had proposed a meeting of churches at the High Hills of Santee on the last Sunday in April "in order to choose delegates to attend the Continental Association" to press the cause of religious liberty.[23] This initiative by Baptists was extended to include dissenting members "of all denominations."[24] At the April meeting delegates were appointed

---

[21]Ibid., 284.

[22]In his account of South Carolina Baptists in 1772, Morgan Edwards lists twenty-four organized churches with forty-nine meetinghouses, and about the same number of ministers, licensed preachers, and exhorters.

[23]Welsh Neck Church Book, 8 March 1776, microfilm copy, SCBHS, Furman University.

[24]Anne King Gregorie in her *History of Sumter County*, 41, says that this meeting was "probably called by Furman." This, however, contradicts the Welsh Neck Church Book, which credits Elhanan Winchester with having proposed the meeting; see Townsend, *History of South Carolina Baptists*, 277. Furman's church at the High Hills was centrally located and therefore a convenient place to meet.

and instructed "to obtain our liberties and freedom from religious tyranny or ecclesiastical oppression."[25] From this meeting came the "Dissenters' Petition." It went before the Commons House of Assembly in
January 1777 and, after prolonged debate, resulted in disestablishment
of the Church of England and equality for all churches.

Though the proceedings of the High Hills meeting itself are lost to
history, in attendance was probably the most prestigious interdenominational gathering of clergymen yet assembled in South Carolina history. Furman was then only twenty-one years of age. Other Baptists at
the meeting included Oliver Hart, whose presence would lend distinction to the gathering; Evan Pugh, who had just completed an interim
pastorate of the Welsh Neck church;[26] Elhanan Winchester, then pastor of the Welsh Neck church;[27] Joseph Reese, from the Congaree church
beyond the Wateree; J. B. Cook, the young man from the Countess of
Huntingdon's school in England; perhaps Edmund Botsford, who would
succeed Winchester as pastor of the Welsh Neck church and later move
on to Georgetown; Timothy Dargan, close friend and traveling companion of Furman on their preaching missions around "the middle
country" of South Carolina; and yet others from the twenty-eight Baptist churches then in South Carolina. The number of dissenting churches
in South Carolina early in 1777 was given by William Tennent as sev-
enty-nine.[28] The Presbyterians would certainly include Thomas Reese,
a greatly revered pastor then in his third year as pastor of Salem Black
River Presbyterian Church; and most prominent of all, William Tennent, the Presbyterian minister of the Independent church in Charleston, who had been on the 1775 mission to the backcountry with William
Henry Drayton and Oliver Hart.

---

[25]Welsh Neck Church Book, April 1776, quoted in Townsend, *History of South
Carolina Baptists*, 152.

[26]John Stout, *Historical Sketch of the Welsh Neck Baptist Church, 1738-1888, For the
220th Anniversary of the Church* (Greenville SC: Hoyt and Keys, 1889; Columbia: State
Printing Co., 1963) 8.

[27]Ibid.

[28]Edward McCrady, *History of South Carolina in the Revolution, 1775-1780* (New
York: Russell and Russell, 1901) 210. H. T. Cook in his *Biography*, 63, distributes
these, "subject to correction," as thirty-eight Presbyterian, twenty-eight Baptist, eight
Lutheran, and five unclassified.

Tennent was selected to lead the fight in South Carolina. Then thirty-six years of age, "of majestic and venerable presence," he was the foremost Presbyterian or Congregational minister in South Carolina. Like Hart and Furman, the leading Baptists, he was a committed leader in the Revolution.[29] On 11 January 1777, after the "Dissenters' Petition" had been presented by Christopher Gadsden, Tennent made an eloquent speech in the Commons House on behalf of religious equality. Laws, he declared,

> . . .which made odious distinctions between subjects equally good ought not to be tolerated. . . . Would it content our brethren of the Church of England to be barely tolerated, that is, not punished, for presuming to think for themselves? With the new Constitution, let the day of justice dawn on every rank and order of men in this State. . . . Yield to the mighty current of American freedom and glory, and let our State be inferior to none on this wide continent in the liberality of its laws and in the happiness of its people.[30]

The key passage in the petition read:

> There shall never be an establishment of any one Denomination or sect of Protestants, by way of preference to another in this State. That no Protestant inhabitant of this State, shall by law, be obliged to pay towards the maintenance and support of a religious worship that he does not freely join in or has not voluntarily engaged to support, not to be denied the enjoyment of any civil right merely on account of his religious principles, but that all Protestants demeaning themselves peaceably under the government established under the constitution shall enjoy free and equal privileges, both religious and civil.[31]

Efforts to obtain some privilege for Episcopalians without financial support for their church were beaten down seventy to sixty after a prolonged debate. Rawlins Lowndes and Charles Pinckney contended for

---

[29]Wallace, *South Carolina: A Short History*, 279.

[30]Ibid., 279-80.

[31]Cited in H. T. Cook, *Biography*, 54-55; see also McCrady, *History of South Carolina in the Revolution*, 212-13.

retention of the Anglican establishment, but Charles Cotesworth Pinckney stood with the dissenters. Disestablishment was then given a unanimous second reading. The new legislated constitution was printed in pamphlet form and left for public consideration for a year.[32]

On 3 February following this action, the Charleston Baptist Association met and adopted a circular letter in which Baptist support for the new constitution was strongly urged.

> We are likely to have a most excellent civil government in this State; settled upon the most equitable foundation, securing liberty and property to all well affected subjects of the same and, as this excellent Constitution is intended for our safety and happiness, in common with others, we recommend to you all to endeavor to support it to the utmost of your power.
>
> We are happy in being able to say that there is not one in this Association but heartily joins in the measures taken by America in general and this state in particular, to secure our liberties. . . . We heartily congratulate you on the prospect of obtaining universal religious liberty in this state; an event which must cause every generous mind to rejoice. . . . [33]

The letter was signed by Evan Pugh, moderator, and Oliver Hart, clerk.

Since the High Hills church was not a member of the Charleston Association until 1778, Furman was probably not present for the meeting at which this action was taken. But one week later, Hart sent him a copy of the minutes, including a personal letter in which he spoke of "the bright prospect that we shall obtain religious liberty, in its full extent, in this State." This cannot fail, he said, "if we dissenters will be careful to attend the next meeting of the Assembly. . . ." Hart added that "your father will inform you of the particulars."[34] Wood Furman

---

[32]Wallace, *South Carolina: A Short History*, 280.

[33]Oliver Hart to Richard Furman, 12 February 1777, SCBHS; H. T. Cook, *Biography*, 56-57; *Minutes of the Charleston Baptist Association*, 3 February 1777, microfilm copy, SCBHS.

[34]Oliver Hart to Richard Furman, 12 February 1777, SCBHS.

was a member of the second session of the General Assembly when the "Dissenters' Petition" was presented.[35]

The Constitution was given a third reading in March 1778. By its provisions, the Anglican Church was disestablished but retained all its property. Protestantism was declared the "established religion" in South Carolina, with any Protestant church electing its own pastor being entitled to incorporate.

Due credit must go to William Tennent. In his *History of the Presbyterian Church in South Carolina*, George Howe says of him, "He employed his pen from time to time in the public prints in the cause of civil freedom and on the eleventh of February, 1777, he delivered an eloquent speech in the House of the Assembly, Charleston, advocating a petition penned by himself to which had been attached the signatures of many thousands against the church establishment that the Church of England had always enjoyed under the Colonial government."[36]

But Tennent was only one of the many dissenters who joined in the effort. The choice of Tennent to lead the fight and act as their spokesman was logical. He was both an influential and eloquent spokesman and thoroughly committed to the cause. Equally important, he was a member of the General Assembly where the issue would be debated. Internal evidence, however, points clearly to a joint effort originating with Furman's church at the High Hills meetings of April 1776. Thirty years later, Furman made reference to "the petition from the numerous body of citizens who had been Dissenters."[37] But Tennent himself added the clinching evidence in his own speech when he declared, "It is our birthright that we prize. . . . We seek no restitution. . . . Will the danger arise from the dissenting denominations? No: it answers the prayers of their petitions. Will the danger arise from the Church of England? Many of them have signed the petition. Many more have declared their sentiments in the most liberal terms. . . ."[38]

---

[35]William Edwin Hemphill, Wylma Anne Wates, and R. Nicholas Olsberg, eds., *Journals of the General Assembly and House of Representatives, 1776-1780* (Columbia: University of South Carolina Press, 1970) 321.

[36]Howe, *History of the Presbyterian Church in South Carolina*, 1:372.

[37]H. T. Cook, *Biography*, 62.

[38]Howe, *History of the Presbyterian Church in South Carolina*, 1:371.

This was Tennent's final public function. In the summer of 1777, he went to New York to bring his widowed and aged mother to his home in Charleston. Upon returning and reaching Bloom Hill, the plantation home of William Richardson in the High Hills of Santee, he contracted a fatal nervous disorder. From his home, Furman went to Tennent's bedside and remained there until his death. "I was with him," he later wrote to Mrs. Tennent, "in his last moments—his life went gently from him, almost without a struggle or a groan. He told me in almost the last words that he spoke, that his mind was calm and easy, and he was willing to be gone."[39] On hearing of Tennent's death, Oliver Hart delivered a sermon to his Charleston congregation from 2 Samuel 3:38: "Know ye not that there is a great man fallen this day in Israel?"[40]

Twin motives for supporting the Revolutionary cause—civil and religious liberty—were now merged in the state constitution. Three months after adoption of a temporary state constitution in March 1776, the American Declaration of Independence settled the question of whether colonial rebellion was intended to sever ties with Great Britain or merely seek a redress of grievances without severance. The cause was now broader than that argued by Furman in his November 1775 letter to the disaffected residents between the Broad and Saluda rivers. It focused upon a free country and a free church.

WAR REFUGEE

In May 1780 Charleston fell to the British, and Cornwallis fanned his troops out across the state. In August they passed through the High Hills and established themselves in Camden. There in August Cornwallis met and defeated General Horatio Gates, the hero of Saratoga. It was an American disaster without parallel in the Revolution. With Charleston in hand and a string of British forts established across the state from Georgetown and Cheraw to Ninety-Six, complete British subjugation of South Carolina appeared militarily certain.

At his home in the High Hills, Furman watched the gathering storm with alarm for the safety of himself and his family. His friend Oliver

---

[39]Ibid., 1:372.

[40]Hart's Diary, *Yearbook, City of Charleston, S.C.,* 1896, 393; *Collections of the Historical Society of South Carolina*, South Carolina Historical Society, 1858, 64.

Hart had fled from Charleston in February when the British fleet appeared off Stono Bar and moved into the lines before Charleston. It was his last farewell to the city he had served since 1749. At Welsh Neck on the Pee Dee he was joined by Edmund Botsford.[41] The two traveled together for 700 miles until they parted in Prince William Parish, Virginia, with Botsford remaining as a refugee in that state and Hart moving on to Hopewell, New Jersey.[42] Similar circumstances had befallen J. B. Cook, pastor of Euhaw church near the coast. The invasion of the state exposed his coastal situation and subjected him to such losses and distress that he moved to the interior part of the country "for greater safety."[43]

Furman had special reason for concern. His zealous activities as a patriot had reached the ears of Cornwallis, who, it is said, offered a thousand pounds for his capture, declaring that he feared Furman's prayers more than the armies of Generals Francis Marion and Thomas Sumter.[44]

The Furman home was just off the road leading to Camden, twenty miles away from where Cornwallis established his headquarters in the summer of 1780 in the two-story home of merchant Joseph Kershaw. This road was the main British supply route between Charleston and Camden. The American disaster at Camden in August would surely have

---

[41]Hart's Diary, *Yearbook, City of Charleston, S.C., 1896,* 400.

[42]Benedict, *General History of the Baptist Denomination,* 2:324.

[43]Ibid., 286.

[44]This story is legendary, and efforts to document it from an original source have failed. But it appears in numerous published accounts, including the Furman biography edited by Cook. A story appearing in *Baptist Memorial and Monthly Chronicle,* vol. 15, 1856, attributes to Furman his own affirmation of the story in a conversation with James Monroe in Washington; this will be discussed later. Loulie Latimer Owens, authoritative South Carolina Baptist historian and author, surmises that a price was on the head of all well-known zealous patriots and that Cornwallis did not single Furman out as more objectionable than others. But it is not improbable that a copy of Furman's anti-British letter to the residents between the Broad and Saluda may have fallen into the hands of Cornwallis, which gave him special reason to focus on the young preacher. As Cornwallis became disabused of his earlier belief that he had South Carolina under his heel and began to look for scapegoats, none was more convenient than Furman, who, "as an ardent advocate of rebellion," had preached it everywhere, "on stumps, in barns, as well as in the pulpit" (H. T. Cook, *Biography,* 72).

been an unsettling thing in the Furman household. News must have reached them earlier that South Carolina's President (Governor) John Rutledge, while fleeing from Charleston, had narrowly missed being captured at Rugeley's just above Camden, and that Lieutenant Colonel Banastre Tarleton had massacred Buford's Virginians in the Waxhaws in present-day Lancaster County.

Deep gloom had settled over South Carolina, even more so because its citizens were divided between Whigs and Tories, and the war had become civil as well as revolutionary. Under these circumstances, Furman believed it best to follow the course of Hart, Botsford, and Cook and seek safety elsewhere. He took his young family into North Carolina where he settled near the Virginia line on the Mayo River.[45]

The circumstances that dictated his decision are illustrated by an incident described by one of his sons, probably James. He was fleeing from a party of Tories and was in danger of being taken. The night was upon him; darkness favored his escape, but it also exposed him to unseen forces.

> A discharge of musketry at a little distance increased his apprehension as he judged it must proceed from the firing of British soldiers who were encamping for the night, or were in pursuit of prisoners. Either view was sufficiently unfavorable to the feeling of safety; he quickened his pace in order to escape from the dangerous vicinity. He had not gone far when he heard the tramp of horses' feet; and was soon accosted by a man whom he perceived by the clanking of his armor to be heavily armed.
>
> Who are you? said the stranger, the click of his pistol accompanying his words.
>
> A friend, responded Mr. F.
>
> A friend to whom? rejoined the interrogator.
>
> A friend of the country, was the truthful and intrepid reply.
>
> The unknown captor now recognized Mr. Furman's voice and informing him that he was himself making his escape from the enemy, inquired from what direction he was coming. Upon learning this he

---

[45]The Mayo is a small stream forty-five miles long that originates in the Virginia Piedmont and empties into the Dan River a few miles into North Carolina below the Virginia line. See Richard Furman to his wife, Dorothea Furman, 18 October 1819, SCBHS.

informed Mr. F. that he had passed within a very short distance of a party of British soldiers into whose hands, had he been a few moments earlier, he must have inevitably fallen, as they had a short while before crossed the road over which he had just passed.[46]

In selecting the Mayo River in the borderline area between North Carolina and Virginia as a place of refuge, Furman was deep in the western Piedmont area of the state, an area relatively undisturbed by the war, which, unlike in South Carolina, had been largely confined to the east. Ironically, it would not remain so. In 1781 Cornwallis pursued General Nathanael Greene into the very area where the Furmans resided and won a Pyrrhic victory in the celebrated Battle of Guilford Courthouse. It was probably during that time, as Cook points out, that Furman "frequently visited and preached to the troops."[47]

This had been Baptist country. It was where the Separates under Shubal Stearns, Daniel Marshall, and the Sandy Creek church had initiated the Separate Baptist religious movement before the Battle of Alamance. For more than a year Furman remained a refugee, traveling and preaching among the churches as far down as Rowan County in North Carolina[48] and up into Henry County, Virginia. He formed a strong attachment to the people wherever he preached, and they, in turn, demonstrated their affection for him and his family by many acts of kindness.[49] In Virginia, he established a friendship with Patrick Henry, then living on his Leatherwood plantation in Henry County[50] following three terms as governor of Virginia. The celebrated Virginian, who already had a long history of friendly relations with the Virginia Baptists, was a sometime listener to Furman's sermons and was so impressed with his preaching that he gave him two volumes of Ward's *Oratory* with the inscription "Richard Furman, his book, presented to him by the Hon-

[46]MS fragment, unsigned, undated, Furman Papers, SCBHS.

[47]H. T. Cook, *Biography*, 12.

[48]Benedict, *General History of the Baptist Denomination*, 2:12.

[49]MS fragment, unsigned, undated, Furman Papers, SCBHS.

[50]Norine Dickson Campbell, *Patrick Henry: Patriot and Statesman* (New York: David Adair Company, 1969) 282.

orable Patrick Henry, late Governor of Virginia, May 5th, 1782."[51] The homes of the Furmans at Mayo River and the Henrys at Leatherwood were in adjacent North Carolina and Virginia counties. Years later, when Furman was returning from the organizational meeting of the Triennial Convention in Philadelphia, he would drive sixty miles out of his way to visit the widow of Patrick Henry.[52]

In 1782 the British had been pressed back into Charleston and their evacuation of that city appeared imminent. At Mayo River, Furman was eager to return home and resume his ministry. In October he wrote his father of his "earnest desire to live near you once more" and of his intention to return to South Carolina that fall unless he received more unfavorable accounts of the situation than he had "at present." Latest information "in these parts from the northward," he said, was that the French fleet "which was damaged and not taken in action with Rodney" lay at Boston, General Washington had a respectable army near King's Bridge, the French fleet had received a reinforcement of seven ships of the line and 18,000 troops in the West Indies, and Governor Martin had lately received an official account from Congress informing him that John Adams was received as the American ambassador at The Hague and "was negotiating [or had done so] a Treaty of Commerce." Furman had kept up with the news.

He accompanied this letter with another to the church inquiring about the "safety and expediency" of his return, adding that should the British continue in Charleston "and the robberies which I have heard of continue to be practiced about the Hills," the prospect would be "rather discouraging." The church was ready and a Mr. Hamilton had offered to come for him in a wagon caravan. Furman feared this would be an inconvenience, but hoped it would be in his power "sometime or other to make compensation for so great a favour." He advised that whoever should come "would come armed."[53] Accordingly, a well-armed party

---

[51]MS fragment, unsigned, undated, Furman Papers, SCBHS.

[52]Richard Furman to his wife, Dorothea Furman, 18 October 1814, SCBHS.

[53]For the details cited in this and the foregoing paragraphs, see Richard Furman to Wood Furman, 17 October 1782, postdated at Mayo River, contained in the Furman Papers, SCBHS. Numerous published accounts, including H. T. Cook's, record that Furman fled to Virginia and North Carolina. I find no original source, however,

of his friends formed protective coverage for his return.[54] He arrived in the autumn of 1782, and was welcomed affectionately by his family and joyfully by his church. The war interlude had passed. There had been years of danger and separation, but civil liberty had been won, and religious freedom was the constitutional law of the land.

In Alexander Garden's *Anecdotes of the Revolutionary War in America*, published in 1822, three years before Furman's death, he pays Furman the following tribute:

> With great delight I mention a faithful servant both of God and of the Republic, who still lives an ornament and blessing to society. In the field a hero, in private life, I know no man, that by the uniform display of talent and virtue, does greater honor to humanity than Doctor Furman. Strenuous in opposition to the invaders, he fought and he preached with energy and effect, and the recollection of his zeal to promote unanimity and steady resistance to the encroachments of the enemy, who but a little time since, should have again disturbed the tranquility of his country, demonstrated that the patriot fire that warmed his youthful bosom, burns even in advanced life with all its pristine purity and effulgence.[55]

---

to indicate that he resided in Virginia, while Furman himself speaks of residing at Mayo River, and Benedict, *History of the Baptist Denomination*, 2:112, says that he "resided and preached" in the Sandy Creek Association "during a part of the revolutionary war." It therefore seems probable that he traveled across the North Carolina line into Virginia and preached in that state, but resided in North Carolina.

[54]MS fragment, unsigned, undated, Furman Papers, SCBHS.

[55]Alexander Garden, *Anecdotes of the Revolutionary War in America* (Charleston: R. E. Miller, 1822) 205.

CHAPTER 4

Final Years
at the High Hills

None of the many military actions that occurred in South Carolina during the war took place in the immediate environs of the Furman home in the High Hills, but the fighting swirled all around that area. The final general battle in South Carolina was fought in September 1781 at Eutaw Springs, some thirty miles south. After the battle, General Greene led his troops to Bloom Hill in the lower High Hills for rest and regrouping. Thereafter, the British, pressed by units of Greene's army, gradually retreated into Charleston and evacuated that city in December 1782.

East of the Wateree, north of the Santee, and down along the Pee Dee, place names like Halfway Swamp, Nelson's Ferry, Jack's Creek, Cheraw, Black Creek, Long Bluff, Kingstree, Pocotaligo, Salem, Snow's Island, Georgetown, Singleton's Mill, the Waxhaws, and Camden had entered the lexicon of war memories, while other names like Cornwallis, Tarleton, Wemyss, Rawdon, and east-of-Wateree Tories like the Harrisons on Lynches Creek, Daniel McGirt, David Fanning, and William Rees stirred bitter memories that resulted in confiscation of land and amercement of property. Through the Pee Dee and over the northern part of the state, westward to Ninety-Six, down into the Congarees, and across the lower part of the state, the war between Loyalists and Revolutionaries had been devastating.

The Furman property in the valley of the Wateree between the river and the old Catawba Path had apparently escaped unscathed. From his fields, the aging Wood Furman furnished provisions for Continental troops and state militia, as did his son Josiah. On 27 June 1781 Brigadier General Francis Marion certified that "eighteen bushels of rice and property of Mr. Wood Furman" had been provided to "a detachment commanded by Major James." In November 1783, acting as executor of the Wood Furman estate, Richard Furman swore to war claims of Wood Furman concerning forage given to the Continental Army in 1780-1781. An indent for provisions furnished by Josiah Furman in 1781 and 1783 included two horses "pressed by the public in 1779, potatoes, corn, peas, corn blades, pork, corn meal."[1]

Surviving Baptist church records of this period leave an almost complete blank. Congregations appear to have been torn apart by bitterness. Religious services had been difficult to maintain when congregations were divided. "The war made sad havoc of friends and property, and as for religion, it was almost forgotten."[2] St. Mark's Church was too exposed on the military highway between Charleston and Camden to escape being burned by the British. A similar fate appears to have befallen Salem Black River Presbyterian Church. Its pastor, the Reverend Thomas Reese, went into exile in North Carolina, and his congregation fell victim to pillaging and murder by Tories led by the Harrison brothers on Lynches Creek.[3] The High Hills church, somewhat removed from the British supply route, appears to have survived British depredations. Its congregation, though depleted by the war and the absence of a minister, remained to welcome their returning pastor and restore regular services.

It was a harsh time. Continued enmity between Whigs and Tories bred disorder and lawlessness. Private grudges against Tory neighbors

---

[1]South Carolina Archives M8, AA 2621, and M8 2620.

[2]C. D. Mallary, *Memoir of Elder Edmund Botsford* (Charleston, 1832) 60-63, quoted in King, *A History of South Carolina Baptists*, 94.

[3]Gregorie, *History of Sumter County*, 57.

led to laws passed for the banishment of Loyalists and the amercement or confiscation of property. In 1783 the state permitted the return of seventy-seven banished Loyalists. The following year 125 were exempted from penalties, but feeling still ran high. Many who ventured back were made to suffer from the wrath of their neighbors.[4]

In 1783 the seven circuit districts were subdivided into counties so that resident magistrates might relieve the overcrowded dockets of circuit courts and thus hasten the return of peace and tranquility to the state. Thomas Sumter headed a list of seven commissioners appointed to lay off the Camden district. Assisted by surveyors—of whom Furman, trained in surveying by his father, was probably one—they established the boundaries of seven counties.

When Furman returned to South Carolina, he found his parents in good health. But four months later, in February 1783, his father died at the age of seventy. In the absence of a minister to conduct the funeral, Furman himself performed the sad task. Wood Furman had been a strong influence in the formation of his son's character. A man of industry and cultivated tastes, he had instructed his son by word and example. The assiduous manner in which young Richard studied the classics early in his life may be attributed to the presence of these works in his father's library. Nor was religion neglected in the home. Wood Furman, a church vestryman, directed a study of the Bible, and daily read portions of the Old and New Testaments in family prayer and devotional times.[5]

When Wood Furman made his Last Will and Testament in 1777, he had accumulated, by grants and purchases, 2,000 acres of land and numerous slaves. This gave him planter status and provided his wife and children with an inheritance that left them generally comfortable.[6]

---

[4]Ibid., 58.

[5]*Memoir of the Reverend Richard Furman, D.D.*, unnamed author, James P. Boyce Library, Southern Baptist Theological Seminary, Louisville, Kentucky.

[6]Wood Furman's will, made in August 1777, mentioned approximately 2,000 acres of adjoining land, including the 250 acres originally granted by Lieutenant Governor William Henry Littleton in 1756; also three slaves are mentioned by name—Sirrah, Glasgow, and Jinny, and their issue—and cows, horses, hogs, ewes, "one ram," and farming utensils (Sumter County Estates, Bundle 119, Pack 14, South Carolina Archives).

He served as surveyor, schoolmaster,[7] church vestryman,[8] and representative of the district east of the Wateree in the second, third, and fourth South Carolina Assemblies, where he served with such distinguished South Carolinians as William Henry Drayton, Christopher Gadsden, Daniel Horry, Benjamin Huger, Joseph Kershaw, Henry Laurens, Rawlins Lowndes, Thomas Lynch, Arthur Middleton, and William Moultrie.[9]

As early as 1775, his name appears among those signing a Declaration of Rights submitted to the First Provincial Congress, pledging themselves "by the most sacred of all obligations, the duty of good citizens toward an injured country," to "go forth and be ready to sacrifice our lives and fortunes to secure her freedom and safety," and further, that "this obligation is to continue to full force till reconciliation shall take place between Great Britain and America upon constitutional principles, an event we most ardently desire. . . . "[10] When Charleston fell to the British in 1780 Wood was sixty-eight years old and unfit for military service, but during the years 1780, 1781, and 1783, his plantation in the High Hills furnished provisions for troops of the state militia and the Continental Army.[11] His other positions of public service

---

[7]Gregorie, *History of Sumter County*, 174.

[8]Hugh Charles Haynsworth, "Richard Furman: Pastor and Educator," *Sandlapper Magazine* (January 1974): 33.

[9]*Biographical Directory of the South Carolina House of Representatives, 1693-1973*, ed. Walter B. Edgar (Columbia: University of South Carolina Press, 1974) 1:175, 180, 187.

[10]The name of Wood Furman appears as a signature to this document in Hugh Charles Haynsworth, *Haynsworth-Furman and Allied Families*, 40, along with the full text of the Declaration (ibid., 39-40). The Declaration, or Resolution, appears also in full text (*Extracts from the Journals of the Provincial Congresses of South Carolina, 1775-1776*, ed. William Edwin Hemphill and Wylma Anne Wates [Columbia: South Carolina State Archives Department, 1960] 26), followed by an order "to be signed by the members; and that the deputies for each parish or district be furnished with two copies, or more if necessary."

[11]Wylma Ann Wates, ed., *Stub Entries to Indents Issued in Payment of Claims Against South Carolina Growing Out of the Revolution* (Columbia: Printed for the Historical Commission of South Carolina by The State Company, 1910) 33-34.

were as an early clerk of Claremont County,[12] and a justice of the peace for the Camden district.[13]

The High Hills of the early postwar period was changing from its appearance during Richard Furman's boyhood years. In 1783 General Sumter formed a company with those who had served with him in the Revolution and purchased land on which he laid out the village of Stateburg around the old High Hills tavern.[14] Its central location, it was hoped, would make it a likely choice for the new state capital when it was moved from Charleston. Meanwhile, Sumter moved his residence from lower St. Mark's Parish into the High Hills and in 1784 purchased, "perhaps for his Stateburg home," a hilltop place now called The Ruins.[15]

Stateburg did not become the state capital, but it did become the county seat of Claremont County and remained so for the fifteen years of the county's existence. For a brief period it had a newspaper called the *Claremont Gazette*. In 1786, on what was probably one of his visits to Charleston to supply the pastorless Charleston church, Furman carried copies of the paper, as duly noted in the *Charleston Morning Post*.[16]

During that same year, Furman and his brother, Josiah, joined Sumter and others in organizing the Claremont Society. The Society, in turn, established a school known as Claremont Academy. Heading the teaching staff was William Humphries, who earlier had taught in the Waxhaws district, where he had a future president of the United States, Andrew Jackson, as one of his pupils.[17] The academy provided

---

[12]Gregorie, *History of Sumter County*, 60; Claremont County was later incorporated into the Sumter district.

[13]William Edwin Hemphill, et al., *Journals of the General Assembly and House of Representatives, 1776-1780*, 14.

[14]Gregorie, *History of Sumter County*, 62.

[15]Ibid.

[16]C. S. Brigham, *History and Bibliography of American Newspapers, 1690-1820* (Worcester MA: American Antiquarian Society, 1947) 2:1053.

[17]H. T. Cook, *Biography*, 15; Gregorie, *History of Sumter County*, 63. A petition for the academy was addressed to the General Assembly, circa 1778, asking for a "seminary of learning in the High Hills of Santee" and justifying it as follows:

a boardinghouse and a separate department for girls, but it did not prosper and is believed to have closed in 1788.[18] Furman also worked with Sumter in the formation of a library society, which maintained a circulating library. This proved more successful than the academy; it survived into the next century and in 1817 received a title for its own building.[19]

The pastor of the High Hills church was by now more than a young preacher and respected citizen of Stateburg; he was entering that period

---

That a great number of inhabitants in this part of the state are exposed to many inconveniences and disadvantages for want of a proper seminary of learning for the education of youth. Children of indigent parents and helpless orphans being thereby left in a state of almost entire ignorance, though often possessed of extraordinary natural endowments, even though in affluent circumstances put to a great deal of trouble and expense to obtain any tolerable degree of education for their children. Although societies have been formed and incorporated in other parts of the state, the wants of your petitioners are not likely to be removed as the course of the rivers and swamps which lie between them and these places are often impassable; that the healthy and beautiful as well as central location of the High Hills makes for advantageous place for erecting a seminary of learning.

Your petitioners have formed themselves into a society for the purpose of erecting an academy upon the High Hills, and ask that they may be allowed the priviledge of incorporation (MS, Caroliniana Library, University of South Carolina).

Apparently, war conditions prevented pursuit of the plan and the school did not get underway until the war had ended. In the *South Carolina Gazette*, Charleston, dated 24 April 1786, the following advertisement appeared over the names of Thomas Sumter and Richard Furman:

In compliance with the request of several gentlemen who have engaged in the design of erecting a Seminary of Learning at the High Hills of Santee, the subscribers take the liberty to inform the public, that a scheme of education has been formed, and is now opened at Statesborough under different instructors, where besides the common branches of learning taught in the English schools, the learned Languages, French, the Mathematics in all its branches, and (should design meet with proper encouragement) the other usual parts of polite and useful Literature, will be taught, with the utmost care and attention, together with a due regard to the morals of youth. The price of education is three guineas per year for an English scholar, and five Guineas for one in the languages. A Boarding House is provided at the place, where, it is designed, all suitable accommodations will be furnished for eleven Guineas.

The Gentleman who will preside in this Seminary, has produced authentic vouchers of an uncommon progress in Classical Learning, together with recommendations from persons of note in the learned world, both in Europe and America: This circumstance, added to the healthy, pleasant, and beautiful situation of the Seat of Learning (in which, perhaps, it is inferior to none on the Continent) most undoubtedly weigh, with persons who have the care of youth, in favor of this institution.

[18]Gregorie, *History of Sumter County*, 63.

[19]Ibid., 63-64.

of his life when he would be the acknowledged and respected "leader of South Carolina Baptists, and the Baptists of the South."[20] To ministerial duties and his involvement in civic work he added renewed emphasis upon serious self-improvement. Now reassociated with his friend Dr. Howard, he again studied medicine under Howard's tutelage. On his pastoral visits, he carried with him, in addition to his Bible, a supply of medicines "suitable to the more common disorders." These he "gratuitously administered . . . when a physician could not be procured."[21]

Under his leadership, the High Hills church became the mother of churches—among them Upper Fork of Lynches Creek, Ebenezer, Second Lynches Creek, Bethel, and Swift Creek, all within reasonable itinerating distance. He also frequently supplied the Charleston church, which had been pastorless since the departure of Oliver Hart. This connection with Charleston led to developments not then foreseen by Furman but prophetic of a forthcoming larger ministry.

On 14 April 1783, when the church in Charleston had recovered sufficiently from war conditions to call a permanent pastor, Hart was invited to return.[22] Then sixty-three years of age, he had been gone from Charleston for six years and was settled at Hopewell, New Jersey, "on a pretty little farm; capable with good management of producing a great variety of things."[23] He declined the Charleston call in June 1783, giving as his reasons "the providential direction he had received to Hopewell—the strength of mutual attachments—the pleasing prospects of the church he then served—his own better health—his opinion that a younger and more active man was necessary for them—and his com-

---

[20]William J. McGlothlin, *Baptist Beginnings in Education: A History of Furman University* (Nashville: Sunday School Board, Southern Baptist Convention, 1926) 28.

[21]H. T. Cook, *Biography*, 14.

[22]The invitation was written by Richard Furman, who was then in town on a visit from the High Hills. It was extended on behalf of the church through the trustees—Patrick Hines, John Gourlay, John Hamilton, and Thomas Screven (Basil Manly, *Mercy and Judgment, A Discourse Containing Some Fragments of the History of the Baptist Church of Charleston, South Carolina* [Knowles, Vose and Co., 1837] 47 and note, found in SCBHS, Furman University. Hereinafter referred to as Manly, *Discourse*).

[23]Oliver Hart to Anne Hart, 12 June 1781, Caroliniana Library, University of South Carolina, cited in Loulie Latimer Owens, *Oliver Hart, 1723-1795: A Biography* (Greenville SC: South Carolina Baptist Historical Society, 1966) 20.

parative want of success during the latter part of his residence in Charleston."[24] He also advised that until the church became better able to provide for the material comforts of a pastor they should be content with occasional supplies from their own and other denominations.[25]

The situation continued into 1784 when on 8 March the trustees of the church extended a call to Furman,[26] but he rejected it out of consideration for the needs of his High Hills congregation. The invitation to Hart was then extended again. After some delay, he requested that they renew the call to Furman, describing him as "a prize of inestimable worth." At the same time, he urged Furman to accept the call.[27] Troubled by this development lest it have a negative effect on Hart's decision about Charleston, Furman felt constrained to give "an account of the whole transaction." This he did in a letter written from Charleston in January 1785 in which he lamented "the weakness of our brethren here" in not pursuing the matter with Hart more carefully, including full assurance of their desire that he return, and making it clear "what could be advanced toward your support." He had urged them, he told Hart, not to consider "obtaining another minister until they had the fullest answer" from him. While Hart remained indecisive, the church communicated with him again in the spring of 1785. In his reply, he urged them to seek another minister, adding, however, that he was not yet clear as to how he should respond to their call.

In the meantime, church members, discouraged by Hart's ambivalence, renewed their call to Furman. While Furman deliberated, he received yet another letter from Charleston advising him that they had again heard from Hart and that he had declared himself still uncertain of his duty. Would Furman, therefore, delay any response to their call until Hart's "mind could be fully made?" The potential for an embarrassing dilemma thus became abundantly clear. Furman explained the situation in a letter to Hart.

---

[24]Manly, *Discourse*, 47.

[25]Ibid.

[26]Ibid., 49 and note.

[27]Ibid., 49.

I therefore returned an answer that I had not determined upon the subject of their first letter. When the second came to hand such an answer as I had intended was rendered unnecessary; that their making application to me before a final answer from you had given me much concern and requesting them to use their utmost endeavor to persuade you to return, also that if you did not return I was in hopes that they might be supplied with one more able than myself. It is easy to see that had I accepted the call and put myself in posture to remove to Charleston, the reception of the second letter might have been very mortifying and must have placed me in a ridiculous light to the world, especially to the people I would be leaving.[28]

Furman's feeling of obligation to the High Hills church was expressed in a letter to Hart in 1786. Hart had finally concluded not to return to Charleston, and the church had again extended a call to Furman. He could not, he told Hart, see his way clear at that time to make the move. Under the leadership of Francis Asbury, Methodism was then establishing itself in South Carolina.[29] The Methodists had become active among his people "at the Hills," he explained, which led him to expect a revival among his people more "at present than for many years." Under these conditions, and with "a number . . . making serious inquiries," he could not, he said, "consistently leave them right now." But he added significantly, "perhaps later."[30]

[28]Richard Furman to Oliver Hart, 26 January 1785, SCBHS.

[29]Francis Asbury, the founder of American Methodism, first appeared in South Carolina in 1785. He entered the state from North Carolina at Cheraw and traveled to Charleston through Darlington and Williamsburg counties to Georgetown and thence to Charleston, preaching as he traveled. Formation of early Methodist circuits included the Pee Dee, the Santee, and the Broad River circuits. The Santee circuit began near Charleston and was made to include all the territory on either side of the Santee and Wateree rivers to within ten miles of Charleston. Early South Carolina Methodist circuit riders passed up the principal rivers where the chief settlements were, "and left behind them foot-prints distinctly to be traced on the banks of the Pee Dee and Yadkin, Santee and Wateree, Congaree and Broad rivers, even to the remotest limit of population" (Albert M. Shipp, *The History of Methodism in South Carolina* [Nashville: Southern Methodist Publishing House, 1884] 158-59; *The Journal and Letters of Francis Asbury*, ed. Elmer T. Clark [London: Epworth Press, 1958; Nashville: Abingdon Press, 1958] 1:482).

[30]Richard Furman to Oliver Hart, 23 May 1786, SCBHS.

Furman's final decision to accept the Charleston call came in 1787. In November of that year he and his family, accompanied by his widowed mother, moved into the parsonage on Church Street. Determined to make a "full proof" of his ministry in the Hills area before leaving, he traveled among the churches in a thirty-mile radius conducting preaching services and holding meetings for the promotion of "Christian knowledge and experience."[31] Frequently, he catechized on subjects selected for "mental and spiritual improvement,"[32] with questions presented at one meeting to be answered "verbally or in writing" at the next. A surviving manuscript illustrates the practice.

> What is meant by our Blessed Saviour's being called "The End of the Law for Righteousness to everyone that believeth?"
> What by its saying, "Ye are not under the law, but under grace?"
> Is it the Duty of every Person that hears the Gospel whether Saint or Sinner to be baptized?
> How may we know the witnessing of the Spirit from Delusion?[33]

Doctrine and belief were at the creative center of church fellowship and Christian experience during this period of church history.

Five months before moving to Charleston, Furman's wife of thirteen years died on 15 June 1787, after several months of declining health. Ironically, she had never made a "profession of religion."[34] But she had been a faithful wife, bearing her husband four children and "adding to the social and domestic virtues" the "ornament of a meek and quiet spirit."[35] She had shared with Furman his experiences while taking refuge during the war and had assumed the practical responsibilities of life in a frontier society that otherwise would have handicapped her husband in pursuing his pastoral duties. As he had done for

---

[31]Richard Furman to Oliver Hart, 4 July 1788, SCBHS.

[32]H. T. Cook, *Biography*, 16.

[33]MS fragment, unsigned, undated, Furman Papers, SCBHS.

[34]H. T. Cook, *Biography*, 17.

[35]Ibid.

his father, Furman conducted her funeral service and saw her laid to rest in the plantation burial grounds of the Furman family.[36]

He carried the burden of her death with him to Charleston. To Oliver Hart he wrote of the "agonies in my heart" attributed to the loss of "the companion of my life."[37] He confided that he found life "to be the scene of trial, sorrow, and disappointment," which, despite promising "future prospects" in his new pastorate, his "sober judgment" told him that he "might expect it to still be what I have found it."[38] To his friend he exclaimed, "Oh for an opening of happenings beyond the grave and for a heart already resting in heaven."[39]

Many of Furman's letters reflected the harsh realities of eighteenth-century society. Epidemics of smallpox and yellow fever wrought tragic decimation of the population, even in his own family. Besides, he carried with him the burden of the churches, the usual low state of religion, and the concerns of his family members in Charleston and back at the Hills.

During his closing months at the High Hills a disturbing episode involving himself, the Reverend Beverly Allen, and John Singletary occurred. H. T. Cook calls this "the only known and open attack upon Furman's character," one which he repelled, however, "with modesty, firmness, and conscious truth."[40]

Allen was a Methodist preacher assigned to the South Carolina Santee and Pee Dee circuits,[41] which included the High Hills. In February

---

[36]To the right of the Old Garner's Ferry Road leading to the Wateree River is a mound believed to have been the Furman family cemetery on the estate once owned by Wood Furman. This site was left undisturbed at the time earth was taken from around it for use in building a causeway through the Wateree swamps in the 1930s. Some Furman descendants buried there were moved by Dr. Chandler Baker to the Sumter cemetery in the early 1900s. Location of the family cemetery site, as above indicated, conforms to a statement found in Hugh Charles Haynsworth, *The Haynsworth-Furman and Allied Families*, 123.

[37]Richard Furman to Oliver Hart, 4 July 1788, SCBHS.

[38]Ibid.

[39]Ibid.

[40]H. T. Cook, *Biography*, 16.

[41]*The Journal and Letters of Francis Asbury*, 2:669n.

1786 he married Anna Singletary, youngest daughter of John
Singletary[42] of Bull Head Plantation in St. Thomas and St. Dennis Parish.[43] As an exponent of the Methodist cause, he was both powerful and
popular. Furman listened to critical remarks about Allen and passed
them on—among them that he had married Anna Singletary much
against the wishes of her father, John Singletary, and that he had once
been a member of the Baptist church but had been expelled for "certain
misdemeanors." Singletary was furious. In the *Charleston Morning Post
and Daily Advertiser* he labeled the charges

> slanderous . . . the Reverend Richard Furman of the High Hills of
> Santee . . . has . . . reported that the Reverend Beverly Allen . . . has
> married my daughter against my consent, etc., I think it is my duty
> to assure the public that it is notoriously false . . . it appears that this
> gentleman [Furman] had not given full vent to his spleen and there-
> fore affirmed that Mr. Allen had once been a member of the Baptist
> church but for certain misdemeanors was expelled thence. I shall not
> take notice of this charge since I apprehend it is proved false in the
> Stateburg papers. . . .

Allen had made a public matter of the affair in the Stateburg *Claremont Gazette* in which he threatened to take the case to the Charleston
papers and possibly bring suit against Furman.[44] But Furman remained
discreetly silent until Singletary's letter appeared in the Charleston paper on 30 October. Three days later, he responded that the letter appearing over Singletary's signature contained the language of Allen, not
Singletary. Furman wrote,

> I cannot, and will not, consider him [Singletary] the author of that
> abusive piece. The language is Mr. Allen's and it is the accomplish-
> ment of what he lately promised the public in very polite terms in the
> *Claremont Gazette*, that he would post me in the Charleston papers.

---

[42]*South Carolina Historical and Genealogical Magazine*, 20:53.

[43]Ibid., 58:85.

[44]No copy of the *Claremont Gazette* is known to be extant, and the only proof of
its use by Allen is from internal evidence in correspondence relating to the affair.

Furman's distaste for this public dispute was felt with "the most painful sensations" lest it be interpreted as "unfavorable to Christianity." Still, he considered it essential "in my own defence." What he had said of Allen's character, he wrote, "was chiefly to the people of my charge at a time when he was endeavoring to gain an undue influence over them, and if putting a people with whom I was so nearly connected on guard by relating unfavorable circumstances respecting his character" was the charge against him, he acknowledged to be "indeed chargeable with it."

Concerning Allen's marriage to Singletary's daughter, he said he had

> never intended to convey the idea which is presented to the public to any who were spoken to on the occasion, who were very few, and most of them were persons who had first mentioned it. . . . What I related was the same I received from her father's friends . . . that "the union was, I was informed, very disagreeable to Mr. Singletary, and he had seriously endeavored to prevent it."

He also acknowledged that he may have been in error concerning Allen's dismissal from the Baptist church, but he "had reason to believe it from common report and by what he has acknowledged."

Both Singletary and Allen responded with published letters in December. Singletary did not deny that the language of his former letter was Allen's but assured the public "that the piece which appeared in my name was published at my request," that it contained "in truth the very sentiments of my mind. . . . " As far as the extant record goes, Singletary and Allen had the last word on this unhappy subject.[45]

---

[45]For a full account of the public exchange between Furman, Allen, and Singletary, see 30 October, 7 November, and 1 December 1786 editions of the *Charleston Morning Post and Daily Advertiser*. Allen was one of the original Methodist elders ordained in 1784. He introduced Methodism in Salisbury, North Carolina, in 1783, and was the first preacher appointed to Georgia in 1785. In 1786 he was one of the first elders designated by appointment, being assigned to the South Carolina Santee and Pee Dee circuits with three preachers under him. In 1791, while on the Edisto circuit in South Carolina, he was expelled for a "flagrant crime." He then went to Georgia, where he and his brother operated a store in Elbert County. In 1795, while buying goods in Augusta, a warrant was secured against him by a creditor. Allen armed and barricaded himself in his hotel room. When a U.S. Marshal, Major Forsyth, forced the door, Allen shot and killed him. He was arrested for murder but escaped and fled to his home in Georgia. There the sheriff arrested him by setting fire to the house and

This had been one of the sadder experiences of Furman's career, yet there is no evidence that it damaged his relationship with his congregation. His final message was a "pathetic and solemn farewell discourse."[46] For thirteen years he had been their pastor. Under his leadership the church had been extended to numerous branches in the Santee and Pee Dee regions. Sacred memories were associated with it as the place of his conversion to the Baptist faith and his ordination into the ministry. There and in surrounding areas he had worked for political and religious liberty, and from there he had gone as a refugee during the latter years of the war. It had been the home of his parents for seventeen years. From its wilderness surroundings they had carved a plantation, beginning with the original 250-acre grant and added to by purchases from Samuel Bacot, Bernard Beckman, Thomas Evans, Joseph Forgatis, and Tunis Tiebout.[47] By inheritance, Furman was now owner of 750 acres of his late father's plantation, and a codicil to his father's will gave him equal rights with his brother, Josiah, to build and operate a mill on Beech Creek. His sister, Sarah Haynsworth, and her husband, Henry, lived east of the ridge where Thomas Sumter and associates had carved out a village around a tavern. When he moved to Charleston, he left much of himself behind, including a congregation loved by him that loved him in return.

---

lodged him in jail. But Allen's popularity as a preacher and political circumstances involving the federal courts in unpopularity caused public favor to side with him. When the sheriff tried to remove Allen to another prison, word spread that a mob would attempt a rescue. On the following night the Elbert jail was attacked by two hundred men, and Allen was released. He then went to Kentucky where he practiced medicine and became a Universalist (*The Journal and Letters of Francis Asbury*, 2:669n; see also Albert M. Shipp, *The History of Methodism in South Carolina*, 147-48). Singletary had been an acquaintance of the Furman family since the Furmans lived in St. Thomas Parish. On 5 November 1767 an indenture between Wood Furman and John Singletary mortgaged 500 acres to Singletary and Samuel Wells for 500 pounds for the purchase of a 250-acre tract of land granted to Tunis Tiebout in 1760. The Tiebout land adjoined Furman's original 250-acre tract in St. Mark's Parish. The mortgaged property probably combined this original grant plus the acreage purchased from Tiebout (*Register of Mesne and Conveyances*, Book 3, 313, Charleston County Records).

[46]H. T. Cook, *Biography*, 19.

[47]Wood Furman will, Sumter County Estates, Bundle 119, Pack 14, South Carolina Archives.

On the day of his departure, affectionate and weeping friends filled the house to bid him farewell.[48] He was then thirty-six years of age, a man of fine presence, six feet in height, dark hair and eyes, grave manners,[49] and no longer the boy preacher whose ministerial career had begun almost immediately after his conversion. The years at High Hills had prepared him in many ways for the more significant years of his Charleston pastorate. By study, pastoral work, preaching experience, associational leadership, and ministerial fellowship, he was ready to enter the most fruitful years of his life.

In addition to his mother, his family then consisted of his daughter Rachel, age ten, his son Wood, age eight, and his son Richard, age five. Accompanying them to Charleston were servants—probably two Negro men, Sirrah and Glasgow, and a Negro woman, Jinny. His father had willed them to his mother, plus any issue from Jinny, for the duration of her life.

---

[48]H. T. Cook, *Biography*, 10.

[49]Townsend, *History of South Carolina Baptists*, 30; Tupper, *Two Centuries of the First Baptist Church of Charleston, 1683-1883*, 174.

CHAPTER 5

To Charleston

The Charleston Richard Furman moved to was recovering from two and a half years of British occupation. It was an elegant city built on the lower end of the peninsula formed by the Ashley and Cooper rivers. During the war a line of fortifications had extended across the peninsula, generally along present-day Calhoun Street. As the city grew, a new line was built, which by the time of the War of 1812 ran along Line Street. Some villages grew up outside these lines, while others appeared inside, their names usually affixing the term "borough" to the name of the developer—as Radcliffeborough, Wraggsborough, Mazyckborough.[1] Within these boroughs, spacious houses were built as the summer homes of planters who came into the city to escape the miasma of summer heat and disease then so prevalent on Lowcountry plantations.

The city's intellectual center was the Charleston Library Society, organized in 1748 by seventeen citizens hoping "to save their descen-

[1]George C. Rogers, Jr., *Charleston in the Age of the Pinckneys*, 65.

dants from sinking into savagery."[2] An analysis of its 1770 catalogue indicates the quality of reading and the sources from which well-bred Charlestonians acquired their literary culture. Among the library's holdings were whole sets of contemporary magazines, such as *Critical Review, Gentlemen's Magazine,* the *Annual Register, Monthly Review, British Magazine,* and periodicals like the *Tatler,* the *Rambler,* and the *Spectator.*[3] The primary sources of Charleston's eighteenth-century culture were Britain and Europe.

Charleston's dominant family was the Pinckneys, originating with two brothers, Charles and William. Both had died before Furman moved to Charleston, but through offspring, intermarriage, and friendship with families having names like Horry, Izard, Rutledge, Lucas, Ravenel, Pringle, Gadsden, and Manigault, they influenced the shaping of Charleston society throughout the eighteenth century into the nineteenth. As a frequent supply pastor for the Charleston church during the post-Oliver Hart years, Furman had come to know many of Charleston's foremost families.

Politically, South Carolina was in a golden period, and Charleston was its political and intellectual center. When it was still a British province, Morgan Edwards described it as "the polite and wealthy province of South Carolina; a province whose planters are nabobs, whose merchants are princes and whose inhabitants (for the most part) have slaves to wait on them."[4] He was speaking of the age of the Pinckneys, of rice and indigo, and of sailing ships exporting and importing to and from the world's near and distant ports.

The Baptist church in Charleston was organized at Kittery, Maine, in 1682, and migrated to South Carolina, along with its pastor, William Screven, in 1696.[5] In 1699 one of its members, William Elliott, deeded to the congregation Lot 62 on Church Street for the building of

---

[2]Ibid., 99.

[3]Ibid., 100.

[4]Morgan Edwards, *Materials Toward a History of the Baptists,* bound MS, SCBHS, 5:3.

[5]For a discussion of the founding date of the church and the arrival of William Screven about 1696, see Robert Andrew Baker, *The First Southern Baptists* (Nashville: Broadman Press, 1966) 51; Townsend, *History of South Carolina Baptists,* 10-11.

a church.[6] A meetinghouse was erected no later than 1701. When
Screven's declining health forced his retirement in 1706, he purchased
property at the head of Winyah Bay and settled on land that would be
laid out as the site of Georgetown. He returned to Charleston for a brief
period upon the death of his successor, a Reverend Mr. White, but continued failing health soon forced his return to Georgetown, where he
died in 1713 at the age of eighty-four.

From then until the arrival of Oliver Hart in December 1749, ob-
scurity marks the history of the church. In 1752 a disastrous gale and
inundation from the sea destroyed all church records, leaving a virtually
blank period for historians to ponder. In 1733 a doctrinal schism split
the congregation. Led by William Elliott, Jr., the schismatics adopted
Arminian views and aligned themselves with the General Baptists over
against the Particular Baptists, who held to strict Calvinism. A legal
battle over ownership of the church property followed, resulting in a
court decree in 1745 under which the two groups were given equal title
to the meetinghouse. The Particulars rejected this arrangement, purchased another lot, and in 1745 or the following year erected a brick
church thereon.[7] In later years this became known as the Mariner's
Church. In this new church the Particulars first met every other Sunday
and used the old church alternately with the General Baptists. But on
9 October 1758, an agreement was reached by which the General Baptists would have sole use of the meetinghouse and the Particulars sole
use of the parsonage on the same lot as the church.

Almost simultaneously with Furman's acceptance of the call to
Charleston, the church obtained entire possession of Lot 62, including
the church building and parsonage. General Baptists by then being extinct, a petition was signed on 14 February 1787 by thirty-three members of Furman's congregation asking the legislature to rescind its former
action and place sole ownership in the hands of Particular Baptists. The
legislature concurred, but a few years later the Charleston City Council,

---

[6]Townsend, *History of South Carolina Baptists*, 10.

[7]The lot, purchased from Mrs. Martha Fowler, was described as "bounded to the
westward on Church Street, and known in the plat of the town by the number 102."
Basil Manly, *Discourse*, 26; Henry A. M. Smith, "Charleston—The Original Plan and
the Earliest Settlers," *South Carolina Historical and Genealogical Magazine* 9 (1908): 12
and map, for sites of Lots 62 and 102.

supposing that one-half of the property was liable to fall to the state, passed a resolution directing the city's recorder to take the necessary measures to secure it for the benefit of the Orphan House. The church responded by naming a committee chaired by Furman to appear before Council on behalf of the church's claim. That body, accordingly, backed away from its previous action and placed on record that sole ownership of the church belonged to Particular Baptists.[8] Resolution of this old controversy provided a pleasing circumstance for the beginning years of Furman's Charleston pastorate.

Another development ended an old division as Furman entered upon his Charleston work. The terms Separate and Regular ceased to designate Baptist groups in South Carolina. As early as 1773, Separates were present at the association meeting in Charleston to consider uniting the two groups. But the Separates' insistence upon retaining their peculiar practices resulted in nothing being accomplished. On their part, Charleston Regulars, being Calvinist in doctrine, considered the Separates too Arminian for their fellowship. Two years later, the Charleston Association turned down a proposal from the Congaree Association that "the several associations in this Province" unite.[9] South Carolina Regulars and Separates did merge, however, without formal action, after North Carolina and Virginia Regulars and Separates united in 1787 under the Philadelphia Confession of Faith.[10]

Though converted under the Separatist preaching of Joseph Reese, Furman was not a Separate in the Stearns-Mulkey-Reese tradition. His conservative background and intellectual development made unacceptable the radical revivalistic practices of the Separates. He wrote to Dr. John Rippon of London about "evils which attend Separate revivals that give pain to one who feels a just regard for religion."[11] But he was realistic enough to know that physical demonstrations in religious services during that period of the backcountry's cultural development were a natural expression of religious enthusiasm in a social setting basically frontier in character. He was thus able to identify with the Separates

---

[8]Manly, *Discourse*, 54.

[9]Lumpkin, *Baptist Foundations in the South*, 138.

[10]Ibid., 143.

[11]Howe, *History of the Presbyterian Church in South Carolina*, 2:110.

doctrinally without sharing in the fire and fervor of their religious practices.

That the Regulars needed the zeal and enthusiasm of the Separates may be observed by noting Baptist progress in South Carolina before they came. Regular Baptists had been in the Charleston area for seventy-five years before Shubal Stearns came to North Carolina, but they had organized only the four small Baptist churches that constituted the Charleston Baptist Association, established in 1751. Under the influence of the Separate movement, their number increased to 27 churches in 1784 and 154 in 1812, with a total membership of 11,325.[12]

Within a few years following the Separate-Regular fusion, Baptists presented a united front from Georgia to Maine. Furman's arrival in Charleston coincided with this early period of denominational unity and expansion, which would feature a religious revival in the South comparable to the Great Awakening of the mid-eighteenth century in New England. Under these circumstances, "the church needed a master-hand, directed by consummate prudence, to grasp the situation and wield effectively the agencies within reach. These elements were combined in Richard Furman. . . ."[13]

SECOND MARRIAGE

A personal event of these early Charleston years was his marriage to Dorothea Maria Burn, daughter of Mary Glas Burn McDonald of Charleston. Mrs. McDonald was a woman of Scottish ancestry whose first marriage, in 1772, was to Samuel Burn, an English gentleman lately come to America. Her second marriage, probably between 1776 and 1780, was to Charles McDonald, born in Dunfuilen Castle, Isle of Skye, in 1774. A family tradition connects him with Flora McDonald either as a brother or a nephew.[14] At the fall of Charleston to the British in 1780, Charles McDonald was among those placed on a prison ship

---

[12]Newman, *A History of the Baptist Churches in the United States*, 315.

[13]B. F. Riley, *History of the Baptists in the Southern States East of the Mississippi River* (Philadelphia: American Baptist Publication Society, 1898) 115.

[14]Elizabeth Furman Tally Papers, Manuscript Division, University of North Carolina Library, Chapel Hill.

and removed from the city. Where he was taken is not known, but his wife went to Philadelphia and was there when Cornwallis surrendered in 1781. Dorothea Maria was then eight years old and recalled so vividly the time of that event that she would often tell her children of the excitement when an old Dutchman's cry making his rounds was "All ish well, Cornwallis ish taken."[15]

Following the war, the McDonalds returned to Charleston in 1784 when Dorothea was eleven years of age. Mrs. McDonald was a friend of the Oliver Harts, then in Hopewell, New Jersey, and of the Edmund Botsfords, whose acquaintance was made during his visits to Charleston as a supply preacher for the Charleston church. On his own supply visits, Furman frequently stayed with the McDonalds, and Mary McDonald developed an affection and appreciation for him that approached reverence. In July 1785 she wrote to Botsford, addressing him in the formal salutatory fashion of that day as "Reverend and Dear Sir." After cataloging a list of complaints, she wrote,

> Two great and Particular Blessings and Mercies I must not omit, which is Mr. Furman and my daughter Nancy being inoculated for the smallpox and are both of them happily recovered except a swelling in Mr. Furman's shoulder which I hope will soon be brave. It pleased the Lord to have mercy upon him and not on him only but on us also, for I greatly feared lest the disease should prove mortal to him, his life being necessary and useful made me often expostulate and say Why should his sun go down so soon?[16]

Mr. McDonald soon became engaged in business at Wrightsborough, Georgia, near Augusta, leaving his family in Charleston because of the feeble condition of Mr. McDonald's mother. In a letter written in 1786—internal evidence suggests it was addressed to Furman—Mary McDonald spoke of an "unexpected visit from Mr. McDonald" who "stayed six days" before returning to Wrightsborough. Recent supply preachers for the church, she said, had been Mr. Lewis, Mr. Palmer, and Mr. Redding, but they had gone and Mr. Botsford had then arrived

---

[15]Ibid.

[16]Ibid., 8.

"last Saturday."[17] "He tells me," she wrote, "he expects you will be in town soon, if so, if your old habitation is agreeable I shall be exceedingly glad for you to accept it again. . . . "

Furman was then wrestling with the question of the Charleston church and its interest in him as a pastor while still uncertain about Oliver Hart's intentions. "I trust the Lord will direct you in the important matter agreeable to his will, and may I add," Mrs. McDonald declared, "Oh that it may be his will for you to come and dwell among us."[18]

Mrs. McDonald's daughter, Dorothea Maria, was then thirteen years old, but in May of 1789, two years after the death of Furman's first wife, Dorothea became his second wife. She was sixteen and he thirty-three. Furman's established record as a preacher and his Revolutionary War record brought satisfaction to Mary McDonald that her "lovely Dolly" was married to such a person.[19] Her estimate of him never changed. Fourteen years later, after the McDonald family had moved to Georgia and was living at a home called "Vintage" near Sparta, she wrote to a Mrs. Roositer, "This night makes fourteen years since my dear Dorothea Maria was united to one of the best of men. How good the Lord has been to me . . . in providing for my orphan child such a partner as Dr. Furman."[20] The first of thirteen children by the second marriage was born on 2 April 1790.

DELEGATE TO THE STATE CONSTITUTIONAL CONVENTION

By then Furman had established himself so well in Charleston as both minister and citizen that he was chosen as a delegate from Charleston to the state constitutional convention for framing a new state constitution. Following his habit of keeping Oliver Hart informed about

---

[17]Furman, Palmer, Botsford, Pugh, and Cook supplied the church for periods of one month each during stated months in 1785 and 1786. They were appointed by the Charleston Baptist Association in 1785 in response to a request from the Charleston church for supply ministers. Townsend, *History of South Carolina Baptists*, 27.

[18]Tally MS, 12.

[19]Ibid., 13.

[20]Ibid., 29.

personal, church, and family affairs, he wrote, "I can just send you a few hasty lines being in a great hurry in preparing to set off for Columbia to attend the state convention for modelling a new state constitution, my fellow citizens elected me to represent them in that body."[21]

As a representative from the parishes of St. Michael's and St. Philip's, Furman was among those of prominent social and historic strata. From the older parishes there were Pinckneys, Draytons, Rutledges, a Pringle, a Kinloch, a Bull, a Heyward, a Grimke, a Porcher, a Seabrook, a Moultrie, a Manigault, a Laurens, a Washington, and the old firebrand of the Revolution, Christopher Gadsden.[22] Notably present were the three militia chieftains whose leadership in the field during the Revolution played such a large role in winning American independence—Francis Marion, "The Pee Dee Swamp Fox"; Thomas Sumter, "The Gamecock"; and Andrew Pickens, the stern Presbyterian elder from the Upcountry who, beginning with the Battle of Cowpens, became the third member of that famous trilogy.[23] Yet others who were lesser luminaries but bright potential stars of the young aristocracy were John Chestnut, John Kershaw, Lamuel Benton, William Bratton, William Hill, Hugh Giles, and the Reverend Evan Pugh. All totaled, they numbered in excess of 200 representatives from the older parishes and the newer election districts.

South Carolina had never before held a constitutional convention. The 1778 constitution had been created as a temporary expedient by the legislature. From discussions concerning the need for a new constitution and how to obtain it, the concept of a convention emerged as a means of embodying the sovereign will of the people.[24] Belief in the Upcountry that "a convention brings the people back to first principles, according to which all are equal," and therefore exhibits true democracy in action, was unacceptable political philosophy to Lowcountrymen whose emphasis was on privilege rather than rights.

---

[21]Richard Furman to Oliver Hart, 8 May 1790, SCBHS.

[22]Wallace, *South Carolina: A Short History*, 342; *Journal of the Constitutional Convention of South Carolina, May 10, 1790-June 3, 1790*, ed. Francis M. Hutson, Historical Commission of South Carolina, 1946 (hereinafter referred to as *JCC*).

[23]*JCC*, 4, 6, 10.

[24]Wallace, *South Carolina: A Short History*, 341.

The distribution of representation illustrated the point. The judicial districts of Charleston, Beaufort, and Georgetown, with one-fifth of the state's population—18,644 white inhabitants in 1790—and three-fourths of the wealth, were in control of the convention.

The Upcountry-Lowcountry controversy, pre-Revolutionary in origin, was destined to reach an "alarming crisis" at the convention of 1790. Its personnel reflected the differing social and historic characteristics of the state's upper and lower divisions. Essentially, the controversies at the convention were a battle over the reapportionment of representation. As D. D. Wallace says,

> The just demands of the Up Country were neglected because of the Low Country's ignorance of conditions as well as because of the human propensity of those possessing power to retain it, and the equally natural contempt for the new by an old wealthy and cultured society, which recognized in the newcomers their rawness more readily than their virtues.[25]

As hotly contested as representation was the issue of the location of the state capital. In the years before the convention, the Upcountry-Lowcountry controversy had been heightened by a decision to move the capital to Columbia, in the center of state, where the constitutional convention met. However, many Lowcountry delegates wanted to move the capital back to Charleston. This issue was a crucial test for Furman. Keeping the capital in Columbia would establish a growing city within forty miles of his property at Stateburg, with obvious personal economic benefits. But Charleston was his home, and the influence of Charleston society and Charleston culture created tension between his duty as a representative from that city and his personal economic interests. Some of his associates at the convention believed the latter would influence his decision.[26] However, when the vote was taken and Columbia won 109 to 105,[27] Furman was among the 105 losers who voted

---

[25]D. D. Wallace, *The History of South Carolina* (New York: American Historical Society, 1934) 2:347.

[26]H. T. Cook, *Biography*, 20.

[27]*City Gazette and Daily Advertiser*, 1 June 1790.

for Charleston. As Cook suggests, the raw, undeveloped state of Columbia at that time must have persuaded him that the move was "premature" and should await a time when it was further developed and offered more advantages and greater dignity as the capital of a sovereign state.

The convention assembled on Monday, 10 May. On the following Saturday a unanimous request was made that Furman "perform divine services in the Convention Chamber" on Sunday morning at ten o'clock.[28] There is no extant copy of his sermon, but the first order of business when the convention next met, after reading the journal of Saturday's proceedings, was a resolution thanking "the Reverend Mr. Furman for the able and well chosen discourse delivered to the Convention yesterday forenoon in pursuance of their request."[29]

With Upcountry delegates coming to win their rights and those from the Lowcountry trying to hold on to their privileges, Furman was an advocate of conciliatory measures and proposed concessions. He supported, and the constitution included for the first time, absolute religious equality, which removed certain parochial distinctions and left no provisions for Protestants to occupy a favored position.

An article drawing his opposition excluded ministers from a seat in the legislature.[30] Furman sought no special privilege for ministers, but he believed that a minister should not be denied a right granted to other free citizens. Against his argument that ministers were frequently better qualified by intelligence, character, and experience to serve as public officials, an opponent countered by pointing to the potential danger of overinfluence by the presence of such a body of men of proven ability and seasoned eloquence.[31] The number of ministers serving as delegates illustrated the point. Besides Furman, there were the Reverends Nathaniel Walker, Richard Shackleford, and Evan Pugh, all Baptists, and the Reverend Dr. Henry Purcell, Episcopal rector of St. Michael's in Charleston and former chaplain to the American army.[32]

---

[28]*JCC*, 14.

[29]Ibid., 16.

[30]Article 1, Section 23, 1790 South Carolina Constitution.

[31]H. T. Cook, *Biography*, 21.

[32]*JCC*, 3, 5, 6, 11.

This was the only occasion on which Furman served as a member of a secular political body, but it was not the only time he involved himself in politics. Earlier examples were the debates over constitutionally granted religious liberty and the disestablishment of the Established Church. A later example came in 1808, when Charles Cotesworth Pinckney and James Madison were candidates for the presidency of the United States. In support of Pinckney, the Federalist candidate, Furman addressed a letter to his "Fellow Citizens" recalling Pinckney's support of religious liberty when the question was debated at the Constitutional Assembly of 1777: "To me it appears just and requisite that our Citizens at large and those of South Carolina, in particular, should know and at this time remember that General Pinckney was in the American Revolution an early and influential Advocate of religious as well as Civil Liberty." Furman followed with a eulogy of Pinckney, which concluded that "a laudable self-love calls for her [South Carolina's] attention to her distinguished son. . . . Gratitude for services requires no less."[33]

In spite of Furman's efforts, Pinckney did not win the election. An increase in voting strength in the newer areas of the South and the expanding West had shifted popular support toward the Republican party. Federalists, associated in the average American mind with aristocratic and educational elitism, did not adapt and gain new strength. When the vote was counted, Madison had 120 votes, and Pinckney had 47.

The relationship between Furman and Pinckney was more than casual. Each admired the other and enjoyed the amenities of friendship. In Pinckney's library was a copy of Gale's reflections on Walls' *History of Infant Baptism*, which at one time he offered to loan to Furman. In the meantime, however, he misplaced the book. Not until "some years" later, when "having some reason to look over military books," did he find that "Gale had got among them." He then wrote Furman that "if Gale were alive, he would be astonished to find himself in such company and would be very happy to exchange it for yours."[34] In the same light vein Furman replied that "if it appears that Mr. Gale should have

---

[33]Original in Baptist Historical Collection, Furman University; quoted in H. T. Cook, *Biography*, 59-60.

[34]Charles Cotesworth Pinckney to Richard Furman, 6 March 1792, SCBHS.

got among Gentlemen of the military character, it is not less extraordinary, and to me a flattering instance of unmerited attention that General Pinckney . . . should for years pay respect to a promise so transiently made."[35] Years later, during a season of torrid heat and sickness, Pinckney, noting that the summer "had been more productive of bile" than he had known in thirty years, delivered to Furman two dozen bottles of "unadulterated Madeira," with a note that read, "I have found a few glasses . . . the best corrector . . . and take the liberty of recommending the same medicine to you. . . ." He dutifully added that "the dozen marked O.M. is ten years old; that marked M is five years old."[36]

CHANGE IN CHURCH GOVERNANCE AND FINANCING

Important church actions marked Furman's initial pastoral years in Charleston. One action concerned the adoption of a new system of church governance, the other a change in the system of financial support. Previously, management of church affairs—even the call of a pastor—had been in the hands of trustees who consulted the congregation only occasionally. Now, however, a more systematic plan of organization was introduced by the adoption of constitutional rules and bylaws under the charter obtained in 1778. A seven-member committee—consisting of Furman, Thomas Screven, William Inglesby, Thomas Rivers, E. North, Isham Williams, and John McIver—was named to draw up governing provisions. Their adoption on 21 August 1791 marked the introduction of a more democratic procedure in church life.[37]

Church funds had been obtained as needed by subscription, but at the beginning of Furman's pastorate, he introduced the system of pew rents as more equal, regular, and efficient.[38] Thirty-four years later, in response to a request from the then organized Baptist State Convention to "take decided and effectual measures for providing a regular support for the Gospel ministry," Furman recommended to the churches that they, too, adopt the pew-rental system as the "most easy . . . to give

---

[35]Richard Furman to Charles Cotesworth Pinckney, 26 March 1792, SCBHS.

[36]Charles Cotesworth Pinckney to Richard Furman, 8 July 1825, SCBHS.

[37]Manly, *Discourse*, 54.

[38]Ibid.

the most regularity, and permanence to the undertaking, of any we are acquainted with." He told the convention,

> The writer of these observations . . . is well aware, that usage, and prejudice, in a great part of the country, are against it: But he feels assured that where it is tried . . . it will be approved by all, at least by those who are of liberal minds. The persons who take seats, feel that they have a right in the concerns of the congregation; and if they are pleased with its sentiments and administrations, naturally feel a particular attachment to its interests. To the person holding a seat, . . . he can, if he has a family, have them together with him in the house of God, and his children under his eye; so that his concern for their safety and convenience, as well as for their good behaviour, can at once be gratified. . . . By the seats, also, being rated, at a different valuation, according to their situation, etc., persons of different circumstances in life, can be accommodated, according to their circumstances. For the poor and strangers, seats can be assigned; and particularly, in galleries, where they exist in a building. . . .[39]

His argument reflected the aristocratic affluence of Charleston culture and accorded with the master-servant class society of his day—a society profiled in every edition of the Charleston gazettes. Their pages positioned notices of ship departures and arrivals, private academies for instruction in "scholastic and collegiate literature," and entertainment by professional artists in the same context as notices of runaway slaves and "prime Negroes" for purchase. It disturbed no social conscience to read such notices as: "For sale, a healthy wench, with a fine boy about six and one half years old . . . an excellent cook, washer and ironer as any in the state . . . will be sold low for cash"; or, "To be sold before our store near the Exchange . . . about 20 prime slaves, chiefly country-born, among whom are house servants, field Negroes, and a good cooper belonging to the estate of the late Major Joseph Darrell."[40] The contradictions of this society were not concealed; they were simply ignored.

---

[39]*Minutes of the State Convention*, 1822, SCBHS, 4.

[40]*South Carolina Gazette*, 9 November 1787.

In such a social climate, denoting status in the church by the pew-rental system was not considered inconsistent with a Christian profession. The results, however, were not always as desired. In 1808 Furman wrote to his son Wood, then in Rhode Island, that a "trip to the northward" was in question since "the pew rents . . . are but very partially collected"; a Mr. Harper had made an "advance in money to pay the first quarter's salary in this year and the last quarter is wholly unpaid for."[41] Still, on balance, the system worked and survived long after the Furman pastorate had ended. A debt incurred when the meetinghouse was enlarged during the latter part of the pastorless years was not finally discharged until the pew-rental system was put into practice.[42]

For the church's bicentennial celebration in 1883, Dr. W. H. Williams, a former pastor, testified to the influence of the pew-rental system on the family. "One of the reminiscences of our early years," he said, "running back to the latter years of the pastorate of Richard Furman . . . is that of a long pew occupied by the Tuppers, with the father's lithe form and the mother's expressive face and the group of bright children all silently attesting that they had learned at home how to observe the decorum which became the house of God. There was a large accumulation of energy and intellect in the family flock which gathered at that pew destined to be felt in other spheres." Among those mentioned was H. A. Tupper, a son, who would later serve as corresponding secretary of the Board of Foreign Missions of the Southern Baptist Convention. To use Williams's words, " . . . he was one of that bevy of bright children who once filled their places in that staid old pew."

NEW ACQUAINTANCES

An early consequence of Furman's move to Charleston was his broadened contact with ministers he had not previously known. His letters began to include men like Dr. James Manning, of Providence, Rhode Island; Dr. Samuel Stillman, Dr. William Rogers, and Thomas Ustick, of Philadelphia; Dr. John Rippon, Dr. John Ryland, and the Reverend Samuel Pearce, all of England; and the Reverend Benjamin

---

[41]Richard Furman to Wood Furman, 21 June 1808, SCBHS.

[42]Manly, *Discourse*, 53n.

Foster, of New York. A more illustrious group of clergymen during that period of Baptist history could scarcely have been found.

A graduate of Princeton, Dr. James Manning was the first president of Rhode Island College and the pastor of the First Baptist Church of Providence for twenty years.[43] Another correspondent of Furman, Dr. Samuel Stillman, moved to Charleston with his parents when he was eleven years old. He was converted under the preaching of Oliver Hart and in 1759 was ordained as a minister in Hart's church. He moved north to New England, where he became pastor of the First Baptist Church of Boston and served it with such distinction that it was said he probably had no superior in all of New England.[44]

Dr. William Rogers was from Newport, Rhode Island, and a graduate of Rhode Island College. Licensed to preach in August 1771, in March 1772 he received a unanimous call from the First Baptist Church of Philadelphia. From 1789 to 1812, he was professor of English and oratory, first in the College and Academy of Philadelphia and subsequently in the University of Pennsylvania. From 1816 to 1817, he was a member of the Pennsylvania State General Assembly.[45] Thomas Ustick, reared in the Episcopal church, turned to the Baptist church as a result of association with Baptist friends and the influence of the Reverend John Gano, pastor of the First Baptist Church of New York. At the beginning of the Revolutionary War, when it appeared that New York might be occupied by British troops, Ustick went to Connecticut and was pastor of churches there until 1781. Upon the recommendation of Dr. James Manning of Rhode Island College, Ustick became pastor of the First Baptist Church of Philadelphia and served there for twenty-one years.[46] After serving churches in Rhode Island and Massachusetts, Benjamin Foster became pastor of the First Baptist Church of New York and remained there until his death in 1798.[47] In his *His-*

---

[43]William Sprague, *Annals of the American Pulpit* (New York: Arno Press and the *New York Times*, 1969) 6:89-95.

[44]Ibid., 71-75.

[45]Ibid., 145-47.

[46]Ibid., 165-67.

[47]Ibid., 191-92.

tory of Baptists, David Benedict says that as a scholar, particularly in the Greek, Hebrew, and Chaldean languages, Foster had "few superiors."[48]

Dr. John Rippon was educated at Bristol Academy, England, entered the ministry, and in 1773 became pastor of the Baptist church in Carter Lane, London, as successor to Dr. John Gill. Like the majority of English Baptists, Rippon was warmly sympathetic with the cause of American independence and was in correspondence with leading Baptists in America. From 1790 until 1802, he edited *The Baptist Annual Register.* He is best known as the compiler of a *Selection of Hymns from the Best Authors.*[49] A native of Warwick, England, Dr. John Ryland began preaching at sixteen and was formally admitted into the ministry in 1771. In 1793, he became minister of Broadmead Chapel in Bristol, combining with this post the presidency of Bristol Baptist College. In 1792 he joined in founding the Baptist Missionary Society, and acted as its secretary from 1815 until his death at Bristol in 1825.[50] Samuel Pearce studied at Bristol Baptist College and in 1790 was appointed minister of Cannon Street Baptist Church, Birmingham, England, where he remained until his death in 1799. He was one of the twelve ministers who, on 1 October 1792, signed the resolution founding the English Baptist Missionary Society.

A common denominator between these men of distinction and Furman was their interest in or association, directly or indirectly, with Rhode Island College. Rhode Island was the only American Baptist institution of higher learning then engaged in educating young Baptist ministers in Baptist faith and practice.

Furman was pleased with his larger ministerial associations, especially when correspondence brought him sermon material, religious pamphlets, reports on the progress of religion, and scriptural expositions. In a letter to his mother, then back at the High Hills, he mentioned "letters and presents in pamphlets from new correspondents in England."[51] From Oliver Hart, on behalf of the Charleston Associa-

---

[48]Benedict, *General History of the Baptist Denomination,* 2:304.

[49]*The Dictionary of National Biography,* ed. Sir Leslie Stephen and Sir Sidney Lee (Oxford: Oxford University Press, 1967-1968) 16:1204.

[50]Ibid., 17:544-45.

[51]Richard Furman to Rachel Brodhead Furman, 8 October 1782, SCBHS.

tion, he requested the number of associations and the places of their meetings in New England because of the Charleston Association's desire to know of the "general state of religion on the continent," and for supporting "an extensive correspondence with these Baptist churches."[52] By then the Charleston Association had already opened correspondence with an association in England from which "a large packet had lately come to hand."[53]

Being pastor of the Charleston church elevated Furman's rank as a religious leader and improved his visibility among Baptist leaders in both America and England. It also brought him academic recognition. In 1792 Rhode Island College conferred on him the Master's degree. "Would you believe," he wrote his mother upon learning of the degree, that Rhode Island College, "by whose instance I cannot tell, have, no doubt, in a very good-natured mistake, thought proper to confer a Master's Degree on your unqualified son?" He then added, with uncommon levity, "Conferring an honor or exposing to ridicule: which shall we say?"[54]

He apparently experienced some hesitancy in accepting the degree, for Oliver Hart wrote insisting that he "own the Title which R. I. College has conferred upon you. If the Corporation had a right to bestow it, you have a Right to receive it. It is an honorary title, frequently bestowed on Persons who have not had the advantage of a liberal education."[55] Eight years later, Rhode Island also conferred on him the degree of Doctor of Divinity.

The list of his new acquaintances and correspondents would grow to include others of equal prominence among Baptists of that day—men like Isaac Backus of New England, minister, author, and champion of religious liberty; Robert Semple of Virginia, a lawyer turned minister, educator, and historian who became one of the most distinguished Baptist leaders of his day; and Jonathan Maxcy of Massachusetts, who succeeded Dr. Manning as president of Rhode Island College, and subsequently, upon the recommendation of Furman, became the first

---

[52]Richard Furman to Oliver Hart, 4 July 1788, SCBHS.

[53]Ibid.

[54]Richard Furman to Rachel Brodhead Furman, 8 October 1792, SCBHS.

[55]Oliver Hart to Richard Furman, 30 May 1793, SCBHS.

president of South Carolina College, now the University of South Carolina.

WILLIAM STAUGHTON

Twice in the spring of 1788, Furman went on preaching missions to Georgetown, sixty miles up the coast from Charleston. To Oliver Hart he wrote of these missions that "there seems to be a work of grace begun." The evidence was in baptisms he had conducted, the "solemnity" attending administration of the ordinances, and "a new place of worship in tolerable good order," which he hoped would lead to the constitution of a church.[56] So effective was the work that a church of thirty-six members was established in 1794,[57] with William Staughton, lately arrived from England, assisting in constituting it and serving as supply pastor.

Staughton calls for special note. During the early part of 1793, Furman wrote to Dr. John Rippon in London requesting a "young man of promise and character," willing to come to America to supply the Georgetown church. The letter was read at a meeting of ministers, and the name Staughton immediately came to mind.[58] Rippon replied, "one of our junior ministers is disposed to cross the Atlantic, and you have, in my opinion, described him in every respect, except his name." He termed Staughton an "acceptable, evangelical, and popular minister" whom he considered "above par" among "our English brethren" and one for whom Providence had "designed great and good things."[59]

Among others acquainted with this request was the Reverend Thomas Dunscombe of Bampton in Oxfordshire, England. Though unacquainted personally with Furman, he knew him by reputation, and, to use his own words, "felt no apprehension" in replying to his request.

---

[56]Richard Furman to Oliver Hart, 4 July 1788, SCHBS.

[57]Wood Furman, *History of the Charleston Baptist Association* (Charleston, 1811) 57; Townsend, *History of South Carolina Baptists*, 59.

[58]S. D. Lynd, *Memoir of the Rev. William Staughton, D.D.* (Boston: Lincoln, Edwards and Co., 1843) 28 (hereinafter referred to as *Staughton Memoir*).

[59]John Rippon to Richard Furman, 18 July 1793, SCBHS.

> About ten days ago, I was on a visit to Dr. Rippon (between whom and myself the intimacy and affection of Brothers has grown up, unblasted and unabated from infancy). He read to me a letter he had just received from you; on hearing the part which solicits his furnishing, if possible, a proper person from England to supply a branch of the church under your care, a man "possessed of piety, education, good abilities and politeness, with popular talents, who is willing to come to America," I instantly thought and said to Dr. Rippon that a Mr. Staughton who has lately quitted the Academy at Bristol, and was requested to succeed Dr. Ryland at Northampton answers perfectly this description.[60]

On the same day, Dunscombe told Furman, he had learned that Staughton had already "taken on board the *Minerva*" for Charleston and that he would arrive there soon, "if Providence preserves him on this voyage." He then added, without clarification, "the cause of his quitting England he will fully explain to you."[61] The rest of the story must be pieced together from bits of surviving correspondence.

Arriving with Staughton was an English lady, Maria Hanson, to whom he was married almost immediately by Furman. Staughton told him of circumstances attending his decision to leave England; specifically, that Ms. Hanson had left behind a former husband from whom she had presumably been divorced. In the meantime, Furman had received such warm recommendations of Staughton from English brethren that he accepted Staughton's information and, without hesitation, married him to Ms. Hanson. In a letter to John Waldo, principal of an academy in Georgetown and member of the Georgetown church, Furman shared this information and requested that Waldo, in turn, share it with members of the church.

In reply, Waldo acknowledged receipt of the letter and added, "Agreeable to your request I have laid it before the principal members of the church. They express their approbation of Mr. Staughton's making a visit and giving us an opportunity of having a trial of his gifts among us. The principal circumstances which have brought Mr.

---

[60]Thomas Dunscombe to Richard Furman, 28 July 1793, SCBHS.
[61]Ibid.

Staughton to this country must be considered unfortunate, but no more
so than to himself and lady."[62]

Staughton visited Georgetown, was received cordially, and became
their pastor. Sometime after his arrival in America, Furman, on
Staughton's behalf, requested for him a letter of dismission from the
church in Birmingham, England, where he held membership. His request included a proposed plan by which the Birmingham congregation
could feel justified in granting dismission in good standing. The details
of that plan are not known, but reference to it appears in a letter to Furman from Samuel Pearce, pastor of the Birmingham church at that time.

> The plan you propose, with the peculiarity in his case stated, re-
> ceived my most hearty concurrence, and I hoped it would have been
> acceded to by our church. In this presumption, I drew up a letter of
> dismission upon your plan and after reading at a church meeting that
> part of your letter relating to Mr. Staughton, I submitted what I had
> prepared to the consideration of the brethren. It was the first time since
> I became their pastor that I found popular opposition. I reasoned on
> the dubious nature of the case—the variety of sentiment entertained
> by wise and good men upon it—the probable dependence of Mr.
> Staughton's usefulness . . . on their acquiescence . . . [that] we had
> to believe that although Mr. Staughton had (in our opinion) acted
> wrong, yet he had not acted dishonestly and contrary of his con-
> science, and therefore in the (spirit) of Christian candor, I urged their
> compliance with your request.
> I must do our people the justice to say that they appeared quite
> free from all prejudice and disaffection toward Mr. Staughton. Yet they
> said they could not accede. Their reasoning may be thus concentrated:
> we all think ourselves warranted from the scriptures to pronounce Mrs.
> Staughton barred by the law as long as her husband lives, and to assert
> that although she is not forbidden to live apart from him, yet she is
> in that case expressly commanded "not to marry." (1 Cor. 7:11) It is
> not probable therefore to regard her cohabitation with another man in
> any other than an adulterous light. Such leaven we are exhorted to
> purge out from us. (1 Cor. 5:7) Nor when duty calls are we to consult
> our feelings or probable consequences in living up to our part, al-

---

[62]John Waldo to Richard Furman, 6 November 1793, SCBHS.

though with regret, and leave the issue to him by whose authority our proceedings are regulated.[63]

Neither Furman nor Georgetown was deterred by this action or by the letter of the scriptural law. The congregation accepted Staughton as pastor, and for seventeen months he served them as an able and popular minister. With the assistance of Furman, the congregation was constituted as a church in 1794. However, Staughton finding the climate unfavorable to his health, and both he and his wife being unable to accept the system of slavery, they moved to New York in 1795. The marriage matter, apparently quiescent in Georgetown, followed him there and initially raised questions among Northern ministers. "A Mr. Staughton is in New York," Samuel Stillman wrote Furman from Boston in December 1795,

> whom I am informed you married to a woman who came with him from England who has a husband living there. I am told he is a man of fine abilities, but, sir, there appears to be something wrong respecting him. Dr. Foster of New York has not asked him to preach on account of it and assured me he cannot ask him. I wish for some information concerning him. Was she divorced legally from her former husband? If so, for what, seeing our Lord allows no separation of married people except for cause of fornication. If her former husband was not then guilty how can she leave him and marry again? Now, my dear sir, as you married them you must be acquainted with the circumstances, I presume. I'm anxious to be informed that I may know how to treat him should he come this way.[64]

Furman's reply is not known, but upon Staughton's departure for the North in June, he had with him a letter from Furman warmly recommending him and Mrs. Staughton "to the attention of friends and correspondents, where providence may cast their lot, as persons . . . for whose welfare he feels particularly concerned." "These are to certify," the letter read,

---

[63]Samuel Pearce to Richard Furman, 10 July 1794, SCBHS.

[64]Samuel Stillman to Richard Furman, 11 December 1795, SCBHS.

that the bearer hereof, Rev. William Staughton, is a licensed gospel preacher of the Baptist church, sent out to the important work of the ministry by the Baptist church of Birmingham, in Great Britain. He was a student of the Bristol Academy, where he studied languages, philosophy, and the belles lettres, and came to America with ample recommendations from persons of the first respectability in the Baptist connection. Dr. Rippon, of London, Mr. Pearce, of Birmingham, Mr. Hinton, of Oxford, and Mr. Dunscombe, of Coate, have particularly interested themselves in his behalf, in letters to the subscriber in which they recommend him as their much esteemed and amiable friend. During more than eighteen months' stay in South Carolina, principally Georgetown, Mr. Staughton's conduct has justified the recommendations given him by his European friends, and procured him the love and respect of his acquaintances in general, who esteem him as a man of piety, and a gospel minister of eminent abilities.

Mrs. Staughton is also of the Baptist church. She had employed a considerable part of her time in keeping a boarding school for young ladies, for which she is considered as eminently qualified, and has taught with reputation in this country as well as in Europe.

They are now about removing from Carolina to the Northern States, in expectation that the climate and mode of living there will be more agreeable to them than in the Southern.[65]

Furman's treatment of the Staughton marital matter demonstrated liberalism uncharacteristic then of Baptist conservatism, and persisting so in a milder manner until this day. It was also a significant contribution to the Baptist cause. Staughton became one of the most influential and eminent ministers among American Baptists. His greatest service was in the North. Before his death in 1828, he had served as pastor of the First Baptist Church of Philadelphia and the Sanson Street Baptist Church in that city. In 1822, he was installed as the first president of Columbian College (now George Washington University) in Washington, D.C.

Staughton's popularity as a preacher may be measured from the initial reaction to him by the Charleston church soon after his arrival from England. Its members were so impressed that some wished to obtain

---

[65]Richard Furman to Whom It May Concern, 19 June 1795, *Staughton Memoir*, 36-37.

him as an assistant minister. This troubled Furman, whose design for
him was Georgetown. "There is a proposal in circulation," he wrote his
mother at the High Hills, ". . . for getting another minister under the
character of an assistant: Mr. Staughton, you may suppose, is the man,
and this has been brought forward in such a manner as to be an obstacle
to his going to Georgetown; he is, however, gone there on a visit, and
it is not yet known how it may determine, but it seems pretty certain
we are at the eve of an eventful period."[66]

There is no evidence that Staughton was a party to the proposal, or
that there arose any misunderstanding between him and Furman because of it. But it was of such consequence as to create a temporary division in the church and call for adroit handling by the pastor. Furman's
concern was indicated in a letter to the Reverend J. Hinton of Oxford,
England, one who had recommended Staughton upon his coming to
America. In his reply, Hinton spoke of the "mingled sensations of pain
and pleasure" the letter had raised.

> I am glad to find that you are sensible of the virtues as well as the
> talents of my friends [the Staughtons]. I think both have virtues and
> if in any instance their conduct should be contrary, perhaps Charles-
> ton people rather than themselves are to be blamed. The conduct of
> some of your friends appears to have been highly incautious. Charles-
> ton is a tempting situation, and popularity is enchanting. Mrs. S.
> would naturally express a wish on account of her school to fix where
> handsome offers were made to her, and Mr. S. has been used in En-
> gland to Bristol, Birmingham, and Northampton congregations,
> highly respectable as well as numerous. Now while they are instructed
> to believe that Mr. F. as well as his people would favor their residence
> in Charleston, we cannot wonder they are pleased.[67]

When the 150th anniversary of the church was observed in 1832,
Basil Manly, Furman's successor, recalled the Staughton experience in
delivering a history of the church.

---

[66]Richard Furman to Rachel Brodhead Furman, 18 December 1793, SCBHS.

[67]Jay Hinton to Richard Furman, 1 May 1794, SCBHS.

It has, perhaps, never fallen to the lot of any congregation to be long and entirely free from discontented and restless spirits. . . . Dr. Furman . . . did not escape what usually falls to the lot of those ministers who have long and faithfully served the same people. About the year 1794, an attempt was made by a few persons connected with the congregation, to induce a very popular clergyman, the Reverend Mr. Staughton, then a young man recently arrived from England to settle in Charleston; and hints were not obscurely given for a desire to have him made Co-Pastor of the church. But the more staid and reflecting portion of the congregation frowned indignantly on the effort; and the consummate prudence, and varied excellencies of Dr. Furman, displayed on this trying occasion, gave him even a stronger hold than before on the estimation of all parties; and no similar trouble ever after occurred.[68]

COMPLAINT FROM THE HILLS

A matter of less consequence than the Staughton affair surfaced during Furman's first year in Charleston. While at High Hills his dress was in character with the more primitive life of backcountry settlements. But when he moved to Charleston, he adopted the costume of Revolutionary times—described as "coat with pockets in the skirts opening outwardly under a lapel, waistcoat reaching the hips, knee-breeches and long stockings, the latter protected in foul weather or a journey by high-topped boots." This typical dress for Charleston men of that day contrasted with the attire of the backcountry men, which was made of cotton and animal hides, shaped to size and form in tanneries and by spinning wheels.

When the Association met in Charleston in October 1788, a query came down from the High Hills church conveyed by its messengers, William Hampton and Peter Mellett. "What rule ought we to observe," it asked, "respecting the strange fashion of apparel which come up among us?" After the Association had completed its business, Furman wrote his sister at the Hills.

---

[68]Tupper, *Two Centuries of the First Baptist Church of Charleston*, 147.

I find by Mr. Hampton's account that considerable offense has been taken at the Hills on account of my dress and appearance in Charleston. . . . This . . . I can say, my appearance and behavior here are accommodated to the prevailing customs, in no higher proportion than they were at the Hills to those prevailing there. It is the opinion and desire of my friends that I should appear as the other ministers of the city in whose company I often have to appear in public occasions. And I acknowledge it is a principle I have long acted upon that it is proper to conform in a moderate degree to the prevailing customs in the place where we live . . . the reason is obvious, as it is the means of avoiding an odious singularity, and of conciliating the minds of associates to a free and familiar intercourse.[69]

The Association's answer was a masterpiece of diplomatic double-talk. "We think," it read, in the matter of dress, "that both extravagance and neglect should be avoided, that due respect be paid to the age, circumstances, and stations of persons, and to the customs of the place were we reside; also our income should not be exceeded, as we are under moral obligations to improve our substance for necessary and useful purposes."[70]

The dress matter was in the larger context of the sharp distinction persisting between society in Charleston and that in backcountry settlements. The struggle for district courts in the interior waged in the 1760s, the greater war burden that had been borne by small yeoman farmers in the middle and upper state, and the concentrated political power in Charleston were factors that gnawed at the vitals of backcountry folk to create sectional tensions from which not even the churches were immune. For their minister, beloved in the High Hills, to adopt the dress of Charleston society strained the tolerance of his former parishioners.

In a small way, this incident illustrates the advisory character of the Association. Among historical items prized for their insight into the religious thought of the times are surviving associational circular letters and minutes. At each session of the Association, a minister was designated to prepare a circular letter for distribution along with minutes of

---

[69]Richard Furman to Sarah Haynsworth, 29 October 1788, SCBHS.

[70]*Minutes of the Charleston Association*, 29 October 1788, microfilm copy, SCBHS.

the meeting. Queries, generally on matters of conduct or of practice, were frequently submitted by churches for open discussion and answers. Both queries and answers were dutifully recorded in the minutes for the benefit of all the churches. Thus, the Association was more than an annual meeting to obtain a report from the churches. It instructed in doctrine and policy, and served as a kind of corporate counselor and conscience on matters of particular and general concern. But it advised only; it exercised no final authority.

REENTER HART

No sooner had Furman become settled in Charleston than Oliver Hart planned to attend the 1778 annual meeting of the Charleston Association. Still fresh in Hart's mind was the struggle through which he had gone in finally rejecting Charleston's call to return as pastor. Scenes familiar during his long Charleston pastorate, the memory of old friends, a strong desire to see family relations still there, and the pull of nostalgia associated with age drew him southward by sulky on 2 September 1788. By the time he arrived in Baltimore on 24 September, misfortunes of travel, including fatigue, bad roads, the breakdown of his sulky, and a horse gone lame discouraged his going farther. His return trip to Hopewell, where he arrived on 23 October, was so beset by other difficulties that he described it as "the most trying and fatiguing journey that I ever took."[71] Disappointment in Charleston was keenly felt at his failure to arrive, "especially," wrote Furman, "when we had been so particularly informed that you had set off at an early season and had pleased our place with the prospect of enjoying a large share of your company."[72]

Hart continued to think of Charleston. Frequent letters were exchanged with Furman, who kept him informed about affairs in Charleston—births, deaths, marriages, and the state of religion in churches of the Association. Hart reciprocated with letters in a similar vein. The cold New Jersey climate was damaging to Mrs. Hart's health, and she desired to return to Charleston. In a letter to Colonel Thomas Screven,

---

[71]Loulie Latimer Owens, *Oliver Hart*, 21.

[72]Richard Furman to Oliver Hart, 12 April 1789, SCBHS.

Hart hinted that he might return if a place could be found for him. When Furman learned this, he wrote Hart that it "had occasioned several pleasing and anxious thoughts in my people, pleasing in the hope that we might once more enjoy the happiness of your company and assistance among us; anxious on account of the difficulties of finding a place suitable to our wishes and your advantage."[73]

Furman surveyed the possibilities and laid them and their problems before him. The High Hills church remained without a pastor, but it had been too deficient in the support of a minister to offer encouragement. The Edisto Island church was too divided; the climate at Georgetown was too sickly. The church on St. Helena Island needed a minister, but he had very little to go on by way of encouragement. Concern for his friend then asserted itself in a selfless offer.

> What shall I say of Charleston? It has been seriously in my thoughts. Would Mr. Hart be willing to resume his old station here? Could he go through the labor of preaching three times on the Sabbath? And lecture in the week besides? These things are expected here at present. Besides the constant visiting among fifty or sixty families, which I find very fatiguing. I feel willing to obey the call of Providence and should it appear to be the will of the ever-blessed God you should return and be again settled here, I should without reluctance seek some other place as my field of duty in the gospel service.[74]

Hart was then sixty-seven. It troubled Furman that "at your advanced period of life you should be straightened [sic], together with the anxiety suffered by Mrs. Hart removed as she is from her children and relatives." Furman urged Hart to let him know his real feelings about returning to Charleston and declared his intention "to make further inqueries to see what can be done at any place that appears promising."[75]

Whatever Hart's thoughts, he was never to see Charleston again. He remained at Hopewell until his death at the age of seventy-three on 31 December 1795. On 7 February following, Furman preached a me-

---

[73]Richard Furman to Oliver Hart, 17 August 1790, SCBHS.

[74]Ibid.

[75]Ibid.

morial sermon in his church entitled *Rewards of Grace Conferred on Christ's Faithful People.* Following an extended discussion of the sermon subject, he drew upon his and Hart's long and intimate acquaintance in a glowing eulogy of his friend.

> No person who heard his pious experimental discourses or his affectionate, fervent addresses to God in prayer, who beheld the zeal and constancy he manifested in the public exercises of religion, or the disinterestedness, humility, benevolence, charity, devotion and equanimity of temper he discovered on all occasions, . . . could for a moment, doubt of his being not only truly but eminently religious. He possessed in large measure, the moral and social virtues, and had a mind formed for friendship. In all his relative connections, as husband, father, brother, master, he acted with the greatest propriety, and was endeared to those who were connected with him in the tender ties.

Hart had initiated the educational movement of which Furman had become the heir. They had not seen each other since both had left South Carolina as refugees from the war, but their friendship had been kept alive through correspondence and an exchange of associational minutes. They had not always agreed on matters of practice. Upon receiving a copy of the minutes of the Association of 1788, Hart complained to Furman of their "trifling, crude, and undigested queries and answers." Furman thought his criticism "unjust" and set forth his reasons in a long reply.[76] But differences aside, Hart had been one of the true shapers of early South Carolina Baptists, and no one appreciated and respected him more than Furman.

GEORGE WASHINGTON COMES TO CHARLESTON

In May 1791 President George Washington arrived in Charleston on his famous Southern tour. He came by way of Georgetown, where an elaborate welcome was accorded him. Among those awaiting his arrival was Mary Bullein Johnson, who presented her young son, Wil-

---

[76]Richard Furman to Oliver Hart, 25 July 1789, SCBHS.

liam Bullein Johnson, to the president.[77] Baptists would hear about young Johnson. Like Furman, who assumed the mantle of Oliver Hart, Johnson would do the same for Furman.

From Georgetown, Washington moved on to Charleston by way of Hampton Plantation, home of the Daniel Horrys and much later to become the celebrated home of South Carolina Poet Laureate Archibald Rutledge. The country through which Washington passed consisted of extensive plantations, pine woods, fertile fields, moss-hung trees, virgin forests, and slave labor. Himself a planter, he was much impressed. Later in Charleston, he told Governor Charles Pinckney that he did not know such perfection of agriculture existed anywhere in America.

The entourage arrived in Charleston early in May. The city was in a festive mood. Furman was with other members of the clergy in the procession reviewed by Washington from a platform erected within the balustrade of the Cotton Exchange, situated a short distance from the Baptist parsonage.[78] This was Furman's first and only view of the man he had followed in the struggle for American independence. Eight years later when Washington died at his Mount Vernon home, Furman delivered a memorial sermon in his Charleston church at the invitation of the American Revolution Society and the State Society of the Cincinnati. On that occasion, he rose to his eloquent best. Nothing during his long career drew from him such majestic flow of language as this tribute to his fallen hero. The words flowed in resonant cadence.

> The character of the General . . . has been . . . so often the subject of eulogy, that it is not necessary that we should enter into a particular investigation: and were we to attempt it, the limits of a volume would be found too confined. Where also should we find the Raphael-hand that could draw it to the life, and present it to our view in all its pleasing attitudes and glowing colors?
>
> He was the true, the generous patriot. For her welfare he consecrated the services of his early youth, of his manly prime, and of his

---

[77]Hortense Woodson, *Giant in the Land: A Biography of William Bullein Johnson* (Nashville: Broadman Press, 1950) 4.

[78]Archibald Henderson, *Washington's Southern Tour* (Boston: Houghton Mifflin Company, 1923) 158. Furman's presence in the procession is an assumption based on the official order of march arranged by the reception committee, which listed the clergy as thirteenth in line among participants.

declining years. . . . He sought no rewards but the rewards of virtue! He labored only to render his country free, independent, and happy! What opportunities had he at the head of the army, for amassing wealth, had this been his object? And what rewards might he not have received had he yielded, like the traitor Arnold, to the overtures which proposed his betraying the cause of liberty?

. . . had he lived much longer, he must, according to the common course of nature, have suffered those infirmities and decays which impair, if not destroy, the comfort and usefulness of life. . . . Greatness in ruins is a mournful sight. To himself, therefore, this might be the most desirable time for his departure.

. . . he had for his own honor, and the honor of his country, completed a long course of great and dignified actions, without tarnishing his reputation; in such a manner as to give him full rank, if not precedence, among the great characters of ancient or modern times; and to make his example useful to future ages. Did Greece boast of Solon, Aristides, Leonidas, Timoleon, Epaminodes, and Aratus? Or Rome, of Romulus, the Bruti, Cincinnatus, Fabius, Scipio, the Antonines, or Cato? Does modern Europe glory in her Frederick, Gustavus Adolphus, Malborough, Hampden, or Sidney: as heroes, statesmen, or patriots? It is sufficient for America that she has had a Washington. Heaven has made him to us both a Moses and a Joshua. His example will live, though his body returns to its primeval dust.

For a full hour he engaged in flights of eloquence before an audience hanging on his words. He spoke of others who had gone before: of his friend Patrick Henry, "the Demosthenes of Virginia, the friend, the compatriot of Washington," whose "bold, unconquerable spirit, fired with the love of liberty and his country's fights, stood forth the first to oppose the encroachments of usurping power, in a manner that astonished patriots themselves"; and of John Rutledge, "the amiable, the eloquent, the accomplished . . . our late, honored governor, an early, tried, and steadfast patriot, the Tully of Carolina. . . . "

The man, the moment, and the subject had met for the fullest expression of Furman's oratorical powers. It was a high experience in his career as a citizen. At the request of the Society of the Cincinnati and the Revolution Society, the sermon was published. It survives under the title *Humble Submission to Divine Sovereignty: the Duty of a Bereaved Nation.*[79]

SAVANNAH AND HENRY HOLCOMBE

The Savannah church would not be constituted until 1800, but a stirring of Baptist interest six years earlier initiated a movement to erect a Baptist meetinghouse. Among leaders in this design were David Adams, a deacon of Furman's church in Charleston, and Furman himself. In 1795 Furman wrote to his sister, Sarah Haynsworth, at the High Hills,

> The most news of any importance respecting religious interest is what relates to Savannah. A respectable minister from Wales, Rev. Morgan J. Rhees,[80] was here some time ago and from representations made by himself, was induced to go to Savannah. His preaching has been much attended to and the building of a place of worship undertaken. In consequence, for the latter a lot has been given them and several hundred pounds subscribed. I'm just on the point of going there to pay them a visit long promised.[81]

---

[79]Southern Baptist Theological Seminary Library; SCBHS.

[80]Sprague, *Annals of the American Pulpit.* Morgan Rhees, born in Glamorganshire, Wales, in December 1760, prepared himself for the Baptist ministry at Bristol College, and after leaving was ordained at the Church of Peny-garn, in Monmouth. The French Revolution so excited his interest that he went to France immediately after the fall of the Bastille to participate in the triumphs of liberty. However, soon disillusioned with the chief actors of that drama, he returned to Wales where he established a magazine called *The Welsh Treasury*, in which, with eloquence and biting sarcasm, he exposed the policy of the English ministry. Being compelled to relinquish it, and knowing himself suspected of being friendly to the French pursuit of liberty, and the Tory government needing only a fair pretext to subject him to persecution, he came to America in 1794. Here he traveled extensively through the Southern and Western states, where his preaching attracted large and enthusiastic response. For a sketch of the history of the Savannah church written by Henry Holcombe, see *Georgia Analytical Repository*, November-December 1802, 177-85, James P. Boyce Library, Southern Baptist Theological Seminary.

[81]Richard Furman to Sarah Haynsworth, 1 April 1795, SCBHS.

The proposal to build was first made in 1794, but Baptists in Savannah were so few in number, and generally poor, that any prospect for success was dim until Rhees arrived. Furman's preaching there was attended by large audiences, among them "the first characters of the place." On a Sunday before returning to Charleston he was invited to preach in the Episcopal church by its rector, the Reverend Mr. Ellington. Despite rainy weather, "not less than 500 hearers" were in the audience.[82] Before he left, Furman had drawn up a plan for a building and assisted in initiating a movement for soliciting funds. By the end of the year, a house fifty by sixty was erected.[83]

Such was the ecumenical spirit in Savannah that when fire destroyed the Presbyterian church in 1796, Baptists rented them their meetinghouse. In 1799, a short while before expiration of the rental term, pew holders of the meetinghouse invited the Reverend Henry Holcombe, then residing at Beaufort, South Carolina, but pastor of the Euhaw church, to move to Savannah. He accepted their invitation and for a time was pastor of a congregation of both Baptists and Presbyterians. But early in 1800, the Baptists elected to have an organization of their own. A church was duly constituted, and Holcombe became its pastor.

Furman's interest in Savannah precipitated an unfortunate misunderstanding between him and Holcombe about the time Holcombe was settling into his new charge. The reasons are not entirely clear, but it appears that Joseph B. Cook, a graduate of Rhode Island College in 1797, was Furman's choice for Savannah, and that he recommended Cook without consulting Holcombe. Holcombe took exception to the slight and made his feelings known to Furman. Furman did not reply in haste, but when he did he informed Holcombe that, contrary to his recollection, they had indeed conversed on the subject. "If we did I cannot recollect it," Holcombe replied, "but I still think the subject was never mentioned to me, because from the interest I should have felt in it, my memory certainly would have retained, at least, some traces of it." It is probable, Holcombe continued, "that I am not, in this, mis-

---

[82]Richard Furman to Sarah Haynsworth, 28 September 1795, SCBHS; H. T. Cook, *Biography*, 45.

[83]Benedict, *General History of the Baptist Denomination*, 2:185.

taken, from the reasons which you have thought proper . . . for recommending Mr. Cook to Savannah in the most independent manner. These show that you supposed . . . that no recommendation of him, besides your own, would have operated as an additional advantage."

Among Furman's contentions was that "until lately," those who had done most toward providing a place of worship for Savannah Baptists had been members of his Charleston church. Holcombe disagreed.

> I am apprized [sic] from undoubted authority that no member of the Charleston Church was concerned in the origin of this business, and . . . that it appears from the original subscription before me that the three and the only members of this church [Charleston] who contributed toward building a place of worship here made up 43 pounds, six shillings, and three pence, which tho' generous sacrifice for the worthy persons who made them, were not equal to what was contributed by an individual Baptist who belonged to another church, and who was equaled in his liberality by a worthy person in this place who is an ornament to another denomination.

That Furman did not know of Holcombe's interest in Savannah when he sent Cook down, Holcombe acknowledged as "certain." "I had no more idea or desire when we conversed respecting my affairs in Beaufort of changing my place of abode than of going to the South Sea Islands," he told Furman. "But an unexpected series of events as much from under my influence or control as the rising of a cloud disconnected the plans of usefulness which I mentioned to you, and placed me here."[84] What, then, was Holcombe's problem, if, by his own admission, Furman was unaware of Holcombe's interest in Savannah when he sent Cook down? Distances being long, communication slow, and a considerable time lag occurring between correspondence, Furman may not have known that Holcombe had left Beaufort.

Other reasons may have entered. Holcombe's was an artistic and, therefore, sensitive temperament—"no doubt a poetic genius," Fur-

---

[84]These details are contained in a letter from Holcombe to Furman written in Savannah on 16 July 1800, SCBHS. Furman's letter on the subject has not survived, hence its contents must be surmised from evidence found in Holcombe's letter to Furman.

man called him.[85] According to Edmund Botsford, he was also vain. "As you have not mentioned having seen a piece lately published by Dr. Holcombe, I suppose you have not seen it," he postscripted a letter to Furman from Georgetown. "I saw it at Mr. Marshall's in Georgia. I wish I had not seen it. Why so, say you. Because it discovers so much vanity—for a person to say so much of his wonderful performances shows his fears that his biographer will not do him justice. It quite sickened Mr. Park and myself, as also Mr. Marshall."[86] Botsford was plainspoken, down-to-earth, and sometimes painfully frank.

A health problem also plagued Holcombe. "Our valuable brother, Holcombe, is in a poor state of health," Joseph Cook, father of Joseph B. Cook, informed Furman in 1789. "His disorder seems to be of a lethargic nature . . . A more promising man I know not. It appears to me that the people with whom he now labors are not worthy of a good man as they do not do their duty to him."[87]

We are left without knowledge of the series of events that turned Holcombe's thoughts toward Savannah, but whatever their nature, when he wrote Furman about the Cook affair he was a troubled man. Among other things, he believed himself slighted in the minutes of the 1800 Charleston associational meeting, which he did not attend, since no mention was made of his "distressing affliction," or the "embarrassing circumstances attending my removal from one, and settlement in another state." Mention of these he considered necessary to explain why he did not write the circular letter as requested. He was also troubled about arrangements for Cook's ordination. "I never was officially consulted," he said, "or honored with a line on the subject, 'til the evening before. . . . I was much disappointed in not hearing from you, as well as others on this subject."[88]

---

[85]Richard Furman to Oliver Hart, 2 June 1792, SCBHS.

[86]Edmund Botsford to Richard Furman, undated, SCBHS. The Mr. Park referred to was Thomas Park, son-in-law of Botsford and professor of language at South Carolina College. The Mr. Marshall was either Daniel Marshall or his son, Abraham, who pioneered Baptist work in Georgia.

[87]Joseph Cook to Richard Furman, 21 February 1789, SCBHS.

[88]Henry Holcombe to Richard Furman, 16 July 1800, SCBHS.

The whole affair was a test of Furman's tact and diplomacy in dealing with a difficult problem in human relations. That he succeeded is Holcombe's own testimony after he had unburdened his sensitive soul.

> Your explanation . . . especially your candid declaration as to your never having cherished a thought that led to any disrespect or neglect of your friend give me entire satisfaction. . . . Be assured that there is no man on earth whom I more highly respect, and would go greater lengths to serve, than Mr. Furman.[89]

Despite these gracious remarks, there is mild evidence that their friendship may have suffered. In 1802, when Holcombe initiated what is believed to have been the first American Baptist periodical, the *Analytical Repository*, Furman was less than enthusiastic. To Dr. William Rogers of Philadelphia, he confided that Holcombe was "too hasty" in his publication plans, that "the work will meet with little encouragement in Charleston," and that either Philadelphia or New York would be a more "eligible" place for such a venture. He did, however, add that "should it go on and be well conducted, it will give me much pleasure."[90] His judgment proved prophetic. Holcombe's publication failed to receive adequate support and folded after two years.

In 1814 Furman spent the night in Holcombe's home and dined with him on several occasions while attending the first meeting of the Triennial Convention in Philadelphia, but he spent most of the time with William Staughton.[91] Surviving correspondence shows little communication between the two after Holcombe went to Savannah, and eleven years later to Philadelphia.

Georgetown and Savannah were but two churches encouraged in their organization by Furman early in his Charleston pastorate. As he had done at the High Hills, he traveled extensively in the Lowcountry, assisting established churches and encouraging the formation of new

---

[89]Ibid.

[90]Richard Furman to William Rogers, 22 April 1802, SCBHS.

[91]Richard Furman to Dorothea Furman, 8 June 1814, SCBHS.

ones. Among new churches credited to his work were Beaufort, 1804,[92] Goose Creek and Mount Olivet, 1812,[93] and Edisto Island.[94] The Edisto Island church was long considered a meetinghouse branch of the Charleston church. As early as 1807, Furman's missionary interest attracted him to the island, situated across the Ashley River from Charleston and inhabited largely by Negroes—so many that the need for a meetinghouse was met in 1818 by the benevolence of Mrs. Hephzibah Townsend, a zealous lady remarkable for her good works. The house was opened for worship in 1818 with Furman preaching the dedicatory sermon. It remained a branch of the Charleston church until 1829 when it was constituted as the Edisto Island Baptist Church.[95]

No work came more naturally than these missionary endeavors in unchurched areas, and none pointed more clearly to the need for training young ministers.

FAMILY MATTERS

In 1790 the first child of Richard and Dorothea (Dolly) Furman was born. They named him Richard, but apparently did not call him Richard, Junior. Two years later another son, Samuel, was added to the family. The number now was four: Rachel and Wood by his first wife, and Richard and Samuel by his second. The family was growing, and would continue to grow until the children numbered seventeen.

Ironically, Furman had had little success in making religious converts of his family members. His first wife had died without professing religious faith. His oldest child, Rachel, was now seventeen years old and had made no profession, nor had his wife, Dolly. What religious impressions Wood experienced are not clear, but he was troubled with

---

[92]Richard Furman, *Extract of a Letter from the Rev. Dr. Furman of Charleston, (S.C.) to a Minister in Boston*, 12 March 1804, cited in J. Alvin Reynolds, "A Critical Study of the Life and Work of Richard Furman" (Ph.D. dissertation; Rochester NY: American Baptist Historical Society, 1962) 60.

[93]*Minutes of the Charleston Association*, 1929, SCBHS, 23; Manly, *Discourse*, 56.

[94]*Minutes of the Charleston Association*, 1929, SCBHS, 28.

[95]Ibid.; Manly, *Discourse*, 56-57.

religious doubts for most of his life.[96] Furman wrote to Oliver Hart in 1793 that "the mercy I have enjoyed this year of having two so near to me as my wife and daughter brought into the church is exceeding great and claims my warmest gratitude."[97]

But these early Charleston years brought sorrow also. In the fall of 1794, his mother, Rachel Brodhead Furman, died at the age of seventy-three.[98] She had moved to Charleston with her son and remained there during the first period of his Charleston pastorate, but after his marriage to Dorothea Burn she returned to the High Hills family home.

Like Furman's father, his mother exercised a strong influence in the shaping of his character, both spiritually and intellectually. Her early religious experience had been under the preaching of Presbyterians in New York, and George Whitefield, when he was in New York. She dated her real conversion, however, to the time when the Wood Furman family was living on Daniel's Island and an epidemic of smallpox was sweeping Charleston, causing many to flee the city to escape its scourge.

Among these refugees was an elderly lady, an acquaintance of the Furmans, who became a guest in their home. Being accustomed to the Charleston social whirl, she soon changed the normally serious atmosphere characteristic of the Furman home to one of levity. Then tragedy struck: She contracted smallpox and died. The family, shocked and frightened, decided that Wood Furman and Richard, then eight years of age, should leave to avoid further exposure to the disease. Rachel Furman was left behind with the servants and her only daughter, Sarah. Disconsolate and fearful, she became deeply troubled by thoughts of the deceased and the change that had come over the family during the lady's presence, especially because she had been a participant "in the last scenes of the other's folly and thoughtlessness." In her distress, Rachel engaged in earnest daily prayer until the burden of guilt was lifted. Of that experience she would later say, "As I returned to the place of my abode, the heavens, the earth, the trees, the grass, and all nature around

---

[96]Loulie Latimer Owens, *The Family of Richard Furman*, typescript copy, SCBHS.

[97]Richard Furman to Oliver Hart, 3 September 1793, SCBHS.

[98]*City Gazette*, 22 October 1794; *South Carolina Historical and Genealogical Magazine*, 22:120.

seemed to smile on me in token of the divine favour; and to unite in one general song of praise to God, infinitely good and merciful."[99]

At the 1793 meeting of the Charleston Association, which included the High Hills church, Furman preached the annual associational sermon, using as his subject unity and peace. His mother came up from her home in the Wateree valley to attend the meeting. With what pride and satisfaction she must have listened as her son expounded on the virtue of unity and peace in the Christian church and the Christian community.

> The proper consideration of the subject will naturally lead us to make a distinction between pure religion and the abuse of it. The gospel of Christ is holy and peaceful in its nature, inspires all who truly receive it with the most noble and generous sentiments; and its faithful ministers are men of . . . eminent virtue and piety. But the corruptions of it have furnished an example of quite the contrary, particularly in the middle and dark ages, and too much in the present, in some countries, where it has been used as a state engine of oppression and prefecting rage, or of superstition and imposture; used by civil leaders to accomplish the purposes of ambition and tyranny; and by voluptuous, intriguing men, under the character of priests, or ministers of religion, who, instead of instructing mankind in the knowledge of God, and the amiable principles of Christianity, have wrested from the key of knowledge; taught them to be the tame subjects of arbitrary power and priestly oppression, and the fiery zealots of superstition. . . . It is greatly to be lamented that many of those from whom better things have been expected . . . have, on many occasions, exercised a spirit of intolerance toward their brethren, and even pursued them with persecuting rage, of which not only the history of the world, but even the early part of the American, furnished melancholy proof. This conduct has principally originated in the unnatural union of civil authority with the power of the church; and an idea that persons who were the servants of God, had a right to compel others to conform to their sentiments in religion, or punish them for not conforming. For a considerable time, the contests, not only between papists and protestants, but between sectaries of the latter, seemed to be who had a right to force the conscience of others. These examples fur-

---

[99]The details of Rachel Furman's religious experience and conversion appear in an obituary in Rippon's *Register*, 2:281-83.

nish an awful and interesting lesson to mankind, and should be considered as a warning to us, to keep the faith in all its purity; to exercise
the genuine spirit of the gospel, and preserve its unity in peace.

The Puritan intolerance of his own ancestral roots in the Massachusetts Bay Colony was clearly on his mind, as was the persecution of Baptists in Virginia by the Church of England. Before him, too, were visions
of Old World struggles, of religious wars in the seventeenth and eighteenth centuries, and at that moment, the violent excesses of the French
Revolution in the name of liberty. Furman was aware of human history.
There among the hills of the Santee, in a backcountry church and among
a people known and loved by him, he employed the full range of his
intellectual power and experiential knowledge of the Scripture to em-
phasize how Christianity, when truly applied, makes for unity despite
differences, and peace despite diversity.

It was the last time his mother would hear him preach. Eleven and
a half months later, she was buried beside her husband in the family
burial grounds on Furman Plantation. In February of that same year,
another grief came. A son, John Gano Furman, died. He bore the name
of a cherished friend who, at the invitation of Oliver Hart and the
Charleston Association, had come down from the Philadelphia Association to conduct pioneer missionary work in the interior of the Southern colonies.[100]

STRENGTHENING YEARS

These early Charleston years had strengthened Furman's role as
minister and citizen. The contrast with life in the High Hills had been
sharp and distinct. The cultural life of Charleston suited his cultural
taste and his intellectual interest. Through his friendships with the city's
leading citizens and his contributions to state constitutional development, he had participated in the political structuring of South Caro-

---

[100]Gano's work was so successful that he is said to have been "only slightly less
effective than Whitefield" (King, *A History of South Carolina Baptists*, 65n). He worked
chiefly in the Yadkin valley region of North Carolina, began the merger of Regular
and Separate Baptists in North Carolina and Virginia, and was instrumental in causing several North Carolina churches to affiliate with the Charleston Association.

lina. As pastor of one of the most influential Baptist churches in America, he had come into position for strong leadership in shaping Baptist ecclesiology, missions, and education.

CHAPTER 6

The Great Revival

The final years of the eighteenth century and the first years of the nineteenth are known in American religious history as the period of the Great Revival. For the major religious denominations in the South, they were transition years. The Anglican church had emerged from the American Revolution in an enervated and precarious condition, due largely to its failure to relate its ministry to the needs of people, its "dry-as-dust sermons, lackadaisical piety, and the fopperies of tidewater society."[1] Times had changed and the state church, with its Tory label and its aristocratic past, was no match for evangelical Baptists, Presbyterians, and Methodists. When released from enforced support of the Church of England, the rustic people of the backcountry transferred their loyalty to denominations with a religion of heartwarming relevancy and simplicity. The Episcopal church, deprived of state support and sterotyped as employing stuffy rectors, was no match for fervid evangelicals who preached a simple, direct message with unrestrained emotion.

---

[1]John B. Boles, *The Great Revival, 1787-1805* (Lexington: University of Kentucky Press, 1972) 1.

Despite the presence in the South of three evangelical denominations, there was no regionwide revival until the Great Revival around 1800. The Separate Baptist movement during the mid-eighteenth century was confined largely to Virginia and North Carolina, with some overflow into South Carolina. Presbyterianism, dedicated to an educated clergy, produced schools, academies, and learned ministers, but inevitably it made for a shortage of ministers among the simple folk of the backcountry. "In a South overwhelmingly rural, simple in taste, and habituated to little government supervision of any kind, the immense Presbyterian influence was to be dependent upon a relatively small group of unusually able men," and Presbyterianism did not therefore become "the archetype of the southern church."[2]

Organized Methodism reached the South in 1773 when Robert Williams arrived in the southeastern Virginia parish of Devereux Jarratt, an Anglican with evangelistic zeal whose sermons to his people were hard-hitting and emotional. Jarratt, a Methodist in everything but name, threw his support behind Williams and permitted the new Methodist congregation to use his barn as a meetinghouse. With Jarratt's aid, Methodism grew rapidly in Virginia and spilled over into North Carolina. Jarratt was joined by Thomas Rankin, and both itinerated widely in Virginia. The revival they began lasted into the American Revolution. After the Revolution, a conference of Methodist ministers met in Baltimore in December 1784 and established the Methodist Episcopal Church independent of the Church of England. Under the leadership of Thomas Coke and Francis Asbury, American Methodism adopted an abbreviated liturgy, a de-Calvinized theology, and an evangelistic hymnody. Methodism's subsequent meteoric rise would dominate American Protestantism in the nineteenth century.

These local periods of religious revival had more than local meaning. They prepared the background and the leadership for the Great Revival that would engulf the South as the nineteenth century began. But in advance of revival floods, a religious drought, frequently referred to as a "declension of religion," became a troubling concern of devout clergymen. In a letter to his sister, Sarah Haynsworth, written on 23 August 1792, Richard Furman described the state of religion as

---

[2]Ibid., 3.

"truly melancholy," but felt assured that some remained who feared God, and "as the Lord is great in his mercies, we are hereby encouraged to hope, that he will once more return and look with Mercy on his languishing and almost expiring Church."[3]

In the 1793 circular letter of the Charleston Baptist Association, from the meeting at the High Hills church, Furman addressed himself to "the threatening or warning dispensations of providence, and the declension in religion so apparent among churches and individual professors." He noted the "calamities of war and internal commotion, which ravage the fertile fields, desolate the cities, and convulse the nations of Europe" (the French Revolution). Closer home, he spoke of the "most poignant sensations" experienced when contemplating "the situation of the most noted, and lately, the most populous, opulent, and flourishing city of the American Union (Philadelphia), now almost desolated by the flight and death of her inhabitants, and covered with a deep and melancholy gloom, by the prevalence of an inveterate and pestilential fever . . . to which has been added very general and distressing sickness through the body of the southern states, even in the most healthy parts." Religion, he said, is in "a low and languishing state throughout the continent, admitting a few exceptions, and that it is greatly so with us, is evident from the best testimony and our own observation."[4]

At the 1794 meeting of the Association, "the languishing state of religion in our churches, and the country at large," claimed the "most serious attention" of the delegates, resulting in agreement for the churches to hold monthly meetings in the interests of "the honor of God, the interests of their own souls, and the souls of others." In 1799 the Association requested that Furman prepare a circular letter on the "probable causes of the present languishing state of religion among us in these southern states." The Association also directed the churches to join with the Georgia Association, "to unite with them in solemn humiliation and prayer for a revival of religion."[5]

For many other Southern clergymen—Baptist, Presbyterian, Methodist—the final years of the eighteenth century were freighted with

---

[3]Richard Furman to Sarah Haynsworth, 23 August 1792, SCBHS.

[4]*Minutes of the Charleston Baptist Association*, 1793, SCBHS.

[5]*Minutes of the Charleston Baptist Association*, 2 November 1799, SCBHS.

despair. A circular letter of the Georgia Baptist Association noted the prevalence of "coldness and formality," along with worldliness, dissipation, materialism, and total absence of Christian piety.[6] Jeremiah Norman, an itinerant Methodist minister in North Carolina, made references in his diary to a religious slump in that state,[7] while Lemuel Burkitt, in a letter to Richard Furman on 11 January 1798, lamented that he saw no evidence that piety was returning. After the revival began he would speak of "the long and tedious night of spiritual darkness and coldness in religion" when "the churches appeared to be in general decline."[8] Edmund Botsford, then pastor of the Welsh Neck Baptist Church in the South Carolina Old Cheraw district, became quite desperate over his situation in the spring of 1796. "I was in hopes sometime ago," he lamented, "it was midnight with us, but I now begin to fear I was mistaken . . . in cold winter nights, it often seems a long time from midnight to morning, especially to those who are upon the watch."[9]

In his 1799 circular letter to the churches of the Charleston Association at the Congaree church, Richard Furman dealt with the dilemma concerning both the individual church member and the churches. Of the causes within the churches, he cited this evidence:

> First sending out persons, as ministers, who are not well qualified for the work without using proper means for their improvement. Secondly the too general neglect of members to improve themselves, by reading and other means which are attainable, and which would render them respectable and influential among the people with whom they are connected. Thirdly, inattention to their congregational interests: Which includes neglect of proper means for uniting their members, and those connected with them as worshippers, in such measures as

---

[6]Georgia Baptist Association Circular Letter, 1801, in C. D. Mallary, *Memoirs of Elder Jesse Mercer* (New York, 1844) 141, cited in Boles, *The Great Revival*, 13-14; Reverend John Newton to Reverend Samuel Wilson, 14 July 1794, L. C. Glenn Collection, Southern Historical Collection, University of North Carolina, Chapel Hill.

[7]Jeremiah Norman, Diary, 935, 938, 943, 963, Stephen B. Weeks Collection, University of North Carolina, Chapel Hill, cited in Boles, *The Great Revival*, 14.

[8]Cited in Boles, *The Great Revival*, 14.

[9]Edmund Botsford to Richard Furman, 10 April 1796, SCBHS.

would enable them to erect decent and convenient houses for public worship, and to support the gospel ministry among them in a permanent manner. Fourthly, that prevailing spirit of moving from place to place, just as fancy, whim, or supposed interest may dictate, without a due regard to the call of providence, or the interest of religion; by which churches are often greatly weakened, or, as it were, wantonly, and sacriligiously [*sic*] broken up.

In contrast to Furman's letter, Silas Mercer's circular letter for the Georgia Baptist Association in 1795 portrayed the low state of religion as evidence of how God deals with his people.[10]

By the time Furman became pastor in Charleston, the denominations that would mold the future religion in the South—Presbyterian, Methodist, Baptist—had shaped their personalities and organizational structures. Except for casual and short-lived instances, there was little evidence during the next decade that the Southern climate would support sustained piety. The big issues of these years concerned political activity, constitutional theorizing, ratification debates, land grabbing, British impressment, the French Revolution, Hamiltonian economics, and Jeffersonian democracy.

Westward, virgin land set in motion a migration that saw thousands of the venturesome and footloose swarming along the trailways that led into and beyond Appalachia. "Our roads have been lined with emigrants for sometime past for the Western territory," Mary Glas Burn McDonald wrote from Georgia, as late as 1817,[11] to her son-in-law, Richard Furman. A Tennessean noted, " . . . to a person who observes the migration to this country, it appears as if North and South Carolina, and Georgia, were emptying themselves" into Tennessee.[12] Older churches along the Southern seaboard were therefore left without many of their active members who had joined in the westward migration. One South Carolinian explained that "congregations are not very stable in

---

[10]Jesse Mercer, *History of the Georgia Baptist Association* (Washington GA, 1838) 145-46, cited in Boles, *The Great Revival*, 29.

[11]Mary Glas Burn McDonald to Richard Furman, 1 April 1817, SCBHS.

[12]Boles, *The Great Revival*, 9.

this country at this time. [A] spirit of emigration prevails."[13] Perhaps that was the motivation that led Furman in 1795 to propose "a Society in Charleston for encouraging Emigration of virtuous citizens from other Countries." To his sister, Sarah Haynsworth, he reported that the Society had "met with remarkable success" with "most of the notable characters in Charleston . . . embarked in the Design," among them, Dr. David Ramsay, John Rutledge, Jr., Judge J. F. Grimke, and Henry W. DeSaussure, who with Furman formed the rules of the Society.[14]

The revival began among Presbyterians in Logan County, Kentucky, where James McGready, a Presbyterian minister, had arrived from North Carolina in the autumn of 1796, and in January 1797 had taken charge of three small congregations—Red River, Muddy River, and Gasper River. Preaching repentance, faith, and regeneration, McGready's sermons so moved his listeners that some conversions occurred during the spring and summer, but by winter there was a general falling away. McGready and a few steadfast members of his congregations then adopted a covenant that bound them to pray for revival.

The year 1800 would see revival fires that had begun in Kentucky sweeping that state and spreading across the South. As John B. Boles says in *The Great Revival*, "This was the first revival common to the whole South, and the first in which all denominations shared simultaneously. In a very real sense, this was the South's 'Great Awakening.' " A special characteristic was the camp meeting, a religious phenomenon that would become indigenous to Southern rural revivalism of the nineteenth century.

At his citadel of Regular Baptists in Charleston, Furman received reports of these revivals. To Dr. William Rogers in Philadelphia he wrote, "The revival or religious stir in North Carolina I understand continues and increases. They have had several meetings lately, quite in the Kentucky stile; many ministers and their congregations collecting at one place, and continuing Night and Day on the Ground, for

---

[13]Robert L. Wilson to Reverend Samuel Wilson, Abbeville, South Carolina, 27 March 1798, L. C. Glenn Collection, University of North Carolina, Chapel Hill; Boles, *The Great Revival*, 9n.

[14]Richard Furman to Sarah Haynsworth, 1 April 1795, SCBHS; H. T. Cook, *Biography*, 45.

several Days together; falling down, etc. It seems this is chiefly among the Presbyterians, who have been wont heretofore to ridicule the disorderly Baptists." But as for Charleston, he reported, " . . . we remain much the same as we have for a number of years."[15]

Furman's initial eyewitness encounter with the revival was in May 1802. At a huge camp meeting in the Waxhaws district on the South Carolina side of the border between the two Carolinas, South Carolina experienced the first outbreak of "those bodily affections, which have been experienced at Kentucky, North Carolina, and at other places, where the extraordinary revivals in religion within this year or two have taken place." The Waxhaws district, halfway between Charlotte, North Carolina, and Lancaster, South Carolina, was due north of the High Hills, and Furman was on a business trip to the High Hills family plantation when the Waxhaws meeting began.[16] Before returning to Charleston, he went the seventy miles to the Waxhaws meeting and remained long enough to witness extraordinary demonstrations, and to leave one of the most vivid surviving descriptions of the camp meetings of that period. He described the meeting in a letter to Dr. John Rippon of London.

> Having promised you some information respecting the extraordinary meeting at the Waxhaws, to which I purposed going at the time I wrote in May, and having accordingly attended it, I now sit down to perform my promise.
>
> . . . The place of meeting is about 170 miles from Charleston, in the midst of a large settlement of Presbyterians, but not far distant from some congregations of Baptists and Methodists. . . .
>
> . . . A place was chosen in the forest for an encampment. The numbers which assembled from various parts of the country formed a very large congregation . . . variously estimated . . . to be 3000, or perhaps 4000 persons; but some supposed there were 7000 or 8000.
> . . .
>
> . . . The encampment was laid out in an oblong form, extending from the top of a hill down the south side of it, toward a stream of water. . . . Lines of tents were erected on every side of this space; and

---

[15]Richard Furman to William Rogers, 22 April 1802, SCBHS.

[16]H. T. Cook, *Biography*, 26.

between them, and behind, were the wagons and riding carriages placed, the space itself being reserved for the assembling of the congregation, or congregations, to attend public worship. Two stands were fixed on for this purpose: At the one, a stage was erected under some lofty trees, which afforded an ample shade; at the other, which was not so well provided with shade, a wagon was placed for the rostrum.

The public service began on Friday afternoon . . . with a sermon by the Reverend Dr. McCorkel, of the Presbyterian church; after which the congregation was dismissed: but at the same time the hearers were informed, that they would be visited at their tents, and exhorted by the ministers, during the course of the evening. To this information an exhortation was added, that they would improve the time in religious conversation, earnest prayer, and singing the praises of God. . . . many sermons were preached . . . in the evening; and the exercises continued . . . till midnight. . . .

On Saturday morning, the ministers assembled after an early breakfast, and appointed a committee to arrange the services for that day and the two following. . . . They soon performed the work of their appointment, and assigned the several ministers present their respective parts of the service. By this arrangement two public services were appointed at each stand for that day; three for the Sabbath, together with the administration of the communion, at a place a little distant from the encampment; and two at each stand again for Monday. . . . Most necessary business calling me away on Sunday evening, I did not see the conclusion of the meeting.

This I can say, it was conducted with such solemnity, while I was at it; and the engagedness of the people appeared to be great. . . . The preaching and exhortations of the ministers . . . were well calculated to inspire right sentiments, and make right impressions.

In the intervals of public worship, the voice of praise was heard among the tents in every direction, and frequently that of prayer, by private Christians. The communion service was performed with much apparent devotion, while I attended, which was at the serving of the first table. The Presbyterians and Methodists sat down together; but the Baptists, on the principle which has generally governed them on this subject, abstained.

Several persons suffered at this meeting those bodily affections. . . . Some fell instantaneously, as though struck with lightning, and continued insensible for a length of time; others were more mildly affected, and soon recovered their bodily strength, with a proper command of their mental powers. . . .

In a few cases there were indications . . . of enthusiasm, and even affectation; but others a strong evidence of supernatural power, and gracious influence. Several received the impression in their tents; others in a still more retired situation, quite withdrawn from company. . . .

Some . . . had gone 70 or 80 miles from the lower parts of this State to attend this meeting . . . since their return to their homes, an extraordinary revival had taken place in the congregations to which they belong. It has spread also across the upper parts of this State, in a western direction. . . .

. . . These general meetings have a great tendency to excite the attention, and engage it to religion: Were there no other argument in their favour, this alone would carry great weight with a reflecting mind. . . . At the same time it must be conceded that there are some incidental evils which attend them, and give pain to one who feels a just regard for religion. . . . However, I hope the direct good obtained from these meetings will much more than counterbalance the incidental evil.[17]

Though eminently orthodox and conservative, Furman was tolerant of camp meeting demonstrations as long as they were an expression of heartfelt religion. In a letter to Edmund Botsford he termed "the Revival in the Back and Middle Country . . . a blessed visitation from on high" and prayed that it might be extended to the Seacoast: " . . . that you, that we, and Thousands more may partake of its Blessedness and Joy."[18] Botsford did not approve of the "irregularities," but as "ye land was overrun with infidelity," it seems, he said, "as if something extraordinary was necessary to arouse people from such a state." Botsford wished, he wrote John Roberts from Georgetown, "we had something to move us in this place. I confess it would please me best to see and be ye instrument of work, still, calm, yet powerful—like it was in New England—however, a rushing mighty wind, rather than such a miserable languid state in which we still continue."[19]

---

[17]Richard Furman to John Rippon, 11 August 1802, Rippon's *Register*, 4:1102-1105.

[18]Richard Furman to Edmund Botsford, 12 October 1802, SCBHS.

[19]Edmund Botsford to John M. Roberts, 17 August 1802, SCBHS.

In 1800, when the revival was sweeping across Kentucky and into Tennessee, North Carolina, and Virginia, Furman stressed as an "important point in religion" the ability to "strike the proper line, both in judgment and in practice, between Christian zeal and wild enthusiasm; and between the moderation that is directed by wisdom, or indifference. . . ." With his mind obviously on the physical excesses reported from revival scenes, he cautioned, "Let it be our earnest care to choose the happy medium which truth and duty point out in these cases, and in every other where we are liable to run into dangerous and hurtful extremes."[20]

An example of such "dangerous and hurtful extremes" occurred at a camp meeting in 1802 in Rutherford County, North Carolina. David Gray, an inhabitant of Rutherford who was present, included in his description of the meeting the following account:

> One of the most mysterious exercises among the people was what was called the jerks. . . . Sometimes their heads would be jerked backward and forward with such violence that it would cause them to utter involuntarily a sharp, quick sound similar to the yelp of a dog; and the hair of the women to crack like a whip. . . .[21]

The Reverend James Jenkins, a Methodist minister whose preaching style caused him to become known as "Bawling Jenkins," wrote to Bishop Asbury on 30 June 1802,

> Hell is trembling, and Satan's kingdom failing. Through Georgia, South Carolina, and North Carolina, the sacred flame and holy fire of God, amidst all the opposition, are extending far and wide. I may say with safety, that hundreds of sinners have been awakened and converted this year in the above-named states.[22]

---

[20]*Minutes of the Charleston Association*, 1800, SCBHS.

[21]Shipp, *The History of Methodism in South Carolina*, 274.

[22]James Jenkins, *Experiences, Labours and Sufferings of the Rev. James Jenkins of the South Carolina Conference* (Columbia: State Printing Co., 1842) 115. The camp meetings that covered the upper part of South Carolina are well documented. See Benedict, *A General History of the Baptist Denomination*, 2:165-67; Shipp, *The History of Meth-*

Jenkins tells of passing a Baptist gathering in Union County while on his way to a Methodist meeting. He describes it as "a good meeting but for want of some one to nurse our converts, the Baptists reaped the fruits of our labours."[23] That, however, is not the picture more frequently given of ubiquitous Methodist circuit riders of that period. In his account of the great revivalists, Bernard A. Weisberger described circuit riders as "a superbly mobile force, ready to go anywhere, at any time, where sinners were in need of the saving word. No settlement was too rundown or too remote for them. . . . They went almost literally everywhere."[24] When blizzards howled or the rains poured down, there was a folk saying that "nobody was out but crows and Methodist preachers."[25]

At a general meeting in South Carolina's Spartanburg County, called by Presbyterians for Friday, 2 July 1802, five or six thousand people gathered, along with thirteen Presbyterian ministers and an unknown number of Baptists and Methodists. Three days of intensive religious exercises were followed by a Sunday evening service that continued through the night. The service is described as progressing as usual until about dark when there commenced "one of the most sublime, awfully interesting and glorious scenes which could possibly be exhibited on this side of eternity."

> The penetrating sighs and excruciating struggles of those under exercise, the grateful exultations of those brought to a sense of their guilty condition, and to a knowledge of the way of salvation; mingled with impressions which are naturally excited by the charms of music and

---

odism in South Carolina, 273, 398-400; Richard Furman to Edmund Botsford, 12 October 1802, Botsford Papers, SCBHS; Edmund Botsford to Richard Furman, 11 June 1803, SCBHS; Edmund Botsford to John Roberts, 24 November 1802, SCBHS; and Townsend, *History of South Carolina Baptists*, 297-305.

[23]Jenkins, *Experiences, Labours and Sufferings*, 118.

[24]Bernard A. Weisberger, *They Gathered at the River: The Story of the Great Revivalists and Their Impact Upon Religion in America* (Boston: Little, Brown and Company, 1948; New York: Quadrangle/New York Times Book Co., 1958) 45.

[25]Ibid.

the solemnities of prayer on such occasions . . . were sufficient to bow the stubborn neck of infidelity, silence the tongue of profanity, and melt the heart of cold neglect. . . . Some are more easily and gently wrought than others, some appear wholly wrapped in solitude while others cannot refrain from pouring out their whole souls and exhortation to those standing round;—different stages from mild swoons to convulsive spasms, may be seen. . . .[26]

From its beginning in Logan County, Kentucky, in 1800, camp meeting revivalism spread rapidly throughout the Southern states. Indicating its prevalence, the Reverend Stith Mead wrote of twenty-three camp meetings he had attended in Virginia between March 1804 and April 1805, at which there had been more than one thousand converts.[27] In South Carolina, the revival spread across the whole state and continued several years, with the high point coming in the backcountry in 1802-1803. In 1802 alone, a total of 1,156 members were added to five churches. Constitution of new churches and formation of branches followed rapidly. During the years 1802-1804, thirty-five churches and branches came into existence, concentrated chiefly in four counties.[28] Similar results were experienced in Georgia and North Carolina.

Churches of the Charleston Baptist Association felt the reviving influence that had swept into South Carolina from other states and stirred camp meeting revivalism in the backcountry. But while benefiting from increased baptisms, they also viewed with concern its attending physical demonstrations and emotional outbursts. How gravely the Association observed the revival phenomenon is suggested by the subject assigned for the circular letter of 1803: "How may enthusiasm be distinguished from the influence of the spirit and Grace of God on the Heart?" Because Furman was the most influential minister in that Association and, as its moderator for most of the years of his ministerial

---

[26]Ebenezer H. Cummins to a friend in Augusta, Georgia, 7 July 1802, quoted in Catherine Cleveland, *The Great Revival in the West, 1797-1805* (Chicago: University of Chicago Press, 1916) appendix 3, 165-72; *Georgia Analytical Repository* (1802) 94-95, James P. Boyce Library, Southern Baptist Theological Seminary, cited in Townsend, *History of South Carolina Baptists*, 298-99.

[27]Boles, *The Great Revival*, 29.

[28]Townsend, *History of South Carolina Baptists*, 201.

career, a living spiritual extension of that body, the query must be considered an assertion of Furman's fear that the camp meeting tended to sacrifice sincere religion; or, as he had said, it seemed to miss "the happy medium between truth and duty" in an orgy of emotional excitement.

The circular letter, written by Joseph B. Cook, took the narrow road between endorsement and condemnation. Declaring the query to be "very interesting, particularly at this time," Cook noted with satisfaction the revival of religion "after a long wintry season." He then added that "so strangely have both the minds and the bodies of many been affected . . . particularly at some extraordinary meetings, that it had been doubted, not only by the irreligious, but also by some very pious persons, whether these effects are produced by the Spirit of God, or merely by enthusiasm."[29] Undoubtedly, Cook expressed the sentiments of Furman. Nothing could please Furman more than a genuine demonstration of sincere religion, by whatever means or in whatever form it manifested itself. On the other hand, nothing could disturb him more than a corruption of religion by shabby, physical demonstrations, emotionally based hysteria, or delusive aberrations. He was enough Separate Baptist not to condemn, and enough Regular Baptist to be concerned.

Because of the expansive success of this revivalistic movement, a millennial idea began circulating, causing concern within the mainstream churches. There were two schools of millennial thought: one believed the millennium would begin with the return of Christ to earth, and the other believed that the thousand-year reign of the godly would precede the Second Coming. Hence the terms premillennial and postmillennial. Whether the actual millennium would begin as an evolutionary process or with a cataclysmic event was a question for theological speculation.

The revival movement convinced many that the millennium had already begun. In 1802 a South Carolinian wrote, ". . . the new thought of the Millennium comes on well in these parts and many signs and wonders appear which testify who is at the head of the business."[30] Sim-

---

[29]*Minutes of the Charleston Association*, 1803, SCBHS.

[30]Alexander Porter to John Hemphill, 7 September 1802, B. R. Hemphill Papers, Duke University, Durham, North Carolina, cited in Boles, *The Great Revival*, 103.

ilar expressions of chiliastic optimism appeared from Kentucky to
Georgia. Henry Holcombe's *Georgia Analytical Repository* published letters emphasizing millennial hopes, and in 1803 it ran an article entitled
"Analysis of Prophecy," which declared people to be "living in the last
days" with God working "to prepare the righteous remnant of the church
for the Kingdom of Christ."[31] Such hopes created a belief that the Great
Revival was the beginning of history's glorious culmination, rather than
a temporary resurgence of religion. Even when these hopes were dashed,
the millennial idea remained.

From his church in Charleston, Richard Furman considered these
things with the detachment of an intellectual not given to flights of
emotion. Not unimpressed by revival experiences, neither was he one
to interpret them explicitly as millennial demonstrations. He chose to
see events as ongoing, progressive manifestations of God in history, and
particularly American history. As a patriot of the Revolution, he deeply
believed that Providence had determined its outcome and that God had
a special mission for America as a world-evangelizing nation. "From
what has transpired and exists," he said, "it seems reasonable to conclude, that it [America] was originally designed as an asylum for religion and liberty; and a theatre on which the power and excellency of
both were to be exhibited to the greatest advantage." He saw the United
States as a country where, if people remained virtuous and Christian and
chose their leaders well, a millennial future of almost unblemished
character lay ahead.

The advantages with which the nation has been blessed, he said,

> . . . encourage us to look forward, with pleasing hopes, to a day
> when America will be the praise of the whole earth; and shall partic-
> ipate largely, in the fulfillment of those sacred prophecies which have
> foretold the glory of the Messiah's kingdom . . . when there shall be
> an abundance of peace . . . when God shall build the cities and cause
> them to be spread abroad; when righteousness shall dwell in the fruit-
> ful field, and the wilderness shall rejoice and blossom as the rose.[32]

---

[31]Boles, *The Great Revival*, 105 and note.

[32]Richard Furman, *America's Deliverance and Duty: A Sermon Preached at the First
Baptist Church of Charleston, on the Fourth Day of July, 1802*, Richard Furman Papers,
Furman University, SCBHS.

Speaking in the context of the Great Revival, he linked it with the happy circumstances of the early period of national history and determined that America's manifest destiny was to lead the world into the millennium. Toward that end, and in part from the excesses of the Great Revival, he saw an urgent need among Baptists for a trained and educated ministry. In his circular letter to the churches in 1799, he had listed as a first cause for the languishing state of religion the practice of "sending out persons, as ministers who are not qualified for the work without using proper means for their improvement," and "the general neglect of members, to improve themselves, by reading and other means which are attainable, and which would render them respectable and influential among the people with whom they are connected." He would see the same need arising from the excesses of religion as from its languishing state. He had long since committed himself to meeting that need.

CHAPTER 7

Pioneer Beginnings
in Education

Richard Furman's understanding of the social, educational, and cultural needs of his time inevitably made him a conspicuous eighteenth- and nineteenth-century leader in promoting the cause of education. While providing religious education for ministers was his initial and primary thrust, neither interest nor effort was confined to this objective. He also saw a pressing need for a state institution offering college-level instruction for the state's rank and file. He, therefore, became an influential figure in a move that led to the founding of the first state institution of higher learning in South Carolina—now the University of South Carolina.

The story of ministerial education actually begins with Oliver Hart. In 1755 he organized the Baptist Religious Society in Charleston to assist young ministers in preparing for the ministry. Until then there existed no Baptist organization in America for educating young ministers. A young man wishing to prepare himself for the ministry would serve an internship with some older pastor who would permit him to use his library, instruct him in study, and offer him practical experience in pastoral duties. Such a trainee would be licensed to preach during the training period. At a point of sufficient maturity, he would then be ordained to accept the call of a church.[1]

Hart's Society began with evening lectures at the homes of individual parishioners.[2] From that practice came an organization "for promoting Christian knowledge and practice." When rules were later formulated, rule twenty-seven stated: "[The] principle end and aim of this Society is to educate . . . youths for the ministry."[3] But as late as 1791 Furman wrote to the Reverend George W. Pearce of Birmingham, England, that "a great part of our ministers as well as members are illiterate." He termed this "a great hindrance" to Baptist influence in the state, and the cause "in many instances" for "enthusiasm and confusion" among ministers in the interior.[4]

When the Charleston Baptist Association met in 1786, Furman had written the circular letter and called upon churches to cultivate "a thirst for divine knowledge," to "pay particular attention to the education of children . . . and where it had pleased God to call any of his young servants to the work of the ministry . . . to furnish the necessary means for that end."[5] The letter also took note of several young men who had entered the ministry, and of the developing program of Christian efforts in Great Britain and in different parts of America.

During the 1785 meeting of the Association at the High Hills, he had introduced a proposal to incorporate under state law in order to hold and administer funds and property for educational purposes. The matter was discussed again in 1786, when a covenant was prepared supporting incorporation, and a committee, chaired by Furman, was named to petition the legislature. Before the next meeting, however, some be-

---

[1]Robert A. Baker, *The Contributions of South Carolina Baptists to the Rise and Development of the Southern Baptist Convention*, unpublished manuscript, SCBHS.

[2]Townsend, *History of South Carolina Baptists*, 21.

[3]*Rules of the Society for Promoting Christian Knowledge and Practice*, MS Copy, SCBHS.

[4]Richard Furman to George W. Pearce, 12 February 1791, in H. T. Cook, *Biography*, 42.

[5]Circular letter to the churches, in microfilm copy of *Minutes of the Charleston Baptist Association*, 1786, SCBHS; Howard M. Kinlaw, "Furman as a Leader in Baptist Education" (Ph.D. dissertation, George Peabody College, 1960) 40-41; Furman, *History of the Charleston Baptist Association*, 19.

gan to express doubts. Among them was Edmund Botsford. Then at Welsh Neck, he communicated the matter to Hart in New Jersey. Upon receipt of Hart's reply Botsford told Furman that he was more convinced than ever of the impropriety of incorporation. "Now," he said, "I despair of ever being convinced . . . and am pleased I bore my testimony against it."[6]

Botsford respected and admired Furman, as their copious correspondence shows. "I really have a more sincere regard for you than I ever had in my life, as a minister of Christ, as a master of a family, as a Christian gentlemen," he had written Furman while the question of incorporation was under consideration.[7] In their correspondence, he "wished not to offend [his] brother" and promised not to oppose the matter when it was brought before the Association. But in all honesty, he added, he hoped "it will not take place during my day."[8]

At the 1855 meeting of the Charleston Association, Basil Manly, Furman's successor as pastor of the Charleston church, drew upon letters written between 1786 and 1790 to explain reasons for opposition. Among these reasons were the advisory-only character of the Association, with no right or power to interfere with the independence of the churches; the extended Association boundaries "from the seaboard to the mountains . . . and even into North Carolina"; differences among associational constituency regarding education and funds for its promotion; and antirevolutionary prejudices among Separates in the Upcountry against anything originating with Baptists in the Charleston area.[9]

Furman understood the opposition logic and, though disappointed, he retracted from incorporation to try another approach. He and other friends of education determined to create a corporation in close relationship with the Association,[10] one to collect and manage funds for

---

[6]Edmund Botsford to Richard Furman, 31 August 1789, SCBHS.

[7]Edmund Botsford to Richard Furman, 11 January 1789, SCBHS.

[8]Edmund Botsford to Richard Furman, 31 August 1789, SCBHS.

[9]H. T. Cook, *Education in South Carolina Under Baptist Control* (Greenville SC, 1912) 13-14, SCBHS.

[10]McGlothlin, *A History of Furman University*, 31.

objects approved by the Association without exercising control over or being controlled by it. A stroke of Furman genius bridged differences within the Association without losing sight of objectives.

Furman went to the 1790 associational meeting at Black Swamp Church prepared to urge support for ministerial education in a way that would not prejudice the Association as a purely advisory body. His core objective was to establish a "respectable and permanent fund for the education of candidates for the ministry. . . ."[11] The Association concurred and named a committee—consisting of Furman (chairman), Silas Mercer, Benjamin Moseley, and Henry Holcombe—to draft a plan and present it at the next meeting.[12]

The presence of Silas Mercer on the committee is interesting. Mercer was the father of Jesse Mercer, whose name is associated with the founding of Mercer University. The elder Mercer had appeared at the 1785 associational meeting as a messenger from the lately formed Georgia Association.[13] A man of "strong mind and argumentative habits, of undoubted piety and unextinguishable zeal," he came prejudiced against education, believing it to be a hindrance to religion.[14] One must suppose that Furman was at his persuasive best, for Mercer left not only a committed and exemplary student himself but also a zealous promoter of learning the remainder of his life.[15]

This committee of Furman, Mercer, Moseley, and Holcombe merits a special place in the history of Baptist education. Its work became the germ of an organized program of higher education among Baptists in the South. Its report to the associational meeting at Welsh Neck in 1790 was as follows:

> That the following abstract be considered a general plan for forming, supporting, and supplying the fund.

---

[11]Furman, *History of the Charleston Baptist Association*, 21.

[12]*Minutes of the Charleston Baptist Association*, High Hills, 1790, microfilm copy, SCBHS.

[13]Furman, *History of the Charleston Baptist Association*, 18.

[14]H. T. Cook, *Education in South Carolina Under Baptist Control*, 15.

[15]Ibid.

First, that once a year a charity sermon be preached in each church, at which time collections made from the congregation at large, to be brought into the common fund, for the express purpose of assisting pious young men designed for the ministry, and destitute of other assistance, in obtaining an education; together with such other religious and public uses as may be approved by the churches, should it finally prove sufficient.

Secondly, a committee shall be formed, consisting of a delegate from each church, to convene at the same time and place of the Association's meeting, who may be at the same time a member of that body. They shall receive the collections, determine upon the manner of applying the funds according to the above rule, and examine candidates for the churches' bounty, all applications to be made to them for that purpose. Delegates from nine churches to be a quorum, or capable of business.

Thirdly, particular rules to be thereafter formed to regulate the whole business, by the committee, subject to the inspection of the Association.[16]

Although the plan was unanimously adopted by the Association, it ran into opposition from some churches. In the circular letter of 1790, Holcombe urged all the churches to support the program to help relieve the disadvantages to the Baptist cause, especially in the South Carolina backcountry, from lack of trained leadership. For several years opposing voices were heard at associational meetings, but on every occasion supporters defended the plan with zealous argument. By this time, Botsford had overcome his objections and was satisfied with the plan and worked for its acceptance. But he was afraid, he wrote Furman, that several churches would not cooperate.[17]

Ironically, Evan Pugh, the first to benefit from Oliver Hart's Religious Society, had opposed incorporation of the Association when the idea was first advanced by Furman in 1784. At least, Furman would

---

[16]Furman, *History of the Charleston Baptist Association*, 21-22; McGlothlin, *A History of Furman University*, 32; Kinlaw, "Furman as a Leader in Baptist Higher Education," 55-56; *Minutes of the Charleston Baptist Association*, 1790, microfilm copy, SCBHS.

[17]Circular letter to the churches, *Minutes of the Charleston Baptist Association*, 1790, microfilm copy, SCBHS.

later report, he "entertained some doubts respecting its propriety."[18] But when the substitute plan was presented by Furman's committee, Pugh gave it his approval.

The Association met at Welsh Neck in 1791 with Pugh as moderator. Furman reported for the Education Fund that "they had a system of Rules under consideration, though not fully matured: that they agreed, when the rules were completed, to apply to the Legislature for incorporation, and that they conceived it might be proper to invest the Committee with power to recover and take into their possession any glebes or other property belonging to the churches . . . which either are or may become extinct when liable to revert back to the public, or become private property, and apply the same to the interest of the union."[19] The Association approved both the report and the plan for incorporation, with the predictable provision that the Committee would not at any time interpose its authority over the churches as independent bodies.

The Committee, referred to as the General Committee, went into its first session before the associational meeting was over. The following persons were present: Richard Furman, Henry Holcombe, Edmund Botsford, Robert Ellison, Gabriel Gerrald, Josiah Cockfield, George Hicks, John Golwire, and Joshua Palmer.[20] Furman was elected chairman, a post he would hold for the thirty-five remaining years of his life. Note was taken that a plea for funds during the preceding years totaled fifty-seven pounds, eighteen shillings, and eight pence from the following churches: Charleston, Euhaw, Welsh Neck, Ebenezer, Lynches Creek, and Black Swamp.[21]

Matthew McCullers, recommended by Henry Holcombe[22] for ministerial education, became the first person approved as a recipient of the Committee's bounty, and he was placed under the instruction of

---

[18]Richard Furman to Oliver Hart, 26 January 1785, SCBHS.

[19]*Minutes of the Charleston Baptist Association*, 1791, microfilm copy, SCBHS.

[20]Ibid., December 1791.

[21]Kinlaw, "Furman as a Leader in Baptist Higher Education," 59.

[22]Joe M. King, *A History of South Carolina Baptists*, 161.

Furman.[23] Another candidate, Joseph B. Cook, son of the Reverend Joseph Cook, pastor of the Euhaw church, was also approved for financial help and instruction, if needed.

This event was important in the history of Baptist education. It was the first "such gathering solely for educational purposes ever to be held by Baptists in the South."[24] Through the whole process, from the time Furman had first recommended that the Association be incorporated, he had been the guiding force.

Some minor amendments were made to the rules at the 1792 meeting. The legislature was petitioned for and immediately granted incorporation. Permanent officers were elected as follows: Richard Furman, president; Henry Holcombe, secretary; Thomas Screven, treasurer; Thomas Rivers, John Gourlay, John Hart, Henry and William Inglesby, assistants.[25] When finally ratified on 7 November 1792, the rules bore the title "Rules of the General Committee, for Forming, Supporting, and Applying a Fund amongst the Baptist Churches in the Charleston Association, South Carolina." They carried the signatures of Richard Furman (chairman), Henry Holcombe (clerk), Edmund Botsford, Alexander Scott, Bradley Rhame, Benjamin Moseley, Stephen Nixon, Isham Gardner, and James Sweat.[26] Before the meeting ended, Jesse Mercer, son of Silas Mercer, was examined and approved to benefit from the fund in the amount of ten pounds and books for his studies.

Oliver Hart's Religious Society had placed young men of promise under the tutelage of older and experienced ministers, with pay provided for expenses incurred. Furman's General Committee now added a new dimension: it made use of available schools run by professional tutors. Among these was St. David's Academy at Welsh Neck on the Pee Dee, a private school organized by St. David's Society at Long Bluff (now Society Hill) in 1777 for the purpose of "founding a society for educating youths in Latin and Greek languages, mathematics, and other

---

[23]Ibid.

[24]Kinlaw, "Furman as a Leader in Baptist Higher Education," 59.

[25]Townsend, *History of South Carolina Baptists*, 120.

[26]The full text of the Rules is contained in Appendix B. Original manuscript is in SCBHS.

branches of learning."[27] Another was Ebenezer Academy, petitioned for
by twenty-six persons living on Jeffries Creek who were "deeply impressed with a belief that the proper education of youth contributes much
to the prosperity, respectability, and efficiency of any government and
that the youth cannot be properly educated without the establishment
of seminaries of learning adequate for that purpose. . . ."[28] Still another
was located at Salem Black River and was operated by the Reverend
Thomas Reese, a Presbyterian minister and friend of Furman from his
High Hills days. Reese was a native of Pennsylvania who came with his
parents to North Carolina. A graduate of Princeton in 1786, be began
a preaching career at the Salem church on Black River that continued
for twenty years. There he conducted a school and pursued studies in
divinity, moral philosophy, and other branches of scholarship essential
to "the formation of a complete theologian."[29]

There was also Rhode Island College, now Brown University.
Founded in 1764 at Warren, Rhode Island, and relocated in Providence
in 1770, it originated with the Philadelphia Baptist Association out of
concern that there existed no "public seminary" in America where Baptist youth could "enjoy equal freedom and advantages with others."[30]
Support for the college was solicited as far south as South Carolina. It
was on such a mission to Charleston, mentioned earlier, that the Reverend Hezekiah Smith met and influenced young Richard Furman,
whose family was then living on Daniel's Island.

As chairman of the General Committee, in 1794 Furman sent two
of his first students to Rhode Island College—Joseph B. Cook and John
M. Roberts. Both were admitted to advanced standing. They were the
first of many to be supported by the General Fund and sent there during

---

[27]*Minutes of St. David's Society*, original copy held by the Darlington County Historical Commission, quoted in James A. Rogers, *Theodosia and Other Pee Dee Sketches*
(Columbia: R. L. Bryan and Co., 1978) 163.

[28]From *Memorial to South Carolina Senate by the Washington Society*, original held by
the Darlington County Historical Commission, photostatic copy is in James A. Rogers, *Ebenezer: The Story of a Church* (Columbia: R. L. Bryan and Co., 1978) 25.

[29]Ramsay, *History of South Carolina*, 2:267-68.

[30]Reuben A. Guild, *History of Brown University, with Illustrative Documents* (Providence RI: privately printed, 1867) 113.

the next thirty years of Furman's life. Cook and Roberts are believed to have been the first native South Carolina Baptist preachers to attend college.[31]

ROBERTS ACADEMY

Following his ordination in 1799, John M. Roberts became pastor of the High Hills church. In the same year, when the Association met with the Congaree church, he was elected secretary of the General Committee.[32] He stood where Furman had stood twenty-five years earlier at the beginning of his pastoral career. Sometime before 1 November 1800, he established Roberts Academy. Although it was a private school, it was adopted by the Association as "the chief agency for the education of beneficiaries of the General Committee."[33] The associational minutes of 1800 urged the churches to give it their "most firm and vigorous support."[34]

The close tie between the Association and the academy was further demonstrated in 1802 with authorization for the General Committee to purchase "a complete theological library" for the school. Furman reported the following year that forty-eight pounds had been sent to Europe for that purpose and that a "very valuable" collection had arrived and would "in a short time" be placed at the academy. The books, he said, had been purchased "to great advantage," and "would furnish the students with essential and extensive aid in all the important parts of their studies, both in science and in divinity."[35]

The first students to be admitted under the General Committee were William Jones and Sydenham Morton. Jones had been admitted conditionally by a special committee authorized to consider applications between associational meetings. Before the Association's unanimous approval of him at the 1800 meeting, he had been studying at the acad-

---

[31]McGlothlin, *A History of Furman University*, 35.

[32]*Minutes of the Charleston Baptist Association*, 1799, bound copy 1799-1817, SCBHS, also microfilm.

[33]McGlothlin, *A History of Furman University*, 36.

[34]*Minutes of the Charleston Baptist Association*, 1800, SCBHS.

[35]Ibid.

emy for several months.[36] Some unanswered questions about Morton resulted in his acceptance conditionally at the same time Jones's conditions were removed.

Roberts's school became widely known for its scholarship. In David Ramsay's *History of South Carolina*, the following reference appears: "An Academy of great reputation is kept by the Reverend Mr. Roberts. Several pupils educated by him have entered the sophomore and some the junior class in the South Carolina College."[37] Among those attending the school was young William Capers, later to become Bishop William Capers, foremost leader of the Methodists in South Carolina during the antebellum period. He and his brother, Gabriel, entered the academy in September 1801 from their home on an island plantation near Georgetown.[38] Capers attended the academy from 1801 to 1805. He found Roberts

> . . . a man for one to love and honor . . . a most estimable man and a good scholar, but an imperfect teacher . . . In recitation, our too easy instructor seemed more apprehensive of detecting the deficiency of his pupils, than we were of being exposed. His manner was that of one who might not expect us to know what we ought to have known; and asking us only questions as to points of obvious instruction, he reserved to himself the parsing of all difficult passages.[39]

---

[36]Ibid.

[37]Ramsay, *History of South Carolina*, 2:304.

[38]From Capers we get the best description of the exact location of Roberts Academy. In an autobiographical sketch he says that his first "boardinghouse" was a Mrs. Jefferson's "on the main road between Statesburg and Camden, just three miles from the former place, and touching the road." The academy, he says, was "a mile and a half" from Mrs. Jefferson's, on the summit of a hill—Prospect Hill, where Roberts lived. Later, his boarding place was changed to the home of Roberts, who lived, says Capers, "hard by the academy." Thus, Roberts Academy was adjacent to the Roberts home on Prospect Hill east of and overlooking the Stateburg-Camden road about three miles from Stateburg. No trace of the building can now be found, nor is there any surviving tradition that identifies the hill as Prospect Hill. In his correspondence, however, Roberts gives his address as Prospect Hill. See William M. Wightman, *Life of William Capers, D.D., One of the Bishops of the Methodist Episcopal Church, South, Including an Autobiography* (Nashville: Publishing House of the Methodist Episcopal Church, South, 1858) 40, 44.

[39]Wightman, *Life of William Capers*, 39-40.

This "somewhat unfavorable opinion of his [Roberts's] ability as a teacher . . . may have been due in some measure, it has been suggested, to the fact that young Capers failed in his effort to make the junior class in South Carolina College."[40] Roberts's scholarship in the Greek and Latin classics, however, was not in question. Latin textbooks included Corderius, Erasmus, Caesar, Virgil, Cicero's *Orations*, Cornelius, and Horace's *Odes* and *Art of Poetry*, while Greek was taught from the Greek grammar, Homer, Xenophon, Schrevelius, and the Greek New Testament.[41]

More than any other man of his time, Roberts had imbibed the spirit of Richard Furman in his concern for education generally, and ministerial education in particular. Through Roberts, Furman's work in establishing the incorporated General Committee bore special fruit. A product of the Committee's educational assistance, he, the educated, became, in turn, the educator, and his institution became an instrument of the General Committee in the performance of its mission. At Furman's suggestion, the Charleston Association, meeting at Welsh Neck in 1806, took "graceful and public acknowledgement" of Roberts's "disinterested and generous conduct" in providing tuition-free education to its beneficiaries.[42]

Sometime prior to 1810, the academy appears to have been closed. In that year the Association, in annual session at the Ebenezer church, entertained the following query from the High Hills church: "Is it not desirable, and expedient, that the Charleston Baptist Association should establish and patronize a charitable academy, in some healthy, central part of the state: and would not the High Hills of Santee be the most eligible place for such an institution; and the present the most favorable time for establishing it?"[43] The query was referred to a committee "to digest a plan for such an undertaking, devise ways and means for its

---

[40]McGlothlin, *A History of Furman University*, 37; Wightman, *Life of William Capers*, 47.

[41]Wightman, *Life of William Capers*, 46-48.

[42]*Minutes of the General Committee*, 1806, SCBHS.

[43]*Minutes of the Charleston Baptist Association*, 1810, SCBHS.

execution, estimate its expense, form an opinion of a suitable site: and report back to the Association the following year with a satisfactory judgment." Furman, in his usual role as moderator, appointed Roberts, David Collins, and W. B. Johnson to the committee.[44] Their report the following year declared the proposal to be "ineligible at present." The Association agreed, and thus the first attempt to establish an institution under Baptist auspices and control failed.

DEATH OF JOHN ROBERTS

For nearly twenty-five years the name John M. Roberts stood alongside Richard Furman's as a leader in every forward movement of South Carolina Baptists. Like Furman, Roberts began his ministry at the High Hills church and there he remained throughout his pastoral career. Like Furman, too, he never missed a meeting of the Association. He and Furman later joined their efforts in 1819 to initiate a movement that would lead to the organization of the South Carolina Baptist Convention. His life's tragic ending in 1822 is one of the sad stories in Baptist history.

The first reference to the tragedy is found in the 1821 minutes of the Charleston Association, meeting at the Congaree church. In the course of the year, Roberts's health had failed him, and for the first time in his career he was not present for the meeting. On Wednesday, the fourth and final day, his absence was noted with the following reference:

---

[44]Collins, an active minister, was ordained in 1793 and for a time was a beneficiary of the General Committee, from which he retired in 1803 to study in private owing to domestic concerns (Townsend, *History of South Carolina Baptists*, 253n). Johnson was of a family whose names had been associated with South Carolina Baptists from earliest years. Born on John's Island in 1782, he lived in Georgetown during his formative years, practiced law in Beaufort, and became a religious convert in 1804 during the Great Revival of the early nineteenth century. Upon the death of Furman, he assumed the mantle of his leadership and was his successor as president of the South Carolina Baptist Convention—a position he held for twenty-seven years (Hortense Woodson, *Giant in the Land*, 7, 8; *Minutes of the South Carolina Baptist Convention*, 1979, historical tables, 250). In 1810, when Johnson was appointed to the committee to respond to the query from the High Hills church, he was chaplain of South Carolina College.

The Association learn[s] with deep regret that the Rev. Dr. Roberts, a well known and excellent minister of this body, continues to be awfully afflicted by the hand of God. They sympathize sincerely and affectionately with the distressed church and family of their afflicted brother, as well as with himself, and feel it their duty to recommend his case to the particular notice of the churches of this body, as the subject of earnest prayer, that God may be pleased to remove the affliction, and to restore this worthy man, in the right use of his intellectual powers, to his family, to the churches of Christ, and to society at large.[45]

Before the next meeting, the worst had happened. Roberts, deranged in mind, had ended his life by his own hand. Thus was brought to an end the life of an early statesman among South Carolina Baptists. It surely was a severe blow to Furman. Together the two had walked hand-in-hand in the cause of education. At his death, Roberts had fulfilled his "firm determination" stated in a letter of gratitude written to the Association in 1797: ". . . to use his best exertions to obtain every suitable qualification, and to devote himself to the great work."[46]

Near the front door of today's High Hills Baptist Church, a white obelisk marker memorializes Roberts. The simple inscription reads: "To the memory of John M. Roberts who was born June 30, 1775 and died March 22, 1822." Richard Furman, his benefactor, mentor, colaborer, and friend, would survive him by three years.

SOUTH CAROLINA COLLEGE

Furman knew that private schools like Roberts Academy were short of the real need and that only education at the institutional level of higher education would suffice. For thirty years, he had sent students to Rhode Island, while nursing a dream that would broaden the base of Baptist educational opportunity. In the meantime, his thoughts were directed to the cause of secular education.

The English along the South Carolina coast, the Swiss along the Savannah River, the German Protestants on the Edisto River, the French

---

[45]*Minutes of the Charleston Baptist Association*, November 1821, SCBHS.

[46]*Minutes of the Charleston Baptist Association*, 1797, SCBHS.

Protestants on the Santee River, and the Scotch-Irish in Williamsburg had established their own schools and were sending their sons to the best universities in Europe and the North.[47] But in the Upcountry beyond the state's geologic fall line, population was on the rise, educational opportunity was minimal, and frontier society offered no encouragement, economically or culturally, to patronize European universities.

In Charleston, some had foreseen much earlier that as Upcountry wealth and population increased, changes in government more favorable to that region would be necessary. Some sought to delay the change as long as possible, while others believed that the inevitable could be avoided or delayed by a "unification of outlook."[48] Thus began a move to establish a common system of colleges. The most important result was South Carolina College, established in 1801.

Among the Lowcountry Federalists, self-interest and self-preservation brought fear that government might fall into the hands of illiterate and untrained backcountry politicians. In a letter to Thomas Jefferson, one prominent in the service of the state expressed his concern over the rise of a democratic spirit. "Our government," he wrote, "tends too much to Democracy. A handicraftsman thinks apprenticeship necessary to make himself acquainted with his business. But our back countrymen are of the opinion that a politician may be born as well as a poet."[49]

Furman believed that a heterogeneous population divided by sectional interests could best be united by bringing students together to study under the same faculty at a state institution centrally located to serve both the Upcountry and Lowcountry. He therefore threw his support behind enactment of the law establishing South Carolina College. His role is best documented by his association with and influence upon powerful members of the legislature—men like Charles Cotesworth

---

[47]J. C. Hungerpiller, "A Sketch of the Life and Character of Jonathan Maxcy, D.D," *Bulletin of the University of South Carolina* 58 (July 1917): 22.

[48]John Harold Wolfe, *Jeffersonian Democracy in South Carolina* (Chapel Hill: University of North Carolina Press, 1940) 48.

[49]Ralph Izard to Thomas Jefferson, 10 June 1785, *South Carolina Historical and Genealogical Magazine*, 2:197.

Pinckney, Henry W. DeSaussure, John Drayton, James Lowndes, Adam Gilchrist, Henry Middleton Rutledge, Robert Barnwell, Elias Horry, Theodore Gaillard, and Peter Porcher, Jr.—and further, by his record in sending South Carolinians to colleges in the North in the absence of institutions of higher learning in the South.

In the latter role, he had become acquainted with Dr. Jonathan Maxcy, who at the age of twenty-four had become president pro tempore of Rhode Island College in 1792 as successor to Dr. James Manning, and became full president in 1797. Maxcy was a Rhode Island Baptist and a graduate of Rhode Island College in the class of 1787, the same year that Furman had become pastor of the Charleston church. Immediately after graduation he was named a tutor in the college. Four years later he resigned his tutorship to become pastor of the Providence Baptist Church and later president of the college. Through his patronage of Rhode Island College, Furman corresponded frequently with Maxcy concerning his students, including his son, Wood, and other matters of mutual interest. When the college was struggling financially and had not officially adopted a permanent name, the trustees passed a resolution stating that any person giving six thousand dollars by the next commencement would be entitled to name the college. "Have you no rich man among you who would be so disposed?" Maxcy queried Furman, and added, "Is not Dr. Ramsay a great patron of literature?"[50] No such donor was found to meet the time schedule of the resolution, but in 1804 Nicholas Brown, Jr., made a gift of five thousand dollars for the foundation of a professorship of oratory and belles lettres, and the trustees adopted the name Brown University "in consideration of this donation, and others that had been received from him and his kindred."[51]

The act establishing South Carolina College was passed on 19 December 1801, and the school admitted its first students in 1805. The president of the Board of Trustees was instructed "to write to the principals of the various colleges in America, and to all others he may think fit to apply, requesting them to recommend such persons as they think

---

[50]Jonathan Maxcy to Richard Furman, 16 December 1795, SCBHS.

[51]Reuben Aldridge Guild, *Early History of Brown University, Including the Life, Times, and Correspondence of President Manning* (Providence RI: Snow and Farnham, 1897) 442.

best qualified to fill the offices of principal and professors in the South Carolina College."[52] Among the recommendations received was one from Furman about his friend Maxcy. He wrote to the president of the Board of Trustees concerning "the reputation which Dr. Maxcy has acquired as a man of science, of talents, and of virtue: his great experience as the President of a college . . . his eminent oratorical accomplishments . . . and especially his excellent capacities for governing youth." One authority reports that then "all eyes turned to Maxcy, who had filled the presidencies of two colleges, and whose genius and learning had attracted the admiration of the entire country."[53] Because Maxcy was a Federalist, political partisanship asserted itself in the deliberation of the trustees. "We must have a republican at the head of the college or all is lost," said William D. James, who supported another candidate.[54] On the eve of the election, James sought to convince Colonel Wade Hampton, but Hampton could see no connection between literature and politics, and Maxcy was chosen. No objection was raised to the choice of a Baptist as president, though both the state and the Board of Trustees were dominated by Presbyterians and Episcopalians.[55]

No other Baptist in South Carolina stood as tall as Furman across denominational lines, nor had one of any denomination played as many roles in the development of higher educational opportunity. He had initiated a plan that would lead to the founding of a Baptist institution of higher learning, and he had helped shape the beginnings of a state college and the choice of its first president. In recognition of his stature as a civic, religious, and educational leader, South Carolina College

---

[52]Hungerpiller, "A Sketch of the Life and Character of Jonathan Maxcy," 24; Daniel Walker Hollis, *University of South Carolina* (Columbia: University of South Carolina Press, 1951) 1:33.

[53]Maximilian LaBorde, *History of the South Carolina College from its Incorporation, Dec. 19, 1801, to Dec. 19, 1865; Including Sketches of its Presidents and Professors, with an Appendix* (Charleston: Walker, Evans and Cogswell Co., 1872) 100.

[54]Hollis, *University of South Carolina*, 1:34.

[55]Orin F. Crow, "The Control of the University of South Carolina, 1801-1926, A Case Study of University Control" (Ph.D. dissertation, George Peabody College for Teachers, 1931), cited in Hollis, *University of South Carolina*, 1:34.

awarded him the degree of Doctor of Divinity at its first commencement in 1807. Until this point, his career had been one of fruitful works. Yet, the future held still greater works.

CHAPTER 8

Missionary Thrust and the Triennial Convention

The Charleston Baptist Association met with the High Hills church on Saturday, 6 November 1802. As usual, autumn had painted the hills many colors. The road up from Charleston, along the old Catawba Path, was a familiar one to Furman. Northward from the Nelson's Ferry crossing of the Santee River, the Hills spread gloriously wide and beautiful. Furman was always pleased when the Association met with his former church. Being there brought back many memories of his parents and his childhood home, of boyhood days roaming the fields of his father's plantation, and, of course, of the preaching of Joseph Reese that led to his conversion and entrance into the ministry.

There was special reason for him to be pleased to return on this occasion. Earlier that year he had settled an old property mortgage on the plantation inherited from his father by himself, his brother, Josiah, and his sister, Sarah. In August he had reported to Sarah that as executor of the estate he had acted to sell the property at a sheriff's sale and had purchased it back himself at two dollars per acre.[1] To satisfy a judgment

---

[1]Richard Furman to Sarah Haynsworth, 17 August 1802, SCBHS.

against the estate and to cover interest on a note formerly given, he had borrowed money representing a purchase price of "nearly 20 pounds per acre," which was "the utmost" he had intended to give for it.[2] The property was now unencumbered by the old debt, and for the first time since his father's death the plantation was secure against loss. With the estate problem settled, he could now walk over the land with a real feeling of belonging—it to him, his brother, and sister, and they to it.

On Saturday morning, forty-four messengers representing twenty-three churches assembled for the fifty-first annual meeting of the Association. The first two days were spent "in exercises of public devotion." Two sermons were preached on Saturday and three on Sunday, with the Lord's Supper closing "the solemnities of the latter."[3]

MISSIONARY VISION

For the ninth time, Furman was chosen moderator. Letters were read from twenty-three member churches and from corresponding associations—the Philadelphia, the Warren (in Rhode Island), the Bethel, the Neuse (in North Carolina), and the Elk Horn (in Kentucky). The Bethel Association reported "a glorious revival" in which 703 persons had been baptized since the last meeting. Though no letters were received from the Hephzibah and the Georgia associations, private reports told of "a great revival in the upper parts of Georgia" and of "a happy work of grace progressing under the ministry of Rev. Mr. Holcombe in Savannah."[4] Meetings of the Association were always joyous and solemn occasions. This one marked the beginning of a new period in Baptist history. The change was suggested in a query brought by Furman from his Charleston church.

> Is it not in our power at this time to send out a missionary or missionaries, well qualified for the work, to preach the gospel to the many destitute people in various parts of our land; and do not zeal for the

---

[2]Ibid.

[3]*Minutes of the Charleston Baptist Association*, 1802, SCBHS.

[4]Ibid.

cause of God and love to the souls of men, require of us strenuous exertions in such an undertaking?[5]

Until the 1800s the vision of the churches had been largely limited to their own communities. But Furman had been following with much interest how William Carey had inspired English Baptists to initiate the modern foreign mission movement among English-speaking peoples—a work begun almost simultaneously with the organization of the General Committee of the Charleston Association.[6]

In 1800 Furman had brought a similar query from his church.

> Is there not, at this time, a call in Providence for our churches to make the most serious exertions, in union with other christians of various denominations, to send the gospel among the heathen; or to such people who though living in countries where the gospel revelation is known, do not enjoy a standing ministry, and the regular administration of divine ordinances among them?[7]

The Association replied,

> . . . there appears, indeed to be a general call in Providence, for all the churches of Christ to make serious exertions to diffuse gospel light and liberty among the heathen . . . but the particular call to us, seems to be to turn our attention to . . . multitudes in our own land, who have not the gospel statedly preached to them . . . it is greatly to be lamented, that being placed in such circumstances, we have very few ministers, comparatively, to send out into the the gospel harvest; especially of such who are well qualified to undertake the work, as able pastor and missionaries. . . .[8]

There followed a recommendation that

---

[5]Ibid.

[6]McGlothlin, *A History of Furman University*, 41-42.

[7]*Minutes of the Charleston Baptist Association*, 1800, SCBHS.

[8]Ibid.

our ministers . . . make their best exertions to supply destitute churches, and to preach the gospel among people, who have not yet been brought into a church state; And . . . "to pray the Lord of the Harvest, to send forth labourers into his harvest"; and to give their most firm and vigorous support to the institution, under the direction of the general committee; by contributing liberally to the fund. . . .[9]

Furman envisioned a cooperative effort among Christian churches and denominations in a program of both home and foreign missions. But at that time, two areas of domestic missions claimed attention—the Catawba Indians, on both sides of the Catawba River in upper South Carolina, and the large number of churches without pastors. In the Charleston Association alone in 1802, twelve churches were pastorless.[10]

Twin actions in 1802 eased Furman's concern for missions. One action employed the Reverend John Rooker, pastor of the Sugar Creek Baptist Church in the Catawba Indian land,[11] to visit and preach to the Catawbas at least once a month and to examine the feasibility of a school among them. Another instructed Furman "to employ a suitable person . . . if such an one can be found" to visit with and preach to pastorless churches at an annual salary of fifty pounds. At the same meeting, he was asked to superintend the Indian mission. In these roles, he thus became, in effect, the first superintendent of home missions among Baptists in the South.[12] Here, then, was the initial idea for combining missions and education as a Baptist objective, and Furman was cast in the leading role. Later, with the conversion of Adoniram Judson and Luther Rice to Baptist views on baptism, Baptist involvement in world missions would have its "morning hour."

For his work among the Indians, the Association promised Rooker "suitable compensation" and left it to Furman to determine the amount. The next year Furman reported that "after making the proper inquiries" the annual sum of forty pounds sterling had been fixed upon, and

[9]Ibid.

[10]*Minutes of the Charleston Baptist Association*, 1802, Tabular State of the Churches.

[11]Townsend, *History of South Carolina Baptists*, 255n.

[12]*Minutes of the Charleston Baptist Association*, 1803, SCBHS.

the Association agreed unanimously.[13] With these decisions, the churches began contributing to the General Fund for both missions and education. In 1803 Furman reported that $293.33 had been contributed to missions and $408.42 to education. Older churches—like Charleston, Welsh Neck, High Hills, Euhaw, and Ebenezer—gave to both, while numerous backcountry churches less disposed to education contributed only to missions.[14] At the 1804 meeting, the churches were reminded that mission work was not intended to curtail contributions to education.

These years marked the beginnings of organized support for domestic missions among Baptists within the framework of home mission societies. Furman had been missionary in spirit since his conversion, but not until the early 1800s, during the Great Revival period, did there emerge formal instruments for supporting mission activity. Significantly, while Furman and the Charleston churches were thus engaged, two Boston churches, under Doctors Samuel Stillman and Thomas Baldwin, were establishing within the Warren Association of New England the Massachusetts Baptist Missionary Society, the first such society among Baptists in America.[15]

The Catawba Indian mission met with only moderate success. A school was established about 1805 and continued with some difficulty until 1807 when it was temporarily suspended for lack of sufficient operating funds. This undoubtedly was a blow to Furman. Grasping at every straw to keep the school open, he informed the Association that in conversation with Governor Charles Pinckney, the governor had expressed the belief that, if applied to, the state would furnish an annual sum of money to keep the school open. The governor offered to present the matter to the legislature, if so requested. This seeming infringement of the principle of separation of church and state apparently raised no question. Furman was asked to write the governor "to signify the willingness of this association to accept any such aid as the generosity

---

[13]Ibid.

[14]Ibid.

[15]Albert L. Vail, *The Morning Hour of American Missions* (Philadelphia: The American Baptist Publication Society, 1907) 96-97.

of the state would afford; and to request his excellency to lay the subject before the legislature as he had proposed."[16]

The associational minutes do not indicate whether South Carolina came to the rescue of the school. In 1808, at the request of the Indians, the school was revived and continued until 1812 when debt and poor attendance were given as reasons for discontinuing it "at least for a time," but with the mission itself to be continued.[17] In 1817 the mission was discontinued "in consequence of the diminution of the tribe, its wandering habits, the nearness of white churches, and, perhaps most of all, the demoralizing influence of bad whites."[18] Though the tangible results of this work could not have been encouraging to Furman, it was creditable in view of the failure of all others in South Carolina to enter the field of Indian missions.[19] In his South Carolina history, Dr. David Ramsay wrote, "It is truly honorable to the Baptists that they have done so much for the instruction of the Indians."[20]

BROADER HORIZONS

The conversion of Luther Rice and Adoniram Judson to the Baptist faith is one of the watersheds of Baptist history. En route to India by separate passage as missionaries under the auspices of New England Congregationalists, each became convinced that baptism by immersion was according to the Scriptures. Following his baptism in 1812 into the fellowship of a Baptist church in Calcutta, Rice returned to America in 1813, temporarily he thought, for the purpose of organizing American Baptists in the financial support of Burmese mission work under the Judsons.

The 115 American Baptist associations reported a membership of 175,000 in their churches, "scattered from Maine to Georgia and from the Atlantic Seaboard to the frontier stockades of Kentucky and Ten-

---

[16]*Minutes of the Charleston Baptist Association*, 1807, SCBHS.

[17]Ibid., 1812.

[18]Vail, *The Morning Hour of American Missions*, 188.

[19]Ibid., 189.

[20]Ibid.

nessee."[21] Within these broadly scattered churches there were a few small missionary groups organized in urban churches, engaged mainly in raising funds for the support of the English Baptist Mission in India. Only one—the Massachusetts Baptist Missionary Society—was a state society.[22]

Rice's first problem was to unite American Baptist leaders in financial support of the mission work of Judson and his wife, Ann Haseltine Judson. He appealed first to leaders in Boston, where Baptists considered themselves the rightful and logical leaders of the denomination.[23] The Boston leaders were so pleased with Rice's report that they gave him letters of commendation and introduction to leaders in Philadelphia. Leaving Boston in September 1813, Rice traveled to New York and from there to Philadelphia where he met with the Philadelphia Association and arranged the formation of the Philadelphia Baptist Missionary Society. He then went on through Baltimore, Washington, and Richmond, and thence to South Carolina, where he arrived in time for the meeting of the Charleston Baptist Association at Welsh Neck.

Accompanied by his twenty-one-year-old son Samuel, Furman arrived at Welsh Neck from Charleston about midday Saturday after Rice was already there.[24] At their first meeting, Furman found Rice to be a "considerable preacher and an amiable man."[25] In a letter to his wife, Dolly, on the third day of the meeting, he spoke of "a considerable degree of seriousness" that "appeared to be excited among the people at large." Worship services conducted "by candlelight" were attended by "not less than 300 persons at each of them," and on Sunday by an estimated crowd of 2,000.[26]

The business session began on Monday. Following a prayer by Furman, letters were read from thirty-one churches, and the names of their

---

[21]Rufus W. Weaver, "The Place of Luther Rice in American Baptist Life," *The Review and Expositor* 32 (April 1936): 135.

[22]Ibid.

[23]Ibid.

[24]Richard Furman to Dorothea Furman, 8 November 1813, SCBHS.

[25]Ibid.

[26]Ibid.

delegates were enrolled. Furman then officially presented Rice as a member of the church of Serampore, India, and Rice, in turn, handed his written address to Joseph B. Cook, the moderator, along with letters of recommendation obtained on his route southward from Boston. The minutes record that he "was received with great affection."

Following the reading of the circular letter, the Association listened to the reading of Rice's address on the subject of foreign missions. On the next day he was invited to speak on "the state of religion in India; and concerning his views of the openings for missions at other places; particularly at the Isle of France, Madagascar and the Brasils." Here, from the minutes of the meeting, is a summary of his remarks.

His account of the state of religion in India corroborated those given in the *Baptist Missionary Magazine*; in the writings of Dr. Buchanan, etc., especially the former, with respect to the interests of the Baptist mission at Serampore. On these he stated that the excellent Dr. Carey, and his pious, able Associates, were proceeding with indefatigable zeal and constancy in translating and printing the Scriptures in 18 languages of the eastern nations, comprehending hundreds of millions of human beings, now held in a state of idolatry or gross superstition. That many Hindus, some of whom were Bra[h]mins, had embraced the gospel, apparently with an unfeigned faith. That a considerable number of churches are formed in that extensive country; one, in a flourishing state, at Calcutta; and that Missionary establishments are affected at various places there, to the extent of 2000 miles—That about forty Ministers are now employed, in connection with the Mission in preaching the gospel; many of them natives, who were lately idolaters—and that the call for Ministers is great and urgent.—He also confirmed the accounts contained in the *Magazine* before referred to, and mentioned in his recommendations—That, Mr. Judson and himself, who had been sent out as Missionaries to India, by our congregational brethren in New-England, had, from the conviction of their own minds, in consequence of searching the scriptures, embraced Baptist principles, and had been together with Mr. Judson's wife, baptized in India. To which he added, that he had left Mr. Judson and his wife at the Isle of France; and had returned to the United States to see, whether the baptist churches here will do any thing toward sending Missionaries among these Heathen Nations, to which the providence of God seems so directly to point.[27]

---

[27]*Minutes of the Charleston Baptist Association*, 1813, SCBHS.

John B. Miller, associational clerk from the High Hills church, recorded that "these communications were received with much satisfaction."

Among listeners with special cause for "much satisfaction" was Richard Furman. Rice was echoing Furman's interest in missions as expressed in 1800 with the query from his Charleston church asking if the time had not come "to make the most serious exertions, in union with other christians of various denominations, to send the gospel among the heathen. . . ."[28] That vision was now being projected onto broad horizons.

The documents brought by Rice contained outlines for a concerted missionary effort recommended by ministers in Boston, Philadelphia, and other cities on his journey south. A committee was appointed—consisting of Furman, Tristam Thomas, and Joseph B. Cook—to consider the matter and, "if in their judgment it be found expedient," to report back a plan for the Charleston Association to act upon, consistent with "the general theme" of the documents gathered by Rice.

The committee met and reported the following day that a united effort among American Baptist churches on behalf of foreign missions would be both "laudable and expedient." There followed the presentation of a plan, unanimously adopted, calling for the "formation of Societies by voluntary Association, in the bounds of the churches, or in any part of the State," to support foreign missions. The incorporated General Committee of the Association was designated the "centre of . . . union" for the societies and the medium of communication with other bodies similarly formed.

Since Furman was listed first when the committee was named, one may assume that he was the spokesman. The expeditious manner in which the plan was prepared and presented reflected the thoughtful manner in which he had developed it while contemplating the time when Baptists would assume the responsibility of foreign missions. He did not then foresee the extent to which it would be applied to a total program of foreign missions in that century and the next. But he had, in

---

[28]Ibid., 1800.

fact, planted a germinal idea of what would become a legacy of Richard Furman to American Baptists.

The meeting adjourned on Wednesday, and Rice traveled on to a meeting of the Savannah River Association, carrying a letter of introduction and recommendations from the Charleston Association to the Georgia brethren. Before adjourning, the Association assigned John M. Roberts the task of preparing the next circular letter on the obligations of Christians to support the cause of missions. They also declared "a day of Humiliation, Fasting, and Prayer" on the first Wednesday of March 1814, "to beseech . . . the Great Arbiter of nations . . . to defend us from our enemies; and to restore us to a state of peace and national prosperity."

When the Charleston Association called for a day of humiliation and prayer at its 1813 meeting, the War of 1812 was then in its second year, while the South had been visited by a bloody tragedy of unprecedented proportion. Two months before the meeting, southern Alabama had experienced the most dreadful Indian massacre in American history; the entire country was horrified at the news. Against this background of Indian war and the larger war with England, associational delegates concluded that the judgments of God were "remarkably abroad in the earth" as evidence of divine controversy with his people.[29] In this troubled national context, Baptists were responding to the call of foreign missions. Before the war was over they would be united for that purpose in the first national organization of Baptists.

BAPTISTS COMING TOGETHER

Morgan Edwards should probably receive the credit for being the first to propose a national organization of Baptists. Of the Philadelphia Association he had said he wished to see it become the prototype for a "combination of Baptist churches universal on this Continent."[30] Luther Rice's return from India was the catalyst for setting in motion such a combination, but the idea of national union had been advanced by

---

[29]Ibid., 1813.

[30]William Wright Barnes, *The Southern Baptist Convention, 1845-1953* (Nashville: Broadman Press, 1954) 9, cited in Owens, *Saints of Clay*, 61.

Baptist leaders, including Furman, years before Rice came onto the scene.

As early as 1795, Dr. Jonathan Maxcy was thinking of a committee "appointed by all the Baptist Associations of America" for the support of ministerial education.[31] The Charleston Association meeting of 1800 had undertaken domestic missions among pastorless churches. At that same meeting, the Association responded to a proposal from the Philadelphia Association for a general union of Baptists throughout the United States, saying that if a "well-digested" plan should be set forth, with general concurrence by the churches, the Association would be disposed to support it.[32]

Upon Rice's return, the time and the idea had come together to form a united Baptist front for a common cause. Preparatory work began with the formation of missionary societies at principal Baptist centers on Rice's journey south. He attributed the concept of a national organization to a conversation between himself and William B. Johnson, pastor of the First Baptist Church of Savannah, Georgia. In a letter to Jesse Mercer, Rice recalled that after he had established mission societies on his Southern journey, he and Johnson discussed a "general combination or concert of action among them." Johnson agreed and suggested Philadelphia as a meeting place, whereupon Rice wrote to all societies then formed, urging upon them the importance of the meeting and requesting them to appoint delegates. He reported to Jesse Mercer that all the societies from Maine to Georgia had agreed.[33]

---

[31]Jonathan Maxcy to Richard Furman, 26 October 1795, SCBHS.

[32]*Minutes of the Charleston Baptist Association*, 1800, SCBHS.

[33]Luther Rice to Jesse Mercer, editor of the *Christian Index*, dated Mercer Institute, Georgia, 20 June 1835, published in I. M. Allen, *The Triennial Baptist Register*, 1836, 2:48, North Carolina Baptist Historical Collection, Wake Forest University Library. Johnson says that Rice was requested by "our brethren at the North . . . to travel through as many states as would be practical to engage the Baptists to form societies, whose delegates would meet at Philadelphia in May, 1814, to organize a Baptist Foreign Missionary Society for the United States" (William Bullein Johnson, *Reminiscences*, Caroliniana Library, University of South Carolina, quoted in Hortense Woodson, *Giant in the Land*, 33). It would thus appear that the meeting had been proposed and the meeting place and time suggested before Rice began his journey

After leaving the Society Hill meeting in November, Rice spent one Sunday in Georgetown with Edmund Botsford, another in Charleston, and traveled on to Savannah in time for the meeting of the Savannah Association.[34] He had written to Furman about the formation of the Savannah Baptist Society for Foreign Missions, and declared,

> . . . it is expected that at least one delegate if not two will be sent from this Society to Philadelphia as early as the latter part of May next to meet with delegates from other similar Societies for the purpose of forming a General Convention, or of devising and adopting some other practical method to elicit, combine and direct the energies of the whole Baptist denomination in the United States in one sacred effort to diffuse among idolatrous nations the glorious light of the gospel of Salvation. . . . I very strongly wish it might be found practical for Dr. Furman to be one of the number of these delegates . . . from my conviction of the great importance particularly of the first meeting of the "General Committee." . . .[35]

Following events in Savannah, Rice returned northward to make arrangements for the Philadelphia meeting in May. En route he spent several days with Furman in Charleston and stressed the importance of his presence at this first general meeting of American Baptists. Furman was then fifty-eight years of age. His health had begun to fail as early as the years 1802-1803, when he contracted a fever that endangered his life. In the spring of 1805, he and Mrs. Furman spent six weeks in the

---

south where he met Johnson. On 17 December 1813, William Staughton wrote to Rice, "With respect to the place of meeting of the general committee, I think our society ought to be passive. I was conversing last evening with Dr. Rogers on the subject, who is of the opinion with myself that the societies which exist at the greatest distance from some central point should decide for themselves. I am persuaded our society will acquiesce with cheerfulness in such a decision. Were we to consult personal convenience and gratification, we could at once recommend Philadelphia" (James B. Taylor, *Memoir of Rev. Luther Rice, One of the First Missionaries to the East* [Baltimore: Armstrong and Berry, 1840] 145-46).

[34]Luther Rice to Richard Furman, 30 December 1813, SCBHS.

[35]Luther Rice to Richard Furman, 20 December 1813, cited in H. T. Cook, *Biography*, 92.

Georgia interior where her mother and other relatives lived.[36] He was frequently urged by members of his church and others in the community to go north for the improvement of his health, but pastoral, denominational, and family duties at home held first claim upon him. To one in New England who expressed the wish of many to see him there he wrote, "I am obliged to friends for their expression of kindness, [and] desire of seeing me. However, I think, in general, it would be a matter of no great advantage, and probably with most, of disappointment. They would not find me to be what at a distance they suppose."[37]

JOURNEY TO PHILADELPHIA

At this point, Furman was under great pressure to go to Philadelphia. In addition to making a "liberal contribution for his use," his church gave him a leave of absence until winter.[38] "As so many persons and concurring circumstances unite to urge my going on the proposed journey," he wrote to Edmund Botsford, "I have finally determined to attempt it; and I shall probably set out next Wednesday, taking Stateburg on the way."[39] For his sermon text on the Sunday preceding his

---

[36]H. T. Cook, *Biography*, 29, says this visit occurred in 1806. It seems probable, however, that it was made in 1805 since Furman made reference to it in a letter to his sister, Sarah Haynsworth, dated 30 June 1805. A few days earlier Sarah had informed him of the death of "the good old lady, our mother-in-law," and expressed the desire of herself and her husband that the Furman family would spend the summer with them; to which Furman replied, "The first subject claims a tear; the latter requires expression of our gratitude of your kindness. Permit me, however, to inform you that I do not think it would be right for me to leave Charleston for so long a time and that I hope it is not necessary on account of my health. I have always found an absence from Charleston for some weeks has had an unfavorable influence on the state of the congregation, and it is very visible at this time in consequence of our journey to Georgia. What then might be expected from a summer's absence?" In a concluding paragraph he says, "We have had a communion season since my return from Georgia." These references to his trip to Georgia, dated in June 1805, appear to be conclusive evidence that Cook's date of 1806 should be 1805 instead.

[37]H. T. Cook, *Biography*, 28.

[38]Ibid., 30.

[39]Richard Furman to Edmund Botsford, 1 April 1814, SCBHS.

departure, he used Acts 20:22—"And now, behold, I go bound in the spirit to Jerusalem, not knowing the things that shall befall me there."

He began his journey on 15 April accompanied by Judge and Mrs. Matthias B. Tallmadge. Tallmadge would distinguish himself as the most important layman at the convention. A native of New York, he was graduated from Yale in 1795 and had served in a state constitutional convention and in both branches of the New York legislature before being named district judge for the Northern District of New York in 1810. His wife was the daughter of George Clinton, governor of New York and vice-president of the United States. In 1812 he united with the Baptist church of Poughkeepsie, after a loss of health turned his thoughts to religious matters. For health reasons he found it necessary to spend winter months in a milder climate; hence his presence in Charleston, where he formed a fast friendship with Furman and shared with him his concern for missions. Both Furman and Tallmadge were named accredited delegates to the Philadelphia Convention from South Carolina, though neither Tallmadge's residence nor his church membership was ever removed from New York.[40]

Representing Georgia was William B. Johnson, then thirty-two years of age, the southernmost representative at Philadelphia and the one who traveled the greatest distance to get there.[41] Johnson arrived in Columbia on his way to Philadelphia on 16 April and there found a letter from Edmund Botsford under whose ministry in Georgetown he had formed a close bond of friendship that grew into a spiritual father-son relationship. Botsford had followed Johnson's career with the fatherly interest of one always ready to impart the wisdom of age and experience. For this special occasion in Johnson's life, Botsford wrote,

---

[40]Vail, *The Morning Hour of American Missions*, 371-72.

[41]In a letter to William Rogers, dated 13 May 1805, Furman said, "There are two Members of the church at Beaufort, who have come into it by Baptism since the Revival began; who are called to the Ministry—The one is Thomas Fuller, Esq., a gentleman of Fortune and high Respectability, some what advanced in life. . . . The other is William Bullein Johnson; a young Gentleman bred to the Law, for which he has gone through a regular Course of Studies; but had not entered on the Practice. He has Talents, particularly for eloquence; is zealous, and preaches with much acceptance, though it is very lately since he began in the important work" (Original MS in the South Caroliniana Library, University of South Carolina).

. . . This journey may be of singular advantage to you, if you improve it . . . the people among whom you are going are a free, plain people. No doubt you may meet with some eccentric characters; yet even from these you may obtain knowledge . . . Be not too forward, at any time, to give your opinion; neither be backward where it appears duty. Remember you are yet a young man; you will, therefore, attend to the observations and reasoning of those, who have the advantage of years and experience. . . . You'll see Dr. Staughton, Dr. Rogers, and Dr. Holcombe; Mr. Benedict, Mr. Rice, Dr. Baldwin and Dr. Gano. . . .

All of these were towering names in the Baptist fellowship, but Botsford told Johnson to "be sure to consult Dr. Furman on every occasion."[42]

In addition to Furman, Tallmadge, and Johnson, thirty others would meet in Philadelphia—twenty-three ministers and seven laymen—among them Henry Holcombe, William Staughton, William Rogers, Thomas Baldwin, Robert B. Semple, Lewis Richards, and, of course, Luther Rice. Rogers was born in 1751 to Baptist parents in Newport, Rhode Island, entered Rhode Island College in 1765, was licensed to preach at the age of twenty, and was pastor of the First Baptist Church of Philadelphia from 1772-1775. Four years before going to the Philadelphia meeting, he had concluded twenty years as professor of English and oratory at the University of Pennsylvania. Baldwin, a native of Connecticut, had been pastor of the Second Baptist Church of Boston for twenty-three years when he rode down to Philadelphia for the convention. As editor of the *Baptist Missionary Magazine*, he sent the churches correspondence that made his acquaintance with them superior to that of any other during this early period of Baptist mission work. Semple was the son of Scottish parents, wealthy Episcopalians of Virginia. After a period of infidelity, he was converted, became a Baptist preacher, and in 1790 began a forty-one-year pastorate of the Bruington, Virginia, church. By the time of the Philadelphia Convention, he had been offered and declined the presidency of Transylvania University and had written and published a catechism and a book, *History of Vir-*

---

[42]Mallary, *Memoirs of Elder Edmund Botsford*, 187-88.

ginia Baptists. Richards, a native of South Wales, was the same Lewis Richards who had come to South Carolina from Lady Huntingdon College, was baptized by Furman at the High Hills church, and later ordained at Charleston. He had been pastor of the First Baptist Church of Baltimore for thirty-nine years. Rice could claim royal lineage. He was a direct descendant of William the Conqueror through the Duke of Cornwall, and a kinsman of John Quincy Adams, the sixth president of the United States. Others of eminence who would follow him in his family line would be Samuel Morse, inventor of the telegraph; Henry Wadsworth Longfellow, the poet; Gamaliel Bradford, the biographer; Julia Ward Howe, author of the *Battle Hymn of the Republic;* Frances E. Willard, the leader of American women in the promotion of temperance reform; and Clara Barton, founder of the American Red Cross.[43]

Viewed as a whole, this Philadelphia gathering was an eminently select group from the 112 Baptist associations scattered from Maine to Georgia and from the Atlantic to the frontier beyond the Alleghenies. When compared with the number of Baptists they represented—nearly 200,000[44]—their number appears too few for significance. But taking into consideration the comparatively late decision on the selection of a time and place for the meeting, the difficulty of travel over poor to nearly nonexistent roads, and the fact that the country was in the latter stages of a war, the number of prominent Baptist leaders is remarkable. They were the ablest and most distinguished body of Baptists yet brought together on the American continent. Writing in 1907, Albert L. Vail, in his *Morning Hour of American Missions*, says that "as a deliberative body, adequately handling great issues, it stands out colossal and distinguished."

Since the beginning of his residence in Charleston, Furman had been in regular correspondence with Baptist leaders in the North, exchanging sermons, sharing circular letters and associational minutes, giving and receiving information on the state and progress of religion, and cultivating acquaintance and friendship through the written word passed

---

[43]Weaver, "The Place of Luther Rice," 131; for a more detailed biographical sketch of these and other delegates to the Philadelphia Convention, see Vail, *The Morning Hour of American Missions*, 311-75.

[44]Vail, *The Morning Hour of American Missions*, 309.

along the post roads, or more frequently by coastwise sailships between the port cities from Charleston to Boston. These activities and his long patronage of Rhode Island College notwithstanding, there is no record that he had traveled north of Virginia since his parents had moved to South Carolina in 1775.

He and the Tallmadges left Charleston on 15 April, traveling in separate coaches.[45] They arrived in Richmond on 4 May after a nineteen-day journey. To his wife, Dolly, he wrote that they were two hundred and sixty miles from Philadelphia "by the usual route." He described Richmond as "a considerable place" with "a number of good buildings . . . considerable trade," and "said to contain 10,000 inhabitants."[46]

Thirteen days later he arrived in Philadelphia in time for the opening of the convention on 18 May. Having traveled in the rain for several days, the resulting dampness made him unwell, with some fever, for the first four days of the convention. Nevertheless, he immediately became so involved in convention proceedings that he wrote no letter home until 8 June when the convention itself and his immediate postconvention responsibilities were behind him.[47]

CONVENTION IN PHILADELPHIA

At the time Furman went to Philadelphia, he was perhaps the most influential Baptist in America and among the best-known Baptists in both America and England. In that nascent period of the English Baptist missionary movement, he was one of its most active agents in America, both in arousing American support and in transmitting American offerings. He was foremost in the advocacy of an educated ministry, but he equally urged the literary and theological education of all Christians.[48] His superior intellectual faculties were well known

---

[45]This is the inference from reference to "the Judge's coachman" in Furman's letter to his wife upon their arrival in Richmond. See Richard Furman to Dorothea Maria Furman, 5 May 1814, SCBHS.

[46]Ibid.

[47]Richard Furman to Dorothea Maria Furman, 8 June 1814, SCBHS.

[48]Vail, *The Morning Hour of American Missions*, 314-15.

among his brother ministers. "There are few men, it is believed," said Dr. William R. Williams, "who had their minds more richly stored with the fine passages of Milton, Young, Pope, Addison, Butler, and other great authors than Dr. Furman. From them he could quote properly and appositely for almost every occasion what was most beautiful and eloquent."[49]

It was, therefore, logical that he be "called to the Chair" and later elected president of the convention when it began on 18 May in the First Baptist Church. The minutes record that he "opened the meeting with an appropriate prayer, in which the feelings of all present appeared to be solemnly united." After Dr. Thomas Baldwin of Boston was named secretary, the delegates presented their credentials by states in the following order: Thomas Baldwin and Lucius Bolles, Massachusetts; Stephen Gano, Rhode Island; John Williams, Thomas Hewitt, Edwin Probyn, and Nathaniel Smith, New York; Burgiss Allison, Richard Proudfoot, Josiah Stratton, William Boswell, Henry Smalley, Matthew Randall, John Sisty, and Stephen Ustick, New Jersey; William Rogers, Henry Holcombe, William Staughton, William White, John K. Peekworth, Horatio G. Jones, Silas Hough, Joseph Mathias, Pennsylvania; Daniel Dodge, Delaware; Lewis Richards and Thomas Brooke, Maryland; Obadiah Brown, William Gilmore, and Luther Rice, District of Columbia; Robert B. Semple, Jacob Grigg, and John Bryce, Virginia; James A. Randalson, North Carolina; Richard Furman and Matthias B. Tallmadge, South Carolina; and William B. Johnson, Georgia. Gilmore and Brown, of the District of Columbia, and Bryce, of Virginia, did not attend.[50]

Later writers variously attribute delegate credentials to missionary societies, churches, and other Baptist organizations, but no authorities contemporary with that period make any attribution except for Bolles, Baldwin, Furman, and Tallmadge. The *Baptist Missionary Magazine* attributes Baldwin's credentials to the Boston Society for the Propagation of the Gospel in India and Other Foreign Parts, and Bolles's to the Salem

---

[49]Cited in ibid., 315-16.

[50]*Proceedings of the Baptist Convention for Missionary Purposes, Held in Philadelphia, May, 1814*, printed copy, Southern Methodist University, Dallas, Texas; also American Baptist Historical Society, Rochester, New York.

Baptist Translation Society. Furman and Tallmadge were accredited by the Special Committee of the General Committee of the Churches of the Charleston Association. Other delegates were probably accredited by the missionary societies to which they belonged.[51]

By the constitution adopted, the organization was named "The General Missionary Convention of the Baptist Denomination in the United States of America, for Foreign Missions." Though limited in design, it was a watershed event in American Baptist history. The two standing foremost in this gathering were Luther Rice and Richard Furman—Rice for being the catalyst in dramatizing the cause of foreign missions before a national Baptist constituency, and Furman for his recognized standing as a Baptist leader.

The first item of business after the seating of delegates was an agreement that "a meeting of solemn prayer" would be held on the following Saturday evening "to implore the direction and blessing of the Holy Spirit, on our measures." Following frank discussion on "the most eligible plan" for realizing the objective of the Convention, a fifteen-member committee was appointed to prepare a plan and report back to the convention "without delay." The committee consisted of Furman, Baldwin, Bolles, Gano, Williams, Allison, Holcombe, Rogers, Staughton, Dodge, Richards, Rice, Semple, Randalson, and Johnson. Every state with a delegate or delegates present—from Massachusetts to Georgia—plus the District of Columbia, was represented on the committee.[52]

Additional actions of this first session were, first, a request to Furman, Baldwin, and Staughton to prepare an address on foreign missions and "the general interests of the Baptist denomination," to be circulated among the Convention's constituents and throughout the Union and, second, the appointment of a committee of Holcombe, Gano, and Rice "to collect and report information relative to the encouragement already afforded by Societies and Associations in behalf of Missionary Interest."

Thus ended the first afternoon of the Convention. That evening, at the request of the Convention, Furman preached a sermon that so im-

---

[51]Vail, *The Morning Hour of American Missions*, 467.

[52]Ibid.

pressed the delegates that on Saturday afternoon a resolution was passed requesting him to prepare it in abstract for publication with the minutes. Since he apparently was not asked to preach until after he arrived at the Convention,[53] he wrote it down only after it had been delivered. Using as his text Matthew 28:20—"And lo, I am with you alway, even to the end of the world"—he developed the theme with such logical sequence and homiletical precision as to set the tone and direction for that historic gathering of Baptists. In a flight of climactic oratory, he drew to a conclusion with reference to the great things being divinely accomplished in the earth and the greater things yet to come, then added:

> These considerations stimulate to vigorous exertions in the cause of Christ, and apply with equal force to the circumstances of our present meeting. . . . Electrified, as it were, by the considerations which the united voice of Scripture and Providence have presented to our minds, we have suddenly assembled, from almost every state in the American Union, to represent multitudes of our Christian friends, who feel with us, to speak and act with them in the best of causes. . . . Let faith, gratitude, and love unite their influence and call all the energies of our souls on this solemn occasion. . . . Let the wise and good employ their counsels; the minister of Christ, who is qualified for the sacred service, offer himself for the work; the man of wealth and generosity, who values the glory of Immanuel and the salvation of souls more than gold, bring of his treasure in proportion as God has bestowed on him; yea, let all, even the pious widow, bring the mite that can be spared; and let all who fear and love God, unite in the prayer of faith . . . and unceasingly say, "Thy Kingdom come," And O! let it never be forgotten, that the Son of God hath said, "Lo, I am with you alway, even to the end of the world."[54]

On the second day the Convention resolved itself into a committee of the whole, with Stephen Gano in the chair, to hear the report of the constitutional committee. The minutes do not identify the committee

---

[53]In his *Reminiscences*, W. B. Johnson says that no provision had been made for a convention sermon.

[54]*Proceedings*, Triennial Convention, 1814.

chairman, but it was probably Furman—an inference drawn from the fact that Gano was in the chair so that Furman could make the report, and from the further fact that Furman returned to the chair after the articles of the proposed constitution had been twice read and "freely debated." The session ended on an uncertain note, with the committee reporting progress but requesting and receiving permission to sit again.

That afternoon the Convention again resolved itself into a committee of the whole and resumed its work. Although silent on the character and content of the discussion, the minutes imply disagreement so sharp that the Convention requested the committee to ask that it be dissolved and a new five-member committee be named to draft another constitutional plan. The five members selected were Furman, Gano, Semple, Baldwin, and White.[55] In this first general meeting of American Baptists, their historic propensity for disagreement was illustrated. The fifteen-member committee was obviously too large and by its dimensions represented too many points of view to reach a consensus. There were also sharp differences between Holcombe, Staughton, and Rogers,[56] whose names are conspicuously absent from the new committee. White, pastor of the Second Baptist Church of Philadelphia, was the only member of the new committee who had not served on the larger one. Vail takes note of a "personal and ecclesiastical" controversy between Holcombe and Staughton, which had already begun and would prove demoralizing to Philadelphia Baptists. Their estimate of White was part of the problem. Holcombe believed him to be a disreputable character; but Staughton defended him.

A greater problem was the difference between the associational and societal plans for doing mission work. Until around 1800, American Baptists generally used the associational plan for mission work, but by 1814 separate societies had largely replaced the associations as mission vehicles,[57] due, likely, to the "excessive sensitiveness in behalf of church independency then characteristic of Baptists."[58] At Philadelphia, some

---

[55]Ibid.

[56]Vail, *The Morning Hour of American Missions*, 380.

[57]Robert A. Baker and Paul J. Craven, Jr., *Adventure in Faith: The First 300 Years of First Baptist Church of Charleston, S.C.* (Nashville: Broadman Press, 1982) 231.

[58]Vail, *The Morning Hour of American Missions*, 150.

favored the associational plan and others the more independent societal plan. On this issue, they divided, with those from the South favoring the association and those from the North the society.[59] Not being able to reach agreement, the committee of fifteen was then replaced by the committee of five. The appearance of Furman's name first on the smaller committee suggests that he was its chairman.

This smaller committee presented a revised plan the next morning, and that afternoon the Convention began to discuss it article by article. On the next Saturday, Furman, who had presided throughout the discussion, put the question on third reading: "Shall this Constitution as now read be adopted, as the basis of union, and the rule of conduct to be observed by this Convention and its board of Commissioners?" The delegates rose to a man with their affirmative vote. It was a dramatic and solemn moment in Baptist history. As the states had joined together to form a union under a constitution, so now had Baptists. Writing in 1907, Vail paid tribute to the work of these pioneer Baptists.

> In the light of nearly a half century of impressive manifestations, that vote was an event. We can see as probably none there could, the significance of it. The modifying of this constitution will soon begin, indeed; the responses of the denomination will be comparatively sluggish, fluctuating, and inadequate; sources then unsuspected of disruption will arise, waves of protest and assault will surge against the craft there launched, the ambitions of men, the defections of friends, the deficiencies of missionaries and administrators, will follow each other and combine with each other to wreck the enterprise almost; but that was begun there on which God will lay his hand to steady it when men stumble, and crown it when laurels fail! For that was in some appreciable sense the inauguration of one of the great forces for the salvation of the world. And it may be deliberately questioned whether any Baptist vote ever meant more for the denomination or for mankind.[60]

---

[59]William Wright Barnes, *The Southern Baptist Convention, 1845-1953*, 8f.

[60]Vail, *The Morning Hour of American Missions*, 384-85.

Termed a General Missionary Convention, it would meet every third year; hence the name by which it became popularly known, the Triennial Convention. During recess, a twenty-one-member Board of Commissioners was authorized to transact necessary business. The constitution stated their assignment in the following language.

> To employ Missionaries, and, if necessary, to take measures for the improvement of their qualifications; to fix on the field of their labors, and compensation to be allowed them for their services; to supervise their conduct, and dismiss them, should their services be disapproved; to publish accounts, from time to time, of the Board's Transactions, and an annual Address to the public; to call a special meeting of the Convention on any extraordinary occasion, and, in general, to conduct the execution part of the missionary concern.[61]

On Monday afternoon, a Board of Commissioners was elected as provided. Again the name of Furman headed the list. Others on the committee were William Rogers, Henry Holcombe, William Staughton, Thomas Baldwin, Burgiss Allison, James K. Peekworth, William B. Johnson, Robert B. Semple, Stephen Gano, Lucius Bolles, Lewis Richards, Matthias B. Tallmadge, Jeremiah Vardeman, H. G. Jones, and William Moulder.

The Convention adjourned Tuesday morning following an address by Furman and the appointment of a committee consisting of Furman, Baldwin, and Staughton "to receive for safe-keeping such monies as have been transmitted from the several Societies, until placed in the hands of the treasurer-elect."[62]

Immediately thereafter, the Board of Commissioners, officially termed the Baptist Board of Foreign Missions for the United States, convened with sixteen of the twenty-one members present. Furman was chosen president, but declined because of his distant residence from the seat of the board. Baldwin was then elected president; Holcombe and Rogers were elected first and second vice-presidents, respectively; and Tallmadge was elected treasurer. Tallmadge, too, declined due to the

---

[61]*Proceedings*, Triennial Convention, 1814, 4; full text of Constitution is in Appendix C.

[62]Ibid.

delicate state of his health. That position was then filled by John Caldwell of New York. The Board adjourned and resumed again at three o'clock when Staughton was elected corresponding secretary, White recording secretary, and a committee consisting of Tallmadge, Bolles, and Johnson was named to prepare bylaws.

The concluding meeting was on Wednesday. With all the officers present, and eight other members, including Furman, Allison, Johnson, Williams, Gano, Randalson, Bolles, and Peekworth, the real task of the newly formed convention of Baptists was initiated. Luther Rice was named the Board's first missionary, but was requested "to continue his itinerant services, in these United States, for a reasonable time; with a view to excite the public mind more generally, to engage in Missionary exertions; and to assist in originating Societies, or Institutions, for carrying the Missionary design into execution."

Adoniram Judson, then in India, was named missionary "under the care and direction" of the Board, with provision made for his support and the transmission of one thousand dollars "by the first safe opportunity." The Board also resolved to communicate the proceedings of "the late Convention to the Baptist Missionary Society in England . . . assuring them that it is the desire of this board to hold an affectionate intercourse with them, in the work of the Lord; that they will be ever grateful for any information which the extensive experience of their brethren may enable them to impart on the subject of fields of Missionary action, etc., etc., and will derive joy from the reflection, that though in these transactions their respective seats of council be remote from each other, their hearts and aims are harmonious."[63]

The first meeting of the Triennial Convention and its executive board thus ended with an emphasis on a world vision. The final address on Tuesday, delivered by Furman, afforded an eloquent climax to a historic gathering.

> Four hundred million of our fellow creatures spread over the countries of Hindostan, Siam, Tartary, China and its neighboring islands, various parts of Africa, America, and the isles of the Pacific Ocean are involved in the darkness of Paganism. Their idolatry is associated with customs, absurd, sanguinary and obscene. The female character is sunk

---

[63]*Proceedings*, Triennial Convention, 1814, 13-14.

in servility in wretchedness. Millions in Europe, Africa, and Asia are revering the Arabian imposter as a messenger from God and the Koran as their guide to Paradise. Ten millions of our race are Jews, scattered throughout every nation, and are everywhere resting in their law and rejecting the Messiah. In many sections of our globe, where Christianity is publicly professed, it has been so mixed with vain superstitions, its doctrines so misinterpreted, its duties so mistaken, and the means by which it has been propagated and maintained, so repugnant to its pure and gentle spirit, that even Christendom itself presents scenes for pious exertion, which for ignorance and misery, are in heathen regions scarcely exceeded.[64]

In such a sweep of world vision, couched in oratory that reverberated through the meetinghouse of Philadelphia's First Baptist Church, Furman appealed to his audience to accept the challenge of the purpose for which they had gathered.

Some question has arisen about the authorship of the address. As mentioned earlier, the Convention appointed Furman, Baldwin, and Staughton "to prepare an address on the subject of foreign missions and the general interests of the Baptist denomination, to be circulated among the constituents of this Convention and throughout the Union." Fifty years later, Baron Stow wrote that "internal evidence" points to Staughton as the author. Vail declares the authorship to be uncertain, but agrees that Staughton, as corresponding secretary, may have written it. Robert A. Baker finds the language more like that of Furman than of Staughton. He notes that it bore the name of Furman, was attested to not by Staughton but by Baldwin, and was "most certainly the ecclesiology of Furman after the pattern of the General Committee of the Charleston Association."[65]

The probable explanation is that it was a collaborative effort between Furman and Staughton, with the eloquence of both written into it. In a letter to his wife, written after the Convention had adjourned, Furman suggests that Baldwin played a lesser role. "The Convention sat a week," he wrote, "and I was appointed one of a committee to digest, and prepare the minutes of their transactions, and of the Board of

[64]Ibid., 40.

[65]Baker and Craven, *The First 300 Years of First Baptist Church*, 399.

Missions which they had established for publication; to draw up an address to their constituents and the public on the subject of their meeting, and to furnish the substance of the sermon on the occasion for the same purpose. *The weight of this business has fallen on Dr. Staughton and myself.*"[66] Further supporting the Furman-Staughton collaborative authorship is the fact that Furman stayed with the Staughtons during the Convention, thus affording special opportunity for fulfilling their committee assignment.[67]

By two omissions, the Convention did not go as far as Furman had hoped. The Convention did form a foreign mission society, but Furman had visualized "a general denominational body to promote ministerial education and domestic missions in addition to foreign missions."[68] His wish that ministerial education have its rightful place in Baptist denominational emphasis was expressed in a concluding observation.

> It is deeply to be regretted that no more attention is paid to the improvement of the minds of pious youth who are called to the gospel ministry. While this is neglected, the cause of God must suffer. Within the last fifty years, by the diffusion of knowledge and attention to liberal science the state of society has become considerably elevated. It is certainly desirable the information of the minister of the sanctuary should increase in an equal proportion. . . . While we avow our belief that a refined or liberal education is not an indispensable qualification for ministerial service, let us never lose sight of its real importance, but labour to help our young men by our contributions, by the origination of education Societies, and if possible, by a general theological seminary, which learning and mature studies can afford, to qualify for acting the part of men who are set for the defence of the gospel.[69]

This is believed to be the only suggestion at that time concerning expansion of the foreign mission society into a general denominational body for promoting ministerial education and domestic missions in ad-

---

[66]Richard Furman to Dorothea Maria Furman, 8 June 1814, SCBHS.

[67]Ibid.

[68]Baker and Craven, *The First 300 Years of First Baptist Church*, 401.

[69]*Proceedings*, Triennial Convention, 1814, 42.

dition to foreign missions.[70] The vision and the thought were right out of the mind of Furman as he had nurtured and cultivated them for many years through the General Committee of the Charleston Association.

The Philadelphia Convention had met under conditions of international warfare. In Europe, the French Revolution had escalated into the Napoleonic Wars. These, in turn, forged a European alliance against Napoleon, forced his retirement to the island of Elba, and restored the Bourbon monarchy. In America and on the high seas, the War of 1812 was moving toward an uncertain conclusion. Furman had traveled to Philadelphia by the more difficult land route to avoid danger from British warships on a voyage by sea. He learned of the overthrow of Napoleon while still in Philadelphia bringing together the loose ends of the Convention. The consequences, he feared, would be a buildup of British forces against the United States, with veterans of Wellington's army, freed from service in Europe, joining forces with British troops against American arms.

> We yesterday received here the momentous news of the disposition of Bonaparte and the restoration of the Bourbons. . . . It will evoke very strong emotions in the minds of the American public. To some it will occasion painful disappointment and mortification. I hope however these are events directed by Providence in the way of mercy; and that we shall be partakers in that merciful design and its results. However if peace is not soon made I think we must expect war in reality as England will have a large force at her command for its prosecution.[71]

His fear was prophetic. With the war against Napoleon finished, England made plans to transfer part of the victorious army from Europe to America. Soon Wellington's veterans were reinforcing British troops on American soil.[72]

The news of Napoleon's overthrow and the effect it might have upon the war in America inclined Furman to return home upon completion

---

[70]Baker and Craven, *The First 300 Years of First Baptist Church*, 401.

[71]Richard Furman to Dorothea Maria Furman, 8 June 1814, SCBHS.

[72]John J. Mahon, *The War of 1812* (Gainesville: University of Florida Press, 1972) 266.

of his work in Philadelphia.[73] But apparently having conceived of this journey as an opportunity to travel to New York and New England, and probably, too, at the urging of his friend, Judge Tallmadge, he chose to pursue his original plans. Tallmadge had left Philadelphia for New York immediately after the Convention and upon arrival had written Furman urging him to come "at once." But to Dolly he wrote, "I suppose however that I shall be detained here a week or more to complete the business of printing, etc." He then added, "But I shall expect my future letters for sometime to be directed to New York."[74] Only H. T. Cook, in his biography of Furman, gives any details of this extension of his trip. Cook's account is taken from a manuscript written, he concluded, by Richard Furman's son, Wood.[75]

POSTCONVENTION JOURNEY

Furman remained in Philadelphia until past the middle of June, then went to New York, and thence up the North River to Poughkeepsie, east of the Hudson, to the home of the Tallmadges. From there he crossed over to Esopus, the place of his birth fifty-eight years earlier. There he slept in the house where he was born and whence he had left before reaching the age of one. Since he had no personal memories of Esopus and its people to cherish, this was not a sentimental journey to relive past experiences. But for the first time he met Brodheads and other maternal relatives not known to him, except through his mother's references to them. Because the time was short and he planned to revisit them before returning south, he remained only briefly, then recrossed the Hudson and pushed on through Connecticut by way of Hartford to Providence, Boston, and Salem. Five generations earlier, his forebears, the Firmins, had pioneered settlements on this part of the continent, and for twenty-five years he had been sending students to Rhode Island College, in Providence, by then Brown University. In Boston he would

---

[73]Ibid.; Richard Furman to Dorothea Maria Furman, 8 June 1814, SCBHS.

[74]Ibid.

[75]Wood Furman's authorship is questioned by South Carolina Baptist historian Loulie Latimer Owens, who reasons that Furman's daughter, Susan, was its author. See Owens, *The Family of Richard Furman*, unpublished manuscript, SCBHS.

certainly visit Thomas Baldwin and probably preach in his church on a subject relating to the missionary objective of the convention they had helped form. On the return trip, he traveled through Worcester to Albany and down the Hudson to Esopus again. This time, he preached in the Dutch Reformed church to an audience that included many of his Brodhead relatives. From there he proceeded to New York and back to Philadelphia.[76]

By that northward extension of his trip, he had been gone more than two months since leaving Philadelphia for New York, traveling, probably, by private means to New York and Poughkeepsie, then by Hudson River passage to Esopus, and by stage to and from Providence, Boston, and Salem. At Poughkeepsie, on his return, he would pick up his own private conveyance, probably left with the Tallmadges, and travel back to Philadelphia. From Philadelphia, the route took the roundabout course through Lancaster, York, and Fredericktown to Washington, in order to avoid Baltimore, then under the British siege that would give birth to "The Star Spangled Banner," by Francis Scott Key.

When Furman arrived in Washington, he found it in shambles. The city had been sacked and burned by British troops in August, the torch having been put to the Capitol, the White House, the Navy Yard, and all public buildings except the Patent Office. Upon seeing this destruction, Furman's thoughts turned to the defense of Charleston. Later at Danville, Virginia, he would find a letter from Dolly awaiting him telling him that their children were assisting in defense work against a possible enemy attack. "I am glad," he wrote in reply, "that the citizens of Charleston are exerting themselves in a plan of defense and that our children bear a part, yet I am afraid that exposure to the sun and labor that they are not accustomed to may make them sick."[77]

In Washington an acquaintance introduced Furman to James Monroe, secretary of state under President James Madison. Taking Furman's hand, Monroe thought for a moment and queried in some puzzlement, "Furman, Furman, of Charleston. May I enquire if you once lived near the High Hills of Santee? And were you the young preacher

---

[76]H. T. Cook, *Biography*, 30.

[77]Richard Furman to Dorothea Maria Furman, 18 October 1814, SCBHS.

who fled for protection to the American camp on account of the reward
Lord Cornwallis had offered for his head?" "I am the same," Furman
replied. With that Monroe would not let him go without introducing
him to his colleagues and hearing him preach in the halls of Congress.
An account of this experience appears in periodicals of the nineteenth
century. According to these sources, "All the elite, the honorable and
the notable of the metropolis were there, including the president, cab-
inet, ministers, foreign ambassadors, etc., for his early adventures and
eloquence had been noised abroad." Preaching from Acts 22:16—"And
why tarriest thou, arise and be baptized"—he is described as having
great liberty of expression as he addressed an audience whose attention
was riveted by his earnest eloquence.[78]

---

[78]Any official record of Furman's preaching before Congress or of his introduction
to James Monroe has eluded research in Washington. The first reference from published accounts is found in *The Christian Secretary*, later republished in *The Religious
Herald*, and still later in *The Baptist Memorial and Monthly Chronicle* 15 (1856): 244-
45 (The Samuel Colgate Baptist Historical Collection, American Baptist Historical
Society, Rochester, N.Y.). H. T. Cook, *Biography*, 73, tells of it and attributes it to
The Christian Secretary. A brief account also appears, undocumented, in Colyer Mer-
iwether, *History of Higher Education in South Carolina* (Washington DC: Government
Printing Office, 1889) 93-94. That Furman was in Washington in October 1814,
when the introduction to Monroe and his preaching before Congress are said to have
occurred, is supported by a letter he wrote to Dolly on 14 October from Danville,
Virginia, when returning from the Philadelphia Convention. In that letter he says,
"Richard's letter I have not received. Wood's letter *sent to Washington I found there* (emphasis mine) and acknowledged from Fredericksburg" (SCBHS). But, oddly, in that
letter, written so soon after he was in Washington, he makes no reference to having
preached before Congress. Research in the Congressional Library, the National Archives, the National Publications and Records Commission, the Senate Historical Office, and in chaplains' offices in both the House of Representatives and the U.S. Senate,
failed to find any record to document the story. Such failure, however, need not be
considered conclusive. In the early nineteenth century, the House of Representatives'
chamber, which today serves as Statuary Hall, was the scene of Sunday services conducted alternately by chaplains of the Senate and the House, and frequently by distinguished but unrecorded visiting clergymen. It is possible, even probable, that
Furman may have been among the latter without any record having been made of his
appearance—especially since keeping records was then a low priority compared with
rebuilding the capital. (See Gaillard Hunt, ed., *The First Forty Years of Washington
Society, Portrayed by the Family Letters of Mrs. Samuel Harrison Smith from the Collection
of Her Grandson, J. Henley Smith* [New York: Charles Scribner's Sons, 1906]; U.S. Senate
Library; also the *Congressional Record*, 25 June 1980, S8219.)

He left Washington in October. Traveling through Virginia, he passed from Alexandria to Fredericksburg and on to Danville. Along the way, he went sixty miles out of his way to visit the widow of "the great Patrick Henry," then the wife of Judge Edmund Winston, a first cousin twice removed of Dolley Madison, wife of President James Madison.[79] To his great disappointment he found Mrs. Winston absent seventy miles away on a visit with some of her children. "I however met with a most friendly reception from the Judge and his daughter," he wrote Dolly, "stayed with them on the Sabbath and preached in the neighborhood in company with a Presbyterian minister."[80]

It was night when he arrived in Danville. He immediately went to the post office and found a letter from Dolly informing him of generally favorable conditions at home. Early the next morning he set out for Mayo River, where he had been a refugee during the latter years of the Revolution. Ten days later he wrote to Dolly from the home of his sister, Sarah Haynsworth, in the High Hills of Santee. John M. Roberts had heard of his probable arrival in advance and announced to those of his High Hills congregation who lived near the Haynsworth home that Furman would preach a charity sermon on the day following his return. Furman learned of this near dark, "while still on the road." Despite this brief forewarning he preached according to the appointment to "a small audience."[81]

It had been six months since he had left Charleston for Philadelphia—the longest time he ever spent away from home—and it would be yet two weeks before the completion of his journey. A letter from Dolly awaited him at the Stateburg post office. It brought the news that their daughter, Anne, youngest of their thirteen children, was suffering with a "complaint distressing and often fatal." Furman took the news in stride. "Sooner or later, it may be expected in such a place as Charleston," he wrote, "and it is to be hoped that with proper treatment she,

---

[79]Richard Furman to Dorothea Maria Furman, 18 October 1814, SCBHS; Charles Campbell, *History of Virginia* (Philadelphia: J. B. Lippincott and Co., 1860) 520n.

[80]Ibid.

[81]Richard Furman to Dorothea Maria Furman, 25 October 1814, SCBHS.

and the rest of the Family, who may be affected by it, may . . . get safely through it."[82]

The 1814 meeting of the Charleston Baptist Association was scheduled for 5 November at the Beulah Church near Columbia. Furman planned to remain at Stateburg "on Business" until that time, then attend the meeting and hope for it to be concluded in time to reach Charleston the following Sunday.[83]

In the meantime, plantation affairs engaged his attention. It had been a bad crop season. Cotton and corn had suffered from dry weather and were in short supply. Cattle had been affected least of all, but all other plantation stock had "diminished." One of his best field hands had been sick and, though improved, his future remained uncertain. There was meal to grind at the mill on Beech Creek, and cotton to be loaded onto wagons for hauling to market at Charleston. But the High Hills were resplendent in fall colors, and after six months of hard travel, Furman found these autumn days of plantation life an invigorating interlude.

REPORT TO THE ASSOCIATION

The Association met as scheduled, and for the sixteenth time Furman was elected moderator. The customary worship service began on Saturday and continued through Sunday. Business sessions followed on Monday and Tuesday. On one of those days Furman made his report on the Philadelphia Convention, presenting the minutes of the Convention, the constitution adopted by it, the address prepared for the public, and the minutes of the Board of Missions. Upon completion of his report, he asked for public expressions from the delegates. "Whereupon," the minutes of that meeting record,

> it was declared, by a unanimous vote, that this Association do approve of the said Constitution and Address, and of the Measures taken by the Board of Missions to bring the Constitution into operation; and that it is their wish, and request, that the Churches for which they are convened will give cordial and firm support to these measures; in or-

[82]Ibid.

[83]Ibid.

der that, through the Blessing of God, the important object proposed, the conversion of the Heathen to the Faith of Christ, may be obtained.[84]

Like a trumpet sounding, John M. Roberts, author of the circular letter, issued a challenge to the churches to support missions as a "sacred, obvious, and delightful duty." In the oratorical passages of this letter is written the missionary fervor of Richard Furman. Prepared by Roberts, it was approved "in its Matter and Spirit" by the delegates. But in response to Roberts's wishes, a committee consisting of himself, Furman, and Joseph B. Cook was appointed to "revise it and make any verbal alterations they might think useful."[85] What changes were made are not recorded, but the letter so circulated articulates in eloquent cadence the same urgency to missionary endeavor as contained in Furman's address that concluded the Philadelphia convention.

> In the records of inspiration, do not precepts command, do not promises encourage, do not examples excite us to labor unweariedly in aid of that blessed work, the spreading of heavenly Gospel light among the unenlightened nations of the earth? Are we not enjoined to be zealously affected in the good cause of the Lord, freely to impart the inestimable blessings of salvation, which we have freely received, and never to be weary in well-doing? . . .

The words flowed toward a climax that would focus upon the example of Christ and the events in Philadelphia.

> Is he not now making the way of duty shine before our eyes by his gracious smiles in our own highly favored country? Has he not, within the space of a few months, kindled a generous flame for the patronage and encouragement of Gospel Missions among our brethren, from New Hampshire to Georgia? In the most central situation has he not assembled a venerable body of our most devout, enlightened, experienced fathers and brethren in the ministry, who by their united counsels, have formed and put into operation, a plan admirably cal-

---

[84]*Minutes of the Charleston Baptist Association*, 1814, SCBHS.

[85]Ibid.

culated to advance the interests of Sion and the glory of God, not only
in this country, but in the remotest parts of the earth?[86]

On that note, the spirit of Philadelphia came down to the churches of
the Charleston Association, and to those of other associations from
Georgia to New England. For the first time in the history of American
Baptists, a general union of Baptists had been formed. Though limited
to a single benevolence and more societal than denominational in character, it had advantages of communication beyond its missionary in-
tent. As Furman had said in his concluding address,

> [I]s it not a fact that our churches are ignorant of each other to a la-
> mentable degree? But for the labours of one or two individuals, it is
> probable that whole Associations might have assembled in different
> parts of our Union without being known or knowing that others ex-
> isted. We have "one Lord, one faith, one baptism," why should our
> ignorance of each other continue? Why prevent us from uniting in one
> common effort for the glory of the Son of God? At the present Con-
> vention the sight of brethren who had never met each other before,
> and who a few months ago had never expected to meet on earth, af-
> forded mutual and unutterable pleasure. It was as if the first inter-
> views of heaven had been anticipated.[87]

Six months after his departure for Philadelphia, Furman arrived back
in Charleston as president of the General Missionary Convention of the
Baptist Denomination in the United States of America for Foreign Missions.

---

[86]Ibid.

[87]*Proceedings*, Triennial Convention, 1814.

CHAPTER 9

Problem Years

Morgan Edwards's perception of the weakness of scattered, unorganized Baptists had caused him to entertain two avowed ambitions—first, to establish a Baptist college and, second, to unify Baptists throughout the continent. The first he achieved by being "the prime mover" in the founding of Rhode Island College.[1] This was the first institutional expression of the cooperation of American Baptists. While the college movement was national, drawing support and enthusiasm from the South as well as from New England and the Middle States, the organization was local and is not to be compared with the general organization embodied in the General Convention. Still, as the first Baptist educational institution, Rhode Island College contributed significantly to molding national unified sentiment among Baptists.

Edwards's other ambition—to unite all Baptists on the continent organically—was expressed in the introduction to his history of Baptists compiled from his *Materials*, as he called it, collected on a journey from New Hampshire to Georgia. Published in 1770, the introduction

---

[1]Guild, *Early History of Brown University*, 12.

declares his purpose to be "the knitting together the several parts of the visible Baptist church of this continent."[2] "The thing is practical," he wrote, ". . . and withal most beneficient. . . ."

Edwards was the statesman among Baptist leaders of the colonial period. But he was also an Englishman and a Tory whose British sympathies during the War for Independence so discredited his reputation among Baptist leaders that the records of the Philadelphia Association, in which he had once been a central and commanding figure, contain no reference to his plan for a general chartered organization of Baptists.

The Philadelphia Convention had been preceded by other efforts in which Baptists reached out for each other through associational correspondence and the formation of general committees,[3] but none had achieved a continental constituency committed to a missionary objective. That was the achievement of the Triennial Convention. It was the first successful movement to establish a national Baptist structure in support of a common cause. The larger task now was to build a true denominational consensus void of conflicting ecclesiology and unimpaired by disparate regionalism.

Religious groups, Baptists included, were hindered in achieving unity of thought and action by the same conditions that affected secular life in early America. As W. W. Barnes points out,

> The first half of the nineteenth century saw tremendous struggles throughout the world. Politically, socially, intellectually, and religiously, the world was in ferment. All of these elements of strife were current in the United States. Westward expansion and the development of new conditions and new political units intensified these conflicts.[4]

As the first president of the first organized national body of Baptists, Furman had leadership over a General Convention consisting of mission societies with individual, state, or associational constituencies. But he,

---

[2]Edwards, *Materials Toward a History of the Baptists*, bound MS, SCBHS.

[3]Vail, *The Morning Hour of American Missions*, 290-306, lists fourteen instances of Baptist organizational efforts prior to 1814.

[4]Barnes, *The Southern Baptist Convention, 1845-1953*, 1-2.

along with others like Luther Rice and W. B. Johnson, wished to see it become truly denominational in character. His wish would not be easily realized. Baptists were moving into a century of differences that reflected conflicts in secular life. Rigid ecclesiasticism, as feared by many, was too reminiscent of the yet clearly remembered struggle for religious liberty for denominationalism to be in favor among some American Baptists. Besides, many rejected the very principle of missions. This fear of ecclesiasticism and opposition to missions combined in many cases to forestall the development of a denominational structure.[5] Geographically, denominational consciousness was present more prominently from Philadelphia southward than northward into New England, where the society plan was generally favored.

Ecclesiology was but one of the problems. Two more immediate ones were a personality conflict within the Board and Rice's failure to rejoin Judson following his early and successful work as agent of the Board. Rice's intention had been to return to the mission field as soon as effective Baptist support for missions could be rallied. To a Baptist minister from Boston while on a stopover in Bahia, Brazil, en route home aboard a Portuguese vessel, he wrote, "I shall be extremely solicitous to return to India as soon as possible. . . . My solicitude is the more keenly ardent in this particular, because, in addition to the loss of time, brother and sister Judson, with whom I have the happiness to be no less united in affection than in sentiment, must remain alone until my return."[6] To Judson he wrote in September 1814, "The Baptist Board for Foreign Missions . . . thought it necessary for me to continue my labors in this country for a time. Of this I am convinced in my judgment, though it is extremely painful in my heart to be thus detained here. I hope however in the course of five or six months to get the Baptists so rallied, that the necessity of my remaining will no longer exist. And I certainly wish not to remain here a moment later than my stay will more advance the mission, than my departure to the field again."[7] That, too, was the understanding of the Board. They had appointed him as mis-

---

[5]Ibid., 4.

[6]*Massachusetts Baptist Missionary Society Magazine*, 3:10 (May 1813): 333, American Baptist Historical Society, Rochester, New York.

[7]Taylor, *Memoir of Rev. Luther Rice*, 149.

sionary "to continue his itinerant services, in these United States, for a reasonable time; with a view to excite the public mind more generally, to engage in Missionary exertions; and to assist in originating Societies, or Institutions, for carrying the Missionary design into execution."[8]

DISSENSION WITHIN THE BOARD

In the summer of 1815, dissension surfaced. Earlier that year, the Board had voted its "very high sense of the services" Rice had rendered in establishing missionary societies, "and that as the way is now opened by the return of peace, for his resuming his missionary labours in India" he should "as soon as possible prepare to embark for that purpose."[9] A month later, however, this action was reversed. The Board concluded that he should continue "for some time longer" as an agent of the Board, subject only to such developments as in the judgment of the Board "may render his continuance in this country no longer requisite, and his removal and missionary station requisite and proper."[10]

A circular letter by William White was sent that summer to members of the Board not present when the vote was taken, asking their view on Rice's remaining longer. The responses favored Rice's staying. At the Board's September meeting, a letter from Judge Tallmadge proposed that "an Agent of talent ought to be employed by the board, none so suitable as Mr. Rice," and that Rice be retained until the following March.[11] Holcombe protested this action, and at the next meeting he, William Rogers, and Daniel Dodge resigned. Subsequently, however, they withdrew their resignations. From that time the lines of division were drawn.

There followed anonymous letters addressed to Staughton, charging him with maneuvering the proceedings of the 1814 Triennial Convention and the board meetings, and attacking Rice for not returning to India. Published in the tract *Plain Truth*, the letters are often attributed to Holcombe. William Rogers, too, was writing derogatory let-

---

[8]*Minutes of the Baptist Board of Foreign Missions for the United States*, 1814, American Baptist Historical Society, Rochester, New York.

[9]Ibid., 6 March 1815.

[10]Ibid., 11 April 1815.

[11]Ibid., 12 September 1815.

ters; and a letter from Asa Messer, president of Brown University, revealed that some were conniving at this early date to unseat Rice as agent of the Board.[12] Part of the problem came from hard feelings between Staughton and Holcombe. Staughton had preceded Holcombe as pastor of the First Baptist Church and had left with some of the First Church members to form the Sanson Street Church. Staughton's popularity as a preacher drew crowds of elite Philadelphians to hear his sermons, a fact not unnoticed by Holcombe. A charge of immoral conduct by William White, pastor of the Second Baptist Church, ranged Staughton and Holcombe on opposite sides, with Staughton defending White and Holcombe condemning him. The controversy continued until White was finally dismissed by his congregation.[13]

Furman was clearly caught in the crossfire that placed Staughton, Rice, White, and others against Holcombe, Rogers, Dodge, and Messer, all strong personalities not free from personal jealousies. It required all the wisdom of his sixty-two years to keep the convention from falling apart on the shoals of internal dissension. The opposing sides held one thing in common: they respected Furman and looked to him for leadership.

In a letter in June 1815, Rogers and Holcombe appealed to his "superior judgment" and earnestly solicited "whatever assistance it may be convenient for your knowledge and experience to afford us." They then set forth in a long letter "a few difficulties which have occurred in transacting the business of our Foreign Mission Society." It charged Rice with deliberately distorting facts in preparing and presenting the Board's first annual report, questioned whether he had departed from his pre-immersion denominational affiliation, expressed doubt that he had ever intended returning to India, and called upon Furman to explain and set forth "the rule of our proceedings, showing how we may correct, or guard against, abuses of the trust reposed in us, and in determining which of our missionaries, if any, should be dismissed from our service."[14]

---

[12]Evelyn Wingo Thompson, *Luther Rice: Believer in Tomorrow* (Nashville: Broadman Press, 1967) 154.

[13]Ibid., 152-53.

[14]Henry Holcombe and William Rogers to Richard Furman, 26 June 1815, SCBHS, cited in H. T. Cook, *Biography*, 93-98.

If Furman replied to this letter, his answer has not survived. But some months later, during the winter of 1816, Rice visited him in Charleston and they discussed these developments. Controversy within the Board over Rice's intention to return to India had reached a point where he, at the request of Judge Tallmadge, had written a declaration of intention and sent a duplicate copy to the corresponding secretary of the Board of Missions. During their Charleston conversation, Furman told Rice that Judge Tallmadge had conveyed to him the impression that the duplicate declaration had been altered to differ from the original before being sent to the secretary. The damaging import of this information did not register with Rice at the time, but as he later considered it he became deeply troubled.

> It is important for me to possess correct information relative to the matter. . . . I do not deem it proper that a subject of this nature which manifestly goes to impeach me with a culpable duplicity of conduct, should be permitted to pass on without investigation . . .
>
> It is far from my inclination to impute to the Judge the malicious design of injuring one whom he had condescended to treat with some degree of attention and kindness; but it is unaccountable to me how he could have been under a mistake in the case. He read the original paper and commented on it. I should think it probable he read the duplicate addressed to the Corresponding Secretary of the Board; and I believe, too, that a copy of the same was sent to him by me; but I am very confident that no such alteration, as that referred to in the conversation at your house . . . was made.
>
> The case, as nearly as my recollection serves, was simply thus: Owing to the clamors of certain persons, the Judge appeared to me solicitous, to obtain something like a commitment from me relative to my return to India and the time of it. The conduct of the Board had not contributed to augment my confidence in the body, nor had it conveyed to my mind any inducement to make a commitment of myself at that time, which I had designedly, and I hope with some sense of responsibility to the Redeemer, abstained from previously making. However, to do everything in my power to satisfy the Judge, I wrote in his house in New York a declaration . . . relative to my intentions of returning to India. At the moment of writing that declaration, the probability of my return, which had been in a fluctuating state before and has been in a fluctuating state since, was as strong as it had been, perhaps at any moment from the sitting of the Convention till that

time. Still I conceived it proper, and continue of the same opinion, to insert an express reservation, leaving the final decision to be predicated on my own views of duty, declaring in substance, simply that it was my intention to return to India, whenever "in my view" it should be my duty to do so.

The Judge immediately pointed out the clause "in my view" as being the only part with which the clamorous persons before alluded to were to be able to find fault. I remarked that it was not possible for me to omit that. He allowed that consistently I could not; and pronounced the whole "amply sufficient". . . .

Dr. Staughton did indeed suggest the propriety of introducing an expression of respect for the Board to which I consented—so that it should read "in my view and that of the Board;" but this obviously does not alter either the character or amount of the reservation. It still does not require me to go on account of its being the view of the Board unless it were also "my view," that it was duty to do so. This merely combines with the express reservation a sentiment of respect due to the Board and could not surely render the whole less acceptable to Judge Tallmadge. . . . I have written to the Judge on the subject to which he has not deigned to reply—at least none has been received. . . .[15]

SECOND MEETING OF THE TRIENNIAL

The time for the second meeting of the Triennial Convention was approaching, and Furman wrote to his old friend Edmund Botsford,

I think it will be an important meeting in its consequences as well as in its nature: either for forwarding the mission and giving rise to other undertakings highly interesting to our churches, and the cause of God; or else of laying a foundation for discord and discouragement among the Baptist churches. . . . I fear that at Philadelphia there is a source of evil which is likely to spread its baneful influence far. In fact I fear that Satan has taken some of our brethren there in a snare, in a manner that they are not sensible of, and that their views and feelings respecting some particular things, excite them to say and do, what is directly contrary to the best interest of religion, and their own true

---

[15]Luther Rice to Richard Furman, 20 March 1817, SCBHS, cited in H. T. Cook, *Biography*, 99.

renown, and Dr. Holcombe has now published a pamphlet against the Philadelphia Association; and churches are likely to form into parties. [16]

Botsford had apparently already learned of the problem in a letter from William Rogers and from an earlier brief reference to it contained in a letter from Furman. To Botsford, Rogers had written,

> The report of the Missionary Board is among many other things a cause of uneasiness among us: it was drawn up by Mr. Rice, except the address by Dr. Staughton, never submitted to the Committee and of course never adopted by the Board; it is probably Mr. Rice's report. We have become a divided Board . . . and without divine interposition, the whole thing bids fair to come to nothing. Such coolness is already produced among the members as a majority or minority that all confidence in one another is gone. [17]

Commenting on this information, Botsford expressed his sorrow to Furman that "misunderstanding should have taken place among those concerned in missionary affairs," and added, "Do my good brother seek, seek heartily for reconciliation. 'Blessed are the peacemakers, for they shall be called the children of God.' I can contribute nothing but my prayers, these you shall have. . . ." [18] As for his own views, Botsford had stronger words.

> To me it has an awful appearance to see those who ought to set the best example, setting the worst. I am very apprehensive Dr. H. is at the bottom of all this disturbance. I received a letter the other day from Dr. Staughton. He says the man from Georgia is trying to rend all that do not bow to him, or words to that import. We Baptists are like

---

[16]Richard Furman to Edmund Botsford, 14 January 1817, SCBHS, cited in H. T. Cook, *Biography*, 99.

[17]Contained in a letter from Edmund Botsford to Richard Furman, original in SCBHS.

[18]Ibid.

the Arabians, against every man, and every man against us, yea we exceed, we are against ourselves.[19]

The names of neither Holcombe nor Rogers appear as delegates to the second meeting of the Convention, or as members of the Board. Both had apparently resigned or been manipulated off as fractious elements standing in the way of convention harmony. Rogers had indicated early in 1816 that he was considering resigning and had so indicated to Furman. Always the balance wheel and harmonizing influence among disparate brethren, Furman had urged him not to turn back "having put your hand to the plow." He added, "I trust the Cause is the Cause of God, and that he will bless those who steadily pursue it in the Gospel Spirit."[20] But Furman's advice, to his regret, was not heeded. When the Board of Managers met in New York in 1816, the rupture between it and Rogers and Holcombe apparently reached a climax that terminated their connection with it. This had been conveyed to Furman by William Staughton. He, in turn, wrote to Judge Tallmadge, "Suppose from Dr. S's representation, that Dr. Holcombe must not only be considered as lost to the Board for the time to come; but as standing in opposition; and perhaps Dr. Rogers also. This is to be lamented, on their own account, if not from other consideration."[21] The propensity for Baptists to disagree, sometimes disagreeably, is written in their history.

The Convention assembled at Staughton's Sanson Street Church for its second meeting on 7 May 1817, and Furman was again elected president. Represented were forty societies, two associations, and one church. To those represented at the Convention could be added one hundred and eighty-seven other societies spread through the several states. Despite the Board's internal strife, the itinerant services of Rice in organizing missionary societies had met with signal success, and the mood of the Convention was upbeat. "The Convention has cause for rejoicing in observing that the support necessary to carry their objectives into full effect, has increased with each succeeding year," William

---

[19]Edmund Botsford to John M. Roberts, SCBHS.

[20]Richard Furman to William Rogers, 18 March 1816, SCBHS.

[21]Richard Furman to Judge Tallmadge, 7 July 1816, SCBHS.

Staughton trumpeted in a message directed to the delegates, "the Associations, Mission Societies, Churches, and religious public throughout the United States."[22] With Furman presiding in a way that won plaudits for "the able and impartial manner in which he has fulfilled the duties of the chair,"[23] the Convention met from the seventh to the fourteenth of May in sessions unmarred by the acrimony he had feared.

In their Address to the Convention, the Board acknowledged having experienced "much embarrassment and obstruction" in the discharge of their duties—an obvious reference to Holcombe and Rogers. It also requested an investigation of their conduct to determine the sentiments of the body whether they should be supported or censured. For that purpose Furman named a committee of seven shrewdly chosen men, with consideration for impartiality and geography: Jesse Mercer, Georgia, chairman; Daniel Sharp, Boston, secretary; John Peck, New York; George Roberts, North Carolina; Archibald Maclay, New York City; William Warder, Kentucky; and Edward Baptist, Virginia. Following their investigation, Mercer reported that their unanimous judgment was that "the Board deserve the explicit approbation and thanks of the Convention for their zealous and unremitting labours," and added, "Your committee are sensible of the embarrassments which have impeded the operations of the Board, and cannot but view, with regret and disapprobation the measures which have been taken by certain individuals to impair the public confidence, and repress the missionary spirit which has been so happily and extensively excited."

At a meeting of the Board following Convention adjournment, the matter came up again—this time in a letter addressed by Rice to the Convention and referred by that body to the Board. In it he solicited "the deliberate sense of the body" on the relations between the Board and himself, and its attitude respecting his return to the mission field. For the consideration of these matters, Furman, Staughton, and Baldwin were named as a committee to make recommendations. Their report was unequivocal. Rice should not, "as yet," rejoin Judson, and should be continued "as agent of the Board in the United States." Fur-

---

[22]*Proceedings*, Triennial Convention, 1817.

[23]Ibid.

man, Staughton, and Mercer were then named "to confer with him, relative to the direction of his ensuing labors."[24]

Thereafter, whether or not Rice should return to the foreign mission field became academic. His problems with the Board were temporarily removed by the departure of Rogers and Holcombe, but a new one arose in which Furman would be more personally and directly involved—one that would create more difficulties for convention leaders and carry over into the fortunes of Columbian College.

COLUMBIAN COLLEGE

The origin of Columbian College can be traced to Furman's educational emphasis as president of the Triennial Convention. Near the close of the second meeting of the convention in 1817, he delivered a presidential address in which he proposed the establishment of a national seminary of learning "at some convenient and central situation" and "as soon as a sufficient fund shall be obtained for this purpose." It was a bold dream based on practical considerations. The most obvious "convenient and central" location was the nation's capital, then a young and small but rapidly growing city with outstanding advantages. Already it had educational, cultural, and medical facilities that could be turned to the institution's advantage. Both Rice and Furman knew this, as did others among Baptist leaders. Moreover, Rice's extensive travels before and after the 1814 organizational meeting of the Triennial Convention had aroused in him the type of educational interest that had long been a primary concern of Furman. Indeed, it is not improbable that the importance of ministerial education may have been impressed upon him for the first time in 1813 at the Charleston associational meeting when he became acquainted with Furman's plan for the General Committee of the Charleston Association initiated in 1791.[25]

For financing the proposed institution, Furman laid before the Convention, "in a speech of considerable length, and great interest,"[26] a plan quite similar to the Charleston plan, which had been in operation

---

[24]Ibid.

[25]Baker and Craven, *The First 300 Years of First Baptist Church*, 237.

[26]*Proceedings*, Triennial Convention, 1817.

for twenty-six years. It proposed that "Baptist churches throughout the United States, and their adherents . . . form themselves into education societies, for the purpose of aiding pious young men of their connexion who appear on good evidence to be called of God to the gospel ministry, in obtaining such education as may fit them for extensive usefulness . . ."; that "a charity sermon be preached once a year, at least, in each church," with the money obtained to be placed in a common fund of the association, or a number of associations; that "part of the monies (say a third part) be conveyed to a General Fund under the care of the Board of Commissioners of the Triennial Convention for the establishment and support of a national theological seminary"; and with the further provision that "as soon as a sufficient fund shall be obtained for this purpose, the Board of Commissioners shall take measures for establishing . . . a Theological Seminary and Library, under the care of learned, pious professors; in which theology shall be studied in its various branches, church history, the Hebrew language, and other oriental languages, the knowledge of which is favourable to a right understanding of the sacred scriptures, as far as the same may be found practical and convenient, together with biblical criticism and pulpit eloquence."[27] The plan envisioned a central school in the nation's capital and eventually feeder schools or academies in each of the states.[28]

Furman's plan was approved by a committee of the Board, and the Convention itself amended its constitution to read: "That when competent and distinct funds shall have been received for the purpose, the Board, from these, without resorting at all to the mission funds, shall proceed to institute a Classical and Theological Seminary, for the purpose of aiding pious young men, who, in the judgment of the churches of which they are members, and of the Board, possess gifts and graces suited to the Gospel ministry." The qualifying phrase—"when competent and distinct funds shall have been received"—would become a cause for division among leaders of the Board and the Convention.

The earnestness of Furman and the practicality of his plan made a profound impression upon the delegates. In its annual report following a meeting in April 1818, the Board said, "The manner in which this

---

[27]The full text of Furman's plan may be found in Appendix D.

[28]Kinlaw, "Richard Furman as a Leader in Baptist Higher Education," 80.

duty (the education of youth) was pressed upon the Convention by the venerated President, at its last session, will not soon be forgotten. All that zeal for the honour of God and the prosperity of the churches, all that correct conception, impressive eloquence and decision of feeling could suggest, were employed to arouse the minds of the brethren to this necessary measure."[29]

But the Convention did not then officially adopt Furman's proposed financial plan, nor one equally practical, as a recommendation to the churches; for this he was disappointed. In June 1818, he wrote to a Board member in Rhode Island,

> I am pleased that a spirit of Zeal in favour of Educational Societies has been awakened in many places in the northern states. I think I see . . . cause for lamenting that the Convention did not agree definitely on a Plan for this Purpose, and recommend it to our churches and the Public, at their session last year. I am told that Episcopalians of high standing in their Connection, have not hesitated to declare that they were induced to undertake the Establishment of a Theological Seminary among themselves, in the consequence of our proposing it in our convention. They came immediately forward with their Plan; and probably, have obtained Thousands of Dollars which might have come to us had we been equally decided in our Measures.[30]

Still another matter troubled Furman. His concentration was upon a single seminary centrally located to serve all Baptists from Maine to Georgia, with special emphasis upon theological education. Any diversion of funds or effort from that objective he viewed with concern. He saw such a diversion in a proposed seminary for Maine. "I fear two things respecting this scheme," he wrote. "First, that it will make a diversion unfavorable to the Plan of having a general Theological Institution among the Baptists in the United States; and secondly, that it will finally sink or prove abortive, for want of sufficient support."[31] For the same reasons, he rejected the idea of a similar plan for three

---

[29]*Fourth Annual Report of the Baptist Board of Foreign Missions for the United States*, 1818, American Baptist Historical Society, Rochester, New York.

[30]Richard Furman to Barnabas Bates, 11 June 1818, SCBHS.

[31]Ibid.

Southern states—Georgia, South Carolina, and North Carolina. Encouraged by the offer of five thousand dollars promised by an unnamed Baptist, a proposal for uniting "the Funds and Exertions of different Bodies" in those states had been submitted to him for consideration. "I have been this Day putting my negative on the question, founded on the reasons I have assigned, for my Fear, in the Case of our Brethren in the Province of Maine."[32]

While putting the "negative" on these diversionary proposals, the Board was acting in advance of convention authority. Since 1813 the Philadelphia Education Society and the New York Education Society had been operating a small seminary at Philadelphia under the supervision of William Staughton. In August 1818 representatives of these societies met in New York and agreed to cooperate in a seminary of the General Convention. By vote of the Convention's Board, the Philadelphia seminary became the official seminary of the Convention, with Staughton as principal and the Reverend Ira Chase as professor of languages and biblical literature.[33]

This beginning was but a prelude to what would follow. Without waiting for Convention approval, or even that of the Board, Rice engaged with three others—Obadiah Brown, pastor of the Baptist church in Washington; Spencer H. Cone; and Enoch Reynolds—to purchase forty-six and one-half acres of land near the White House in Washington, at a cost of six thousand dollars, "for the use of a college, and of a Theological institution under the direction of the General Missionary Convention of the Baptist Denomination in the United States."[34] In a letter to his brother shortly thereafter, Rice said, "We have at present, fifteen students at Philadelphia, in a course of education suited to the ministry, and have bought a piece of land near the city of Washington, on which to place buildings to accommodate the institution. My poor hands are more than full, but I hope much good will be done."[35] In his report to the Convention in May 1820, he referred to the matter as follows.

---

[32]Ibid.

[33]*Fourth Annual Report of the Board*, 1818.

[34]Taylor, *Memoir of Rev. Luther Rice*, 185.

[35]Ibid.

It has afforded me no small pleasure to find it convenient, incidentally to other matters on hand, to bestow some attention on the subject of providing at Washington, a site for the institution to promote the education of the ministry, and ultimately for the foundation of a college, under the direction of the general convention. Considerations of no ordinary influence, induced the brethren Brown, Cone, Reynolds, and myself to open a subscription paper for this purpose. The success has amply justified our calculations.

To pay for the ground, or lot of 46 1/2 acres, to erect a building—to endow a professorship, and for some other points in the general concern, nearly $10,000 have already been subscribed, and part of it paid. This being the result of the incidental attention of an individual, with comparatively little aid from others, and that too, for but little more than half a year, demonstrates the practicability of accomplishing a most important object in a short time. . . . A building has already been commenced, 116 by 47, which will contain rooms enough to accommodate from eighty to one hundred students. It only wants the countenance of the convention, with the blessing of heaven, to insure complete success.[36]

These developments astonished Furman. Opening a seminary, employing a faculty, buying land for two schools in Washington, and taking similar initiatives without securing the approval of the General Convention he believed to be serious mistakes.[37] In a postscript to his letter of 11 June 1818 to Barnabas Bates, written after receiving a copy of the *Latter Day Luminary*[38] and the Fourth Annual Report of the Board of Missions, Furman wrote,

I have read with astonishment that the officers of the Theological Institution are already appointed, and, consequently, that the Institution itself has been established; though no previous information had

---

[36]Ibid., 185-86.

[37]Baker and Craven, *The First 300 Years of First Baptist Church*, 235.

[38]*The Latter Day Luminary* was a missionary publication initiated by Rice for circulating missionary information and keeping constituents of the Convention and its Board of Missions informed of the work of these agencies. Published five times a year, it emanated from Philadelphia, the seat of the Convention.

been given to the Public of the Principles and Regulations of the Plan committed by the Convention to the care and superior wisdom of the Board, nor of the plan they mean to pursue; no measure taken to collect a Fund; to obtain the sense of the Churches; nor even, as I suppose, of the distant members of the Board, respecting the Place, Time, or Manner of forming and organizing the Seminary.[39]

This hasty and unauthorized action by the Board offended Furman's sense of propriety, his practical business judgment, and his experience in collecting funds for education. To Bates he said, "I am indeed a short-sighted, and very imperfect Creature, but I fear the Measures we have taken in this important Business will either render it abortive, or prove so embarrassing, that it will be with much Difficulty anything useful will be affected. As to our Reputation, I fear that is already gone; and that we shall be set down in the Ranks of Children."[40]

This was a traumatic time for Furman. In addition to burdens as president of the Triennial Convention and concern over the action of the Convention's Board of Managers, the death of his wife, Dolly, left him a widower for the second time. She was forty-six years of age at the time of her death on 22 March 1819 and had borne him thirteen children, "all of whom, notwithstanding the delicacy of her constitution, were in their infancy, nourished exclusively at her bosom."[41]

When the Special Committee of the Charleston Association met in Charleston on 12 April 1819, less than two weeks after the death of his wife, Furman presented a document expressing his and the committee's strong opposition to the Board's action. Containing a lengthy set of eleven resolutions approved by the committee, the document voiced the "decided opinion" that no authority had been granted the Board to establish a theological institution until "competent and distinct funds" for that purpose had been obtained, and that any attempt to "make such an establishment, by the election of officers, etc., before such competent funds have been received must be considered not only as premature but as amounting to a nullity." It further advised that involving the

---

[39]Richard Furman to Barnabas Bates, 11 June 1818, SCHBS.

[40]Ibid.

[41]*South Carolina Historical and Genealogical Magazine* 46 (January 1945): 20.

churches in a concerted plan of giving to support the institution was a matter of the "highest importance," and that the plan Furman placed before the Convention at its last meeting had been in successful operation in the Charleston Association "for near thirty years, and has been proved, by time and experience, to be well adapted to accomplish the beneficial purposes for which it was formed."[42] When carried before the Association at its annual meeting, the resolutions received unanimous endorsement.

Not since Furman had addressed dissident residents between the Broad and Saluda rivers on the subject of American independence had he asserted himself more forcefully than in this set of resolutions. He advised suspension of operations until a sufficient fund had been provided and "while wise, firm and dignified measures of preparatory nature are pursued," and further, that the Board of Commissioners "defer establishing the Theological Seminary till the meeting of the Convention in 1820, even though respectable contributions to the fund should be found to have been made by the time of their nearly approaching meeting. . . ."

In the meantime, Furman had written to Staughton lamenting the hasty action, and Thomas Baldwin of Boston, as influential in the North as Furman was in the South, wrote to Rice in November 1819.

> I have been advised of Dr. Furman's dissatisfaction, with the proceeding relative to the Institution. . . . It must be evident to Dr. F. and to every other person upon the slightest observation, that the Institution was not set in motion in conformity to the principle established by the Convention: viz: "When competent and distinct funds shall have been raised for the purpose,—the Board will proceed to institute a Classical and Theological Seminary"—and it will not be pretended that competent funds distinctly assigned for that object had been raised. . . . This hasty, unauthorized procedure is probably the ground of Dr. Furman's objections. . . .[43]

---

[42]H. T. Cook, *Biography*, 107-12; full text of the document may be found in Appendix E.

[43]Thomas Baldwin to Luther Rice, 22 November 1819, New York Historical Society, New York City, cited in Thompson, *Luther Rice: Believer in Tomorrow*, 165-66.

Confronted with such protests, the Board postponed any further ac-
tion until the Convention assembled in 1820. With eighty-five dele-
gates present representing Massachusetts, Connecticut, New York, New
Jersey, Pennsylvania, Delaware, Maryland, Virginia, South Carolina,
North Carolina, Georgia, Kentucky, Mississippi, and the District of
Columbia, the Convention met on 26 April in the meetinghouse of
Philadelphia's Sanson Street Baptist Church. As he had for the two ear-
lier meetings, Furman, then in his sixty-fourth year, had come up from
Charleston, probably in one of the packets plying the coastal waters.

In the opening paragraphs of its report to the Convention, the Board
turned to the subject of the seminary. Referring to Furman's plan presented in 1817, the report read,

> The "Plan" submitted to the Convention was referred to a com-
> mittee of the Board, who, after a delay of twelve months, stated in
> their report, that "they approve, in the main, highly of the Plan the
> President proposed, and are of the opinion that it will, ultimately, in
> substance, probably in a few years, be found in successful operation."
> They, however, stated that "until it can be accomplished; and for its
> accomplishment very ample funds must be obtained; something may
> be done that will prepare the way for more comprehensive mea-
> sures."[44]

The "something" was an apparent reference to the action of the Board
in bringing Staughton's modest Philadelphia seminary under the aegis
of the Convention, and justification for it as a first step toward the goal
of a general theological institution. In a summary of the Board's action
since its previous annual meeting, Robert B. Semple, erudite historian
of Virginia Baptists, reported that eighteen men were already pursuing
their studies, that the recommended location of Washington as a permanent site had many advantages which should "operate as a means of
general union and harmony to our churches," and that the Board had
interpreted "competent and distinct funds" to mean funds "distinct from
those collected for missionary purposes."[45]

---

[44]*Proceedings*, Triennial Convention, 1820.

[45]Ibid.

Furman was still a highly respected leader of American Baptists, but he did not dominate this convention as he did the ones in 1814 and 1817. It was evident from the time the convention began that his make-haste-slowly policy in establishing the seminary was not the majority opinion. Despite the reasoned logic of the remonstrance from the Charleston Association and its Special Committee, as well as objections from other sources, Rice and the Board had done their work so well that there was almost universal approval for the steps that had been taken for adopting Staughton's Philadelphia school as a preparatory step toward what would become Columbian College in Washington, and for confirming acquisition of the Washington site for the college.

As chairman of the committee on education, Furman presented to the Convention a report recommending (1) the basic elements of the plan he had submitted in 1817 and (2) the formation of state conventions or the uniting of associations to establish broad, ground-level financial support for the institution. Together, they projected the essence of his philosophy for the success of the institution; first, that the Convention seriously address itself to its constituents on the importance of education, "with a view of producing excitement to united and vigorous exertions for the attainment of the proposed end," and, second, that "a plan of concert" be adopted to unite efforts throughout the denomination for collecting funds to be applied to missionary and educational purposes.[46]

LITERARY AND THEOLOGICAL SCHOOL APPROVED

The plan approved by the Convention came from Washington pastor Obadiah Brown's committee on finances. It recommended an institution for both literary and theological studies in Washington, approved the prior purchase of the forty-six acres, and directed the Board to "take measures, as soon as convenient, for obtaining legal title to the same. . . ."[47] The plan also suggested that the institution be removed from Philadelphia to Washington, "as soon as suitable accommodations be prepared," and that "sundry persons be employed to go out

---

[46]Furman's Report to the Convention on the Subject of Education, ibid.

[47]Obadiah B. Brown's Report to the Convention on Behalf of a Committee of the Board Concerning Financing, *Proceedings*, Triennial Convention, 1820.

under the authority of this Convention to collect funds for aiding the
education fund."[48] The latter provision was the Convention's nearest
approach to Furman's plan for "producing excitement to united and
vigorous exertions" on behalf of education, but it fell far short of his
basic recommendations.

Furman was not reelected Convention president, not, perhaps, because he supported a plan of education rejected by the Convention, but
because he considered the Board's action too precipitous. The seminary
itself in such a central location as Washington had been his long-stand-
ing vision. He could see it becoming a national center for theological
studies, with feeder institutions in several states. But he was wise and
experienced enough to know that strong financial underpinnings would
be essential to success, and that the only way to insure this was to make
dreams conform to budget limitations.

AUSPICIOUS BEGINNING

The institution could scarcely have had a more auspicious beginning. The theological department opened in the fall of 1821, and the
classical department was added in 1822. In its seventh annual report,
presented in 1821, the Board reported in heady language that at a
meeting in Washington in March for organizing the college, ". . . it
was gratifying, in a high degree, to behold, on one of the most beautiful and commanding sites in the metropolis of the union, a substantial
brick edifice, of 117 feet in front by 47 feet in depth, completely covered in, a large part of the interior carpentry finished, and the whole
promising in a short time to become a nursery of science and of ministerial talent, which shall diffuse its blessings not only around the district of Columbia, but through every section of the United States, and,
by the agency of christian missionaries, to the uttermost parts of the
earth."[49]

In January 1822 there were thirty-three students, and by October
there were forty-six; two years later, in April 1824, there were ninety-

---

[48]Ibid.

[49]*Annual Report of the Board of Managers of the General Convention of the Baptist Denomination in the United States*, 1821, American Baptist Historical Society, Rochester,
New York.

three. They represented twenty-one of the twenty-four states. In 1822 the trustees reported, "Every circumstance indicates the hand of God in all our operations. Daily inquiry shows that this College is becoming a subject of general notoriety, and encourages the hope that it will rapidly extend its usefulness, and obtain, at no distant day, much greater patronage than the hopes of its friends had anticipated."[50] Encouragement came from the highest officials in the land. President James Monroe wished the college well in March 1821,

> The establishment of the institution within the federal district, in the presence of Congress, and of all the departments of the government, will secure to the young men who may be educated in it many important advantages; among which the opportunity which it will afford them of hearing the debates in Congress, and in the Supreme Court, on important subjects, must be obvious to all. With these peculiar advantages, this institution, if it receives hereafter the proper encouragement, cannot fail to be eminently useful to the nation. Under this impression, I trust that such encouragement shall not be withheld from it.[51]

When the Convention met in Washington in 1823, it obtained an audience with President Monroe in the White House and received from him in warmest terms his "great interest and satisfaction" in the development of such educational institutions.[52]

But as early as January 1822, when student enrollment was on the rise and the future of the institution appeared rosy, Furman's fear for its future was gaining substance. The financial load that had been assumed was already casting a cloud. Though then no larger than a man's hand, the debt would grow and grow until the wisdom of Furman became universally apparent.

---

[50]*Minutes of the Board*, 1822.

[51]James Monroe to Obadiah Brown, President of the Board of Trustees, 24 March 1821, *American Baptist Magazine*, vol. 3, James P. Boyce Library, Southern Baptist Theological Seminary.

[52]The Convention's address to the President and his address, in turn, to the Convention may be found in the proceedings of the 1822 Convention.

MOUNTING CRISIS

By the time of the 1823 Triennial, general knowledge prevailed that the college was heavily in debt, and a committee was appointed to "investigate the concerns of Columbian College." Their report showed that the "trustees stated expenditure of $70,000 and debt of $30,000," but in an appendage that only the sanguine Rice could have worded, they added that "all things coming to the college would liquidate the debt."[53]

By 1826 the college was so overwhelmed with debts that Rice apparently used some of the Convention's mission funds to support it, an act clearly prohibited by the action of the Convention in establishing the school. For this he and the denomination were severely criticized. Convention funds were also drawn upon to support Rice's journalistic enterprises—*The Latter Day Luminary* and *The Columbian Star*. He had established *The Latter Day Luminary* in 1818 as the missionary monthly published by the Convention, and later, in Washington, at his own expense, he established *The Columbian Star* as a religious weekly. The objective of the two publications was to mold and unite Baptist public opinion in support of denominational missionary and educational enterprises. He had hoped that proceeds from the *Star* and the *Luminary* would be enough to pay more than their way from their subscription lists and the interest generated in the objectives of the Convention. But in this, as in other things, he was overly optimistic.

"Now is the time," Rice wrote from Augusta, Georgia, in July 1826, "for every possible effort to be made. It is a great crisis. The reputation of the whole baptist denomination is deeply concerned. I wish it were possible for me to express the intenseness of my feelings on the subject."[54] The yellow pages of his journal remain today to testify to the ardor of his labors. His summary of the four months of his travels during the same year that the headquarters of the Convention were moved from Philadelphia to Washington illustrates his efforts at all times. He "travelled 6,600 miles in populous and dreary portions of the

---

[53]*American Baptist Magazine*, 140, cited in Thompson, *Luther Rice: Believer in Tomorrow*, 169.

[54]Luther Rice to Iverson L. Brooks, original copy in William R. Perkins Library, Duke University, Durham, North Carolina.

country, through wilderness and over rivers, across mountains and valleys, in heat and cold, by day and night, in weariness, painfulness, fastings, and loneliness, but not a moment lost for want of health; no painful calamity has befallen my lot; no peril has closed upon me nor has fear been permitted to prey upon my spirits nor even inquietude to disturb my peace."[55]

Before the crisis had reached its zenith, the theological school was turned over to the Massachusetts Baptist Education Society. With the cooperation of other New England states, the Society hoped to provide permanent maintenance. Newton Theological Institution, which subsequently merged with Andover Seminary to form Andover Newton Theological School, thus had its beginning.

The objection to diverting missionary funds to educational purposes was so deep that in 1826 the Convention considered it advisable to separate itself as much as possible from Columbian College, leaving as its only connection the right of nominating fifty persons from whom the trustees would be chosen.[56] In 1827 Rice resigned as treasurer and general agent of the college; he was joined by the entire faculty and part of the trustees. The school operated as a private college until 1898 when it reverted to the Baptist denomination for a period of six years. An act of Congress in 1904 restored its secular status and changed its name to George Washington University, as it is known today. Because Rice was the principal agent of the school and its chief promoter, criticism for its failure fell heaviest upon him. But conditions beyond his control were contributing factors—like the financial panic of 1819 and the depression that followed, the rising tide of opposition to cooperative efforts in missions and education, and divisions in the leadership of the Board.[57] Albert B. Newman records a judgment of Rice now widely held.

> It was commonly agreed that Rice was among the most unselfish men, but was lacking in business capacity and had allowed himself to plan expenditures on a scale far beyond what prudence would have dictated. The accounts of receipts and expenditures were very loosely

---

[55]Weaver, "The Place of Luther Rice in American Baptist Life," 139-40.

[56]Newman, *History of the Baptist Churches in the United States*, 400.

[57]Baker and Craven, *The First 300 Years of First Baptist Church*, 406.

kept, and it was not easy to determine precisely what funds had been given for missions and education respectively. Some were so uncharitable as to suspect Rice and others of a dishonest use of funds; but he showed his disinterested devotion to the cause by giving into the funds of the college not only the money he had been able to save during the twelve years of arduous service at a salary of $400 a year, but also a patrimony of $2000 or $3000. Removed from the responsible agency, he continued till his death, in 1836, to labor assiduously, without remuneration, for the institution that he loved, and when dying requested that his horse and buggy, his only possessions, be sent to the agent of the college.[58]

Rufus W. Weaver wrote of Rice in glowing terms: "He had given his strength, his exceptional talents, his powers of persuasion and his ability to plan, all that he had been able to make and all that he had inherited from his family, to promote the causes that increased the strength and extended the influence of the Baptists of America. No man ever served us so faithfully or gave to us so gladly his all."[59]

Furman would have agreed with these assessments. Both men saw the need for the kind of Baptist educational institution implicit in Columbian College, and both felt that Washington was the proper site. However, Furman thought as a pragmatist, Rice as an idealist. It was an honest disagreement over procedure: They disagreed on how and when to establish the school. Rice rushed in precipitously and obtained the approval of the Convention. Furman advised cautious procedure until the support and resources of the denomination had been marshaled and organized to provide the financial underpinning. The difference lay also in the basic structure of associations in support of multi-benevolent causes. The Convention had been organized as a foreign mission society dependent upon separate and independent auxiliary societies without cohesive strength. There was no center of gravity to pull the whole denomination together in a concerted plan.

LOYALTY OF FURMAN

Despite his objection to the structural form assumed by the Convention and its action in respect to Columbian College, Furman knew

[58]Newman, *History of the Baptist Churches in the United States*, 399-400.

[59]Weaver, "The Place of Luther Rice in American Baptist Life," 144.

the meaning of the democratic spirit and embraced it. He worked within the system as it was formed and gave his best to it. The rejection of his leadership caused no bitterness or reluctance to cooperate in working for success. When the constitution of the South Carolina State Baptist Convention was adopted in 1821, the spirit of Furman shone in Article III.

> In what relates to education, and particularly to the gratuitous education of indigent, pious young men, designated for the gospel ministry, the organization and support of a seminary of learning in this state, under the care of the convention, *and on a plan of accordance with that of Washington {Columbian College},* under the patronage of the general convention, . . . shall be considered as a primary object.[60]

He showed the same spirit at the meeting of the Charleston Association at Camden in November 1820. Furman, elected moderator as usual, gave "an account of the views, spirit and proceedings of that venerable body [the Triennial Convention]," including plans approved for the theological school; and the Association, expressing its "high sense of the importance and usefulness of the measures adopted by the Convention," promised to promote them "to the best of its ability."[61] One year earlier, the Association had endorsed resolutions of its Special Committee protesting action by the Board of the Triennial Convention in exceeding its authority in the matter of a theological school. In this reversal, Furman's influence and counsel were clear. No matter how much he may have doubted the wisdom of the Convention's hasty action and how strongly he may have protested, when the vote was counted and the school became a reality, he gave his cooperation and advised the influential Charleston Association to do the same.

Still further evidence came in an address to South Carolina constituents following the 1820 meeting of the General Convention. The subject then was a proposed state convention for South Carolina Baptists. Under the care of such a convention, he pointed out that an academy might be formed for preparing students to enter Columbian College

---

[60]*Minutes of the South Carolina Baptist Convention,* 1821, SCBHS (italics mine).

[61]*Minutes of the Charleston Association,* 1820, SCBHS.

where the "general interests of the whole denomination, in the United States, are designed to be concentrated."[62]

Furman's death in 1825 removed him from the ill fortunes of Columbian College, but while he lived he supported its interests, and as president of the General Fund of the Charleston Association, he continued to send students there. He also remained a friend of Luther Rice. In 1823, when Rice was under heavy criticism concerning the handling of missionary and educational funds, the Charleston Association, with Furman in his next-to-last year as moderator, recorded in its minutes,

> We feel assured that the moneys collected under the patronage of the convention, are, and will be faithfully applied, to the objects for which they were intended: And we are gratified in learning that the Rev. Luther Rice, of whom jealousies and surmises, which appear to be without just foundation, have been propagated, is continued in the agency of the convention. His unwearied labours, and voluntary sacrifices in the cause of Christ, entitle him, in our opinion, to the best regards of his brethren.[63]

This statement was the mind of the Association asserting itself; but because Furman was the most influential member of that body and its moderator for twenty-five years, the statement also expressed his thoughts.

The same support for the college and belief in the integrity of its officers were expressed by Furman's son Josiah two years after Furman's death. Probably then a Charleston businessman, but later to become an ordained minister, Josiah replied, on behalf of the General Committee, to a letter from Columbian College regarding the account of a student attending the college under the fund of the Committee.

> I trust that the College will be sustained. . . . I have deeply regretted the dissensions which have found existence during the history of the Institution. They have given a handle to evil disposed persons to hurt the Christian name with disrespect—and I am sorry to say that Christians have been too free and unkind with the names and repu-

---

[62]*Minutes of the South Carolina Baptist Convention*, 1821, SCBHS.

[63]*Minutes of the Charleston Association*, 1823, SCBHS.

tations of their brethren. I consider it due to my own feelings to say that the more I reflect upon the subject the more I am convinced that there is nothing to justify suspicion of fraud or impurity of motive on either hand, other than, perhaps, the love of power and influence so inherent in the human heart. But the subject is unpleasant—May a brighter day dawn upon us at no distant hour.[64]

EDUCATIONAL WATERSHED

The educational thrust of the 1817 Triennial Convention, as embodied in the plan advanced by Furman, marked a watershed in American Baptist educational history. Within five years, five institutions that grew into Baptist colleges and seminaries were founded at Hamilton, New York, in 1819; Waterville, Maine, in 1820; Washington, D.C., in 1822; Georgetown, Kentucky, in 1824; and Newton, Massachusetts, in 1825. During the next ten years, five others were founded: Richmond College in Virginia, Wake Forest University in North Carolina, Furman University in South Carolina, Mercer University in Georgia, and New Hampton Institute in New Hampshire.[65]

Southern Baptist historian Robert A. Baker correctly declares that there is enough credit to memorialize all the leaders of the General Convention of 1817, but he adds,

> If any one person must be named, it can assuredly be none other than the pastor of the Charleston church. He was advocating ministerial education by denominational bodies before many of the leaders of the 1817 meeting were born or had attained maturity; he provided the pattern in his plan for the General Committee of the Charleston Association in 1791 that probably called the attention of Luther Rice to Baptist ministerial education for the first time in 1813; the Address to the Public by the committee of the General Convention in 1814, whether Furman's composition or that of someone else, bore his name and reflected his longtime interests; he presented the plan for the na-

---

[64]Josiah Furman to unidentified Columbian College official, 30 October 1827, George Washington University Papers.

[65]H. T. Cook, *Biography*, 104, citing William Cathcart, *Baptist Encyclopedia*, 2 vols. (Philadelphia: Louis Everts, 1883).

tional body's involvement in ministerial education in 1817; and his distinguished character and leadership moved the General Convention in the direction of making it a multi-benevolent body by including ministerial education and domestic missions in its structure. When his influence was removed, the General Convention promptly resumed its character as a foreign mission society only. . . .[66]

Furman's distinguished son, James C. Furman, added his testimony in discussing the history of the First Baptist Church of Charleston.

> . . . the widespread interest in denominational education which shows itself now among our brethren of the North had a Southern origin. There was no Newton, no Rochester, no Hamilton in 1814 when the Missionary Convention was held in Philadelphia. . . . [T]he President [Richard Furman in 1817] was asked to address the assembled delegates on a subject which he held to be of vital importance. From a heart surcharged with concern on the subject of education, especially that of the rising ministry, he made an address, the effect of which was powerful and instantaneous. From [that] day a great idea was born in the Baptist public mind. . . .[67]

Furman's dream of a central theological institution in Washington, with institutions preparatory to it in several states, fell victim to the failure of Columbian College. But inspired by his leadership, the basic dream remained, and while he lived he was the consistent shaper of the form it would take in years after his own life.

---

[66]Baker and Craven, *The First 300 Years of First Baptist Church*, 407-408.

[67]H. T. Cook, *Education in South Carolina Under Baptist Control*, 34.

CHAPTER 10

Family Man,
Minister,
and Citizen

During the middle years of the eighteenth century, when Charleston was under royal rule, the city was a crossroads of trade and a center of British commerce. When vessels left England, they generally caught the trade winds around the Azores, then made for the West Indies, thence sailing into the Gulf Stream and hugging the American coast past Cape Hatteras before veering off to England and northern Europe. Charleston's position on the western edge of this great sailing circle contributed to her prominence and prosperity in the world of trade. This was the Charleston of Furman's early pastorate in that city.

But the later years were marked by change. An era of booming economic expansion that began in the early eighteenth century was followed in the 1820s by economic depression and by sectionalism that gave birth to a nullification crisis. Between these eras was Charleston's golden age. Between them also, its greatness rose, flourished, and declined.

For Furman, these were years of rich experience as pastor, preacher, denominational leader, citizen, husband, and father. By the end of this period his family had grown to fifteen children, two of them, Rachel

and Wood, by his first wife. The first five children born to him and
Dolly were boys—Richard, Samuel, John Gano, Josiah, and Charles—
all born between the years 1790 and 1797. Their first daughter, Maria
Dorothea, was followed by Henry Hart, Sarah Susannah, another son
named John Gano (the first John Gano died in infancy), Thomas Fuller,
James Clement, Anne Eliza, and William Brantly. A large number of
progeny was the best assurance of a continuing family line and a safeguard against family decimation by the violence of disease, fires, hur-
ricanes, and war.

Furman was never happier than when he was surrounded by his
family in their home at 94 Church Street.[1] Returning to them and the
church of his pastorate was always his fondest wish when away on his
travels. To this his letters furnish ample testimony, such as this one
written from Richmond en route to the Triennial Convention of 1814.

> I hope, my dear Dolly, that the Lord will preserve and bless you,
> and all our dear children. . . . Repeated accounts of Death from
> Charleston, in the short time since I left it, and in the circle of our
> particular Connexion . . . produce particular anxiety respecting you,
> our Children, and surviving Friends. . . . I hope Woody and Richard,
> as well as yourself, will write to me. To Woody and his family, to
> Richard . . . Josiah, Charles, Maria, and each of the younger Chil-
> dren, give my special Love. Tell Susan that I hope she goes well with
> her Grammar; and Henry, John and Thomas, that I shall hope to find
> that they attend well with their Books; and tell my little James and
> Ann, that I long to have them on my knee.[2]

---

[1]The Furmans probably lived at only two places in Charleston between 1787 and
1825. The 1790 city directory lists their residence as 19 Church Street, which would
correspond with the site of the church building at 61-63 Church Street. The 1819
city directory lists 117 Church Street as the Furman residence. This is now known as
94 Church Street. The move to this location probably occurred to make way for the
new church building erected during the latter part of Furman's pastorate. See *Dr.
Richard Furman's Residences, A Research Report Prepared by Mr. Robert Stockton for the First
Baptist Church of Charleston, April, 1982*, SCBHS.

[2]Richard Furman to Dorothea Maria Furman, 5 May 1814, SCBHS.

A charming vignette of life within the Furman family and of a child's love for her father is contained in a letter written by sixteen-year-old Sarah Susannah to a friend in Georgetown.

> Maria and myself since you left us have been so engaged first in making preparations for brother Richard's wedding and afterwards for Papa's voyage to Philadelphia [to attend the 1820 Triennial Convention] that we have scarcely had time to think of anything else until a few days past. Papa sailed yesterday morning about 9 o'clock. . . . I hope that he will have a pleasant passage, the weather has been delightful, and the wind quite fair since yesterday. You know by experience how painful it is to part with a dear Parent for a length of time. I felt very reluctant at the idea of Parting with Papa, though I wished him to go . . . .[3]

Among Furman's surviving letters to his children, those to his oldest son, Wood, make reference to Wood's plan to write a history of the Charleston Baptist Association. A graduate of Rhode Island College in 1799, Wood came home to Charleston, married Hannah Bowers on 30 December 1800,[4] and was hired as a schoolmaster in a private academy in 1803 when his wife's failing health required her to go to the New England climate. In November of that year Wood joined her at Sommerset, Rhode Island, near Providence, after leaving his school in charge of his cousin, James.[5] In Rhode Island he apparently both taught and wrote.

His principal writing project was the history of the Charleston Baptist Association. For this purpose he requested the minutes of the Association from his father. Furman replied, "I confess I feel a difficulty in committing the Association book to the danger of the seas, especially at this season of the year when the danger from boisterous weather and head winds is great." However, he added, "I will consider the matter a little more and perhaps send the books, as I would be sorry you should be prevented writing for want of them or fail to obtain the assistance

---

[3]Sarah Susannah Furman to Susan ?, 7 April 1820, SCBHS.

[4]*South Carolina Historical and Genealogical Magazine*, 26:236.

[5]Wood Furman to Sarah Haynsworth, 3 November 1803, SCBHS.

they would afford."[6] One month later, he had sent the minutes, but his anxiety for their safety was still present. "As I feel anxious about the Association record," he wrote, "I shall be glad to hear as soon as possible that it has arrived safely. Should it not I may be charged with using an unwarrantable liberty with it by trusting it to the danger of the seas."[7]

By the spring of 1808, Wood had completed his manuscript and forwarded it to his father for criticism and correction. Furman recorded his comments in a letter to Wood.

> I am in general pleased with it. . . . A few of the vacancies you had left I have filled in, particularly for the collections, dispersements, and amount of the [education] fund, and a sketch of Mr. Dargan's life and character. I should be sorry the publication should take place without a somewhat particular account of Mr. Reese. . . . I also think it would be proper to produce a more full account of Mr. Hart, Dr. Stillman, etc., and not let so much depend on the reference to other publications, some of which will never be seen by many who will read the history of the Association.[8]

The relationship between Furman and his children was a reflection of the Puritan qualities of the family background, with a strong emphasis upon his own religious values. He was the patriarchal figure who held the family together.[9] No one was in better position to know the family than Edmund Botsford. In a letter to Botsford, Furman, speaking of his family, had declared himself no apostle of draconian laws in parental matters, to which Botsford replied,

> I think there is a medium between severity and undue indulgence. I have in different families observed both severity and indulgence car-

---

[6]Richard Furman to Wood Furman, 11 January 1808, SCBHS.

[7]Richard Furman to Wood Furman, 12 February 1808, SCBHS.

[8]Richard Furman to Wood Furman, 5 May 1808, SCBHS.

[9]For a sketch of the family members, see Loulie Latimer Owens's charming family profile contained in her unpublished manuscript, *The Family of Richard Furman*, SCBHS.

ried to extremes and neither answers the purpose. I do not know if you my Brother have hit on the medium—but this I know, and it is with the greatest pleasure I think of it. I never observed in so large a family such affection to parents and to one another from the oldest to the youngest. As a citizen, he who raises such a number of orderly children, is in my opinion entitled to more respect and honour than any other character.[10]

Very little material remains to tell what Dolly was really like. References in Furman's correspondence indicate that she communicated with him faithfully during his absences from home, but only two of her letters have survived. Obviously, she had little time for writing, a fact painfully referred to by her mother, who lived in Georgia.

> Can you remember, my dear daughter, when you last wrote to your mother? Do you reflect for a moment if I were at a place two hundred miles from Maria and Susan should I not like them to write me oftener than once in a year, yea two years, yet this has almost been the case of somebody. If I were not as well assured of the affection of my Dorothea, there remains not the least doubt or jealousy on my mind respecting it, I should be very uncomfortable.

But having given this gentle rebuke, she adds, "I make all the apology I can for you, your being so closely engaged with so large a family and company, so many pressing demands upon your time, withal, delicate health, that if you have a leisure moment you require rest. Yet the tear will trickle down my furrowed cheek at not seeing that dear handwriting more frequent."[11]

Dolly appears to have been a gentle, patient woman of strong character, well qualified to manage the responsibilities of bearing and rearing a large family. Supervising servants, caring for shipments of cotton and supplies from the High Hills plantation, and seeing that returning wagons were laden with salt and bagging were some of her many responsibilities during her husband's absences. However, she apparently

---

[10]Edmund Botsford to Richard Furman, undated, SCBHS.

[11]Mary Glas Burn McDonald to Dorothea Maria Furman, 18 September 1816, SCBHS.

could not overcome a natural shyness, a characteristic noted by her mother, Mrs. McDonald, in a letter to Furman. A Mrs. Bird, a friend of Mrs. McDonald, had moved to Charleston and expected, but had not received, a visit from Dolly. In a letter to Furman, Mrs. McDonald requested that he convey "a few thoughts to my Dorothea." Tell her, she suggested, "to borrow a carriage, for the walk is too great, and call on her [Mrs. Bird] without delay," and tell her also to "try to set aside [her] natural diffidence and be quite sociable . . . not to be ceremonious" and not to "feel uneasy, if when anyone calls, [she is] not just as [she] wish[es] to be; never seem to mind, but be as cheery as possible and care not a fig about fears of remarks."[12]

Botsford admired Dolly deeply. "It is often said," he wrote to Furman, " 'a person must ask his wife if he may be rich,' intimating if she is not economical, nothing can be saved. So in the case of bringing up children if the mother does not act her part, all will not be right. In this you are happy. Mrs. F. has united with you in the pleasing yet arduous task. God indeed has been kind to you . . ."[13]

Her awareness of her impending death is reflected in an obituary that appeared first in the Charleston *City Gazette* and later in the *American Baptist Magazine,* published in Boston.

> During some of her last days, an affectionate farewell was taken of several pious friends, under the impression that they should meet no more on earth; of her children it was taken, individually, on the day of her departure, and united with parental counsels and tender pious wishes for their temporal and eternal welfare. It was extended to the servants. After this . . . she said but little; yet she joined in devotional exercises, expressed her humble hope, and solemnly resigned her soul into the hands of her Saviour and her God—and at 3 o'clock she ceased to breathe; without a struggle or a groan—experiencing one of the most gentle and peaceful dismissions from the frail body which are ever afforded to the immortal spirit of man.[14]

---

[12]Mary Glas Burn McDonald to Richard Furman, postmarked 4 March 1816, SCBHS.

[13]Edmund Botsford to Richard Furman, undated, SCBHS.

[14]A curious postscript to a letter written by one of Dolly's granddaughters de-

Outside his immediate family, Furman's love for his sister Sarah and hers for him is shown in their affectionate correspondence. Little is known, however, of the relationship between him and his brother Josiah. Josiah appears to have owned extensive property in the Camden and Charleston districts, and the few references to him in surviving letters are concerned chiefly with matters of business regarding the estate of their father. A family tradition is that Josiah's wife was an invalid. Assisting them in the home was a widowed housekeeper, surnamed Hutson, who became the mother of two of Josiah's children. [15] After Josiah's death, legal documents were signed by Richard Furman, Dorothea M. Furman, Sarah Haynsworth, and Henry Haynsworth disclaiming any inheritance rights to more than three thousand acres of Josiah Furman's property in the Camden and Charleston districts and investing these rights in "Rebecca Russell and Richard Furman, commonly so-called, otherwise sometimes called Richard Hutson, both the reputed illegitimate children of . . . Josiah Furman for their benefit and advancement, together with other good and valuable consideration. . . ." [16]

---

stroys a misconception held by a doctor grandson that Furman was married three times. "I am sorry to inform you," it says, "(if it is any pleasure to your doctor to think his grandmother was No. 3) that Richard and Elizabeth Furman were married on the 25th of Nov. 1774. The said Richard Furman having been ordained to the ministry the 16th of May in the same year. . . . Richard Furman and Dorothea Maria Burn, were married on the 5th day of May 1789." This, the postscript reads, was copied from Furman's Bible then in possession of Anne E. Furman. This interesting comment follows: "I think the feeling that Grandfather was capable of doing what we of this generation would call a silly performance, was not a third marriage but marrying a child of fifteen! Our grandmother was a little beauty when she married. She was born in 1774. Grandfather's first child was born in 1774. . . . Every two years grandmother bore a child, until 1819—when Aunt Ann[e] said: 'dear mama died of exhaustion, having borne so many children, and having such a large family to care for.' Of course, grandfather was no doubt thinking of biblical heros [sic], but my heart has always gone out to the pretty child whose life was one of pain and service until the tired body found rest in God." Copy of the original postscript, detached from the letter to which it was added, is in the possession of Mrs. Stanley Brittain Duffies III, 101 Belmont Avenue, Greenville, South Carolina.

[15]Conversation with Alester G. Furman, Jr.

[16]The original of these documents is in the Sumter, South Carolina, County Court House, with a copy in the South Carolina Archives, Columbia.

PASTORAL MINISTRY

Furman always carried with him the concerns of his congregation. While in Richmond, en route to Philadelphia in 1814, a stage passenger, who had left Charleston not many days earlier, told him of the death of two members of his congregation, husband and wife. He felt the loss deeply, both for himself and for his church, and asked Dolly to "remember my love to their Children and tell them that I sensibly feel for them; and that I hope the loss they have sustained in the Death of both their pious Parents will induce them more earnestly to seek an Interest in the Favour of the Ever-blessed God, and to choose him for their Friend and Father."[17] While engrossed in the business of the Triennial Convention, a letter from "Woody" told of "the death of Mr. Simons and [of] Dr. Hollinshead's illness."[18] Furman described them as "events in which the public interests of the city . . . are much concerned," then added that "the scarcity of ministers in Charleston requires my being there as much if not more than ever."[19] This was the heart of a pastor speaking.

To his sister Sarah's expressed hope that he could spend time at the High Hills following the death of their mother-in-law, he replied, "I do not think it would be right for me to leave Charleston for so long a time. . . . I have always found an absence from Charleston for some weeks has had an unfavorable influence on the state of the congregation."[20] He particularly disliked being away during the summer season when sickness was prevalent. In 1817 when Charleston was visited with a severe affliction of yellow fever, he was left almost alone among ministers to attend the sick of his and other congregations. Ministers, including three Presbyterians, one Independent, and one Lutheran—all, in fact, "except Dr. Buchan"—had left the city, and Dr. Buchan himself was stricken with the fever and could perform no public services. This meant

---

[17]Richard Furman to Dorothea Maria Furman, 5 May 1814, SCBHS.

[18]Hollinshead was "one of the pastors of the Independent or Congregational Church," H. T. Cook, *Biography*, 22.

[19]Richard Furman to Dorothea Maria Furman, 8 June 1814, SCBHS.

[20]Richard Furman to Sarah Haynsworth, 30 June 1805, SCBHS.

"much additional service . . . in visiting the sick and attending funerals."[21]

Devastating yellow fever epidemics were common during the early and middle years of Furman's life in Charleston. In 1792, following forty-four years with only sporadic attacks, a new era of yellow fever commenced. It raged that year, and during ten other years between 1794 and 1807. In the worst of these—1799, 1800, 1802, 1804, and 1807—there were 829 deaths.[22] In 1807 Furman wrote to his son, Wood, then in Rhode Island, and told him of the sickness within the family and his fear that it might be yellow fever, since it was "prevailing in the city" with such intensity that of twenty cases, seventeen had died. During such times, his visits to the homes of the sick were more than pastoral. The influence of his friend of the High Hill years, Dr. Joseph Howard, so sustained his interest in medicine that he had discovered a medicinal remedy that proved quite successful in the treatment of common ailments.

In September 1807, with the fever raging, he wrote to his sister that he was "so engaged in various ways, especially in attending the sick . . . in the quality of a physician, or a quack," that he had little time to write. The mail having closed before he reached the post office with his letter, he reopened it and added,

> You may think that I have the ambition to appear as a person acquainted with medicine . . . but if I know myself . . . the motive from which I have allowed myself to act is this twofold one, first, a desire to save life while numbers were dying under the hands of some of our best physicians, and second a wish to give publicity, and Evidence, to the Efficacy of a Medicine, or Mode of Treatment which I may say has been Providentially discovered to me, and of which I have proved the Benefit in the course of 14 to 15 years. The Knowledge some had obtained of this, induced them to apply to me; and the Success attending the Practice induced more. Only one had died on whom I have regularly attended, and he had been 16 hours under the Power of a most violent Fever before I saw him . . .[23]

---

[21]Richard Furman to Alexander McDonald, 2 October 1817, SCBHS.

[22]Ramsey, *History of South Carolina*, 47.

[23]Richard Furman to Sarah Haynsworth, 28 September 1817, SCBHS.

During one period of yellow fever, he had more than thirty patients, of whom he lost none. He made it his practice to take his lancet and medicines on his travels away from Charleston, and not infrequently he was called upon to minister to the sick, especially in general meetings of the denomination when some sudden attack of the disease occurred among those in attendance.[24]

Moving testimony of the effectiveness of Furman the pastor is expressed by Eliza Yoer Tupper, who was married by Furman to Tristam Tupper in 1816 when she was sixteen. Two years later, in December 1818, Furman baptized her. Late in life, she still recalled his words as she stepped into the baptismal waters. "My dear child," he said, "how happy your sainted father would have been could he have witnessed this scene." The day after her baptism, she bore a child and named him Samuel. On 9 December she wrote in her diary,

> This day has been a jubilee to me. . . . Dr. Furman came . . . and made a solemn dedicatory prayer for our household, not forgetting the baby Samuel Yoer. He fervently asked God's blessings on our child that he might be like the Samuel in the Bible, and also like his sainted grandfather, whose name he bears. . . .
>
> I remember the first Sabbath I went to church . . . in 1804. Never can I forget my astonishment when I saw in a high pulpit Dr. Furman in a black gown and white bands.
>
> When he lined out the hymns, and the choir (seated around the font) commenced some familiar old-fashioned tune, and the gallery burst forth, it appeared to me like thunder.
>
> The naturally fine voices, and perfect knowledge of the dear old tunes gave them perfect assurance, and they were fully prepared and quite at home when our pastor, in his clear, ringing voice, said, "Let us sing" . . . .
>
> Dr. Furman had a manner peculiar to himself; his voice excelled in melody; grace of action he possessed in an eminent degree. He lived and preached for eternity. He had power to move the affections and to warm the heart. . . .
>
> We had no Sabbath School then, but we had the Baptist Catechism, which we were as familiar with as with the Lord's Prayer. At

[24]Sprague, *Annals of the American Pulpit*, 6:163.

our quarterly season, we, the children of the congregation, repeated the Baptist Catechism, standing in a circle around the font. We numbered from sixty to a hundred. . . . Dr. Furman would in his majestic, winning manner, walk down the pulpit steps and with a book in hand, commence asking questions. . . . We had to memorize the whole book, for none knew which questions would fall to them. I think I hear at this very moment the dear voice of our pastor, saying, "A little louder, my child. . . ."[25]

As a pastor, Furman believed in a strong, united church, preferring a church serving a large area rather than numerous small mission churches established "to suit the convenience of a few; and thus dividing a minister's time and labours." Larger congregations, he reasoned, became "better able to support public worship, and to execute extensive schemes of piety, and Christian benevolence. . . ."[26] Guided by this concept, he concentrated on building a Charleston church commensurate with its influence among American Baptists of that period. Tabulated statistical growth during the thirty-eight years of his pastorate testifies to his success. In 1787 he came to a numerically weak church of 152 members still suffering from the effects of war and subsequent pastorless years. At the time of his death in 1825, the church listed some 780 members, with most of the increase coming from baptisms. During the same period there were 139 dismissals and 66 excommunications.[27]

WORLD MISSIONS

Even before William Carey's *An Enquiry into the Obligations of Christians to Use Means for the Conversion of the Heathen* initiated the English foreign missions movement, Furman had been in correspondence with Englishmen Samuel Pearce of Birmingham, John Sutcliff of Olney, and John Ryland of Northampton, who with Carey and Andrew Fuller constituted the "Immortal Five" who launched the foreign mission enter-

---

[25]Tupper, *Two Centuries of the First Baptist Church of Charleston, 1683-1883*, 293-300.

[26]Ibid.

[27]From the records of the Charleston Baptist Association.

prise in early October 1792.[28] When Carey was appointed teacher (later professor) of Bengali, Sanskrit, and Marathi at a government college in 1801, Furman wondered if his work as a professor would impair his work as a missionary.[29] But as one who understood the importance of communication, he did not minimize the importance of Carey's work as a translator of the Bible into native tongues.

Dating back to the first two decades of the eighteenth century, world missions had been a subject of intercessory prayer in England. Jonathan Edwards took up the theme in Boston in 1746, and in 1748 he published an appeal for a world Concert of Prayer for missionary work, which was reprinted many times during the next century.[30] Furman's awareness of this movement led him to involve his Charleston church by setting aside the first Tuesdays in January, April, July, and October to observe a Quarterly Concert of Prayer for World Missions. By 1795 this was recommended to all the churches in the Charleston Association. After 1810 the Charleston church observed a Monthly Concert of Prayer, following the pattern of the Nottingham Association in Great Britain, where the monthly movement had begun in June 1784.[31]

With the formation of the English Baptist Missionary Society, Furman raised funds to assist Carey and his associate English missionaries, John Marshman and William Ward, in translating the Bible into Indian dialects. The report of the English Baptist Missionary Society for 1806 attributes two thousand dollars to American Baptists and a little less than one-half that amount to Presbyterians. The amount credited to Charleston totaled five hundred and thirty-six dollars, with the note that it was sent by "Rev. Dr. Keith and Rev. Doctor Trueman." Dr. Keith was a Presbyterian, then pastor of the Independent church, and "Trueman" was evidently a misprint for Furman.[32]

In 1807 Furman traveled some forty miles south of Charleston to Edisto Island and preached to some whites and many Negroes. Among

---

[28]Baker and Craven, *The First 300 Years of First Baptist Church*, 221.

[29]Richard Furman to William Rogers, 22 April 1802, SCBHS.

[30]Stephen Neill, *A History of Christian Missions* (New York: McGraw-Hill, 1964) 239.

[31]Baker and Craven, *The First 300 Years of First Baptist Church*, 222.

[32]Vail, *The Morning Hour of American Missions*, 239-40.

his converts was Mrs. Hephzibah Jenkins Townsend, daughter of a Revolutionary War officer, Captain Daniel Jenkins, and his wife, Hephzibah Frampton Jenkins. When Charleston fell to the British, Captain Jenkins was imprisoned in Charleston, and Mrs. Jenkins, frail of body, did not survive his imprisonment. Prior to her death she entrusted her baby to two family slaves who were told to take the child to Edisto Island and give her to the Townsend family. Through winding marsh creeks and across the Ashley River, the two slaves, known only as Jack and Jean, avoided the enemy on a six-day journey from Charleston to Edisto Island.

When Hepzibah Jenkins Townsend reached maturity, her concern for black people reflected what she had learned from her experience as a baby. Although the Townsends were Presbyterians, their adopted child became a Baptist through the influence of Furman's preaching on the island. Subsequently, she attended services with some regularity at Furman's church in Charleston, accompanied by eight black servants who poled dugout boats from the island to Charleston.

Impressed by Furman's missionary sermons, she determined to have a share in mission work. Her plan was simple but ingenious: Building a large tabby oven from crushed oyster shells, she began to bake long pans of brown gingerbread. One day she invited several women friends from Wadmalaw and Edisto islands to her home at Bleak Hill. There, over tea, they talked about missions. When someone reminded her that their husbands controlled the family money supply, she drove them to the tabby oven and let them savor the smell of the freshly baked bread. She then explained that Furman, her pastor, had told of a "mite society" in Boston organized by Miss Mary Webb. Since a mite was all they could give at present, why not organize a mite society, with proceeds from the sale of bread or other handmade items going to missions? They agreed, and from that meeting was born the Wadmalaw and Female Mite Society, the first organized women's missionary society in South Carolina. In 1812 it became the first such society in the South to contribute to the Triennial Convention. The work of Hephzibah Townsend, inspired by the sermons of Richard Furman, marked the beginning of mite societies all across South Carolina and beyond.[33]

---

[33]Loulie Latimer Owens, *Banners in the Wind* (Columbia: The Women's Missionary Union of South Carolina, 1950) 1-10; Baker and Craven, *The First 300 Years of First Baptist Church.*

In 1799 Joseph Hughes, a British minister at Battersea, helped initiate the interdenominational Religious Tract Society. Soon thereafter,
Furman joined with Isaac Keith, a Congregational pastor in Charleston, to organize a similar society in Charleston, and for many years he
served as its president. With the formation of the British and Foreign
Bible Society in 1804, he became an active participant that same year
in organizing the Charleston Bible Society and for the remainder of his
life served as its vice-president.

These small beginnings symbolized Furman's world view of missions and cast him in the role of a leading American Baptist identified
with the work of William Carey and the English Baptist missionary
initiative.

ELOQUENT VOICE

In a city dominated by Anglicanism, it was the pastor of the Baptist
church whose personal piety, pastoral ministries, and human concern
made him revered most among its ministers. If an eloquent voice were
needed to articulate the sentiments of Charleston citizens, they turned
to Furman. When Alexander Hamilton was killed in a duel with Aaron
Burr, the State Society of the Cincinnati and the American Revolution
Society requested that Furman pay tribute to Hamilton in a memorial
sermon, as he had at their request on the occasion of the death of Washington.

The address began as a sermon, continued as a eulogy, and concluded as an attack against dueling, with a call to abolish it by law.
After reviewing Hamilton's life of nearly forty-eight years, Furman described him as "a man of transcendent genius; a refined scholar; an accomplished gentleman; an eloquent, powerful orator; a profound
civilian; a heroic soldier; a great statesman." When the occasion called
for it, Furman could use language with exalted and persuasive eloquence, as evidenced in his tribute to Hamilton and his condemnation
of the duel.

> "How has the mighty fallen?" How! Was it by the act of God that
> this great man fell? Or by the hand of a public enemy, in the tented
> field, and in defense of his country's liberty, when endangered by for-
> eign war, or domestic insurrection? No: It was through the influence

of party-rage; by a practice handed down from barbarous ages and nations; by which even they were disgraced. When, America! When, O
my country, shall these evils cease to afflict thee?[34]

Furman felt compelled to make his voice heard against a practice
"brought so effectively into view" by Hamilton's death. Following a
portrayal of the evils of dueling, he called upon legislators and members
of the two societies to find another "expedient which your wisdom can
devise; which your patriotism and religion will approve; and which your
courage can enforce—to bring this barbarous practice into disuse."[35]

Among those listening was Charles Cotesworth Pinckney. The two
societies named him chairman of a joint committee to draft a memorial
to the legislature calling for an act to abolish dueling. This was published in the *Charleston Courier* and signed by Pinckney, James Kennedy, and William Read as the committee for the Cincinnati, and David
Ramsay, Henry W. DeSaussure, William Allen Deas, James Lowndes,
and Richard Furman for the Revolution Society.[36] The memorial was
widely circulated and was attended by a request that clergymen preach
a sermon against the practice.[37] In November of that same year, the
Charleston Baptist Association, with Furman as moderator, unanimously adopted a resolution declaring that "this Association will unite
with their fellow citizens in the petition to the Legislature of this State
for an Act to abolish the bloody practice of duelling."[38]

Furman was easily the most effective orator in the Charleston of
his day. In 1802, upon invitation from the Cincinnati and Revolution
Societies, he delivered a July Fourth oration entitled *America's Deliverance and Duty*. Only two decades had passed since the treaty with England had officially ended the War for Independence. Fresh in his mind

---

[34]The latter part of Furman's eulogy and his denunciation of dueling appear in H.
T. Cook, *Biography*, 135-55.

[35]Ibid.

[36]*Charleston Courier*, 18 September 1804.

[37]Ibid.

[38]*Minutes of the Charleston Association*, 1804, SCBHS.

were his own experiences during that war and the heroic struggles of his compatriots. In his audience, to use his own words, were "many enlightened citizens, statesmen, and patriotic soldiers, who shared largely in the solicitudes, toils, sufferings and triumphs which attended the contest for liberty."

The occasion evoked his eloquent best. Drawing a parallel between the American fight for independence and the deliverance of the Israelites from Egypt, he saw in both the work of a providential destiny.

> Whatever specific difference may be noticed as existing, between the origin of the Jewish theocracy, and the rise, independence and establishment of the United States; yet it must be acknowledged, there is a striking similarity: and if we have not received an express command from heaven to remember the day of our deliverance; yet, the analogy of holy writ unites with reason and gratitude to declare it a duty. By their united voice, we are directed to recollect the merciful interpositions of the Deity in our favour; and devoutly to acknowledge the obligations we are brought under to his delivering and preserving goodness.

In developing his argument, he was orator, theologian, philosopher, logician, and patriot. He pursued the theme that Providence was on the side of America in the struggle and that certain duties and obligations rested upon American citizens in consequence of divine interposition in their favor. The justice of the cause, the manner in which "our citizens entered on, and supported the cause," the "apparent interposition of Providence, in favor of the revolution," the happy termination of the war, and the apparent design of Providence for the nation's destiny were all developed in orderly and majestic sequence.[39] As a patriotic address on a patriotic occasion before an audience of patriots who shared, along with himself, the bitter struggle for independence, his oration deserves a place among the best of patriotic literature.

---

[39]*America's Deliverance and Duty: A Sermon preached at the Baptist Church of Charleston, South Carolina, on the Fourth of July, 1802, before the State Society of the Cincinnati and the American Revolution Society; and the Congregation which usually attends Divine Service in the Said Church, by Richard Furman, D.D.*, Rare Book Collection, Library of Congress, Washington, D.C.

An earlier illustration of his stature as a citizen and orator occurred in 1796 when he was invited to deliver an address at the seventh anniversary ceremonies of the Charleston Orphan House, a charitable institution founded after the Revolution "for the purpose of supporting and educating poor orphan children, and those of poor distressed and disabled parents who were unable to support and maintain them."[40] Although at this time Furman was forty-one years of age and nine years into his Charleston pastorate, this was probably the occasion that established his reputation in Charleston as a gifted orator for events of general public interest.

Furman's address was delivered before "the Intendant and Wardens of the City, the Board of Commissioners, and a Large Assemblage of the Benefactors of the Institution." He saw the orphanage as an institution for uniting "good men of every denomination in vigorous, and common efforts, to promote the best of causes."[41] The orphanage's anniversary celebration attracted an illustrious audience before whom Furman could speak profoundly. Classical Greek characters and their literature, the founders of Eastern religion, and ancient Roman history were among favorite subjects in his experience of self-education. On this occasion, he compared the moral systems of Pythagoras, Confucius, Zoroaster, and Moses with the example of Christ in terms of generosity, love, kindness, and mercy and found them "as the withdrawing stars before the effulgency of the rising sun; and the improvements in favor of philanthropy which had been in the civil polity of the most civilized nations, whether adhering to the institutes of Solon, Lycurgus, or Hermodorus, bear no comparison to those which have prevailed where the genuine influence of christianity has been felt."[42] The subject moved him, the caliber of the audience inspired him, and the logic favoring the cause of the institution was both spiritually and intellectually stimulating. The result was one of his finest utterances.

---

[40] *Yearbook, City of Charleston, S.C.*, 1880, 40.

[41] *The South Carolina Historical Magazine* 68 (1967): 68.

[42] *An Oration Delivered at the Charleston Orphan House before the Intendants and Wardens of the City, the Board of Commissioners, and a Large Assemblage of the Benefactors of the Institution, Oct. 18, 1796, by Richard Furman, A.M., pastor of the Baptist Church in Charleston*, The South Caroliniana Library, University of South Carolina, Columbia.

IN THE PULPIT

From his High Hills years through his Charleston pastorate, Furman's pulpit ability was admired by contemporaries of all ages. In 1776 Oliver Hart, then fifty-one years of age and pastor of the most important Baptist church in South Carolina, wrote in his diary that he assisted Furman, twenty-one, in ordaining twenty-six-year-old Joseph B. Cook. Furman's age was not a stumbling block for the older Cook and the much older Hart, for they recognized that the youthful Furman was mature beyond his age and a preacher with extraordinary promise.[43]

As a young boy in his Georgetown home, William Bullein Johnson heard Furman preach. Later recalling the experience, he remembered that Furman was "solemn and imposing," more so than anyone he had ever seen and, further, that "in the service of the sacred desk, such was the appropriate solemnity of his manner, that the audience felt themselves to be in the presence of a man of God." He added further,

> I remember hearing him, more than forty years ago, preach from the text, "I am set for the defense of the Gospel"—it was truly a masterful effort. Never shall I forget his solemn, impressive countenance, his dignified manner, his clear statements in support of the Gospel's claim to a Divine origin, the lofty sentiments that he poured forth, the immovable firmness with which he maintained his position, and the eloquence with which he enforced the whole argument.[44]

Furman's physical presence reinforced his pulpit performance. A contemporary described him as "somewhat above the common stature, with a frame robust, athletic, well-proportioned, and remarkably dignified. . . . His face was full, manly, and highly expressive of kindness and penetration. In the pulpit he appeared to the greatest advantage, when the natural force and elevation of his person were rendered majestic by the presence of truth and the solemnity of eternal things."[45]

---

[43] H. T. Cook, *Biography*, 56-57.

[44] Sprague, *Annals of the American Pulpit*, 6:164.

[45] Charles G. Sommers, *Memoir of the Rev. John Stanford, D.D.* (New York, 1835) 411, Library of Congress, Washington, D.C.

Developing a sermon apparently came naturally and easily for Furman. At the organizational meeting of the Triennial Convention in 1814, its leaders realized on Wednesday, the opening day of the Convention, that no one had been assigned the task of preparing a sermon for the occasion. With some feeling of apology, they turned to Furman. That evening he preached on the text "And lo, I am with you alway, even to the end of the world." The sermon occupied ten pages in the proceedings of the Convention. It was a powerful appeal for Baptists to unite their strength on behalf of missions. In a concluding crescendo of eloquence, he called attention to missionary exertions by various denominations in both Europe and America, hailed the work of William Carey and his associates, and urged his hearers to respond in a manner that would let "no difficulties . . . retard, no oppositions withstand."[46]

His sermons usually contained a text, an interpretation, three points, and a section called "Improvement," the latter being the practical application of the message. His choice of words reflected the ornate style of nineteenth-century orators, as in this description of the changes in an individual after death.

> The fine features are clothed with deformity, and the active limbs become inert as congealed water, or the insensible rock. The countenance, in which beauty shone, with all its charms; or in which superior sense, manly virtue and dignity appeared to their highest advantage; no longer beams with love, wisdom, courage, friendship, or benevolence; but is covered with appalling gloom. The eye no longer expresses the feeling of the soul; the ear is no more attuned to meaning and harmony of sound; and the tongue, which was most eloquent, is hushed into perpetual silence. The heart ceases to beat; the fine spun cords of sensation cannot perform their office; nor can the muscles exert their force. The exquisitely curious mechanism of the animal economy is deranged and broken; and man's whole material part (oh, humbling consideration to human pride!) is changed into a mass of corruption . . . the immortal soul, dislodged from its former residence, removed to distant worlds, . . . enters on an everlasting, untried state of being.[47]

---

[46]*Proceedings*, Triennial Convention, 1814.

[47]Richard Furman, *Death's Dominion over Man Considered*, 8-9, cited in J. Alvin Reynolds, "A Critical Study of the Life and Work of Richard Furman" (Ph.D. dissertation; American Baptist Historical Society, Rochester NY, 1962).

Very few of Furman's sermons survive, but those that do portray his ability to think deeply, communicate freely, speak forcefully, and use language with grace and style.

The regard in which Furman was held by his Baptist contemporaries is best described by David Benedict in recalling Furman's fifty years among Baptists. Calling him "the principal minister in our order, not only in his own State, but in all the surrounding region," he added, "I do not know of any one in the Baptist ranks . . . who had a higher reputation among the American Baptists for wisdom in counsel, and a skill in management, in all the affairs of the denomination."[48]

Some of his colleagues felt a sense of awe in being in his presence, or addressing a communication to him. Both old and young frequently referred to him as "the Doctor." Few ministers in the South had then been honored with a Doctor of Divinity degree, and Furman had been so honored twice. Edmund Botsford, much older than Furman, was not one to take "the Doctor" lightly, but neither did he wish his younger brethren to be overawed by him. To Joseph B. Cook, who apparently had made some reference to difficulty in communicating with Furman, Botsford wrote, "Are you not a chicken-hearted fellow, to be afraid of D.D.'s. . . . So you feel cramped when you write to Dr. F. So do I; but I write to him. . . ."[49]

Botsford knew Furman as none of his contemporaries did and often wrote to him in intimate terms. Only he would tell Furman that some people were making light of his singing. In a letter of good-natured candor, Botsford said that some people were saying that Furman was a poor singer who thought himself a good one and was vain about it. Furman admitted that some people might indeed believe, "in all sincerity," that he thought himself a good singer. But as to being vain about it, he labeled that "an entirely mistaken" notion.

> I have considered singing an important part of Divine Worship
> and have also considered it my Duty properly to attempt its promo-

---

[48]David Benedict, *Fifty Years Among the Baptists* (New York: Sheldon and Company, 1860) 48-49.

[49]Mallary, *Memoir of Elder Edmund Botsford*, 1832, 190.

tion. . . . I have on all occasions in conversation positively and candidly declared that I knew myself to be a very bad Singer, and that having neither Reputation to gain or lose as a Singer . . . I have readily attempted it both in Public and in private, either directly in devotional Acts, endeavoring to act in concert with others. . . . If in my very imperfect manner of singing, they would discern any Beauty in it, they might enquire after, get acquainted with, and introduce it into public life. . . .[50]

A NEW CHURCH BUILDING

Since 1748, following litigation over the original Lot 62, worship had been held in what was known as the "Mariner's Church." Between 1787 and 1805, church membership had increased from 152 to 331,[51] making it apparent that a new and larger church building was necessary. With characteristic foresight, Furman anticipated this need. As early as 1805, he donated to the church a parcel of land in St. Paul's Parish valued at one thousand dollars. By the terms of his gift, the land would be sold and the proceeds applied to the construction of a new church when a decision was reached to build.

For the next dozen years funds were collected for building purposes, with Furman himself taking a leading role. Two years after Furman made his own gift of land, William M. Turner gave a lot in Charleston for the same purpose. Money held by the extinct Religious Society of Oliver Hart was also transferred to the church. The church minutes of these years record building fund gifts collected by Furman, his son, Richard B. Furman, and others, totaling more than twenty thousand dollars. Contributions came not only from members of the church but from friends in other denominations as well. In October 1817 a building committee was appointed consisting of Richard B. Furman, William Rouse, George Gibbs, Tristam Tupper, and James Nolan.

In September 1818 the revered pastor laid the cornerstone under the southeast corner of the new edifice on old historic Lot 62. Sealed in

---

[50]Richard Furman to Edmund Botsford, 11 June 1793, SCBHS.

[51]Tabulated growth from *Minutes of the Charleston Association*, cited in Baker and Craven, *The First 300 Years of First Baptist Church*.

it were documents pertaining to the history of the church, including no doubt, notation that this would be the fourth building occupied by the church since its removal from Maine to South Carolina. The first was on King Street, the next a frame building erected in 1699 on Lot 62, with a parsonage on the same lot. On the same premises was the church cemetery, which led to a remark by Furman that he lived "among the gravestones." The third was the Mariner's Church on Church Street; the fourth was built during the Furman pastorate.

A South Carolinian, Robert Mills, who designed the Washington Monument in the District of Columbia, was selected as architect. He was the most distinguished architect of his day. He described the church he designed as

> the best specimen of the correct taste in architecture of the modern buildings in the city . . . purely Greek in its style, simply grand in its proportions, and beautiful in its detail. The plan is of the temple form, divided into four parts; the portico, vestibule, nave, and vestry rooms. . . .
>
> The facade presents a portico of four massive columns of the lightest proportions of the Doric, surmounted by a pediment. Behind the portico (on the main walls) rises an attic story squared up to the height of the roof, and crowned by a cupola or belfry. The side walls of the building are opened by the requisite apertures for windows and doors, and a full cornice runs round the whole.
>
> You enter the vestibule by three doors, on each side of which the gallery stairs ascend; by three opposite doors you pass into the aisles, dividing the pews into blocks; at the extreme end of the nave of the church are the baptismal font and pulpit, lighted by a large vaulted window.
>
> Around three sides of the nave a double colonnade extends, rises up to the roof, and supports the galleries. The lower order of the column is Doric, the upper Ionic; each with their regular entablatures; the whole finished in a rich chaste style, and producing, from the unity of the design, a very pleasing effect. . . .[52]

---

[52]Robert Mills, *Statistics of South Carolina* (Charleston, 1825; Spartanburg SC: The Reprint Company, 1972) 411.

The church was near the Church Street homes of distinguished South Carolinians. Two doors away was the Robert Brewton House, built before 1733 by Colonel Robert Brewton, a wealthy landowner and powder receiver. Beside it was the home of Jacob Motte, city treasurer. At 90 Church Street was the Georgian-style house of Thomas Legare, a prosperous Huguenot merchant. At 94 Church Street was the home of Thomas Bee, a leader in the colonial government and patriot of the Revolution. During the middle years of Furman's pastorate, this house was occupied by Governor Joseph Alston, who married the ill-fated Theodosia Burr, daughter of Aaron Burr. In a second floor drawing room, John C. Calhoun, General James Hamilton, and others huddled around a table in 1832 to draft South Carolina's nullification papers. At 87 Church Street lived Thomas Heyward, one of the signers of the Declaration of Independence.

Few buildings in Charleston were nearer the city's cultural and political life, or more reminiscent of its history, than the First Baptist Church built during the latter years of Furman's pastorate. The elegance of early Charleston architecture that flowered particularly during the Federal period, 1793-1808, was doubtless the inspiring factor accounting for the decision to build a church of such classical design.

Final services in the old Mariner's Church were held on Sunday, 13 January 1822. In later recalling that service, Basil Manly said in 1832,

> In the evening, Dr. Furman, deeply penetrated with the varied reflections which the occasion inspired, and scarcely able to command himself, took leave of the spot, with sobbing and many tears; the feeling of the flock were [sic] scarcely less intense than his own; and the place of their pasture was now literally a Bochim, a place of weeping.[53]

In the stately new building just completed, Furman preached the first sermon on Thursday following the final service in the Mariner's Church. It was the evening when he normally delivered a religious lecture to his congregation. His text was appropriately chosen from 2 Chronicles 6:8—"But Jehovah said unto David my father, Whereas it was in thy heart to build a house for my name, thou didst well that it

---

[53]Manly, *Mercy and Judgment*, 62.

was in thy heart." It was a moving experience for Furman, then in his thirty-fifth year as pastor of the church.

During Furman's career, there had been two wars between the United States and England, the French Revolution and the Napoleonic Wars in Europe, the framing and ratification of the American Constitution, the terms of the first five presidents of the United States, the purchase of Louisiana, the invention of the cotton gin, and the Missouri Compromise. In religious terms, Furman had matured from the youthful pastor of a small rural church in the South Carolina backcountry into an eminent and influential figure among American Baptists from Georgia to Maine. "The wisest man I ever knew" was the accolade given to him by Basil Manly, his successor as pastor of the Charleston church, and later president of the University of Alabama.

Probably at no point in his career did he find greater satisfaction than when he and his congregation entered the noble new church of Greek classical design on Lot 62. Baptists had come of age in a city where Anglicans, Congregationalists, and Presbyterians had historically been the dominant religious influence.

CHAPTER 11

Slave Owner

Any study of Richard Furman must address the system of Southern slavery. He was both landowner and minister when the system was an integral part of the South's society and economy. His own view evolved into a classical defense of slaveholding based on scriptural authority; he sincerely believed that this was solid ground upon which the system could be justified.

Slavery's roots in South Carolina dated back to the arrival of the first shipload of settlers from England in 1670. Earlier, slavery had been sanctioned by the Lords Proprietors in the Fundamental Constitutions drawn up in England for the colonial government. During the first one hundred years of state history, slaves were found chiefly along the coast. As late as 1790, less than twenty-five per cent of the total population living fifty miles inland from the coast was white.[1]

The preponderance of blacks in many areas raised frequently expressed fears among whites about the possibility of internal enemies. Typical was the assertion of Lieutenant Governor Thomas Broughton

[1]Wallace, *South Carolina: A Short History*, illustrative map, 340.

in 1737 that "our negroes are very numerous and more dreadful to our safety than any Spanish invaders." Three years earlier, in 1734, the South Carolina governor, the Council, and the Commons had protested against British merchants who sought to defeat efforts by the province to check slave importation. For several years prior to a serious Negro insurrection in September 1739, public demand had grown for more humane treatment as a safeguard against further uprisings. In 1740 the slave code was revised to add rules for the benefit of slaves. In 1796 the strong and influential voice of Dr. David Ramsay was raised against the system, as was that of Richard Furman, who early in the nineteenth century called it "undoubtedly an evil."[2] While a student at South Carolina College, Basil Manly wrote that "slavery seems to be repugnant to the spirit of our republican institutions."[3] When David Benedict journeyed south early in the nineteenth century to collect material for his Baptist history, he found that "many let it [slavery] alone altogether; some remonstrate against it in gentle terms; others oppose it vehemently; while far the greater part . . . hold slaves, and justify them the best way they can."[4]

What otherwise may have resulted in gradual elimination of the slave traffic was checked by Eli Whitney's invention of the cotton gin in 1791. Three years earlier, South Carolina had produced about 1,500,000 pounds of cotton. Ten years later, in 1801, production had increased to 20,000,000 pounds, and by 1834 to 65,500,000 pounds.[5] With the state's economy geared so effectively to cotton, idealism faded and voices opposing slavery became silenced. Governor Bennett summed up the human predicament when he told the legislature that even though any abstract consideration of slavery would condemn it, the institution was so firmly established and the evil so "entailed" that its continuance was a "stern necessity."[6]

----

[2]Richard Furman, letter to an unidentified person, SCBHS, cited in Owens, *Saints of Clay*, 70.

[3]Basil Manly, *On the Emancipation of Slaves*, 1821, Manly Papers, SCBHS.

[4]Benedict, *General History of Baptists*, 2:207.

[5]Wallace, *South Carolina: A Short History*, 363.

[6]Ibid., 385.

Into this climate of fatalism came two factors that brought the sociopolitical implications of the slave system into sharp and critical focus. One was a rising tide of organized antislavery sentiment in the North; the other was the discovery of a planned slave uprising in Charleston that awakened whites to the danger they had created for themselves. The insurrection was plotted by Denmark Vesey, a free Negro and skilled carpenter, who had lived in Charleston for almost forty years. Not in South Carolina history had there been such an orchestrated plan to burn the city, rob the banks, kill the men, ravish the women, and seize the ships. In all some six thousand slaves were incited to insurrection in a carefully planned uprising for execution in the early summer of 1822.[7]

The public became aware of the plot when a faithful servant turned informer. Arrests followed, trials were held, and thirty-five Negroes were hanged, including Denmark Vesey, the only free Negro among them. Thirty-two others were exiled from the United States.[8] The ease with which a few natural black leaders could unsuspectedly organize such a conspiracy created fear and consternation in the white community.

Furman certainly knew Vesey since his home on Church Street was but a short distance from Vesey's on Bull Street.[9] The right of movement for a free Negro, especially a skilled carpenter who had lived in Charleston longer than Furman, would certainly have brought him to the attention of the pastor of the First Baptist Church, who was caught up in the public fear and retribution attending the aborted Vesey insurrection.

When the newly organized State Baptist Convention met in 1822 at Cambridge in the Edgefield district, grave matters were on the minds of the delegates. The year had been marked by a devastating hurricane sweeping across much of the state, leaving death and destruction in its wake. For this to have occurred when the frightful possibilities of the

---

[7]For an excellent treatment of the Vesey plot, see John Lofton, *Insurrection in South Carolina: The Turbulent World of Denmark Vesey* (Yellow Springs OH: Antioch Press, 1964).

[8]Wallace, *South Carolina: A Short History*, 384.

[9]*The Directory and Stranger's Guide to the City of Charleston*, 1822 (Charleston: James R. Schenck, 1822) 109.

Vesey affair were still fresh in mind created widespread public concern. At an earlier meeting of the Charleston Association in November, a resolution had been adopted authorizing its delegates to the forthcoming state convention to request the governor to declare a day of public humiliation and prayer in gratitude for the "preservation afforded from an intended Insurrection; and distress inflicted by a terrible hurricane."[10] The Convention took the further step of requesting Furman to convey to the governor the sentiments of the Convention "on the lawfulness of holding slaves" from a "moral and religious view."

Predictably, as both slave owner and religious leader, Furman cited the Scriptures in justification of the system. Since "Divine law never sanctions immoral actions," he reasoned that the morality of slavery was upheld by scriptural authority. This was a strong argument for those who wished to own slaves in good conscience. So was the paternalistic argument that a slave was the beneficiary of his enslavement. "The children, the aged, the sick, the disabled, and unruly, as well as those who are capable of service and orderly, are objects of their master's care," he reasoned. His lengthy exposition concluded with a summation defending the right of slave ownership and emphasizing the responsibilities of slave owners.[11]

At the next meeting in 1823, his exposition was read before the delegates, who unanimously resolved the thanks of the Convention to "its venerable President, for the very able and satisfactory manner in which he has discharged the delicate and important duty committed to his trust." They also requested that he take measures to have it published in the *Southern Intelligencer* and the *Columbian Star*.[12] The latter would insure its distribution among Northern brethren.

Perhaps he knew nothing of a letter from William Carey to William Rogers twenty-one years earlier in which the former had expressed shock at seeing "some American newspaper advertisements headed by 'To Be Sold, A Negro Man, etc.' " "I hope," Carey said, "no Christian keeps a slave: if this should be the practice . . . in the southern parts of the United States, it will not be difficult to answer the enquiry . . . you

---

[10]*Minutes of the Charleston Baptist Association*, 1822, SCBHS.

[11]A full text of Furman's "exposition" may be found in Appendix B.

[12]*Proceedings*, South Carolina Baptist Convention, 1823.

sent me, 'why the churches in those parts are in so languishing a state.' I hope everyone who names the name of Christ departs from the iniquity of holding their fellow creatures in slavery. . . ."[13]

Social and economic pressures are profound influences in shaping the human situation. From the time Furman pronounced slavery "undoubtedly an evil" until he wrote his address to the governor in its defense, the South's economy had undergone such a revolution that the Southern pocketbook was so dependent upon slave labor that morals and economics were not easily reconciled. Wagon loads of cotton from his plantation lands in the High Hills illustrated the close tie between slave ownership and the productivity of the soil. The one became so identified with the other that the editor of *The Southern Episcopalian*, published in Charleston, editorialized in his paper,

> The men of the Revolution and of the generation immediately succeeding, regarded it [slavery] in the light of an evil, to be gradually remedied if possible by removal or emancipation. Experience and maturer reflection proved the impracticability of either course, and the assaults of abolitionism induced a more thorough examination into the grounds, moral and religious, on which it rested. The Southern mind became satisfied that the relation was not without a divine sanction, and that under existing circumstances it was the only one which could obtain between the two races brought together upon our own soil.[14]

When Furman addressed the governor,[15] the Missouri Compromise had been in effect for almost three years. This famous piece of legislation focused on the bitter struggle between slave and nonslave states for a law regarding the admission of states carved out of the vast territory included within the Louisiana Purchase. Whether they were to be admitted as slave or free states, and thus establish either slavery or nonslavery in the great West, was the question. It was both an ethical and economic question, but it also involved a deep constitutional principle.

---

[13]William Carey to William Rogers, 30 December 1800; Rippon, *The Baptist Annual Register*, 2:810-11.

[14]Quoted in Wallace, *South Carolina: A Short History*, 432.

[15]Governor Thomas Bennett of Charleston had been succeeded by Governor John L. Wilson of Georgetown.

Did Congress have the power to lay restrictions on new states that were not laid on the original thirteen? If so, would the new states be equal with the old? The Sixteenth Congress will be ever memorable for the famous compromise that emerged from this debate.

One does not need to speculate which side of the debate had Furman's support. He had lived in Charleston too long not to have absorbed the aristocratic character of this chief Southern city. As a Southerner and a slave owner, he understood the political implications of carving the western territory into free states that would give the antislavery opinion excessive representation in Congress. Besides, two Charlestonians, Charles Pinckney and William Lowndes, were leaders in the fight against a free Missouri. Furman was not one to follow blindly, but Pinckney and Lowndes could carry public opinion with them if anyone could. The Missouri Compromise gave temporary surcease to the slavery question. But as the aged ex-President Thomas Jefferson wrote after the compromise line had been settled, "The question sleeps for the present, but it is not dead. . . . This momentous question, like a fire bell in the night, awakened me and filled me with terror. I consider it at once as the knell of the Union."[16]

Furman's view of slavery was scripturally rationalized; he also believed that slavery was an economic necessity for a Southern plantation owner. But his scriptural rationalization of the invisible institution was not motivated solely by economic considerations. Underlying the economics of slavery among Southern evangelicals—Baptists, Methodists, Presbyterians—was a deeply held religious view that slavery was a divinely approved system, and further, that it afforded a mission opportunity to convert slaves and nurture their religious experience through continuing instruction. Strong argument can be made that the latter was a consequence of the first, that economic realities became so dominant in a Southern cotton society that moral justification for the slave system became equated with economic survival. In 1790 Baptists declared slavery "a violent deprivation of the rights of nature and inconsistent with a republican government."[17] This was a prevailing view

---

[16]Henry Wilson Nelson, *History of the United States* (New York: The McMillan Company, 1920) 462n.

[17]*Minutes of the Baptist General Committee at their Yearly Meeting, Held in the City of Richmond, May 8, 1790* (Richmond: T. Nicholson, 1790) 7, cited in Donald G. Mathews, *Religion in the Old South* (Chicago: University of Chicago Press, 1977) 69.

among Southern evangelicals during the latter part of the eighteenth century. But the success of the cotton gin and a rising tide of Northern antislavery agitation forced the South into a new posture for justifying slavery. Among evangelicals, Baptists included, this found expression in concern for religious conversion of the Negro and acceptance of him on church membership rolls. One estimate reports that black membership in Baptist churches increased from about 18,000 to 40,000 between 1793 and 1813.[18] Accelerating this growth was the religious fervor of the Great Revival.

The danger posed by the Vesey affair, followed in rapid sequence by the Nat Turner insurrection, provided a new sense of urgency for a lately formed institution known as the Mission to the Slaves, which best exemplified the Southern evangelical ethic and afforded a substantial claim of respect and leadership for creating an orderly, benevolent social system in the slave South. Though the Mission was detached from the churches, it was a reflection of Southern religion as it confronted a mission challenge on one side, an attempt to satisfy the conscience of the South on another, and abolitionist pressure on yet another.[19] The Mission postdated Furman's lifetime, but it was an extension of his perception of the slave system. Like Furman, it sought to balance authority over the slave with responsibility for his religious well-being. Years later, James C. Furman would say to one suspected of mistreatment of a male servant, "We who own slaves honor God's law in the exercise of our authority."[20]

Richard Furman's own treatment of his slaves was in the best tradition of the kind master. They were given the consideration due human beings in a family relationship. To his own son Wood, then in Providence, Rhode Island, he spoke of "the white part of the family and

---

[18]Charles Colcock Jones, *Religious Instruction* (New York: Harper and Row, 1930) 53, cited in Albert J. Raboteau, *Slave Religion: The "Invisible Institution" in the Antebellum South* (New York: Oxford University Press, 1978) 131.

[19]For a discussion of the Mission, see Donald G. Mathews, *Religion in the Old South* and Albert J. Raboteau, *Slave Religion: The "Invisible Institution" in the Antebellum South*.

[20]James C. Furman to W. E. Bailey, 18 December 1848, Furman Family Papers, SCBHS, cited in Mathews, *Religion in the Old South*, 136.

of the Negroes."[21] To William Rogers of Philadelphia, he referred to
the sickness of his own children and the death of a Negro boy in the
same context.

> Smallpox, measles, and some other contagious diseases, pleu-
> risies and other inflammatory diseases from cold have been preva-
> lent. My family have [sic] been visited among others with them,
> several of which have been very sick and one of the number, a very
> promising little negro boy six years old have [sic] died lately, either
> from the effects of the measles or worms. The death was sudden and
> unexpected as death often is. He went to market with his mother
> in the morning and by three o'clock was a corpse. Our little daugh-
> ter is still sick with the consequences of the measles, though it is
> hoped on the recovery. . . .[22]

When returning home from a meeting of the Association at Cheraw
Hill in November 1816, he spent some days on his High Hills plantation tending to plantation affairs—among them seeing that the Negroes were provided with suitable winter clothes and surveying the corn
and cotton harvest. To Dolly he wrote, "The Negro clothes arrived in
safety . . . and were delivered the next day to the satisfaction of their
possessors. They seem to fit as well as if they had been made from their
measure." He was happy to find that despite a week of "remarkably cold
weather," there had been no suffering among them, since "their last
year's clothes were yet in general pretty good."[23]

Yet beneath a veneer of paternalistic concern lay always the economic fact that slaves could be bartered, sold, purchased, and otherwise
dealt with according to an owner's wishes or needs. To the pastor of the
First Baptist Church of Baltimore, Furman once wrote for assistance in
finding a Negro "wench" for purchase. Included in this inquiry was a
listing of the qualifications he wished. He received the following reply:
"I have made what inquiry I could among my acquaintances but cannot
find any person who owns such a wench who is willing to part with her

---

[21]Richard Furman to Wood Furman, 5 May 1808, SCBHS.

[22]Richard Furman to William Rogers, 22 April 1802, SCBHS.

[23]Richard Furman to Dorothea Maria Furman, 15 November 1816, SCBHS.

for scarcely any reasonable sum of money, which makes me conclude that such an one cannot be purchased here at all."[24] When a judgment against the family estate was threatened in 1799 unless a bond given to "Fisher and Edwards" was discharged, Furman arranged for the sale of nine Negroes in the hope that the better price then being paid for slaves would discharge the bond.[25] Earlier, in 1790, when there appeared to be danger of execution against the estate to satisfy mortgages, he had written to his sister Sarah that he would consider selling the Negroes to prevent their being seized on execution.[26] Thus ran the contradiction always present in the slaveholding ethic. It was a contradiction Furman never successfully resolved.

Furman would not live to see how the crisis would divide the Union long before the opposing sides took to the battlefield. In his lifetime he was comfortable with a society that looked upon slavery as scripturally supported and believed it to be economically, socially, and even politically essential.

Thirty-five years following Richard Furman's death, his son, James C. Furman, then president of Furman University, would echo in different but solemn tones his father's views on slavery. By then, Abraham Lincoln had been elected president of the United States, and the loud cry of Northern abolitionism was on a collision course with the Southern doctrine of states' rights. In anger, South Carolina called a convention to meet 17 December 1860 to decide what should be done in consequence of the success of the Abolition party in the presidential election. On 22 November a mass meeting convened in the Greenville courthouse to hear addresses on the subject in preparation for the naming of five delegates from the Greenville district to attend the December statewide meeting. Among speakers the name of James C. Furman was foremost. He spoke with the fervor of a man committed to secession. While the constitutional principle on which he stood was states' rights, the real issue was Southern slavery and Northern determination to abolish it.

---

[24]Lewis Richards to Richard Furman, 26 June 1798, SCBHS.

[25]Richard Furman to Sarah Haynsworth, 4 March 1799, SCBHS.

[26]Richard Furman to Sarah Haynsworth, 7 January 1790, SCBHS.

One of the first ends of public justice is security to the rights of property. And what has been the fate of our right of property under the Constitution? I say nothing of the protective tariff system by which the wealth of the South has been converted to the means of building up Northern capital against the complaint and remonstrances of the suffering States and ask how it has been with our property in slaves? The South has thus been annually robbed of hundreds of thousands of dollars. It will not do to say that the thing has been done by individuals. This is true, but the States of which these individuals are citizens have endorsed their acts. Obstructions have been thrown in the way of Southern citizens attempting to recover their slaves, and the blood of South Carolinians has been shed and their lives sacrificed in the attempt to recover their property. The laws of the United States demand the rendition of fugitive slaves, but eleven states have nullified these laws. This fact virtually dissolved the Union, the compact was broken by states solemnly pledged to support justice, and public justice instead of being secured, has been trodden down with a violated Constitution as the mire of the street.[27]

Among the delegates chosen from the Greenville district to attend the secession convention was this same James Furman. There he "received a liberal share of the votes for permanent president, and there, also he cast his vote in the unanimous action by which South Carolina seceded from the Union."[28] Richard Furman would doubtless have been proud of his son.

[27]H. T. Cook, *The Life and Work of James C. Furman* (Greenville SC, 1926) 194, 197.

[28]Ibid., 201, 202.

CHAPTER 12

Father and Founder
of State Baptist
Convention

In November 1819 the Charleston Baptist Association met at Mechan-
icsville near Evan Pugh's old Cashaway Church just east of the Great
Pee Dee River. It was an unlikely place for a historical event. Twenty
ordained ministers, two licensed preachers, and thirty-seven laymen
registered as delegates. The Association had grown to include thirty-
six churches,[1] thirty-three of which were represented.

As was his unbroken practice, Furman was present, and according
to custom, he was elected moderator. The first two days—Saturday and
Sunday—were given to worship and observance of the Lord's Supper.
On Monday, the business of the Association began. Fraternal letters were
read from other associations all the way from Georgia to Massachusetts.
In turn, delegates were designated to correspond with them on behalf
of the Charleston churches. It was their way of keeping in touch with
Baptist work throughout America.

With these matters behind, John M. Roberts, already showing signs
of the affliction that would soon terminate his life, addressed a query

---

[1]Table with *Minutes of the Charleston Baptist Association*, 1819, SCBHS.

from the High Hills church that would be a milestone in the development of Baptist denominational life. "Would not," it asked, "the formation of a General Association, composed of delegates from the several Baptist Associations in South Carolina, be desirable, and advantageous to the Baptist denomination, and the advancement of the Redeemer's kingdom in general?"[2] As moderator, Furman then brought forward a plan for promoting educational and missionary interests, accompanied by an address to sister associations. Both the spirit and design of his plan were approved and a committee—composed of Furman, Roberts, and Cook—was appointed to select a time for the proposed meeting, sign the address in behalf of the body, and send it to the different associations concerned.[3]

The address sets forth in the strongest terms certain "defects and deficiencies" among the churches that injure "the cause of God" and "too often" result in its being cast "in an unfavorable light before men of discernment." The blame for these evils was fixed "partly in practice, partly in sentiment, and partly in disposition," but was summed up "under the character of neglect, where intellectual and religious improvement is called for in the use of rational means. . . ."[4]

Few documents from that period stress more strongly the low state of preparedness among ministers and the general neglect of religion. The burden of emphasis was upon the need for an educated ministry. Described as "a subject of the first importance" and for the want of which "other defects we have noticed, are ordinarily more or less connected," the address declared that "ministers who have failed to obtain some share of education are not fitted to take that station in society, or exert that influence which would properly belong to them if they had." At the risk of offense, Furman pressed the point.

> Is not this apparent to persons of common discernment; and are not their defects in language and knowledge, lamented by their friends,

---

[2]*Minutes of the Charleston Baptist Association*, 1819, SCBHS.

[3]Ibid.

[4]Richard Furman, John M. Roberts, Joseph B. Cook, *To the Different Associations of the State Baptist Convention of South Carolina,* 8 November 1820, microfilm copy, SCBHS.

while they become the matter of scoff and derision to their enemies? Do not even children, who have obtained a tolerable portion of regular education, see these defects in them; and when they have made a little advance in knowledge and experience, do they not begin to discover them themselves, and feel embarrassed, especially when they have to speak before an enlightened audience.

When entrance into the ministry is made so easy that any person with warm passions, apparent piety, and little fluency of speech, can easily get into the ministerial character and work just as he is . . . the consequences of these sentiments and their influence in practice is that in a very large proportion of our churches our ministers have but little of the improvement which is to be obtained by rational means.[5]

The conditions cited were preparatory to a concluding call for "a united general meeting of all Baptist Associations in this state" to be held

as soon as the subject can be brought regularly before them, for their consideration; and that a delegation be made of a suitable number of their most enlightened and influential members, men who are governed by the fear and love of God, to concert measures in favor of these general interests . . . and particularly with a view to the work of collecting and establishing funds in favor of educating ministers, and of sending the gospel to the destitute.[6]

The twin causes of education and missions were thus merged in this first call for uniting South Carolina Baptists in a statewide organization. Significantly, both causes "would be conducted in strict connection with the General Convention [the Triennial] in which we consider the interest of the Baptists in America, virtually and happily combined."[7]

It was proposed that the assembly be called the State Convention of Baptists in South Carolina and that the place of meeting be Columbia on the last Tuesday in December of 1821. The document was signed on 8 November 1820 by Richard Furman, John M. Roberts, and Jo-

---

[5]Ibid.

[6]Ibid.

[7]Ibid.

seph B. Cook, in that order. Roberts and Cook were the first students sent by Furman's General Committee to Rhode Island College. Now, with their benefactor and mentor, they formed a trio of hope for an educational structure with its supporting roots extending to all associations brought together in a general convention.

When the convention proposal reached the backcountry churches, most of them responded either indifferently or not at all. At the next meeting of the Association, in 1820 at Camden, there was little encouraging news. Item 14 of the minutes of that meeting reads, "Took into consideration the formation of the State Convention, proposed at our last meeting. Upon inquiry it appeared that the Associations in the interior of the State, who had received the Address from this body . . . had not adopted the plan proposed; but some of them had referred it to the Churches. . . . "[8]

Furman and his associates were not discouraged. The logic for a state organization was too convincing, and the cause of education too important to South Carolina Baptists and the Baptist ministry in general. Further consideration of the subject was postponed while efforts were made to enlist the support of the other associations, which then included the Edgefield, Bethel, Saluda, Broad River, Moriah, and Savannah River—all along the western and northern periphery of the Charleston.

The 1821 meeting of the Charleston Association convened with the Congaree church on 4 November. Furman's mind was flooded with memories in that place. This was the church of Joseph Reese, near the Wateree River and the Hills of Furman's boyhood home, where his parents lay in the revered soil of Furman plantation land.

The meeting opened as usual with solemn worship services on Saturday and Sunday. The attendance was "large and seriously attentive." Thirty churches registered delegates, and for the twenty-seventh time Furman was elected moderator. The delegates were preoccupied with the usual matters of business, except those relating to the theological seminary in Washington and the proposed meeting in Columbia to organize a state Baptist convention.

The liberality of Furman's spirit and his cheerful submission to the democratic process had been demonstrated in the 1820 meeting. De-

---

[8]*Minutes of the Charleston Baptist Association*, 1820, SCBHS.

spite the presence of Luther Rice and his own regret that Rice and the Board of Managers of the Triennial Convention had exceeded their authority in establishing the Washington school in advance of adequate financing, Furman led the Association in applauding the work of the Triennial and in promise of support for the school. Now again, in 1821, after hearing a printed communication from the Board of the Baptist Convention in the United States, the Association unanimously stated its "high regard to the interests of the Theological and Literary Institution in Washington, D.C.; and their determination to prosecute the best measures in their power for affording their support to it, and to the Missionary plans."[9]

It was late Tuesday afternoon when the matter of the state convention came before the body, with appointment of the following delegates to represent the association: Richard Furman, William Dossey, William B. Johnson, Joseph B. Cook, George Scott, Lee Compere, and Richard M. Todd. Of the seven, only Scott failed to appear when the delegates met one month later—4 December—in Columbia.

MEETING IN COLUMBIA

Although Columbia had been the state capital for only twenty-four years, the old James Taylor plantation was already being shaped into the metropolitan center that it would someday become. The Baptist church, a frame building on the corner of Plain (now Hampton) and Sumter streets, had been constituted in October 1809, with thirteen members—nine whites and four blacks[10]—and W. B. Johnson as its first pastor. He was also chaplain for South Carolina College. Visible through tall oaks was the frame construction of the original State House built late in the final decade of the eighteenth century. Among the one hundred or more buildings were a primitive meetinghouse built by the Methodists in 1803, a two-story courthouse, the high brick wall surrounding South Carolina College,[11] and scattered business houses lining Richardson (now Main) Street, the principal business thoroughfare.

---

[9]Ibid., 1820, 1821.

[10]See Woodson, *Giant in the Land*, 18.

[11]Ibid., 17.

When the Baptist church was constituted, Isaac Tucker, a licensed preacher from the Beulah church, preached the sermon,[12] and Jonathan Maxcy, who had recently come to Columbia as college president, served as presiding officer. For Johnson, then residing in Greenville, this was a time to remember that clear blue morning in October 1809 when the congregation gathered on the banks of the Congaree River for the first baptismal service and then retired to the courthouse for the services that constituted the church.[13]

In the "church edifice" built during the Johnson pastorate and dedicated in March 1811,[14] the delegates met—six from the Charleston Association, two from the Edgefield, and one from the Savannah River. In addition to Furman, Dossey, Johnson, Cook, Compere, and Todd from the Charleston Association, John Landrum and Colonel Abner Blocker were there from Edgefield, and Thomas Gillison from the Savannah River. The Broad River, Bethel, Saluda, and Moriah associations sent no delegates.

Conspicuously missing was John M. Roberts. At the 1821 associational meeting note was taken of his illness, and the churches were asked to pray for his recovery. Before the next meeting he had taken his own life. It was a tragic end for the one who had established Roberts Academy. As secretary of the General Committee of the Charleston Baptist Association since 1798, he had befriended many young men in their struggle for an education. "No man except Furman, himself," says Joe M. King in his *History of South Carolina Baptists*, "had done more for the cause of education."[15]

The nine delegates present had no way of knowing to what extent their getting together would shape the history of Baptists in South Carolina and the future larger body of Southern Baptists. They represented more than a hundred churches within their respective associations. As pastor of the most important Baptist church in South Carolina and im-

---

[12]*A Concise Account of the Rise and Constitution of the Baptist Church in the Town of Columbia, S.C.*, First Baptist Church Records, 1809-1840, microfilm copy, SCBHS.

[13]William B. Johnson, *Reminiscences*, South Caroliniana Library, University of South Carolina, Columbia.

[14]Ibid.

[15]King, *A History of South Carolina Baptists*, 172.

mediate past president of the Triennial Convention, Furman stood foremost among them as the natural leader of this historic movement. The very dignity and solemnity of his presence in the president's chair inspired respect.

It was resolved that "this body do consider their union as founded altogether upon principles of Gospel truth, Christian affection and liberality; having for their direct object the promotion of the cause and interest of the Redeemer." This was the expression of pious men when "piety" was a term used to express depth of spiritual commitment. They then turned their attention to the main order of business. Furman, Johnson, and Landrum were named, in that order, to a committee to prepare a constitution, and Furman, Cook, and Compere were to prepare an address "to the several associations in the state."[16]

The Convention continued for three days. On the second day, Furman reported that the committee appointed to prepare a constitution had not completed its work and asked for further time. On the third day it made a report under the title *Constitutional Principles*. On the same day, the committee for preparing an address to the associations reported that they had completed their work "in substance," but that the address needed "the finishing touch." Furman was requested to apply this "touch" at such time as suited his leisure and publish the address with the minutes.

Both *Constitutional Principles* and the address bore the signature of Furman as president and Blocker as secretary. As a member of each committee and probably chairman of both, Furman brought to the work his ripe experience and observation. The principles were clear and concisely stated. The preamble foresaw the Convention as "a bond of union, a centre of intelligence, and a means of vigorous, united exertion in the cause of God. . . ." The "grand objects" were stated as "the promotion of evangelical and useful knowledge, by means of religious education; the support of missionary service among the destitute; and the cultivation of measures promotive of the true interest of the churches of Christ in general, and of their union, love and harmony in particular." In addition, the independence and liberty of the churches, with no arbitrary

---

[16]*Minutes of the State Baptist Convention*, 1821, SCBHS.

interference in their secular or spiritual interests unless requested by them, was stated as a binding policy.[17]

As an object of "primary importance," the organization and support of a "seminary of learning in this State . . . on a plan of accordance with the interests of that established by the denomination at large, in the United States," was given high priority. Columbian College was then in its infancy, and Furman's vision of its usefulness transcended his fear for its financial future. The promotion of missions, the exertion of "vigorous efforts to engage the most able, pious and suitable ministers" in mission enterprises, and the establishment of Sunday schools for the religious instruction of children were other objects declared in principle. For the support of these causes, charity sermons, societies, donations, and bequests were set forth as convention policies.[18]

Here, in essence, was the plan for a multi-benevolent denominational organization that rested upon the associations as the associations rested upon the churches. It provided a central organization to act as a promotional and financial agent for all agencies and institutions supported by the denomination. It successfully outlined what Furman unsuccessfully attempted when he sought to incorporate the Charleston Baptist Association to handle the Education Fund.

The State Baptist Convention illustrated the consistency of Furman's thinking. From the attempted incorporation of the Charleston Association in 1790, through the organization of the Triennial Convention in 1814 and the State Convention in 1821, he never departed from his basic concept that Baptists should form a voluntary association centrally organized from the local church to the national level in support of multi-benevolence.

When he put the "finishing touch" on the address to the associations, it was both a strong appeal and a diplomatic handling of matters having sensitive overtones for many of the churches.[19] The educational

---

[17]*Constitutional Principles Agreed Upon by the Baptist State Convention of South Carolina*, an appendage to the *Minutes of the State Baptist Convention*, 1821, SCBHS.

[18]Ibid.

[19]The full text of this address accompanies the *Minutes of the State Baptist Convention*, 1821, and may be found in the South Carolina Baptist Historical Society Collection. An abridged text appears in Appendix G of this work. It is an important document in considering Furman's place in Baptist educational history.

and missionary objectives of the Convention were clearly set forth—especially the educational. "A respectable academy, at least, if not ultimately a college; and the support of students in the Gospel ministry, under the care of the Convention, or its agents," were emphasized as "special objectives for the Convention."

Was there in this a contradiction between his support for an academy, and ultimately a college, in South Carolina, when, as president of the Triennial Convention, he had earlier opposed an institution in Maine and another proposed for North Carolina, South Carolina, and Georgia out of concern that they might financially weaken the one in Washington?[20] The answer must be rationalized. If a contradiction is assumed, Furman no doubt had further matured his thinking on institutional interrelationship and concluded that success for the Washington school necessitated a strong contingent of institutions on the state level.

> The general interests of the whole denomination, in the United States, are designed to be concentrated in the institution in Washington. . . . Under the care of the State Convention, a respectable academy may be formed, in which the students would be prepared, by an acquaintance with the learned languages and the elementary parts of science, to enter the other institution with advantage.[21]

This was the crux of Furman's thinking at that time. He foresaw a college sufficient unto itself as a distinct possibility. But his eyes were fixed first upon a preparatory academy feeding into Columbian College, and others like it serving the same purpose.

The first convention of the South Carolina Baptists adjourned on the third day of meeting.[22] A bold vision had been proposed with only

---

[20]See pages 181-82 of this work.

[21]Ibid.

[22]This was also the first state convention among American Baptists. The following year, 1822, Georgia Baptists formed the General Baptist Association of the State of Georgia, which, in 1827, changed its name to the Baptist Convention for the State of Georgia (*History of the Baptist Denomination in Georgia: with Biographical Compendium and Portrait Gallery of Baptist Ministers and Other Georgia Baptists*, compiled for the *Christian Index*, 1881, 105-106). In its September 1822 edition, the *American Baptist*

nine men from three associations to project it. "Their names," says Joe
M. King, "deserve to be enshrined forever in the memory and hearts of
South Carolina Baptists."[23] If one whose leadership and influence towered above the rest is to be selected from that group, it would be Richard Furman. Long the guiding genius in broadening the base of South
Carolina Baptists in support of education and other causes, he had also
been a wise architect for voluntary union among American Baptists from
Georgia to New England. For more than thirty years he had been shaping the tomorrows of American Baptists.

SECOND CONVENTION MEETING

The Convention met again on 4 December 1822 at the Fellowship
church near the village of Cambridge in the Edgefield district. The delegates numbered one more than the preceding year. But those from the
Savannah River Association, "four or five in number," failed to attend,
as did William Dossey and Peter Edwards from the Charleston Association, and Richard Carson from Edgefield—these latter due to "in-
disposition." Furman was again elected president, and Joseph B. Cook
was elected secretary. Among the new faces at the second meeting were
John Good, Timothy Dargan, Chesley Davis, Basil Manly, and James
Scott. Good was in the early part of a ten-year pastorate at Ebenezer
Church on Jeffry's Creek. Dargan, one of his members, was the son of
the Reverend Timothy Dargan, the first pastor at Ebenezer and traveling companion of Furman during their evangelistic tours soon after
Furman's conversion. Basil Manly was then a twenty-four-year-old
bachelor destined to succeed Furman as pastor of the Charleston church
and later to become president of the University of Alabama.

Missionary Magazine, published in Boston, took commendatory note of the organization of the South Carolina Baptist Convention. "We cannot but remark," the edi-
tors wrote, "that our brethren in the South have in this as in many other cases, presented
us an example most worthy of imitation. We have long been sensible of the want of
some such organization as this for every state in the Union. . . . Let each one, wherever
he may reside, ask himself, why might not a general convention be established in this
state as well as in South Carolina?"

[23]King, *A History of South Carolina Baptists*, 171.

By appointment, Furman delivered the introductory sermon prior to the business session. Furman, William B. Johnson, and John Landrum were named to draft a constitution on the basis of *Constitutional Principles* adopted at the Columbia meeting. Within the year since the first meeting, Furman had given thoughtful consideration to a document that would enunciate the principles adopted at Columbia and had probably brought the tentative draft of a proposed constitution to this second meeting. On the second day, he reported that progress had been made and that the committee hoped to "bring forward the form of a Constitution, for consideration" on the third day.[24] Their hopes were realized. On the third day, as the first order of business, the proposed constitution was read straight through, then article by article. With some alterations, it was unanimously adopted and ordered to be printed.

This is one of the most important documents in Baptist history. From it would evolve, in the course of time and with appropriate variables, state conventions throughout the South, and eventually the Southern Baptist Convention. Within the fertile mind of Furman and his committee, the future structure of denominational life among Southern Baptists had come to birth.

The beginning and support of a "Seminary of Learning" in South Carolina, under the care of the Convention, was stated as a primary objective, but on the condition that it be "in accordance with that at Washington." A further provision stated that should the General Association of Georgia Baptists, "or other religious bodies out of this State," wish to cooperate in the establishment of a seminary; the support and government of the institution would be "conducted in concert with them."[25] The constitution was signed by Richard Furman, president, and Joseph B. Cook, secretary, by order of the Convention on 4 December 1822.

Full implementation of the Convention into a representative body of South Carolina Baptists was not to be easy. W. B. Johnson was asked to prepare an address to the churches in support of convention objectives and as an answer to critics of the convention plan. His was a classic polemic against ignorance of mind, poverty of spirit, and pervasive sec-

---

[24]*Minutes of the State Baptist Convention*, 1822, SCBHS.

[25]Ibid.

tionalism. One by one he took up objections and destroyed them with devastating, sometimes scathing, argument. Having dealt with each in turn, he called for help in making the Convention a tool of denominational revival. He then added, for those whose minds were closed to cooperation,

> You do not like our plan for attempting to obtain this revival. Come with us and point out a better way, and we will adopt it. Keep not aloft from us, and load us with censure, but meet us in solemn council and prayerful deliberation. . . . If we are right, come join and help us. If we are wrong, show us our error and help us to abandon it.[26]

He had words of special appeal for the churches that had not joined the Convention.

> We have proposed you a plan . . . and invited your cooperation. We have delayed till our present meeting, the completion of our Constitution, in the hope that we should have enjoyed the pleasure of your presence and counsel. . . . We have waited in vain. . . . But we are unwilling to proceed without you. We desire your aid and your counsel. We therefore once more address you . . . affectionately and solemnly. . . . We wish to use plainness of speech, but not to hurt your feelings. If therefore anything should seem to be harsh, or have the appearance of injustice; be not hasty in forming your opinion. Weigh well what is written, and then form your judgment. . . . A man, who is convinced today, that he is wrong, is wiser than he was yesterday; and he who changes his erroneous sentiment or practice today, is better than he was yesterday.[27]

Even so, execution of the convention plan matured slowly.

 In varying degrees the majority of the associations, churches and members opposed foreign missions, domestic missions, ministerial

---

[26]*Address to the Churches, the State Convention of the Baptist denomination, in South Carolina, to their Constituents, and their Brethren throughout the State*, in *Minutes of the State Baptist Convention*, 1822, SCBHS.

[27]Ibid.

education, the General Convention and its theological institution in South Carolina. They argued that all these movements and organizations were unscriptural, that education was dangerous to the spirituality and independence of the ministry, that the money given would not go where it was designated, that too much of it would go out of the state, that there were "heathen enough at home," that the whole tended to foster pride and vainglory in the leaders who would soon be "lording it over God's heritage" like bishops. All that ignorance, fear and cupidity could invent in the minds and hearts of good men was hurled at this effort to enlist the entire denomination in support of the great objects of the kingdom.[28]

But Furman, Johnson, and Manly, and others of that visionary group, though somewhat dismayed at the depth and intensity of the opposition, did not turn back. They had set their course. The next meeting convened at Edgefield on 29 November 1823 and continued through 3 December. Twenty-nine delegates had been appointed from the Charleston, Edgefield, Savannah River, and Saluda associations. The Edgefield church had been constituted in April of the same year, with Basil Manly as pastor. In the meantime, Johnson had moved to Greenville in the Saluda Association, and his presence and encouragement there had resulted in its sending delegates to the Edgefield meeting. But the Saluda Association illustrated the problem of forming a truly viable and representative state convention. At its 1824 meeting, union with the Convention was discontinued after many of its churches expressed unwillingness to continue an affiliation. Not only was the resolution of union rescinded, but a circular letter was also revoked that had been prepared by Johnson based on cooperation of the Association with the Convention.[29]

With this rejection, Johnson prepared a paper entitled *The Alarming Condition of the Churches*, in which he said,

> The present is a season of alarming visitation from the hand of our God. Our churches generally complain of great coldness and declension. Serious troubles exist between some of them, and even between some of

---

[28]McGlothlin, *A History of Furman University*, 52-53.

[29]Woodson, *A Giant in the Land*, 48.

their ministers and venerable fathers in the gospel. Very few have been
the additions to them, and our number, as a body, has suffered a de-
crease, as well this year as the last. In the providential arrangement of
the Divine hand, indications of His displeasure are strongly marked.
The heaven above is as iron, and the earth beneath our feet is as brass.
The bottles of heaven are stopped, and the earth withholds her usual
supply of kindly fruits for the support of men. Brethren, this dearth
of rain upon the earth, and of Divine influence upon the churches, call
for solemn prayer and serious self-examination. . . .[30]

The General Association of Georgia Baptists had communicated by
letter to the 1822 Convention their interest in a cooperative educational
undertaking with South Carolina Baptists, and the Convention had returned "an affectionate, respectful Answer" expressing "readiness to cooperate . . . in any practical measure. . . ."[31] In 1823 Jesse Mercer and
William T. Brantly represented the Georgia Baptists at the Convention. The purpose of their coming was to consider with their South Carolina brethren whether a jointly supported institution might not serve
the needs of each and be both feasible and desirable. On the second day,
this was the principal subject of discussion. The conclusions were that
the two conventions should cooperate in building and maintaining an
institution, and that it should be located in South Carolina within thirty
miles of Augusta, and that ultimately it should embrace a course of
theological instruction and "a general course of literature, scientific, and
classical" studies. A committee was appointed to confer with others from
Georgia to select a site and arrange courses of study. Thirty-two delegates from South Carolina associations were named agents to collect
funds for support of the enterprise.

The immediate results were disappointing. When the Convention
met again in December 1824 at Coosawhatchie, those appointed to collect funds reported that "owing to disasters suffered throughout the state
this year, . . . the majority had attempted nothing."[32] There had been
a severe drought that summer, followed by heavy rains and floods dur-

---

[30]Ibid., 49.

[31]*Minutes of the State Baptist Convention*, 1822, SCBHS.

[32]Ibid., 1824.

ing the fall and winter. In Charleston, sickness had reached a stage of pestilence, and a hurricane had spread destruction across much of the state. Only twenty-five dollars had been collected for the contemplated seminary. A committee named to consult with representatives of the Georgia Association reported that, though a Georgia committee had been appointed to consult with them, the two committees had reached no agreement on a time to meet, and that while the Georgia General Association was sympathetic toward cooperation with South Carolina, "no effectual co-operation could be expected at present." It was proposed, therefore, that a new committee be appointed with authority to act without restrictions relating to Georgia's participation. Specifically, the new committee was asked "to institute inquiries relative to the most suitable place within the limits of the State, collect all the information in their power, with respect to the advantages of particular situations, obtain estimates for buildings of different kinds, and of other expenses for carrying the designed institution into immediate operation . . . and to proceed in the duties of their appointment, though the Committee from Georgia should, for any cause, fail to attend."[33]

Furman was unhappy with the dilatory response of the Georgia people. To Basil Manly he wrote, "I am by no means pleased by what you represent to have been the views and feelings of the [Georgia] association respecting the contemplated seminary of learning. The sentiments and intentions which they have now expressed on the subject appear to me as coming from them with a very awkward grace when it is remembered that they were early in suggesting the subject as one in which they were disposed to cooperate with us in a prompt and decided manner. Indeed, what the delegates urged at our last meeting and their late decision taken in connection with their former communications bear an appearance of quibbling or child's play."[34] These were strong words for Furman, who was normally the most restrained of men.

Among other matters, the Georgia Association had quibbled over the possible negative effect the proposed institution might have upon Columbian College. Furman disagreed. "We surely cannot as a body be charged with doing anything to impair the program of Columbian Col-

---

[33]Ibid.

[34]Richard Furman to Basil Manly, 9 May 1824, SCBHS.

lege," he told Manly, "when it is not only designed but solemnly declared that our intention is to promote its interest, and when the direct use of such institution as we may establish will be for the present and perhaps for a long time to come, if not always, to prepare youth for entering the college. . . . At the same time, it will afford such aid as it can in services, particularly in divinity, to such as can go there, but would not if the contemplated seminary here should never be established."[35]

To those who feared that an institution in South Carolina in cooperation with Georgia Baptists would draw upon the same financial sources as Columbian College, Furman acknowledged that "we hope to get money for this institution from persons who are friendly to the college in Washington," but, he countered, "our principal dependence is on those who will not contribute to the college at Washington, it having been stated by persons entitled to know that many who will not give anything to the Washington institution are willing to contribute to the aid of this. . . ."[36]

While Georgia Baptists temporized and vacillated, the trustees of Edgefield Village Academy, a small school near the Edgefield Court House, offered to deed property, including an academic building, to the South Carolina Baptist Convention. At the 1823 meeting of the Convention in Edgefield, W. B. Johnson, Furman, Manly, and other members of the committee chosen to select a site for a convention seminary met with academy trustees Eldred Simkins, Sr., John S. Jeter, Matthew Mims, Benjamin Fraser, and Whitefield Brooks.[37] Johnson was doubtful about the site. For health reasons, he preferred the higher altitude around Greenville or Pendleton where he then lived.[38] Furman thought otherwise. "As to the superior advantage of extreme upper country in respect to health," he would later write to Manly, "I believe it to be visionary, and that within the limits we have prescribed for the site of the institution, as much health may be found as in any other part

---

[35]Ibid.

[36]Ibid.

[37]Woodson, *A Giant in the Land*, 56.

[38]Robert Norman Daniel, *Furman University: A History* (Greenville SC: Hiott Press, 1951) 14.

of the interior so far as situation is concerned. For my own part, and especially as our Georgia friends are now disposed to withhold a decision at least for the present, I am very much disposed to accept the offer of the trustees of the Edgefield Academy." He then added,

> It will probably be in the power of the convention to give a few hundred dollars to one or two able teachers in addition to the ordinary salaries they would receive so as to render their station both comfortable and respectable, and one of those at least should be qualified to assist young men in the study of Divinity as well as the most useful branches of general science. In this case I wish education societies to be promoted as much as possible to contribute to the support of the young men who may be admitted on the plan of being educated gratuitously, each society having particular regard to the youth it may recommend. This plan, I think, will be attended with more vigor and effect than that of leaving the work altogether to the operation of general collections or the mere application of a general fund.[39]

That was in May 1824. He would not live to see the time when the Convention selected Edgefield as the site for the school. While attending the annual meeting of the Charleston Baptist Association at Society Hill in November, he was stricken by a disease that would prove fatal. During the previous summer an uncommon amount of sickness in Charleston had added heavy additional burdens of pastoral care. From early morning to late night, he was occupied with the physical and spiritual care of patients until his own constitution began to feel the effects of the strain. Still, as time for the 1824 meeting of the Charleston Baptist Association arrived, he followed his unbroken attendance custom and set forth to the meeting place, probably traveling by way of Georgetown and from there taking the Georgetown-Cheraw stagecoach road to Society Hill. Along this same road Francis Marion had led his troops during the Revolution, and over it the much-traveled Francis Asbury had carried the tenets of Methodism into the South Carolina interior.

This would be Furman's final attendance at an associational meeting. He entertained a special affinity for the old Welsh Neck church in

---

[39]Richard Furman to Basil Manly, 9 May 1824, SCBHS.

Society Hill. That year the church was eighty-seven years old, the second oldest Baptist church in South Carolina—second only to his own church in Charleston. It was also one of the four original churches that formed the Charleston Baptist Association and in doctrine had been like the Charleston church, more Regular than Separate. Within the next decade, his son, James C. Furman, would begin a distinguished career as pastor and educator there.

The meeting was well attended, as meetings of the Association were, but the sickly malaise of the summer and fall hung over it like a cloud. "The exhibitions of Divine judgment which have been so awfully made this year in the severe drought of Summer, the excessive rains of Autumn, the overwhelming floods on several of the principal rivers, the ravages of pestilential disease in Charleston, and the devastation of the late tremendous hurricane, through an extensive region of our country" were listed in a resolution as "loud calls in Divine Providence on us, and the whole community for the exercise of humiliation and prayer."[40]

This was Furman's forty-fourth year in attendance. He was again elected moderator and presided through the whole of the sessions, despite painful symptoms of what in the medical terminology of that day was called dropsy. Among matters of business he urged upon the Association was support for the American Baptist Tract Society (now the American Baptist Publication Society) for the circulation of "well-written, compendious, religious Tracts." The Association agreed to recommend the formation of auxiliary societies for support of the parent society in Washington and to establish convenient depositories "where the Tracts may be obtained."[41] In that way Furman added a new dimension to his insistence upon an informed and well-trained ministry. For that session he prepared his last official message to the churches in a circular letter emphasizing the divinity of Christ. Into it he poured a full measure of the wisdom he had accumulated through his long ministry. Joseph B. Cook would term it "a legacy bequeathed unto you by a dying father. It is a rich, invaluable treasure. Prize it as such. Never

---

[40]*Minutes of the Charleston Baptist Association*, 1824, SCBHS.

[41]Ibid.

suffer it to be lost. Induce Your children to read it, and bequeath it to them when you die."[42]

One month later Furman traveled west of Charleston to Coosawhatchie to attend the fourth annual meeting of the State Baptist Convention. On Monday he preached the convention sermon prior to the opening of the business session. On the preceding Saturday he had been elected president for the fourth time. On Sunday, as part of a day of worship, he administered the ordinance of baptism to his third son, Samuel, who lived in the neighborhood.[43] For his sermon text on Monday, he selected a text prophetic of his own early departure. It was taken from 1 Corinthians 3:10—"According to the grace of God which is given unto me, as a wise master builder, I have laid the foundation, and another buildeth thereon; but let every man take heed how he buildeth thereupon."[44] The sermon has not survived, but as Basil Manly would later say, "Having imparted with more than the usual copiousness and solemnity, his latest counsel, he took affectionate leave, expressing his apprehension that he should see them no more."

The minutes of the Coosawhatchie Convention also include an address to the churches strongly presenting the case for an educated ministry. Prepared by J. B. Cook, but revised and approved by a committee consisting of Cook, Furman, Jesse Mercer, and W. B. Johnson, it was signed by Furman as president of the Convention and by Basil Manly as secretary.[45]

Furman was in sight of the promised land of an educational institution under South Carolina Baptists, but he would not be permitted to enter. The committee appointed to select a site reported that they had not "fixed on any spot to be recommended," that no progress had been made in obtaining cooperation from Georgia Baptists, and that "although the General Association of Georgia felt a friendly disposition

---

[42]Joseph B. Cook, *The Good and Faithful Servant Approved and Honoured by His Divine Master, a Funeral Sermon Occasioned by the Much Lamented Death of the Rev. Richard Furman, D.D.*, Southern Baptist Theological Seminary Library, Louisville, Kentucky.

[43]H. T. Cook, *Biography*, 36.

[44]*Minutes of the State Baptist Convention*, 1824, SCBHS.

[45]An abridged text of this address is contained in Appendix H.

towards the contemplated institution," the committee had learned that "no effectual cooperation could be expected at present."[46] It would remain for the next meeting of the Convention, two months after Furman's death, to select a site and proceed with the fulfillment of his dream.

LAFAYETTE IN CHARLESTON

Back home in Charleston, an event of extraordinary civic and patriotic importance would require Furman's services during this final year of his life. In February 1824 President James Monroe invited the Marquis de Lafayette to visit the United States. His coming would demonstrate again the esteem in which Charleston held Furman and show the admiration of the nation for Lafayette.

Lafayette arrived in New York on 16 August 1824. Following a trip to Boston, he traveled leisurely down the east coast. Everywhere along the way, he was greeted by large and enthusiastic crowds of appreciative citizens. In March 1825 he arrived in Charleston. Seated in a carriage drawn by four grey horses, he entered the city in a procession that included the clergy immediately behind the general. Following them, beginning with the Society of Cincinnati, was a broad representation of Charleston, including educational institutions, the military, officers and soldiers of the Revolution, and the numerous Charleston educational, cultural, and industrial societies.[47] Not since George Washington visited the city in 1791 had there been such a lavish and joyous welcome of any visitor.

An arrangement was made for Lafayette to meet the clergy of Charleston and the surrounding environs on the following morning at eleven o'clock, with Furman as their spokesman. Furman's health was declining, but his gift of speech was not. "While all these classes of our citizens hail your safe arrival in Charleston," he addressed the general, "we, the clergy of the city and its vicinity are induced to approach you with a profound respect, uniting our voice with the community at large in presenting to you the most sincere and cordial welcome."

---

[46]*Minutes of the State Baptist Convention,* 1824, SCBHS.

[47]*Charleston Mercury and Morning Advertiser*, 16 March 1825.

It affords us, sir, a refined satisfaction to see you again among us, brought, as you have been in safety through so many vicissitudes and dangers, and in the possession of so much health and vigor, and with the body of our fellow citizens, we feel highly honored by the friendly visit you have made to these United States in general and our city in particular.

It must, General, afford you pleasure to behold the present flourishing state of our country where liberty is happily blended and established with government and laws; where agriculture, commerce, and the arts, are making daily advances in improvement; where science is cultivated with care and success; and where religion, unfettered by those human restrictions which attempt to direct or control the conscience, stands on its own evidence, and divine authority, deriving its doctrines and precepts immediately from the oracles of heavenly truth and wisdom, the sacred scriptures. . . .[48]

As far as surviving evidence indicates, this was the final public occasion on which Furman addressed his remarks to the patriotic impulses of Charleston citizens.

---

[48]Ibid., 17 March 1825.

CHAPTER 13

Death and Legacy

Richard Furman died on 25 August 1825, prior to the meeting of the State Baptist Convention in Camden, 3-6 December of that same year. The malady that ended his life was not dropsy, as first believed, but iliac-passion,[1] a disease of the intestines described as "one of the most obstinate and distressing diseases to which the human frame is liable."[2] He attempted to stay its progress by exertion. He went to Edisto Island, Goose Creek, and Georgetown to preach, though subject to excruciating pain at intervals.

---

[1]Susan Furman to Susan M. Mallory, 1825, cited in H. T. Cook, *Biography*, 38. A case of ileus, describing symptoms precisely like Richard Furman's chronic attacks over a number of years, and eventually causing his death, may be found in James Wyngaarden, M.D., and Lloyd H. Smith, Jr., M.D., eds. *Cecil Textbook of Medicine* (Philadelphia and London: W. B. Saunders Co., 1982) 1:665f. *The American Illustrated Medical Dictionary*, 24th ed., ed. W. A. Newman Dorland, M.D. (Philadelphia and London: W. B. Saunders Co., 1968) describes the ileum as the distal portion of the small intestine extending from the jejunus to the cecum (p. 717). This is not to be confused with the ilium, the haunch bone or flank (p. 718).

[2]H. T. Cook, *Biography*, 38.

At Georgetown, there were warm memories of his old friend, Edmund Botsford. Botsford had died in December 1819, and Furman had preached at his funeral. The two had enjoyed a Jonathan-David relationship involving both personal visits and continuous correspondence. In a letter to Botsford, Furman had once written, "But if I should say, that, amongst my numerous correspondents, there is one whose correspondence affords me the greatest satisfaction, and that this correspondent is Mr. Botsford, I should not err from the truth."[3] In his funeral sermon, he had said to the Georgetown church, "I must . . . necessarily feel for you in no common degree on this mournful occasion when, in your esteemed Pastor, I have lost my most particular friend on earth."[4]

Susan Furman left an account of her father's final days. "The paroxysms of pain which reduced him so rapidly, commenced with intervals from ten days to a fortnight but these gradually diminished to one or two days. . . . He thought it his duty to make use of means for the recovery of his health, but his opinion, as he frequently said, was, that this was his last illness. His last discourse was preached from 'And Enoch walked with God, and was not, for God took him.' . . . He attended public service but one Sabbath after this. . . . He was so much spasmed and so much exhausted by pain on the day of his death that he could speak but little; he maintained however the command of his mind until the last day of his life. . . ."[5] Death came while listening to the reading, at his request, of the Twenty-third Psalm.

On a sultry August day they buried him in the church cemetery. The funeral cortege was a solemn procession, six persons abreast, almost three blocks long. It included civic, social, and religious leaders of the city and rank and file citizens, black and white. The order of the procession was as follows: officiating clergymen, other clergymen of the city not serving as pallbearers, the hearse, pallbearer clergymen, members of the family, members of the Baptist church, members of the Charleston Bible Society, members of the Charleston Religious Tract Society, members of the Revolution Society, and other citizens of the

---

[3]Mallary, *Memoir of Elder Edmund Botsford*, 217.

[4]Ibid.

[5]H. T. Cook, *Biography*, 38-40.

city. On either side of the procession walked the black members of his congregation.[6]

When the line moved out of Church Street onto Broad Street and approached St. Michael's Church, it was halted momentarily by Colonel J. R. Pringle, collector of the port, who said that it must not pass St. Michael's Church until the bells were tolled. This he ordered to be done.[7] The procession then moved solemnly onto Meeting Street, marched down Meeting to Tradd, from Tradd to Church, and to the Baptist church where the body was conveyed along the middle aisle. So crowded was the building that many were prevented access. Officiating clergymen were the Reverend Dr. Henry, minister of the French Protestant church, who led the prayers, and the Reverend William A. McDowell, of the Third Presbyterian Church, who preached the funeral sermon from Matthew 14:12—"And the disciples came and took up the body, and buried it, and went and told Jesus." Nothing was more indicative of Furman's catholic spirit than his choice to have ministers of other denominations officiate at his funeral. Furman probably never learned that a few days prior to his own death, his cherished friend and compatriot, Charles Cotesworth Pinckney, had died, nor that on the very day preceding his death, another friend, Thomas Baldwin, pastor of the First Baptist Church of Boston, had died on his way to attend the commencement exercises of Waterville College in Maine.[8]

Furman's death brought tributes from many sources. The *Charleston Mercury* called him "a man of no common character" on which "nature had formed one of her finest models as to both mind and body." The editor eulogized Furman in glowing prose.

Through a pilgrimage of seventy years he fulfilled in the moral, social, and religious worlds a system of the most comprehensive and useful destinies. . . . Dr. Furman was the patriarch of the Baptist church in South Carolina, the counsellor and guide, the father and friend to whom they looked up for advice and consolation. He was one

---

[6]*American Baptist Magazine* 10:5 (October 1825): 317-18, James P. Boyce Library, Southern Baptist Theological Seminary, Louisville, Kentucky.

[7]H. T. Cook, *Biography*, 125.

[8]*American Baptist Magazine* 10:5 (October 1825): 318.

of the main pillars of the denomination in the United States, and whenever he appeared in the councils of the General Convention, the unanimous voice always placed him in the first post of dignity and responsibility. He was one of the framers of the constitution of that convention and the original projector of the institution for theological, scientific, and classical education which is evolving its infantine honors with so much success at Washington. In his own state he was the father of whatever has reference to the education of the ministers of the Baptist church. . . . His whole life was one of unblemished piety and virtue.

In this city, as the consecrated and beloved pastor of the Baptist church, he universally exhibited a character of exemplary purity, edifying and impressive in the highest degree. . . . The labors which he daily and habitually underwent, the prosecution of his ministerial, parochial and benevolent avocation were great, various, and unremitting. . . .

Dr. Furman united a simple, unaffected dignity, and a countenance indicating a strong and comprehensive intellect . . . and a humility which may be termed sublime. He added the manners of a gentleman rectified and refined by the principles of the Christian, the love, reverence and respect which were always paid him by all classes of people. As a citizen he was exemplary in discharging all civil duties.[9]

At its Camden meeting, the State Convention resolved,

That this Convention are deeply affected by the death of the late Dr. Furman, as a serious calamity to the cause of Christ, and to society in general. In relation to themselves as a Body which, under God, he was the father and founder, they regard his death as a sore bereavement, and awfully afflictive visitation. . . .[10]

In a memorial sermon at the Convention, Joseph B. Cook intoned the sadness of his colleagues in words reflecting the copious style of ministerial utterances of that day.

---

[9]*Charleston Mercury and Morning Advertiser*, 4 September 1825.

[10]*Minutes of the State Baptist Convention*, 1825, SCBHS.

A calamity, of no ordinary character, has fallen on the Christian community of which we are members. The voice of lamentation and woe has reached our ears. Death has entered into the sanctuary of the Most High, and removed, into the silence of the dreary tomb, the loss which the Church of Christ has sustained in the departure of that amiable and excellent man of God, and faithful servant of the Cross, the Rev. Dr. Furman. Yes, our beloved and venerated father in the Gospel, now sleeps in the cold embrace of death. Our hearts are swollen with grief, and our eyes overflow with tears, at the sad reflection.[11]

For an hour and a half, he developed the implications of the text "Well done, good and faithful servant—enter thou into the joy of the Lord" as he applied it to Furman. It was his third time for delivery, with only minor variations in content—first before his own congregation, the Mount Pisgah church, Sumter district; subsequently, before the Charleston Association during its meeting at the Congaree church; and finally at the State Convention in Camden.

At the Congaree meeting of the Association, the delegates termed Furman "a star of the first magnitude in the Church of Christ," whose "active and enlightened mind was almost continuously engaged in forming plans for general usefulness, as connected with this body." The existence of the General Committee "for the education of pious young men, designed for the work of the Gospel ministry" was called "a monument to his praise which, it is devoutly hoped, will last, when every other monument, erected to his memory, shall cease to greet the eye or please the mind."[12]

When the Board of Managers of the Triennial Convention met in October at College Hill, Columbian College, they framed a resolution recognizing the dominant place Furman had filled in denominational leadership in being "among the first to originate and organize the Baptist General Convention."[13] Twenty-five years later, William B. Johnson testified that "by common consent" Furman had been regarded as

---

[11]Ibid.

[12]Ibid., 3.

[13]Cited in Kinlaw, "Richard Furman as a Leader in Baptist Higher Education," 165.

not exceeded by any "as a consistent, uniform and exemplary person, in a community of from twenty to thirty thousand, of whom not a few were upright professors of religion in different denominations." He was, Johnson said, "so eminent . . . for exemplary piety and holy living, that the whole city held him in veneration."[14]

In a tribute by Furman's congregation published six days after his death, expressions of love and grief were declared in superlatives.

> If there was a pastor beloved, if there was a pastor who deserved to be beloved, it was he whose loss we now deplore. . . . Follow him from youth to manhood, from manhood to old age, from old age to the grave, where can you find so much to admire and so entire exemption from everything to censure? . . . He possessed an energy of character, an extent of information, and vigour of eloquence, which powerfully promoted every measure which he advocated, though he urged his opinions with the most unpretending, unassuming modesty; and which were often exerted in the councils of this country, and more than fifty years in the cause of his God. . . . He seldom or never engaged in religious controversy; though he always maintained the doctrines of the church with firmness and energy, yet with courtesy and affability; and if he failed to convince, he never offended. . . . Such was our deceased pastor. But he has fulfilled his day; we are bereaved; and a thousand aching hearts are at this moment testifying their sorrow and his worth.[15]

There followed a resolution that as an expression of the church's "sense of loss" the members of the church "would wear crape on the left arm for a space of thirty days" and that "immediate measures" would be taken for "the preparing of a monument, with a suitable inscription, to be erected in the church to the memory of their venerable pastor."[16] Thirty-two years later when Furman's successor, Basil Manly, presented a history of the church on the occasion of its sesquicentennial, he entered into his diary, "I this morning finished what I last Saturday began, a sermon on the history of the Charleston Baptist Church from its for-

---

[14]Sprague, *Annals of the American Pulpit,* 163.

[15]*Charleston Mercury and Morning Advertiser,* 1 September 1825.

[16]Ibid.

mation in 1682. . . . In . . . speaking of the death of Dr. Furman, my revered Father and Friend, my feelings quite overcame me. I had not the power of utterance. I sobbed out a few of the last words, and was constrained to take my seat and recover before I could conclude the service with prayer."[17]

The curtain had fallen on fifty-one years of ministry, but Furman's influence and leadership had set the stage and established the direction until this day. Henceforth, the causes to which he had given his life and the denominational structure to which his genius had been directed would exceed his dreams in shaping the years that lay beyond.

A zealous patriot in the American Revolution, Furman had championed political independence and shared in the dangers and struggles to achieve that end. A devout proponent of religious liberty, he had helped frame a "dissenters' petition" that gained passage by the House of the Assembly as an act providing for absolute religious liberty freed from favor to any church or denomination. He was a delegate to the state constitutional convention of 1790 when this religious liberty provision was written into the state's first permanent constitution. He considered a free country and a free church essential to a free society.

As the wisdom of organizing a centrally located state institution of higher learning became apparent, he threw his influence behind the establishment of South Carolina College, which later would become the University of South Carolina. Upon his recommendation, the trustees of the college turned to Jonathan Maxcy as its first president.

These were among causes to which he gave himself as a citizen during the nascent years of American statehood. So honored was he in a city of many esteemed families having reputations for national leadership that he was chosen as orator and spokesman by his compatriots on occasions calling for an unusual gift in communicating the mind and heart of his fellow citizens.

But it was among Baptists that the real significance of Furman's life lay. He was in the front ranks of those who gave direction and purpose to the scattered Baptist churches of his day. It should, of course, be observed that most movements of historical consequence spring from a totality of influences more encompassing than the immediate persons

---

[17]Basil Manly Papers, University of Alabama.

involved. A nineteenth-century leader among Southern Baptists spoke to the point when he said,

> Invariable in such matters, the history and results of organic and effective life are due in part to that subtle, pervasive, and complex influence which we call the spirit of the age; in part to some exciting event or series or events; and in part to some leader or leaders, and usually more than one, and the wisdom to guide the forces and the tendencies of the times. In the United States, at the pivotal epoch which includes the late years of the Eighteenth and early Nineteenth centuries, the age, the events, and the leaders joined forces to inaugurate those co-operative measures and agencies which through times and changes since then have carried forward the missionary and educational work of the Baptist churches of our country.[18]

The estimates of Furman's contemporaries and of subsequent Baptist leaders testify that he stood among the tallest and joined with the age and its events to inaugurate what would become the dynamics of Baptist organization and education. Today's structured Southern Baptists and the causes they support trace back to the years when his leadership was a dominant force in shaping Baptist life.

While not the father of education among Southern Baptists—that title belongs to Oliver Hart and his Religious Society—Furman took up where Hart left off and carried Baptist education forward toward institutional development. As early as 1786, while still at the High Hills of Santee church, he called for churches of the Charleston Association to take an annual offering for ministerial education and for ministers to preach supporting sermons. When his proposal in 1785 to incorporate the Association to qualify it to receive and administer educational funds was rejected, he then sought and gained approval to incorporate a committee independent of the Association. This committee—the General Committee—met simultaneously with the Association and reported to it but was not a part of it. By this simple act, the seed of Baptist education was planted. From it would grow Furman University.

---

[18]E. C. Dargan, "Richard Furman and His Place in American Baptist History," *Furman University Bulletin* 3 (July 1914): 17.

Furman was also an early proponent of a centrally located Baptist institution serving Baptists from Georgia to New England. In his role as first and second president of the Triennial Convention, he favored and hoped for the success of Columbian College. But in accurately foreseeing the fatal financial stress of that institution because of inadequate initial resources, he established a Baptist legacy emphasizing fiscal responsibility in support of denominational causes and institutions.

Support for home and foreign missions by American Baptists likewise had its beginnings during the years of Furman's leadership. In 1802 the Charleston Baptist Association began mission work among the Catawba Indians and destitute whites, a work later added to that of the General Committee. Following organization of the Triennial Convention to promote foreign missions, the mission work of the Convention was also added to that of the General Committee within the associations.

When Luther Rice returned to America to enlist the support of American Baptists for foreign missions, he found in Furman one already involved in mission work at home and inspired by the foreign mission work of William Carey and other English Baptists. When the two met for the first time at the Welsh Neck meeting of the Charleston Association, they parted with a mutual commitment to the twin causes of missions and education. As they subsequently made their way toward Philadelphia for the first meeting of American Baptists, new purpose and direction were shaping the Baptist life.

Furman's last work as "father and founder" of the South Carolina Baptist Convention reflected both his disappointment and his consistent thought. He was disappointed with the society plan adopted by the Triennial Convention and wished for a convention plan that would place all the causes supported by Baptists under a single umbrella. The logic of the association voluntarily binding churches together was clear. He visualized associations forming a state convention, and state conventions forming a national convention. Hence was born the structural plan by which Baptists are drawn together from the association through the state to the national level. The convention plan reflected a special Furman genius. No one prior to him had developed a plan to support such an array of benevolent objectives as education, home and foreign missions, Sunday schools, tract societies, religious journals, temperance, and the seminary in Washington through a single agency. His

commitment to these causes and the creation of an instrument for continuing cooperative support is at the heart of the Furman legacy. In time,
the Triennial Convention would be split asunder by North-South differences, but out of the division occurring twenty years after Furman's
death emerged a convention of Southern Baptists with its roots in the
very ideas he had nurtured.

No part of his legacy is better known than his contribution to ministerial education, beginning with the formation of the General Committee of the Charleston Baptist Association. The story carries forward
into institutional development and the founding of Furman University
in 1851 as successor to three preceding institutions—the Furman
Academy and Theological Institution at Edgefield, founded in 1826,
the Theological Institution at the High Hills, and the Furman Institution at Winnsboro.[19]

Historians are not in accord as to whether it was Furman or Luther
Rice who did most in first directing the attention of American Baptists
to the cause of education. Furman was obviously first in point of time;
he was stressing education and assisting young men in preparing for the
ministry before Rice became a Baptist. Rice was but eight years old when
the General Committee of the Charleston Association was formed and
incorporated under Furman's leadership. When the two met for the first
time in 1813 at the annual meeting of the Charleston Association, Furman had been chairman of the General Committee for twenty-two years.

Following the organization of the Triennial Convention, it was
Furman who publicly spoke of his regret that more attention was not
addressed "to the improvement of the minds of pious youth who are
called to the gospel ministry," and he urged that appropriate steps be
taken to remedy this omission. At the 1817 meeting of the Convention
it was Furman who returned to the subject with a plan of education that
was unanimously endorsed by the Convention and referred to the Board
of Foreign Missions "to give it that maturity and publicity which they
shall approve." The address in which Furman unfolded this plan en-

---

[19]For an account of the founding and development of Furman University, begin-
ning with the Furman Academy and Theological Institution at Edgefield, see R. N.
Daniel, *Furman University: A History* (Greenville SC: Hiott Press, 1951) and Alfred
S. Reid, *Furman University: Toward a New Identity, 1925-1975* (Durham NC: Duke
University Press, 1976).

grafted the educational feature in that body and caused "all our later institutions to be but after fruits of the same great educational awakening."[20]

Whether Baptists would have rallied as quickly to the cause of education as a denomination had it not been for the work of Rice is unknown. Rice became the catalyst for doing what Furman probably could not have done for want of a factor to get a movement started. Foreign missions became the factor, and Rice became the catalyst for converting support for missions into support for education. The initial impulse, however, had come from Furman, and through the years it had been sustained by him.

On its present campus in the shade of Paris Mountain in Greenville, South Carolina, where the Piedmont foothills begin rising to the Blue Ridge Mountains, Furman University is a living, dynamic legacy of the man whose name it bears. From it have been graduated Rhodes scholars, a Nobel Laureate, the father of behavioral psychology, renowned scholars, and countless others whose contributions to American business, government, education, literature, religion, and the professions have given broad scope and meaning to Richard Furman's dreams. Five generations of Furmans have invested their talents and resources in its development and added lustre to the legacy of their venerable forebear.

A narrow peninsula that fingers out into the lake on the Furman campus is graced by an exact replica of the Bell Tower that for many years towered above Richard Furman Hall, centerpiece of the original Furman campus in Greenville. Erected as a gift donated by the five children of Alester Garden Furman, great-grandson of Richard Furman, it memorializes the heritage of an honored past and symbolizes in architectural beauty the history of an institution with its roots in the mind of Furman and in the General Committee of the Charleston Baptist Association conceived by him.

On a sprawling campus filled with majestic and patriarchal beech trees in Louisville, Kentucky, is the Southern Baptist Theological Seminary, historically linked with Richard Furman and the university that bears his name. Separation of the theological school from Furman University in 1869 to form the Southern Baptist Theological Seminary ful-

---

[20]Address by Dr. S. S. Cutting in Philadelphia, 1878, cited in H. T. Cook, *Biography*, 105.

filled Furman's dream essentially as he had dreamed it. His plan had called for a central seminary in Washington with feeder institutions in the states. The Baptist constituency was then along the Eastern seaboard from Georgia to New England, making the nation's capital a natural place for an institution centrally serving their needs. But by the time the theological school was moved from Greenville to Louisville in 1877, westward expansion was shifting the population center beyond the Appalachian Mountains, while separation of Northern and Southern Baptists had created a new situation for both constituencies. Furman University and Southern Seminary are thus in direct line of descent from Richard Furman and his convention plan.

Collaterally associated are Mercer University in Georgia and Baylor University and the Southwestern Baptist Theological Seminary in Texas. When the Charleston Baptist Association met at the High Hills church in 1785, Silas Mercer, a leader among Georgia Baptists, was present. As noted in an earlier chapter, he brought with him an unfriendly attitude toward ministerial education. Like many of his contemporaries, he considered it inimical to true religion and a handicap to preaching. However, under Furman's persuasive influence, he changed his attitude. Through his own efforts and those of his son, Jesse, Mercer University was founded in 1833. A student at Mercer from 1833 to 1836 was William H. Tryon. There, under the influence of Jesse Mercer, he volunteered to go to Texas in 1841 as a missionary of the Home Mission Society. In Texas, he became the principal voice in the establishment of Baylor University in 1845, and from that institution emerged the Southwestern Baptist Theological Seminary in 1908.[21]

Furman's real significance historically is not in the finished work of his lifetime but in what he did to shape the future of Southern Baptists and their institutions in the tomorrows of his age. He laid the foundations, set the stage, illustrated the spirit, and established the climate that firmly committed Baptists to a structured denominational program. The commitment remains a guiding and shaping influence more than a century and a half after Furman's death. It asserts itself through the convention principle of voluntary organization in support of a broad range of benevolent interests, with special reference to missions and ed-

---

[21]Robert A. Baker, *The Contributions of South Carolina Baptists to the Rise and Development of the Southern Baptist Convention*, unpublished manuscript, SCBHS.

ucation, twin causes of Richard Furman. Under the convention plan, domestic, home, and foreign missions are today supported nationwide and worldwide, and prestigious Southern Baptist colleges, universities, and seminaries are across much of the United States. Thus have the streams of Furman's influence flowed as a living legacy throughout the years.

Dr. William R. Williams taxed his rhetorical resources to say about Furman, "Of this eminent servant of the Lord it is difficult to express what is just and proper without the appearance of excessive partiality. To represent him in the ordinary terms of eulogy, or to depict his virtues by any common standards of description, would be the direct way to fall short of the truth. The providence of God gives few such men to the world as Doctor Furman. . . . Where others were great, he was transcendent, and where others were fair and consistent in character, he stood forth lovely and luminous in all the best attributes of man. . . . "[22]

---

[22]Vail, *The Morning Hour of American Missions,* 315.

APPENDIX A

An Address to the Residents
Between the Broad and Saluda Rivers
Concerning the American War for Independence
November, 1775

Gentlemen, permit me on this alarming occasion to address you under the endearing character of Friends, Brethren, and Fellow-Subjects. For as it concerns great numbers in the most interesting matters, their Lives, Fortunes (and what is much greater) Consciences being called in question; Suffer me, my Friends, to offer you a few thoughts, that flow from a heart, which thinks it is influenced with the most tender and impartial concern for the good of the whole. I have endeavoured since the present unhappy disputes took place between Great Britain and America, to make an impartial inquiry concerning the transactions of both parties, in order to find the truth; and as we are all liable to be imposed upon, I would willingly offer a few things to your consideration at this critical juncture. I am informed that a considerable number are now met, and encamped near Bush River, but by whose influence, and for what purpose, it is hard to determine, as the accounts are various: but by what I can gather from the sense of the people I have been conversant with, your design is to withstand the operations of the Congress; upon supposition of their acting in rebellion against the King, and designing to enslave the People.

My business therefore, shall be to set matters in a clear light, that an impartial judgment may be passed upon them. I find myself under difficulties (it is true) to go through this work, because what is, and has been said to that end is so much called in question, by people, who have not opportunity to inform themselves, who are prejudiced by false reports, carried about by men, who wish well to neither King nor Country. If the above articles are believed by you, viz: the Congress being in rebellion against the King, and designing to enslave and ruin the People, I shall 1st shew that they do not appear to be true, and then the consequences, that will necessarily flow from your proceedings, if they are not.

1st Then, I am to shew that the Congress (and with them far the greatest part of America) do not appear to be acting in rebellion against the King, nor seeking to enslave the people. This will readily appear if we consider what the Americans oppose, what means of opposition they have made use of, what they have laid themselves open to, in so doing, and how far it is consistent, with Justice and Righteousness to make such resistance.

First then, What do the Colonies oppose? I answer not the rightful power of the King, not the lawful power of any of his officers, but such things as tend to destroy the peace, and happiness of the Nation. The sum of what they oppose, is comprised in that law, that was past some years ago by the British Legislature; That they had a right to bind the Americans in all cases whatsoever!

The taxes, that were afterwards laid upon Glass, Paper, Paint, Tea etc were only consequences of the above law: and therefore their enforcing, and our submitting to one of them, would be as effectual to the enslaving of Americans, as the whole of them would have been. For instance, if a man tells me, that he has a right to do with me or any thing I have got, what he pleases, and therefore demands something of me, either of labour, or part of my estate, if I give it, I then submit to his unlimited power over me; and by my own consent, he has a right to lay upon me, what he pleases. The Parliament, therefore by insisting on the duty of tea (tho' they did take off the other duties) as much claim their unlimited power over America, as they did whilst those acts were unrecalled; As is abundantly manifest, from the resolves of both Houses of Parliament, and it being what the Minister founds his pretentions upon, in sending an army to make us yield thereto. Let it be considered that, for that end, they have taken away the charter of Massachusetts-Bay Province, sent an army and navy to Boston, their capital, who after many provocations and insults, fell upon in a furious manner, and killed eight men before they were resisted. They also passed an act forbidding them to trade to any place whatsoever, excepting Ireland, Great Britain, and the West Indian Islands, or to fish on their own coast; And respecting trade have done the like to almost all the other provinces along the Continent. They have enlarged t[h]e government of Canada, and extended it all along the back of the other provinces, and established the Roman Catholic religion, and made it a Military, Arbitrary and Tyrannick government, intending as the Minister declared in the House of Commons, to have the Canadians as a force always ready to bring down on the back of the other colonies, (should they oppose the designs of Parliament) to subdue them. And should they succeed, we have nothing to assure us, but the Popish religion may be established in all the colonies. They have taken away our birth-right. I mean trials by Juries; so enlarged the power of the admiralty and the Officers thereof, that a man can scarcely call any thing his own that he possesses; for they may break open any man's house, chest etc, on suspicion, without a civil officer to assist: and should they kill anybody in this service, they are not to be tried for it here, but sent to England for trial; and if any man should prosecute another in that court, tho' contrary to law, if the judge but writes on the proceedings, That there was probable cause of action, it shall hinder the owner from recovering damages from the prosecutor.

And now it is intimated, that if they succeed in their attempts, they will make us pay for all the expense of the last war, which they say was undertaken on our account, and cost them Seventy Millions Pounds Sterling, (four hundred and ninety million this money); & yet it stands recorded in the transactions of Parliament, that America did more than their part, and therefore at the conclusion of the peace, they sent them some of the money back.

In the next place let us consider the means of opposition. It first began in their not receiving the tea. Several provinces sent it back. Boston would have done the same, but their governor would not suffer it to go out of the port. While it was thus kept a number of men, said to be about thirty, in disguise, went and destroyed it; probably fearing that as the time was drawing near, that it was (agreeable to the act) to be seized and sold for the duty, some persons might by the governor's influence, buy it, and so Parliament have the plea that they had submitted to the abovementioned law. In the next place, they entered into a resolution, not to trade with Great Britain, and some other of His Majestie's dominions; (at the same time sending the most humble petitions to the King, that he would be pleased to repeal those acts, that were the causes of the unhappy disputes. And this they have continued to do, to this very day.) They also fell upon other measures, to bring any, that should be disaffected among themselves, to a compliance. And here (I believe) thro' the means of some men who were put into public trusts, and did not know very well what to do with power, some things were done, contrary to the designs of Congress, and the genius of the cause. (Had the People been unanimous and exerted themselves, they might have prevented this, by choosing such men, as would have best suited the whole, as it depended upon choice.) The next step of opposition was the taking up of arms, which never was done, till the stroke was struck at Boston, before-mentioned, when it was done purely by way of defence.

The third thing is to consider what the Colonies have laid themselves open to, by opposing the designs of Parliament. And here a due consideration, methinks, will remove those undue suspicions, and jealousies, that arise in the minds of some. In the first place, the rage of the ministry is excited against them, (as was expected). Thro' their means the King seems set against his Subjects, and the British army and, navy have access unto our c[oa]sts. Their trade being stopped, they necessarily encounter with many inconveniences; their crops, that they used to export, through which they obtained their wealth, lying upon their hands. And should Great Britain continue to insist upon subjection, under the necessity of maintaining the expenses of a war, here let it be observed that great men are the chief losers, their estates being along the sea-coasts, their houses in towns, and cities being liable to be burnt, or knocked down by bombs, and cannon; and as they have the most in their hands, the taxes must be heavier upon them. These are a few of the difficulties, that the Colonies have to struggle with, (& these chiefly felt by rich men) whilst they are earnestly seeking for reconciliation. But if, as it is asserted by some, they are struggling for independency, they may not only expect to have Great Britain to encounter with, but other great and war-like powers of Europe, therefore it cannot be true that they are struggling for such a state.

Lastly let us consider the justness, and righteousness of the cause. The righteousness of it appears in their endeavoring to maintain the principles of the Constitution; in which the peace and happiness of the people is safely included. The state of the British empire is a mixt monarchy, where the King and People make laws. The people do this by their representatives, whom they choose. The representatives can agree in no law, but they bind themselves in it. The House of Commons of Great Britain are their representatives, and every thing passed as law there is first agreed to by them. The Houses of Assembly of the province of America, are their representatives. Thus the King and representatives are officers of trust, and accountable for what they do, the people giving them authority. The King can do nothing without the representatives, not the representatives without the King. Neither can the representatives of one part of the Kingdom, represent another part of it. Now the Parliament of Great Britain say they have a right to bind us in all cases whatsoever, tho' they are not our representatives, and so may lay any thing upon us without feeling it themselves. Thus they have broken the principles of the constitution, by taking away the power of our Assemblies, and by establishing Popery, contrary to law, in one of the provinces, which gives us reason to suspect, they have a design to impose the same upon the other provinces; at least they claim that power.

Thus it is to maintain the happy state of the constitution, that America has opposed Parliament; and in so doing has not rejected the King's lawful authority. For what the King does, contrary to the constitution, is not the power, that is of God, spoken of in Scripture, and therefore ought not to be obeyed. For should the King command one man to kill his innocent neighbor, this would be contrary to justice and humanity. He ought therefore, to reject that command; but in everything lawful and just, he ought to yield willing obedience.

Thus, tho' America oppose those things that are wrong, which his Majesty has consented to, yet as they believe him blinded by his ministers, they do not reject him as their King, but desire that he should reign over them. This appears by their petition sent to him, their publick professions of loyalty, and by the constant prayers put up for him, in every religious assembly, and the direction of the Continental Congress so to do; (tho' some audacious villains assert that Ministers dare not in the lower parts to pray for the King, as I was told in your neighborhood.) As I intimated in the beginning of my letter, I feel the greatest difficulty, from the incredulity of so many of the people. But Sirs, for what end should the people in the lower parts of the Province, deceive you? You are their Brethren, and you may depend upon it, that every wellwisher to the cause of America, and friend of Congress, desires your welfare. But what farther evidence would you have, more than may be had? The Acts of Parliament spoken-of may be seen. The debates upon greatest abilities, in the nation, (and which serve for the greatest proof,) have been and are printed in the public Gazettes. Men of the best authority, who have been to England, and returned, assert them to be so. The newspapers brought from thence (which may be seen) prove the same. The very enemies of the cause, who have come from England, do not pretend to deny them. The troops sent into America, all prove the same; not to mention on the other hand that the members of the Continental and Provincial Congresses, and with them the Committees of the several districts, throughout the country, act spending their time and labor, without fee or reward. The Gentlemen in the Towns, and Cities, take their turns in keeping guard; a hardship the Country does not feel.

The second general proposition was to point out a few of the consequences, that necessarily will flow (according to the most probable appearances) from your opposing (especially in violent measures), the proceedings and designs of America, who is seeking to preserve her liberty. Indeed, God may make use of you, as a scourge to the nation, for sin; and so you may succeed in your attempts, altho' their cause be good. But before you engage in this you ought to consider, whether your sins do not call for the same divine displeasure, and whether you had a commission to act as the ministers of the Divine vengeance, or not.

First then, if you succeed in your endeavors, (which no doubt is the thing you would desire,) what would you gain by it? It is not likely this could be done, without the shedding of much blood, and that of your friends, and neighbors! A most awful consideration. But will this be to answer any valuable purpose? Certainly no. It will be to bind yourselves, unde[r] the unlimited sway of Arbitrary power, in the hands of those men, who, to make use of you, for the accomplishment of their purposes, will smile upon you, and promise you fair things; but once they have got their ends, will make you and your posterity feel the heavy hand of their oppression. Perhaps, (as has been intimated by some) you have the promise of obtaining the rebels' (as they are called) lands and estates. But will you act the parts of assassins, and robbers, for these! Surely not. Is there not a day coming, when a righteous judge will make inquisition for these things? But after you have got these, must not the present designs of Parliament, (I mean the corrupt part of it,) be answered by the taxes, that will be laid upon them. Above all, consider that by joining in with the designs of the Ministers, you conspire against the liberty of Conscience, and would extinguish that precious jewel out of the Constitution.

But what prospect have you of success? It is true you have a number of men amongst you, and I doubt not, many of them valiant men, who are associating with you, who, for want of better information, do what they do. But what are they, to the rest of the twenty thousand of South Carolina, and the united power of the other Twelve Confederate Provinces, who are ready to give their aid. Consider how, if once they get to the height of exasperation, not only your own blood may be shed, but also your innocent Wives, and children may share in the unhappy fate. The Indians already vow revenge for the loss of the powder, which, you may be assured, (whatever you may suspect) was sent only to keep them in friendship, instead of bringing them upon you. Who could have acted so inhuman a part?

If you have been privately injured, or your concerns not so tenderly attended-to, as you could desire; remember that taking up of arms is not the most likely way to get redress. Rather fall upon cool measures. Rather join in with the great body of America; and as friend with friend, endeavor to promote the good of the Whole. Should you appoint some sensible and honest men, that you could confide in, to inquire into the truth of those things I have asserted, you may be assured you will find them true.

Thus Sirs I have endeavored to discharge my conscience, in what appeared to me to be my duty, in laying these things before you. What I have said has been impartial. My undertaking has been private and voluntary, not for reward, as you may suppose.

When I was lately among you, I would have come to your camp, and there would have conversed with you about these things, only that I understood you were making some prisoners. If these lines may be a means to convince any and so stop the effusion of human blood, I shall have gained my end. Which that it may be, is my sincere and hearty prayer to Almighty God.

A Loyal Subject
High Hills of Santee
November 1775

APPENDIX B

Exposition
of
The Views of the Baptists
Relative To The
Coloured Population
Of The United States
In
A Communication
To The Governor of South Carolina

Charleston, 24th December 1822

Sir,

When I had, lately, the honour of delivering to your Excellency an Address, from the Baptist Convention in this State, requesting that a Day of Public Humiliation and Thanksgiving might be appointed by you, as our Chief Magistrate, to be observed by the Citizens of the State at large, in reference to two important recent events, in which the interposition of Divine Providence has been conspicuous, and in which the interests and feelings of our Citizens have been greatly concerned—viz: The protection afforded them from the horrors of an intended Insurrection; and the affliction they have suffered from the ravages of a dreadful Hurricane.—I took the liberty to suggest, that I had a further communication to make on behalf of the Convention, in which their sentiments would be disclosed respecting the policy of the measure proposed; and on the lawfulness of holding slaves—the subject being considered in a moral and religious point of view.

You were pleased, sir, to signify, that it would be agreeable to you to receive such a communication. And as it is incumbent on me, in faithfulness to the trust reposed in me, to make it, I now take the liberty of laying it before you.

The Political propriety of bringing the intended Insurrection into view by publicly acknowledging its prevention to be an instance of the Divine Goodness, manifested by a providential, gracious interposition, is a subject, which has employed the serious attention of the Convention; and, if they have erred in the judgment they have formed upon it, the error is, at least, not owing to a want of consideration, or of serious concern. They cannot view the subject but as one of great magnitude, and intimately connected with the interests of the whole State. The Divine Interposition has been conspicuous; and our obligations to be thankful are unspeakably great. And, as principles of the wisest and best policy lead nations, as well as individuals, to consider and acknowledge the government of the Deity, to feel their dependence on him and trust in him, to be thankful for his mercies, and to be humbled under his chastening rod; so, not only moral and religious duty, but also a regard to the best interests of the community appear to require of us, on the present occasion, the humiliation and thanksgiving, which are proposed by the Convention in their request. For a sense of the Divine Government has a meliorating influence on the minds of men, restraining them from crime, and disposing them to virtuous action. To those also, who are humbled before the Heavenly Majesty for their sins, and learn to be thankful for his mercies, the Divine Favour is manifested. From them judgments are averted, and on them blessings are bestowed.

The Convention are aware, that very respectable Citizens have been averse to the proposal under consideration; the proposal for appointing a Day of Public Thanksgiving for our preservation from the intended Insurrection, on account of the influence it might be supposed to have on the Black Population—by giving publicity to the subject in *their view*, and by affording them excitements to attempt something further of the same nature. These objections, however, the Convention view as either not substantial, or overbalanced by higher considerations. As to publicity, perhaps no fact is more generally known by the persons referred to; for the knowledge of it has been communicated by almost every channel of information, public and private, even by documents under the stamp of Public Authority; and has extended to every part of the State. But with the knowledge of the conspiracy is united the knowledge of its frustration; and of that, which Devotion and Gratitude should set in a strong light, *the merciful interposition of Providence*, which produced that frustration. The more rational among that class of men, as well as others, know also, that our preservation from the evil intended by the conspirators, is a subject, which should induce us to render thanksgiving to the Almighty; and it is hoped and believed, that the truly enlightened and religiously disposed among them, of which there appears to be many, are ready to unite in those thanksgivings, from a regard to their own true interests; if, therefore it is apprehended, that an undue importance would be given to the subject in their view, by making it the matter of public thanksgiving; that this would induce the designing and wicked to infer our fear and sense of weakness from the fact, and thus induce them to form some other scheme of mischief: Would not our silence, and the omission of an important religious duty, under these circumstances, undergo, at least, as unfavourable a construction, and with more reason?

But the Convention are persuaded, that publicity, rather than secrecy is the true policy to be pursued on this occasion; especially, when the subject is taken into view, in connexion with other truths, of high importance and certainty, which relate to it, and is placed in a just light; the evidence and force of which truths, thousands of this people, when informed, can clearly discern and estimate. It is proper, the Convention conceives, that the Negroes should know, that however numerous they are in some parts of these Southern States, they yet are not, even including all descriptions, bond and free, in the United States, but little more than one sixth part of the whole number of Inhabitants, estimating that number which it probably now is, at Ten Millions; and the Black and Coloured Population, according to returns made at 1,780,000: That their destitution in respect to arms, and the knowledge of using them, with other disabilities, would render their physical force, were they all united in a common effort, less than a tenth part of that, with which they would have to contend: That there are multitudes of the best informed and truly religious among them, who, from principle, as well as from prudence, would not unite with them, or fail to disclose their machinations, when it should be in their power to do it: That, however in some parts of our Union there are Citizens, who favour the idea of general emancipation; yet, were they to see slaves in our Country, in arms, wading through blood and carnage to effect their purpose, they would do what both their duty and interest would require; unite under the government with their fellow-citizens at large to suppress the rebellion, and bring the authors of it to condign punishment; that it may be expected, in every attempt to raise an insurrection (should other attempts be made) as well as it was in that defeated here, that the prime movers in such a nefarious scheme, will so form their plan, that in a case of exigency, they may flee with their plunder and leave their deluded followers to suffer the punishment, which law and justice may inflict; and that, therefore, there is reason to conclude, on the most rational and just principles, that whatever partial success might at any time attend such a measure at the onset, yet, in this country, it must finally result in the discomfiture and ruin of the perpetrators; and in many instances pull down on the heads of the innocent as well as the guilty, an undistinguishing ruin.

On the lawfulness of holding slaves, considering it in a moral and religious view, the Convention think it their duty to exhibit their sentiments, on the present occasion, before your Excellency, because they consider their duty to God, the peace of the State, the satisfaction of scrupulous consciences, and the welfare of the slaves themselves, as intimately connected with a right view of the subject. The rather, because certain writers on politics, morals and religion, and some of them highly respectable, have advanced positions, and inculcated sentiments, very unfriendly to the principle and practice of holding slaves; and by some these sentiments have been advanced among us, tending in their nature, *directly* to disturb the domestic peace of the State, to produce insubordination and rebellion among the slaves, and to infringe the rights of our citizens; and *indirectly*, to deprive the slaves of religious privileges, by awakening in the minds of their masters a fear, that acquaintance with the Scriptures, and the enjoyment of these privileges would naturally produce the aforementioned effects; because the sentiments in opposition to the holding of slaves have been attributed, by their advocates, to the Holy Scriptures, and to the genius of Christianity. These sentiments, the Convention, on whose behalf I address your Excellency, cannot think just, or well founded; for the right of holding slaves is clearly established in the Holy Scriptures, both by precept and example. In the Old Testament, the Israelites were directed to purchase their bond-men and bond-maids of the Heathen nations; except they were of the Canaanites, for these were to be destroyed. And it is declared, that the persons purchased were to be their "bond-men forever;" and an "in-heritance for them and their children." They were not to go out free in the year of jubilee, as the Hebrews, who had been purchased, were; the line being clearly drawn between them. In example, they are presented to our view as existing in the families of the Hebrews as servants, or slaves, born in the house, or bought with money: so that the children born of slaves are here considered slaves as well as their parents. And to this well known state of things, as to its reason and order, as well as to special privileges, St. Paul appears to refer, when he says, "But I was free born."

In the New Testament, the Gospel History, or representation of facts, presents us with a view correspondent with that, which is fur-nished by other authentic ancient histories of the state of the world at the commencement of Christianity. The powerful Romans, had suc-ceeded in empire, the polished Greeks; and, under both empires, the countries they possessed and governed were full of slaves. Many of these with their masters, were converted to the Christian Faith, and received, together with them into the Christian Church, while it was yet under the ministry of the inspired Apostles. In things purely spiritual, they appear to have enjoyed equal privileges; but their relationship, as mas-ters and slaves, were not dissolved. Their respective duties are strictly enjoined. The masters are not required to emancipate their slaves; but to give them the things that are just and equal, forbearing threatening; and to remember, they also have a master in Heaven. The "servants un-der the yoke" (bond-servants or slaves) mentioned by Paul to Timothy, as having "believing masters," are not authorized by him to demand of them emancipation, or to employ violent means to obtain it; but are directed to "account their masters worthy of all honour," and "not to despise them, because they were brethren" in religion; "but the rather to do them service, because they were faithful and beloved partakers of the Christian benefit." Similar directions are given by him in other places, and by other Apostles. And it gives great weight to the argu-ment, that in this place, Paul follows his directions concerning servants with a charge to Timothy, as an Evangelist, to teach and exhort men to observe this doctrine.

Had the holding of slaves been a moral evil, it cannot be supposed, that the inspired Apostles, who feared not the faces of men, and were ready to lay down their lives in the cause of their God, would have tolerated it, for a moment, in the Christian Church. If they had done so on a principle of accommodation, in cases where the masters remained heathen, to avoid offences and civil commotion; yet, surely, where both master and servant were Christian, as in the case before us, they would have enforced the law of Christ, and required, that the master should liberate his slave in the first instance. But, instead of this, they let the relationship remain untouched, as being lawful and right, and insist on the relative duties.

In proving this subject justifiable by Scriptural authority, its morality is also proved; for the Divine Law never sanctions immoral actions.

The Christian golden rule, of doing to others, as we would they should do to us, has been urged as an unanswerable argument against holding slaves. But surely this rule is never to be urged against that order of things, which the Divine government has established; nor do our desires become a standard to us, under this rule, unless they have a due regard to justice, propriety and the general good.

A father may very naturally desire, that his son should be obedient to his orders: Is he, therefore, to obey the orders of his son? A man might be pleased to be exonerated from his debts by the generosity of his creditors; or, that his rich neighbour should equally divide his property with him; and in certain circumstances might desire these to be done: Would the mere existence of this desire, oblige him to exonerate *his* debtors, and to make such division of his property? Consistency and generosity, indeed, might require it of him, if he were in circumstances, which would justify the act of generosity; but, otherwise, either action might be considered as the effect of folly and extravagance.

If the holding of slaves is lawful, or according to the Scriptures; then this Scriptural rule can be considered as requiring no more of the master, in respect of justice (whatever it may do in point of generosity) than what he, if a slave, could, consistently, wish to be done to himself, while the relationship between master and servant should be still continued.

In this argument, the advocates for emancipation blend the ideas of injustice and cruelty with those, which respect the existence of slavery, and consider them as inseparable. But, surely, they may be separated. A bond-servant may be treated with justice and humanity as a servant; and a master may, in an important sense, be the guardian and even father of his slaves.

They become a part of his family, (the whole, forming under him a little community) and the care of ordering it, and of providing for its welfare, devolves on him. The children, the aged, the sick, the disabled, and the unruly, as well as those, who are capable of service and orderly, are the objects of his care: The labour of these, is applied to the benefit of those, and to their own support, as well as to that of the master. Thus, what is effected, and often at a great public expense, in a free community, by taxes, benevolent institutions, bettering houses, and penitentiaries, lies here on the master, to be performed by him, whatever contingencies may happen; and often occasions much expense, care and trouble, from which the servants are free. Cruelty, is, certainly, inadmissible; but servitude may be consistent with such degrees of happiness as men usually attain in this imperfect state of things.

Some difficulties arise with respect to bringing a man, or class of men, into a state of bondage. For crime, it is generally agreed, a man may be deprived of his liberty. But, may he not be divested of it by his own consent, directly, or indirectly given; And, especially, when this assent, though indirect, is connected with an attempt to take away the liberty, if not the lives of others? The Jewish law favors the former idea: And, if the inquiry on the latter be taken in the affirmative, which appears to be reasonable, it will establish a principle, by which it will appear, that the Africans brought to America were, in general, slaves, by their own consent, before they came from their own country, or fell into the hands of white men. Their law of nations, or general usage, having, by common consent the force of law, justified them, while carrying on their petty wars, in killing their prisoners or reducing them to slavery; conseqently, in selling them, and these ends they appear to have proposed to themselves; the nation, therefore, or individual, which was overcome, reduced to slavery, and sold, would have done the same by the enemy, had victory declared on their, or his side. Consequently, the man made a slave in this manner, might be said to be made so by his own consent, and by the indulgence of barbarous principles.

That Christian nations have not done all they might, or should have done, on a principle of Christian benevolence, for the civilization and conversion of the Africans; that much cruelty has been practised in the slave trade, as the benevolent Wilberforce and others have shown; that much tyranny has been exercised by individuals, as masters over their slaves, and that the religious interests of the latter have been too much neglected by many cannot, will not be denied. But the fullest proof of these facts, will not also prove, that the holding men in subjection, as slaves, is a moral evil, and inconsistent with the Christianity. Magistrates, husbands, and fathers, have proved tyrants. This does not prove, that magistracy, the husband's right to govern, and parental authority, are unlawful and wicked. The individual who abuses his authority, and acts with cruelty, must answer for it at the Divine tribunal; and civil authority should interpose to prevent or punish it; but neither civil nor ecclesiastical authority can consistently interfere with the possession and legitimate exercise of a right given by the Divine Law.

If the above representation of the Scriptural doctrine, and the manner of obtaining slaves from Africa is just; and if also purchasing them has been the means of saving human life, which there is great reason to believe it has; then, however the slave trade, in present circumstances, is justly censurable, yet might motives of humanity and even piety have been originally brought into operation in the purchase of slaves, when sold in the circumstances we have described. If, also, by their own confession, which has been made in manifold instances, their condition, when they have come into the hands of humane masters here, has been greatly bettered by the change; if it is, ordinarily, really better, as many assert, than that of thousands of the poorer classes in countries reputed civilized and free; and, if, in addition to all other considerations, the translation from their native country to this has been the means of their mental and religious improvement, and so of obtaining salvation, as many of themselves have joyfully and thankfully confessed— then may the just and humane master, who rules his slaves and provides for them, according to Christian principles, rest satisfied, that he is not, in holding them, chargeable with moral evil, nor with acting, in this respect, contrary to the genius of Christianity.—It appears to be equally clear, that those, who by reasoning on abstract principles, are induced to favour the scheme of general emancipation, and who ascribe their sentiments to Christianity, should be particularly careful, however benevolent their intentions may be, that they do not by a perversion of the Scriptural doctrine, through their wrong views of it, not only invade the domestic and religious peace and rights of our Citizens, on this subject; but, also by an intemperate zeal, prevent indirectly, the religious improvement of the people they design, professedly, to benefit; and, perhaps, become, evidently, the means of producing in our country, scenes of anarchy and blood; and all this in a vain attempt to bring about a state of things, which, if arrived at, would not probably better the state of that people; which is thought, by men of observation to be generally true of the Negroes in the Northern States, who have been liberated.

To pious minds it has given pain to hear men, respectable for intelligence and morals, sometimes say, that holding slaves is indeed indefensible, but that to us it is necessary, and must be supported. On this principle, mere politicians, unmindful of morals, may act. But surely, in a moral and religious view of the subject, this principle is inadmissible. It cannot be said, that theft, falsehood, adultery and murder, are become necessary and must be supported. Yet there is reason to believe, that some of honest and pious intentions have found their minds embarrassed if not perverted on this subject, by this plausible but unsound argument. From such embarrassment the view exhibited above affords relief.

The Convention, Sir, are far from thinking that Christianity fails to inspire the minds of its subjects with benevolent and generous sentiments; or that liberty rightly understood, or enjoyed, is a blessing of little moment. The contrary of these positions they maintain. But they also consider benevolence as consulting the truest and best interests of its objects; and view the happiness or liberty as well as of religion, as consisting not in the name or form, but in the reality. While men remain in the chains of ignorance and error, and under the dominion of tyrant lusts and passions, they cannot be free. And the more freedom of action they have in this state, they are but the more qualified by it to do injury, both to themselves and others. It is, therefore, firmly believed, that general emancipation to the Negroes in this country, would not, in present circumstances, be for their own happiness, as a body; while it would be extremely injurious to the community at large in various ways: And, if so, then it is not required even by benevolence. But acts of benevolence and generosity must be free and voluntary; no man has a right to compel another to the performance of them. This is a concern, which lies between a man and his God. If a man has obtained slaves by purchase, or inheritance, and the holding of them as such is justifiable by the law of God; why should he be required to liberate them, because it would be a generous action, rather than another on the same principle, to release his debtors, or sell his lands and houses, and distribute the proceeds among the poor? These also would be generous actions: Are they, therefore obligatory? Or, if obligatory, in certain circumstances, as personal, voluntary acts of piety and benevolence, has any man or body of men, civil or ecclesiastic, a right to require them? Surely those, who are advocates for compulsory, or strenuous measures to bring about emancipation, should duly weigh this consideration.

Should, however, a time arrive, when the Africans in our country might be found qualified to enjoy freedom; and, when they might obtain it in a manner consistent with the interest and peace of the community at large, the Convention would be happy in seeing them free: And so they would, in seeing the state of the poor, the ignorant and the oppressed of every description, and of every country meliorated; so that the reputed free might be free indeed, and happy. But there seems to be just reason to conclude that a considerable part of the human race, whether they bear openly the character of slaves or are reputed free men, will continue in such circumstances, with mere shades of variation, while the world continues. It is evident, that men are sinful creatures, subject to affliction and to death, as the consequences of their nature's pollution and guilt: That they are now in a state of probation; and that God as a Righteous, All-wise Sovereign, not only disposes of them as he pleases, and bestows upon them many unmerited blessings and comforts, but subjects them also to privations, afflictions and trials, with the merciful intention of making all their afflictions, as well as their blessings, work finally for their good; if they embrace his salvation, humble themselves before him, learn righteousness, and submit to his holy will. To have them brought to this happy state is the great object of Christian benevolence, and of Christian piety; for this state is not only connected with the truest happiness, which can be enjoyed in time, but is introductory to eternal life and blessedness in the future world: And the salvation of men is intimately connected with the glory of their God and Redeemer.

And here I am brought to a part of the general subject, which, I confess to your Excellency, the Convention, from a sense of their duty, as a body of men, to whom important concerns of Religion are confided, have particularly at heart, and wish it may be seriously considered by all our Citizens: This is the religious interests of the Negroes. For though they are slaves, they are also men; and are with ourselves accountable creatures; having immortal souls, and being destined to fu-

ture eternal award. Their religious interests claim a regard from their
masters of the most serious nature; and it is indispensable. Nor can the
community at large, in a right estimate of their duty and happiness, be
indifferent on this subject. To the truly benevolent it must be pleasing
to know, that a number of masters, as well as ministers and pious individuals, of various Christian denominations among us, do conscien-
tiously regard this duty; but there is great reason to believe, that it is
neglected and disregarded by many.

The Convention are particularly unhappy in considering, that an
idea of the Bible's teaching the doctrine of emancipation as necessary,
and tending to make servants insubordinate to proper authority, has
obtained access to any mind; both on account of its direct influence on
those, who admit it; and the fear it excites in others, producing the effects before noticed. But it is hoped, it has been evinced, that the idea
is an erroneous one; and, that it will be seen, that the influence of a
right acquaintance with that Holy Book tends directly and powerfully,
by promoting the fear and love of God, together with just and peaceful
sentiments toward men, to produce one of the best securities to the
public, for the internal and domestic peace of the state.

It is also a pleasing consideration, tending to confirm these sentiments, that in the late projected scheme for producing an insurrection
among us, there were very few of those who were, as members attached
to regular churches, (even within the sphere of its operations) who appear to have taken a part in the wicked plot, or indeed to whom it was
made known; of some churches it does not appear, that there were any.
It is true, that a considerable number of those who were found guilty
and executed, laid claim to a religious character; yet several of these were
grossly immoral, and, in general, they were members of an irregular
body, which called itself the *African Church*, and had intimate connection and intercourse with a similar body of men in a Northern City,
among whom the supposed right to emancipation is strenuously advocated.

The result of this inquiry and reasoning, on the subject of slavery,
brings us, sir, if I mistake not, very regularly to the following conclusions:—That the holding of slaves is justifiable by the doctrine and example contained in Holy writ; and is, therefore consistent with Christian
uprightness, both in sentiment and conduct. That, all things considered, the Citizens of America have in general obtained the African slaves,

which they possess, on principles, which can be justified; though much cruelty has indeed been exercised towards them by many, who have been concerned in the slave-trade, and by others who have held them here, as slaves in their service; for which the authors of this cruelty are accountable. That slavery, when tempered with humanity and justice, is a state of tolerable happiness; equal, if not superior, to that which many poor enjoy in countries reputed free. That a master has a scriptural right to govern his slaves so as to keep them in subjection; to demand and receive from them a reasonable service; and to correct them for the neglect of duty, for their vices and transgressions; but that to impose on them unreasonable, rigorous services, or to inflict on them cruel punishment, he has neither a scriptural nor a moral right. At the same time it must be remembered, that, while he is receiving from them their uniform and best services, he is required by the Divine Law, to afford them protection, and such necessaries and conveniences of life as are proper to their condition as servants; so far as he is enabled by their services to afford them these comforts, on just and rational principles. That it is the positive duty of servants to reverence their master, to be obedient, industrious, faithful to him, and careful of his interests; and without being so, they can neither be the faithful servants of God, nor be held as regular members of the Christian Church. That as claims to freedom as a *right*, when that right is forfeited, or has been lost, in such a manner as has been represented, would be unjust; and as all attempts to obtain it by violence and fraud would be wicked; so all representations made to them by others, on such censurable principles, or in a manner tending to make them discontented, and, finally, to produce such unhappy effects and consequences, as have been before noticed, cannot be friendly to them (as they certainly are not to the community at large,) nor consistent with righteousness: Nor can the conduct be justified, however in some it may be palliated by pleading benevolence in intention, as the motive. That masters having the disposal of the persons, time and labour of their servants, and being the heads of families, are bound, on principles of moral and religious duty, to give these servants religious instruction; or at least, to afford them opportunities, under proper regulations to obtain it: And to grant religious privileges to those, who desire them, and furnish proper evidence of their sincerity and uprightness: Due care being at the same time taken, that they receive their instructions from right sources, and from their connexions, where they will not be in danger of having their minds corrupted by sentiments unfriendly to the domestic and civil peace of the community. That, where the life, comfort, safety and religious interest of so large a number of human beings, as this class of persons is among us, are concerned; and, where they must necessarily, as slaves, be so much at the disposal of their masters; it appears to be a just and necessary concern of the Government, not only to provide laws to prevent or punish insurrections, and other violent and villa[i]nous conduct among them (which are indeed necessary;) but, on the other hand, laws, also, to prevent their being oppressed and injured by unreasonable, cruel masters, and others; and to afford them, in respect of morality and religion, such privileges as may comport with the peace and safety of the state, and with those relative duties existing between masters and servants, which the word of God enjoins. It is, also, believed to be a just conclusion, that the interest and security of the state would be promoted, by allowing, under proper regulations, considerable religious privileges, to such of this class, as know how to estimate them aright, and have given suitable evidence of their own good principles, uprightness and fidelity; by attaching them, from principles of gratitude and love, to the interests of their masters and the state; and thus rendering their fidelity firm and constant. While on the other hand, to lay them under an interdict, as some have supposed necessary, in a case where reason, conscience, the genius of Christianity and salvation are concerned, on account of the bad conduct of others, would be felt as oppressive, tend to sour and alienate their minds from their masters and the public, and to make them vulnerable to temptation. All which is, with deference, submitted to the consideration of your Excellency.

With high respect, I remain, personally, and on behalf of the Convention,

Sir, your very obedient and humble servant,
RICHARD FURMAN
President of the Baptist State Convention

APPENDIX C

RULES OF THE GENERAL COMMITTEE

RULES of the GENERAL COMMITTEE, for FORMING, SUP-
PORTING, and APPLYING A FUND Amongst the BAPTIST
CHURCHES United in the Charleston Association, SOUTH CARO-
LINA.

Finally ratified on the 7th November, 1792

PREFACE

The importance of the following scheme to the cause of religion,
must forcibly strike the mind of every thinking person at the first view.
To offer labored arguments, in proof of its usefulness, would be to in-
sult the understanding of the serious and enlightened part of the community. It rather may be considered strange, that an expedient of this
kind has not been generally resorted to by the Baptist churches heretofore: Since on their general plan, they not only refuse admittance into
the service of the sanctuary to any who are not esteemed holy persons,
whatever their other qualifications may be; but acknowledge the benefit of learning and study in forming the useful and accomplished
preacher: Especially while there is no great want of ministers thus endowed, and a number of young candidates for the sacred office are daily
rising up among them who do not appear to be deficient either in piety,
zeal, or genius.

The mode of collecting money for the beneficient purpose, as stated
in the following pages, is certainly an easy one, and experience has
proved to those who have tried it, in a candid and determined manner,
that it is successful. Even the mite when thrown in by a number,
amounts to something considerable; but on this occasion there have been

found some generous souls, who, entering into the spirit of the undertaking, and regarding its important end, have come forward and bestowed their contribution with liberal hand.

The charities thus bestowed, have already taken effect, and some promising youth who bid fair to be useful in the ministerial character, are now reaping the benefit. In a word, there is just reason to believe, that such is the regard to religion, such the liberality of a great part of our churches, and other christians with whom they live in friendly connection, that when once they see the channel opened for conveying their generous donations to the proposed end, and the money regularly applied—according to this plan, the yearly address of the charity sermon will be attended with abundant success; and that thereby a source will be formed which will diffuse the firearms of useful and evangelic knowledge, consolation and joy through our American church, and bring a revenue of praise and thanksgiving to the churches' great and glorious head.

The early advocates for this undertaking, and its friends in general, contemplate with satisfaction the success which has already attended it; and view with peculiar pleasure and gratitude, the respect and attention with which it was treated by the legislature of South-Carolina, when submitted to their inspection, and when in its favor, they passed the act of incorporation by which the general committee is made known in law.

RULES, &c.

I.

This committee shall be known and distinguished by the name of "The General Committee for the Charleston Baptist Association Fund."

II.

Once a year a charity sermon shall be preached in each church; at which time, collections shall be made from the congregation at large, which, together with any donations or bequests which may be received for the purpose, shall be applied towards forming and supporting a fund, to assist pious young men designed for the work of the ministry and destitute of other *assistance*, in obtaining education; together with such other religious and public uses as may be approved of by the churches, should the said fund finally prove sufficient.

III.

A committee shall be formed, consisting of a delegate from each church, to be chosen by them respectively for that purpose; which committee shall convene annually at the same time and place with the association, and may, likewise, be members of that body: But are to be considered as invested with a distinct power and trust, as members of the committee. They shall receive the collections, determine on the manner of applying the fund according to the foregoing rule, and examine applicants for the churches' bounty. All applications for this purpose, to be made to them. Delegates from nine churches to be a quorum, or capable for business.

IV.

The committee of the churches thus formed, shall be considered as a standing body, and the election of members shall be for one year, or till a new election takes place; and if found necessary, they shall be impowered to meet occasionally, during the term of their appointment, in the recess of the Association. At their annual meeting they shall choose a President, Treasurer, and Secretary, to conduct the public business of the committee; together with two assistants with the officers, shall form a select committee to transact such business as may be necessary, or which may be committed to them, when the General Committee is not in session. A majority of the select committee shall be equal to business; and of what shall be considered necessary business, the General Committee shall always judge.

V.

The President shall preside in all meetings of the committee, and perform the duties of a moderator or chairman. The Treasurer shall receive and take care of all money collected for the fund, and put it out on interest, or otherwise dispose of it, as the committee shall direct; keeping a regular account of all monies received or disbursed; and for the faithful discharge of the duties of his office, shall give bond to the President for double the value of all monies or specialities lodged in his hands. The Secretary shall keep a fair account of all transactions both of the General and Select Committee, at their regular meetings, which shall be entered in a book kept for the purpose.

VI.

The President shall contract for the education of such persons as are taken on the churches' bounty; and the expenses consequent thereon, shall be paid by the treasurer, on the president's written order.

VII.

No persons shall be admitted on the churches' bounty, but such as come well recommended, and appear, on examination, to be truly pious, of evangelical principles, of good natural abilities, and desirous of devoting themselves to the work of the ministry.

VIII.

Every person received as above, shall be considered as coming under peculiar obligations to submit to the government and direction of the committee, while pursuing a course of study: And to be liable to refund the money which may be laid out on his education, within four years after said education is finished, if he does not enter on the work of the ministry, to the satisfaction of the committee within that time; the committee, therefore, shall take such measures as may be legal and proper to secure the observance of this rule.

IX.

When there are more candidates than can be received on the churches' bounty, preference shall be given, first, to those who are members of churches belonging to the Charleston Association: And secondly, to those who are most promising.

X.

Such persons as are admitted on the churches' bounty, shall be considered as under the care and inspection of the committee, with respect to their moral and religious conduct; and if any of them, while pursuing their education, shall embrace principles subversive of the great truths of the gospel, or abandon themselves to an irreligious course of life, they shall, on proper evidence of the fact, and after suitable endeavours to reclaim them, should these prove ineffectual, be dismissed.

XI.

The churches in the Charleston Association, having invested this committee with a power and right to take into their possession, and under their care, all property of churches which are comprehended in their union, when the said churches are become extinct, and the property liable to revert to the public, or become the property of individuals: The committee therefore, shall use its best endeavors to obtain all such property; which, when obtained, shall be applied by them, to such uses, for the general good of the churches, as shall appear most important and interesting; and in all such appropriations of property, they shall consult the Association. The committee shall be considered as having no power to interfere in any concern of a church, either spiritual or temporal, where power is not expressly delegated to them by the churches.

XII.

Whereas some inconveniences may arise when only a partial collection is made from the churches, and those churches which contribute to the fund are rendered unable to act by their delegates, on account of the inattention of others, according to a foregoing rule: In all such cases, the power of transacting the business of the fund shall be considered as vested, *exclusively*, in those churches who regularly contribute to the fund, or a majority of them; any thing contained in these rules to the contrary notwithstanding.

XIII.

No alterations or amendments shall be made to these rules, but after being moved for in the committee, at an annual meeting, twelve months before such alterations take place, and being agreed to by two thirds of the members.

To all which rules we promise strict and faithful adherence.
As witness our hands this 7th day of November, in the year of our Lord 1792.

RICHARD FURMAN, Chairman.
HENRY HOLCOMBE, Clerk.
EDMUND BOTSFORD,
ALEXANDER SCOTT,
BRADLEY RHAME,
BENJAMIN MOSELY,
STEPHEN NIXON,
ISHAM GARDNER,
JAMES SWEAT.

APPENDIX D

RICHARD FURMAN'S PLAN OF EDUCATION

Proposed Resolutions, including a scheme of Education, having for its object the assistance of pious young men designed for the gospel ministry, which were laid before the Baptist Convention at Philadelphia, in May, 1817.

I.   Resolved, That it be recommended by this Convention, to the Baptist churches throughout the United States, and their adherents to form themselves into education societies, for the purpose of aiding pious young men of their connexion, who appear on good evidence to be called of God to the gospel ministry, in obtaining such education as may best fit them for extensive usefulness in the cause of our Redeemer, and enable them to appear as workmen who need not be ashamed, rightly dividing the word of truth: And likewise for assisting poor ministers, who have families, and have not obtained the advantages which are derived from a suitable education, by gratuitously furnishing them with the most necessary and useful books, to aid them in their endeavours to obtain mental improvement. For the accomplishment of which design the following scheme is submitted to the consideration of the churches.

1st.   Let a charity sermon be preached once a year, at least, in each church, and a collection made expressly for the purposes above specified; and let the monies so collected, together with any other collections, donations or bequests obtained for such purposes, be conveyed by the hands of a person specially appointed as a representative to attend the meeting of the association to which such church belongs, and there to be deposited in a common fund, under the direction of a body of delegates similarly appointed by other churches belonging to that association: or to a number of associations uniting in the same measure as a common cause: excepting always such part of the monies (say a third part) as shall be appropriated to the establishment and support of a Theological Seminary, in our connexion, to be hereinafter described; which last sum shall be conveyed to the general fund, and be placed under the care and direction of the Board of Commissioners connected with the Convention, or such part of them as shall be intrusted with the superintendence of the education department.

2nd.   Let the Body formed by the coalition of churches, as above recommended, be styled the General Committee, or Trustees of the churches united in Association or Associations, and have a President, Treasurer, Secretary, and Assistants, who shall be authorized to transact all necessary business as a special committee, during the recess of the general committee.

3rd.   Let this Committee of the churches be invested with full power to examine applicants for the churches' bounty, with respect to their qualifications, according to the sentiment before expressed; to wit, that ministers must be the subjects of renewing grace, be called of God to the office, and receive gifts of Jesus Christ, the great prophet of the Church, to fit them for the work.

4th.   Let the committee by their proper officer, or officers, contract for the education of the young men so taken under their care, at some convenient seminary; superintend their education and morals, that the former may be promoted by due excitement, and the latter preserved in purity; a departure from which shall be considered as incurring censure and the loss of privilege. It shall also be considered as the object of their care, to secure the return of money to the fund which may have been expended at any time on the education of persons who do not, in a reasonable time after they have completed their studies, enter on the work of the ministry to the satisfaction of the committee.

5th.   After young men thus provided for, have finished their classical studies, or obtained a proper acquaintance with general science, let it be the concern of the churches to place them in a situation favourable to the study of divinity. While in circumstances which prevent their obtaining more ample assistance, let the students come under the care of some pious, well informed, and judicious minister; but when a divinity college shall have been established, according to the provision made in the constitution of this Convention, let as many of them as the respective funds of the societies, or churches, can support, be sent to said seminary; especially those who possess superior talents, together with a desire and aptness for study.

6th.   As it is possible that some churches belonging to the associations may refuse or neglect to make contributions, and that embarrassments may arise from this cause, let the exclusive right of managing the business of the fund be vested in the delegates of those churches which regularly contribute to its support.

II.   Resolved, That as soon as a sufficient fund shall be obtained for this purpose, the Board of Commissioners shall take measures for establishing, at some convenient and central situation, a Theological Seminary and Library, under the care of learned, pious professors; in which theology shall be studied in its various branches, church history, the Hebrew language, and other oriental languages, the knowledge of which is favourable to a right understanding of the sacred scriptures, as far as the same may be found practicable and convenient, together with biblical criticism and pulpit eloquence.

III.   Resolved, That the agents, or missionaries, which may be appointed by the Board of missions to travel in our own country, shall be particularly charged with the important concern of giving information to the churches of our denomination, and the public at large, concerning the true nature and design of the scheme in which the foregoing articles are comprehended, of recommending it to their serious regard, and of affording assistance to those who may be disposed to bring it into operation, in what relates to a right beginning and organization.

APPENDIX E

CIRCULAR LETTER PERTAINING
TO COLUMBIAN COLLEGE

At a regular meeting of the Special Committee of the Baptist Churches united in the Charleston Association, held at Charleston the 12th of April, 1819.

Whereas it is the duty of this Committee to attend with most serious regard to the general interests of the churches represented in the General Committee of the Charleston Association and more especially when the interests of the Baptist churches and of religion at large are concerned in connection with them; this Committee being intrusted with the important concerns of the union during the recess of those religious and highly respectable bodies; and whereas the establishment of a Theological Seminary for the education of pious young men for the Gospel Ministry, as proposed by the General Convention of the Baptist Denomination in the United States of America, is an object of great magnitude and high importance to the interests of the whole denomination; and as the board of Commissioners appointed by the Convention have requested the Constituents of the Convention to give their sentiments on the merits of a plan they have laid before the public relative to this important measure; they having already adopted measures for carrying in to effect the design of the Convention, respecting it according to their views of the subject; and propose giving permanence to the said plan at the next annual meeting of the Board.

Therefore the Committee think it [original defaced], and therefore do with all due respect and affection to the board of Commissioners, submit to them the following resolves, as expressing the sense of the Committee:

First.   It is the decided opinion of this Committee that the Constitution formed by the General Convention of Baptist churches in the United States, does not empower the board of Commissioners to establish the Theological institution which it contemplates, till "competent and distinct funds" for the purpose are in their possession, which also implies the general Knowledge and approbation of a plan and a concert in the measure by the community interested; so that any attempt by the board to make such establishment, by the election of officers, etc., before such competent funds have been received must be considered not only as premature but as amounting to a nullity. And considering the magnitude of the object, and how important to the [original defaced] institution should be well endowed, regularly established and rendered permanent, a very considerable sum, perhaps not less than $100,000 appears to be requisite for the establishment.

Second.   It appears to the Committee that it is of the highest importance to the undertaking that the body of churches be brought to take an active part in it; and as much as possible in their Associated capacity so as to form large Educational Societies on a regular scheme of general consent; thus establishing separate funds to be held under their own direct concert and control and applied at their discretion to the education of pious young men in classical learning, at places the most convenient to them; that they may be thus fitted for divinity studies and be finally sent to the Theological Institution. For which a regular appropriation of a part of their funds should be made and deposited in the general fund, under the direction of the board.

The plan commended by the board, appears to the Committee, to be in this respect radically defective: for though it recommends the formation of Educational Societies, and public collections by means of sermons preached on such occasions, yet it is done in a vague indeterminate manner, without any annexed plan or form of proceedings, for the information of the Ignorant, and the assistance of the willing who may be disposed to act, but feel at a loss how to proceed in such a business with which they are quite unacquainted, and in which they have had no experience: and respects only formation of a fund to be under the immediate inspection of the board.

Third.   Resolved, That the plan laid before the Convention, by the President, at its last meeting, which embraces the article noticed in the former resolve, has, in this respect, been in operation, among the churches with which this Committee are immediately connected, for near thirty years, and has been proved, by time and experience, to be well adapted to accomplish the beneficial purposes for which it was formed, and by its provisions to maintain its operation, notwithstanding the reluctance and tardiness of some in the union, (through the influence of certain motives,) without breaking or even disturbing the peace of the general union; and eventually becoming more generally approved, regarded and effective. A plan therefore which seems to be highly proper for the great body of the Baptist churches, among which so large a proportion are held under the power of ignorant prejudices against learning, and of views, habits and passions, which are unfavorable to generous exertion. It is with regret, therefore, that this Committee reflect, that not only has this plan as a whole been withheld from the public view, but that this important feature of it does not appear in that which the board has published.

Fourth.   [Illegible] as proposed in the plan that the board has published is a regulation which should not be adopted but under careful restrictions; and only in extraordinary cases, when the state of the fund will fully admit it. As it is most natural to conclude that otherwise, the persons admitted to this benefit would ordinarily be those whose residence would be near the seat of learning. In which case those churches, societies, etc., at a distance, who should send youths to the Institution and pay for their support would, by their general contributions, also support the poor young men of that central part of the union, without having their own, in similar circumstances admitted to the benefit. As their distance and poverty would prevent their making application at uncertainties. And this would naturally operate a cause of dissatisfaction and disunion. The regular ordinary course, therefore, certainly should be, that those bodies, of individuals, which send young men to the institution should make ample provision to pay for their support, from whatever quarter they are sent. And if indigent youth are admitted, by the original or immediate act of the board, they should be taken in equal proportion, from the different parts of the Union from which contributions have been regularly made.

Fifth.   Resolved.   That it is the opinion of this Committee a suspension of operations, respecting the establishment of the institution, till a sufficient fund is provided and while wise, firm and dignified measures of a preparatory nature are pursued, to make it a reality, an-

swerable to the character bestowed on it, would both hasten and facil-
itate the accomplishment of the design; by giving satisfaction and
confidence to its enlightened friends, and by inviting the beneficence
of those whose liberality is united with prudence: that on the contrary,
hasty establishment of the institution, or an attempt to establish it,
without the forementioned requisites, will have contrary effects; destroy confidence, repel the hand of liberality, alienate the minds of the
most efficient friends of the design, occasion the turning of their attention to other objects, and thrusting on ruin to the undertaking.

Sixth. Resolved. That in our most deliberate view of the subject, it does not appear to us, that any society formed for the purpose
of giving Education to candidates for the ministry, in these United
States, can be consistently associated with the board in the work of establishing the Theological Institution proposed by the Convention in
any other character than that of auxiliary; not co-ordinate but as sub-
ordinate: that therefore, such society cannot in consistency be admitted
by the Board to vote with them, on any question of general concern, to
the union, in which the board acts as an agent to the Convention; nor
the Society be entitled to have the youth under their care, taken, in virtue of such coalition, or agreement, under the patronage of the board
to be educated by them without said Society's defraying the expense
consequent upon such education.

Seventh. Resolved that though it is certain there are many pious
youths who need and desire that assistance which the proposed Theological Institution is desired to afford, yet it is not the name of such an
institution nor one unendowed which can afford the benefit: it seems
more desirable for the present to proceed on the former plan of assisting
those pious youth by the use of minor institutions; which will not interfere with the general fund, provided for the proposed college.

Especially [?] a contrary line of conduct would so consume the monies collected for that purpose, while the contributions are small, as to
prevent the regular establishment of the Seminary for a long time, keep
it in an embecile, inefficient state; and, from reasons before assigned,
jeopardize the whole undertaking.

Eighth. Resolved that however their intimate acquaintance with
a distinguished character and their affection for that character, together
with the real worth of the person, may dispose a quorum of the board
to decide promptly in the choice of a Principal or Professor for the

Theological Institution; yet considering the magnitude of the office, especially that of the Principal; the rare qualifications necessary in the person appointed to it; the extent of the Union formed through the medium of the Convention; the apparent ground for suspicion respecting the operation of undue motives in cases of hasty action; and the improper injurious use which may be made ultimately by designing men of such a Precedent given by the board, and especially at the time of forming and arranging the Constitution—therefore this Committee are of opinion that three months is a time far too short for giving publicity to an intended election to such cases, and for collecting the sense of the Convention on the momentous subject: on which occasion it would seem necessary not only that all the members of the board be early informed and called upon to give their votes; but that the whole denomination should be early called upon and have time to deliberate.

Ninth.   Resolved that from the combined force of the foregoing and other considerations, it appears to this Committee as most advisable for the Board of Commissioners to defer establishing the Theological Seminary till the meeting of the Convention in 1820, even though respectable contributions to the fund should be found to have been made by the time of their nearly approaching meeting; and to confine themselves to preparatory measures; especially to uniting the churches in common efforts and in enlarging and giving permanency to the Fund; and for this purpose they recommend that a form of Association for uniting the churches in Education Societies be published; together with forms for Bequests and donations to the Treasurer of the Board for the Fund: and to annex to these, some calculations showing the practicability and ease of providing a sufficient fund on a proper plan of concert by the numerous churches and Associations of the Baptist Denomination in the United States: also that an addition of able men of influential character be made, especially in the middle and Southern States to solicit benefactions.

10.   Resolved.   That this Committee feel themselves authorized to assert that the Baptist churches connected in the General Committee and Charleston Association are sincerely disposed to do their part in the important work of forming and maintaining a fund to support the Theological Seminary proposed as are the members of this special Committee in particular, on impartial catholic principles; provided a reg-

ular and constant course shall be pursued by the agents of the Convention in these important transactions.

11.   That the observations here submitted though made with freedom have originated in tender concern for the great object of attention, as connected with the glory of God and the best interests of his Kingdom; and in real respect and affection for the board of commissioners as a body and as composed of individuals for whose happiness they pray and whose usefulness and respectability they wish to see advanced to the highest degree attainable on earth. That they are conscious of their own weakness and liability to err and have not meant to dictate to the board but simply to investigate principles and facts with a view to a right adjustment of interest and measures which they view as sacred to the cause and glory of the Divine Redeemer. That if the board has in any wise erred in judgment or procedure, as they have thought and ventured to suggest, they are disposed to impute it to ardent desires to arrive at once at their object, or in general to that imperfection with which the wisest and best of men are encompassed in this transitory life.

APPENDIX F

CONSTITUTION
OF THE BAPTIST CONVENTION (TRIENNIAL)

May, 1814

(From the Proceedings of the Baptist Convention
for Missionary Purposes
Held in Philadelphia in May, 1814)

We the delegates from Missionary Societies, and other religious Bodies of the Baptist denomination, in various parts of the United States, met in Convention, in the City of Philadelphia, for the purpose of carrying into effect the benevolent Intentions of our Constituents, by organizing a plan for eliciting, combining, and directing the Energies of the whole Denomination in one sacred effort, for sending the glad tidings of Salvation to the Heathen, and to nations destitute of pure Gospel-light, DO AGREE to the following Rules or fundamental Principles, viz.

I.   That this body shall be styled "The General Missionary Convention of the Baptist Denomination in the United States of America, for Foreign Missions."

II.   That a triennial Convention shall, hereafter, be held consisting of Delegates, not exceeding two in number, from each of the several Missionary Societies, and other religious bodies of the Baptist Denomination, now existing, or which may hereafter be formed in the United States, and which shall each, regularly contribute to the general Missionary Fund, a sum, amounting, at least, to one hundred Dollars, per annum.

III.   That for the necessary transaction and dispatch of business, during the recess of the said Convention, there shall be a Board of twenty-one Commissioners, who shall be members of the said Societies, Churches, or other religious bodies aforesaid, triennially appointed, by the said Convention, by ballot, to be called the "Baptist Board of Foreign Missions for the United States:" seven whom shall be a quorum for the transaction of all business; and which Board shall continue in office until successors be duly appointed; and shall have power to make and adopt by-laws for the government of the said Board, and for the furtherance of the general objects of the Institution.

IV.   That it shall be the duty of this Board, to employ Missionaries, and, if necessary, to take measures for the improvement of their qualifications; to fix on the Field of their Labours, and the compensation to be allowed them for their services; to superintend their conduct, and dismiss them, should their services be disapproved; to publish accounts, from time to time, of the Board's Transactions, and an annual Address to the public; to call a special meeting of the Convention on any extraordinary occasion, and, in general, to conduct the executive part of the missionary concern.

V.   That such persons only, as are in full communion with some regular Church of our Denomination, and who furnish satisfactory evidence of genuine Piety, good Talents, and fervent Zeal for the Redeemer's Cause, are to be employed as Missionaries.

VI.   That the Board shall choose, by ballot, one President, two Vice-Presidents, a Treasurer, a corresponding, and a recording Secretary.

VII.   That the president, or in case of his absence or disability, the senior vice-president present, shall preside in all meetings of the Board, and when application shall be made in writing, by any two of its members, shall call a special meeting of the Board, giving due notice thereof.

VIII.   That the treasurer shall receive and faithfully account for all the monies paid into the treasury, keep a regular account of receipts and disbursements, make a report thereof to the said Convention, whenever it shall be in session, and to the Board of Missions annually, and as often as by them required: He shall also, before he enters on the duties of his office, give competent security, to be approved by the Board, for the stock and funds that may be committed to his care.

IX.   That the corresponding secretary shall maintain intercourse by letter with such individuals, societies, or public bodies, as the interest of the institution may require. Copies of all communications made by the particular direction of the Convention or Board, shall be by him handed to the recording secretary, for record and safe keeping.

X.   That the recording secretary shall, ex officio, be the secretary of the Convention, unless some other be by them appointed in his stead. He shall attend all the meetings of the Board, and keep a fair record of all their proceedings, and of the transactions of the Convention.

XI.   That in case of the death, resignation, or disability of any of its officers, or members, the Board shall have power to fill such vacancy.

XII.   That the said Convention shall have power, and in the interval of their meeting, the Board of Commissioners, on the recommendation of any one of the constituent bodies belonging to the Convention, shall also have power, to elect honorary members of piety and distinguished liberality, who, on their election, shall be entitled to a seat, and to take part in the debates of the Convention: but it shall be understood that the right of voting shall be confined to the delegates.

XIII.   That in case any of the constituent bodies shall be unable to send representatives to the said Convention, they shall be permitted to vote by proxy, which proxy shall be appointed by writing.

XIV.   That any alterations which experience may dictate from time to time, may be made in these Articles, at the regular meeting of the Convention, by two thirds of the members present.

                                        RICHARD FURMAN, President

Attest,
       THOMAS BALDWIN, Secretary.

APPENDIX G

THE DELEGATES
of the
BAPTIST ASSOCIATIONS
of
Charleston, Edgefield, and Savannah River,
in
THE STATE OF SOUTH CAROLINA,
Met in Convention at Columbia,
On the 4th day of December, 1821,
To Their Constituents,
AND TO THE OTHER BAPTIST ASSOCIATIONS
In The Said State,
Present Their Affectionate Christian Regards.

(Abridged from *Minutes of the State Baptist Convention*, 1821, SCBHS.)

Beloved Brethren,

. . . You will perceive that we indulge a pleasing hope, that our brethren, who have not yet come forward to take a part in this scheme of piety, Christian benevolence, and noble effort, will not long forbear. . . .

To our brethren who have not met us in Convention, we would say with sincere affection, and respect, that as it would have afforded us great encouragement, comfort and satisfaction, to have enjoyed their company and aid on this occasion; so the want of these has occasioned regret. We, indeed, entered with some reluctance on the business of forming the Convention in their absence; and had it not been for the firm persuasion we felt that the cause we had espoused, was the cause of God; that the call of his Providence, and the interests of his Church required immediate exertion, the tender regard we felt for the sentiments and feelings of our brethren, would have induced us to delay the transaction, till the churches of every Association concerned, had fully matured their thoughts on the subject, and consented to a cordial and vigorous co-operation. We trust, however, from the nature and design of the undertaking, that this will be the result; and in this confidence, we have ventured to make a beginning, relying on the Omnipotent arm and rich grace of Jehovah. . . .

We would wish to obviate certain objections, which have been represented to us as existing in the minds of some persons concerned, whether founded in mistake, jealousy, or any other cause. First, some, it seems, have thought, that the Convention is formed with an intention to establish a governing power over the Associations and Churches. But it will be seen by the outlines of a Constitution, that the Convention not only designs otherwise; but disclaims this power, and provides against all attempts which may at any time be made to establish such coercive power. Secondly, it has been suggested, that the monies which may be contributed to a fund, under the care of the Convention, will be arbitrarily disposed of by them, or placed at the disposal of the General Convention, so that the application of these monies will be made, ordinarily, to objects out of the immediate connexion of the contributors; to the neglect of those interests in which they feel themselves particularly concerned. Here again, referring to the constitutional principles we have agreed upon, we can assert that this objection is without foundation. By these it will be seen, that the right of having money applied according to the will of the donor, only, is expressly secured by a constitutional provision. To which may be added, that among the subjects fixed upon, for special regard, by the Convention, the greater number are such as require the application and use of money among ourselves. These are, the home missions; a respectable academy, at least, if not ultimately a college; and the support and education of students for the Gospel ministry, under the immediate care of the Convention, or its agents.

We are far from saying, however, that this Convention has no regard for the missionary service abroad, or to the support of the theological seminary in Washington, under the care of the General Convention of the Baptist Denomination in the United States. . . .

The general interests of the whole denomination, in the United States, are designed to be concentrated in the institution at Washington; and certainly, by the united exertions of the whole, in providing the means, the most ample provision may be made for affording *there*, the best assistance to students in divinity, and profound erudition. Under the care of the State Convention (and, especially, should generous individuals give their aid, in the manner some have signified they intended) a respectable academy may be formed, in which students would be prepared, by an acquaintance with the learned languages and the elementary parts of science, to enter the other institution with advantage. And it may likewise be of excellent use to others, who from particular circumstances may not find it convenient to go to Washington. In time, also, it might be hoped that, by the blessing of God, it would grow up to a fully organized college; should wise and liberal measures be pursued.

The General Convention, it may surely be expected, will be always so sensible of their high responsibility, and feel such concern for the cause of God; that they will be careful to have the true design of the institution carried into effect; and to have suitable instructors placed at the head of it; so that abuses may be prevented; or should they at any time take place, the disordered state of things be soon rectified. We trust it will be found to the end, to the satisfaction not only of the churches, but of the world, that those who now occupy that station are, not only men of distinguished abilities, but faithful to their trust. This is mentioned the rather, because in some places unfavorable representations have been made, and fears excited. The whole, according to our view, having originated in an unhappy personal dispute; which we lament, with respect to each of the parties. On this delicate subject we certainly should say nothing, were it not that the necessity of the case seems to require its being noticed. But from what has been stated, that it will be the duty of the Convention to see that none but faithful men are placed, or continued at the head of the seminary, every considerate mind will see that a rational and proper security is given, that the institution will be well conducted. . . .

To the foreign missionary service we cannot be indifferent while we regard the Saviour's sacred charge, "Go teach all nations," "Preach the Gospel to every creature" . . .

We trust the end we have in view, is really the Redeemer's glory; which if promoted by this undertaking, or by whatever means heavenly wisdom is pleased to direct, we shall rejoice. If that end is not answered in any undertaking, the undertaking can be of no real value.

Our commencement in this work is indeed, comparatively small; though, through the goodness of God, more than a hundred churches are comprehended in the Associations we represent. But were they fewer, we have great reason to be encouraged; when we reflect that through the blessing of God, great things have arisen from very small and weak beginnings. . . .

Dear brethren, let us remind you, that this is a time of uncommon exertion among Christians of all denominations, and in every quarter of the globe. Much is doing in the cause of truth and holiness; and much is yet to be done, before the promises of the Most High will have their full accomplishment; that the church may come forth in her strength; that she may arise and shine in all the beauty of moral, intellectual, and spiritual excellence; and that the earth may be filled with the knowledge and glory of God. . . .

Let us then entreat you to give it a serious and candid consideration; bear it on your hearts before the Throne of Grace; and seek direction of God, as your duty is concerned in it. And should it appear to your understanding and conscience, that it is such a cause; we must farther entreat you, to suffer no delay. Such is the state of things with and among us, that we may truly say with David, "The king's business requires haste." Israel suffered severe reproof from their God, when they said, "The time is not come: The time for the Lord's house to be built." "Is it time," said Jehovah, "O! ye, for you to dwell in your ceiled houses, and for my house to lie waste?"

Wishing you the choicest blessings of Providence and Grace, and requesting remembrance in your prayers, we remain,

Beloved brethren, yours affectionately in the Gospel,
RICHARD FURMAN, President
ABNER BLOCKER, Secretary

APPENDIX H

ADDRESS TO THE CHURCHES.

The State Convention of the Baptist Denomination, in South-Carolina, convened in the Village of Coosawhatchie, 4th December, 1824, to their constituents, and to other Associations, within the State, present their affectionate Christian salutation.

(Abridged from *Minutes of the State Baptist Convention*, 1824, SCBHS.)

Beloved Brethren in the Lord,

. . . The gospel ministry is certainly a most important and awfully responsible office. Such is its sacred nature, and such its difficult and weighty character, that even an inspired Apostle was induced to exclaim, "Who is sufficient for these things!" But those, who are opposed to preparation for the sacred work, adduce the case of the Apostles in support of their favorite opinion. The Apostles, they say, were unlearned and ignorant men, some of them fishermen, and on account of their poverty and humble occupation in life were but little esteemed; and yet they were chosen by the divine Saviour, and made the instruments of advancing his kingdom, notwithstanding they had to face the learned as well as the ignorant; kings as well as the humble poor. This is in general true: but can they prove that these men, who were illiterate, when called, did not receive suitable instruction previously to their being sent abroad to preach the gospel? Did they not study under the greatest Teacher the world ever knew? Were they not inspired by the Holy Ghost and endowed with miraculous power? Will the opponents to a regular course of instruction, for the work of the gospel ministry, say that men are inspired by the Holy Ghost *now*, as the Apostles were?—Or that they *still* have the power of working miracles? Surely they cannot. If men are not divinely inspired *now*, and *the age of miracles* has past away, then, surely, it is necessary that attention should be paid to the education of those whom God has been pleased to call to this work without it. We live, beloved Brethren, in an advanced period of the world. The arts and sciences are rapidly progressing.—The human mind is daily acquiring strength and refinement. It is greatly to be lamented that many men of profound learning and highly improved intellect are opposed to the Christian religion, and others to some of its most interesting doctrines. They are acquainted with all the subtlety of reasoning and logical deduction. Like the prejudiced Jew and learned Greek, they are wise above what is written; hence, Christ is to one a stumbling block, and to the other foolishness. Give us, say they, in the pride of their hearts, demonstration, and then we will believe. Now, how are the unlettered, the unskilled in human science, to confront such opposers? These candidates for the ministry may, indeed, be men of God: thoroughly established in the faith of the gospel, and useful, to certain extent, in winning souls to Christ; but, not being able to wield the weapons of science, they are unable to meet the enemy on his own ground. . . .

The Unitarians boast of having, on their side, men of superior knowledge. Their ministers are, generally, well educated; depending on the strength and refinement of their reasoning, they are prepared to throw a mask over the fair and beautiful face of truth, and to make her appear in all the deformity of error; whilst error is represented in all the beauty, simplicity and loveliness of truth. Now, who is able to distinguish truth from error? Who stands prepared to strip error of her assumed garments of loveliness, and to make her appear in all her native deformity and vileness? We answer, the man of God; the faithful minister of Jesus Christ; he who believes in his proper Deity, and whose mind, like that of his opponent, has been illuminated by science; who can, by fair and sound argument, parry the thrust of sophistry, and prostrate in the dust, the enemy of truth and righteousness.

Brethren, do you not perceive the necessity of having an enlightened Gospel ministry? Are you willing that error should abound at the expense of truth? Are you concerned for the advancement of the kingdom of God's co-equal Son? Are the best interests of this kingdom to be supported and extended by the volume of Inspiration, and by the appointment of pious, zealous and enlightened men to the work of the Sacred Ministry?

Then let us beseech you, by all that is sacred and dear to you, as Christians, to come up to the help of the Lord, against the mighty powers of darkness. Unite with us, in supporting and educating those pious, excellent young men, whom God hath called to the work of the ministry, that, by the aids of both grace and learning, they may be enabled to put to silence the proud philosopher, the artful sophist, who would oppose Christ's divine character, and many of the essential doctrines of Christianity.

And, here we would recall your attention, to the important objective of our concern, the establishment of a Seminary of Learning, under the care of the Convention. It is undoubtedly an object attainable by proper exertion, and its utility must be obvious to every reflecting mind. It is with pleasure, we observe that amid the various discouragements under which the body of our Constituents have laboured during the present year, some public spirited and generous individuals and congregations, have subscribed, and some of them actually contributed towards the accomplishment of this design. The great majority of them, however, viewing the various public calamities which have afflicted the state, and the actual loss of property its citizens have sustained, have thought it prudent to suspend their exertions for the present, in the hope of a more favourable season for commencing them. And we are happy to learn from various sources, that a friendly regard is manifested by many towards the undertaking.—We hope, therefore, that by the blessing of Providence, at some future and not distant period, we shall be able to carry the interesting design into execution; and, therefore, request that you will take every prudent and laudable measure for giving it effective aid. . . .

. . . Consider the important cause of Missions, both Foreign and Domestic, and the necessity of giving it our most cordial support.

The Great King of Zion, ere he ascended to the throne of his Glory, gave this commission to his apostles, "Go ye into all the world, and preach the Gospel, to every creature. He that believeth and is baptized shall be saved; but he that believeth not, shall be condemned."—They obeyed, and were the first Missionaries who went forth to proclaim the glad tidings of Salvation to sinful men. Since their day, God has raised up many faithful witnesses for the truth in various parts of the world, who have not shunned to declare the whole counsel of God, and whose labours have been abundantly blessed. It is evident, however, that a considerable portion of the earth is yet in a state of moral darkness. Look at Asia, with her four hundred and ninety-eight millions of heathen!—Over that land, where the Sun of Righteousness once shone so resplendently, a dark and gloomy night has long prevailed. Only a small part of it, has hitherto been revisited with the Light of Life. Africa, with her eighty-seven millions, presents to view a still more gloomy picture!—Even in Europe, where the glorious Gospel has been more extensively published than in any other quarter of the habitable globe, there are said to be three millions of heathen! In America, twelve millions are living in pagan darkness! Thus, according to the estimate of those who have carefully investigated the subject, we behold in the aggregate, six hundred millions of immortal souls living under the influence of superstition; devoted to idolatry, and pressing towards the gulf of eternal misery, unapprised of their awful end!

If, returning from this wide survey, we direct our attention to the interests of the Domestic Mission, what an affecting scene is here presented to our view! How many in our own Country and State, are living ordinarily without the word and ordinances of the Gospel: how many churches, even in our own connexion, destitute, and others very partially supplied?—How many children and youth growing up in ignorance of Gospel truth, and in the pursuits and habits of sin? How generally is the Sabbath profaned, being made by many a day of business, idleness or sinful recreation? And how many living in these circumstances, are rushing on to destruction, and, in their ignorance and guilt, sinking into the grave? . . .

Let us then, beloved brethren, seriously and affectionately invite you to put your hand to the work. Imposition and selfish interest, especially on such a subject as this, we hold in contempt. We do not ask for ourselves: And we trust our hearts are influenced by the generous sentiments which the Gospel inspires. But acting in the cause of God, feeling for immortal souls, and regarding the honour of the Church's glorious Head, we call for your generous contribution. We also desire your counsel and co-operation in all that is conducive to the accomplishment of this work of piety and benevolence. . . .

Beloved brethren, be not weary in well doing. Rest assured, your labour of love shall not be in vain in the Lord. Persevere in your laudable undertakings; look up to God for his blessing, and, ere long, we have reason to believe, you shall see Zion breaking forth on the right hand and on the left, and becoming the glory of our land.

To those Associations, who have not united with us, we shall only say, brethren, we love you, and wish you may prosper in the Lord; and we sincerely hope and pray, you may, yet with us, see eye to eye, and become one with us, in what we believe to be the cause and work of the Lord. . . .

Your Brethren and Servants
In the Gospel of Jesus Christ

B. MANLY, Secretary.   R. FURMAN, President

Bibliography

BOOKS

Allen, I. M. *The Triennial Baptist Register*, 1836. North Carolina Baptist Historical Society Collection, Wake Forest University Library, Winston-Salem, North Carolina.

Alley, Reuben Edward. *A History of Baptists in Virginia*. Richmond: Virginia Baptist General Board.

Bailey, J. D. *Reverends Philip Mulkey and James Fowler*. Cowpens SC, 1924.

Baker, Robert Andrew. *A Baptist Source Book*. Nashville: Broadman Press, 1966.

Baker, Robert Andrew. *The Contributions of South Carolina Baptists to the Rise and Development of the Southern Baptist Convention*. Unpublished manuscript, South Carolina Baptist Historical Society Collection, James B. Duke Library, Furman University, Greenville, South Carolina.

Baker, Robert Andrew. *The First Southern Baptists*. Nashville: Broadman Press, 1966.

Baker, Robert Andrew. *Relations Between Northern and Southern Baptists*. New York: Arno Press, 1980.

Baker, Robert Andrew. *The Southern Baptist Convention and Its People 1607-1972*. Nashville: Broadman Press, 1974.

Baker, Robert Andrew, and Paul Craven. *Adventure in Faith: The First 300 Years of the First Baptist Church of Charleston, S.C.* Nashville: Broadman Press, 1982.

Ballantyne, W. *History of the Baptist Institutions of Washington City*. Privately printed, 1867.

Banks, Charles Edward. *The Planters of the Commonwealth*. Boston: Riverside Press, 1931.

Banks, Charles Edward. *Topographical Dictionary of 2885 Emigrants to England*. Baltimore: Southern Book Co., 1957.

Barnes, William Wright. *The Southern Baptist Convention, 1845-1953*. Nashville: Broadman Press, 1954.

Benedict, David. *Fifty Years Among the Baptists*. New York: Sheldon and Company, 1860.

Benedict, David. *A General History of the Baptist Denomination in America and Other Parts of the World*. Boston: Manning and Loring, 1813.

Black, Robert C., III. *The Younger John Winthrop*. New York: Columbia University Press, 1966.

Boles, John B. *The Great Revival, 1787-1805*. Lexington: University of Kentucky Press, 1972.

Bond, Henry. *Genealogies of the Families and Descendants of the Early Settlers of Watertown, Massachusetts*. Boston: New England Historic Genealogic Society, 1860.

Brigham, C. S. *History and Bibliography of American Newspapers, 1690-1820*. Worcester MA: American Antiquarian Society, 1947.

Brodhead, John R. *History of the State of New York*. New York: Harper and Brothers, 1859.

Brown, Stuart Gerry. *Alexander Hamilton*. New York: Twaynes Publishers, Inc., 1966.

Campbell, Charles. *History of Virginia*. Philadelphia: J. B. Lippincott and Co., 1860.

Campbell, Norine Dickson. *Patrick Henry: Patriot and Statesman*. New York: David Adair Company, 1969.

Cathcart, William. *Baptist Encyclopedia*. 2 volumes. Philadelphia: Louis Everts, 1883.

Champlin, Carroll D. *The Movement for a National University in the United States*. Pittsburgh: University of Pittsburgh Press, 1925.

Clark, Elmer T., ed. *The Journal and Letters of Francis Asbury*. 3 volumes. London: Epworth Press, 1958; Nashville: Abingdon Press, 1958.

Clarke, Philip G., Jr., comp. *Anglicanism in South Carolina, 1660-1967*. Southern Historical Press, 1976.

Cleveland, Catherine. *The Great Revival in the West, 1797-1805*. Chicago: University of Chicago Press, 1916.

Clute, Robert F. *The Annals and Parish Register of St. Thomas and St. Denis Parish in South Carolina from 1680 to 1884*. Charleston: Walker, Evans and Cogswell Co., 1884.

Cohen, Hennig. *The South Carolina Gazette, 1732-1775*. Columbia: University of South Carolina Press, 1952.

Collections of the South Carolina Historical Society. Volume 3. Charleston: South Carolina Historical Society, 1858.

Cook, Harvey Toliver. *Biography of Richard Furman.* Greenville SC: Baptist Courier Job Press, 1913.

Cook, Harvey Toliver. *Education in South Carolina Under Baptist Control.* Greenville SC, 1912.

Cook, Harvey Toliver. *The Life and Work of James C. Furman.* Greenville SC, 1926.

Cooper, Thomas, and David J. McCord, eds. *The Statutes at Large of South Carolina.* 10 volumes. Columbia: A. S. Johnston, 1836-1841.

Crow, Orin F. "The Control of the University of South Carolina, 1801-1926, A Case Study of University Control." Ph.D. dissertation, George Peabody College for Teachers, 1931.

Dabney, William M., and Marion Dargan. *William Henry Drayton and the American Revolution.* Albuquerque: University of New Mexico Press, 1962.

Dalcho, Frederick. *An Historical Account of the Protestant Episcopal Church in South Carolina, from the First Settlement of the Province to the War of the Revolution.* Charleston: E. Thayer Theological Books, 1820.

Daniel, Robert Norman. *Furman University: A History.* Greenville SC: Hiott Press, 1951.

Dargan, E. C. "Richard Furman and His Place in American Baptist History." *Furman University Bulletin* 3 (July 1914): 17.

Davis, William Watts Hart. *History of the Hart Family of Warminster, Bucks County, Pennsylvania.* Doylestown PA: W. W. H. Davis, 1867. Caroliniana Library, University of South Carolina, Columbia.

Dunlap, William. *Diary of William Dunlap.* New York: New York Historical Society, 1930.

Easterby, J. H. *A History of the College of Charleston.* New York: Scribner Press, 1935.

Edgar, Walter B., and N. Louise Bailey, eds. *Biographical Directory of the South Carolina House of Representatives, 1693-1973.* 3 volumes. Columbia: University of South Carolina Press, 1974- .

Edward, George N. *A History of the Independent or Congregational Church of Charleston, South Carolina.* Boston: The Pilgrim Press, 1947.

Edwards, Morgan. *Materials Toward a History of the Baptists in the Provinces of Maryland, Virginia, North Carolina, South Carolina, Georgia, 1772.* Bound manuscript, South Carolina Baptist Historical Society Collection, James B. Duke Library, Furman University, Greenville, South Carolina.

Encyclopedia of Southern Baptists. Nashville: Broadman Press, 1958.

Furman, Alfred Antoine, and Phillip Howard Furman. *Memoirs of the Firmin-Furman Family in America.* Bound copy, South Carolina Baptist Historical Society Collection, James B. Duke Library, Furman University, Greenville, South Carolina.

Furman, Wood. *History of the Charleston Baptist Association*. Charleston, 1811.

Garden, Alexander. *Anecdotes of the Revolutionary War in America*. Charleston: R. E. Miller, 1822.

Gillies, John. *Memoirs of the Rev. George Whitefield*. New Hampshire, 1834.

Goodwin, John A. *The Pilgrim Republic*. Boston: Houghton Mifflin Co., 1920.

Green, J. R. *A Short History of the English People*. New York: Harper and Brothers, 1888.

Gregorie, Anne King. *History of Sumter County*. Sumter SC: Library Board of Sumter County, 1954.

Gregorie, Anne King. *Thomas Sumter*. Sumter SC: Library Board of Sumter County, 1954.

Griffin, Edward M. *Jonathan Edwards*. Minneapolis: University of Minnesota Press, 1971.

Guild, Reuben Aldridge. *Early History of Brown University, including the Life, Times, and Correspondence of President Manning*. Providence RI: Snow and Farnham, 1897.

Guild, Reuben Aldridge. *History of Brown University, with Illustrative Documents*. Privately printed, 1867.

Hart, Oliver. *Extracts from the Diary of the Rev. Oliver Hart, from* A.D. *1740 to* A.D. *1780, with Introductory Letter from William G. Whilden*. In *Yearbook, City of Charleston, S.C.* Charleston: Lucas and Richardson, 1896.

Haynsworth, Hugh Charles. *Haynsworth-Furman and Allied Families*. Sumter SC: Osteen Publishing Co., 1942.

Haynsworth, Hugh Charles. "Richard Furman: Pastor and Educator." *Sandlapper Magazine* (January 1974): 33.

Heads of Families, First Census of the United States, 1790, South Carolina. Baltimore: Geneaological Publishing Co., 1966. South Carolina Heritage Series, number 6.

Hemphill, William Edwin, and Wylma Anne Wates, eds. *Extracts from the Journals of the Provincial Congresses of South Carolina, 1775-1776*. Columbia: South Carolina Archives Department, 1960.

Hemphill, William Edwin, Wylma Anne Wates, and R. Nicholas Olsberg, eds. *Journals of the General Assembly and House of Representatives, 1776-1778*. Columbia: University of South Carolina Press, 1970.

Henderson, Archibald. *Washington's Southern Tour*. Boston: Houghton Mifflin Company, 1923.

Hollis, Daniel W. *University of South Carolina*. Columbia: University of South Carolina Press, 1951.

Hotten, John Camden. *The Original Lists of Persons of Quality Who Went from Great Britain to the American Plantation, 1600-1700*. London: Chatto and Windsum, 1874.

Howe, George. *History of the Presbyterian Church in South Carolina*. Columbia: Duffie and Chapman, 1870.

Hubbard, William. *A General History of New England from the Discovery to 1680*. Boston: Chas C. Little, 1848.

Hungerpiller, J. C. "A Sketch of the Life and Character of Jonathan Maxcy, D.D." *Bulletin of the University of South Carolina* 58 (July 1917): 22.

Hunt, Gaillard, ed. *The First Forty Years of Washington Society, Portrayed by the Family Letters of Mrs. Samuel Harrison Smith from the Collection of Her Grandson J. Henley Smith*. New York: Charles Scribner's Sons, 1906.

Hutson, Francis M., ed. *Journal of the Constitutional Convention of South Carolina, May 10, 1790-June 3, 1790*. Historical Commission of South Carolina, 1946.

Jacie, Henry. *Letters of Henry Jacie*. In *Massachusetts Historical Collections*. Volume 1. Boston.

Jenkins, James. *Experiences, Labours, and Sufferings of the Rev. James Jenkins of the South Carolina Conference*. Columbia: State Printing Co., 1842.

Johnson, William Bullein. *Reminiscences*. Unpublished manuscript, Caroliniana Library, University of South Carolina, Columbia.

Kayser, Elmer Louis. *Bricks Without Straw: The Evolution of George Washington University*. New York: Appleton-Century-Crofts, 1970.

Kayser, Elmer Louis. *Luther Rice: Founder of Columbian College*. Washington DC: George Washington University, 1966.

Kennedy, Lionel H., and Thomas Parker. *An Official Record of the Trials of Sundry Negroes, Charged with an Attempt to Raise an Insurrection in the State of South Carolina*. Charleston: James R. Schneck, 1822.

Killens, John Oliver. *The Trial of Denmark Vesey*. Boston: Beacon Press, 1970.

King, Joe M. *A History of South Carolina Baptists*. Columbia: The General Board of the South Carolina Baptist Convention, 1964.

Kinlaw, Howard M. "Richard Furman as a Leader in Baptist Higher Education." Ph.D. dissertation, George Peabody College, 1960.

Kirkland, Thomas J., and Robert M. Kennedy. *Historic Camden*. Columbia: The State Company, 1926.

LaBorde, Maximilian. *History of the South Carolina College from its Incorporation, Dec. 19, 1801, to Dec. 19, 1865; Including Sketches of its Presidents and Professors, with an Appendix*. Charleston: Walker, Evans and Cogswell Co., 1872.

Lofton, John. *Insurrection in South Carolina: The Turbulent World of Denmark Vesey*. Yellow Springs OH: Antioch Press, 1964.

Loth, David. *Alexander Hamilton*. New York: Carrick and Evans, Inc., 1939.

Lumpkin, William L. *Baptist Foundations in the South*. Nashville: Broadman Press, 1961.

Lynd, S. D. *Memoir of the Rev. William Staughton, D.D.* Boston: Lincoln, Edwards and Co., 1843.

Mahon, John J. *The War of 1812.* Gainesville: University of Florida Press, 1972.

Mallary, Charles D. *Memoir of Elder Jesse Mercer.* New York, 1844.

Mallary, Charles D. *Memoir of Elder Edmund Botsford.* Charleston, 1832.

Manly, Basil. *Mercy and Judgment: A Discourse Containing Some Fragments of the History of the Baptist Church of Charleston, South Carolina.* Knowles, Vose and Co., 1837. Copy in the South Carolina Baptist Historical Society Collection, James B. Duke Library, Furman University, Greenville, South Carolina.

Mathews, Donald G. *Religion in the Old South.* Chicago: University of Chicago Press, 1977.

McCrady, Edward. *History of South Carolina in the Revolution, 1775-1780.* New York: Russell and Russell, 1901.

McCrady, Edward. *The History of South Carolina Under the Royal Government, 1719-1776.* New York: Russell and Russell, 1899.

McGlothlin, William J. *Baptist Beginnings in Education: A History of Furman University.* Nashville: Sunday School Board, Southern Baptist Convention, 1926.

McGready, James. "A Short Narrative of the Revival of Religion in Logan County, in the State of Kentucky, and the Adjacent Settlements in the State of Tennessee, from May, 1797, until September, 1800." *New York Missionary Magazine* 4 (1803).

Mercer, Jesse. *History of the Georgia Baptist Association.* Washington GA, 1838.

Meriwether, Colyer. *History of Higher Education in South Carolina.* Washington DC: Government Printing Office, 1889.

Mills, Robert. *Atlas of South Carolina.* A new facsimile edition of the original 1825 edition. Columbia: Lucy Hampton Bostick and Fant H. Thornley, 1938.

Mills, Robert. *Statistics of South Carolina.* Charleston, 1825; Spartanburg SC: The Reprint Company, 1972.

Morgan, Edmund S. *The Puritan Dilemma.* Boston: Little, Brown and Company, 1958.

Morison, Samuel Eliot. *Builders of the Bay Colony.* Boston: Houghton Mifflin Co., 1930.

Morton, James M., Jr. *Leadership of William Bullein Johnson in the Formation of the Southern Baptist Convention.* Baptist History and Heritage, 1970.

Mueller, William A. *A History of Southern Baptist Theological Seminary.* Nashville: Broadman Press, 1959.

Neill, Stephen. *A History of Christian Missions.* New York: McGraw-Hill, 1964.

Nelson, Henry Wilson. *History of the United States of America.* New York: The McMillan Company, 1920.

Newman, Albert H. *A History of the Baptist Churches in the United States.* Philadelphia: American Baptist Publication Society, 1915.

Norman, Jeremiah. *Diary.* Stephen B. Weeks Collection, University of North Carolina, Chapel Hill.

Owens, Loulie Latimer. *Banners in the Wind.* Columbia: The Women's Missionary Union of South Carolina, 1950.

Owens, Loulie Latimer. *The Family of Richard Furman.* Typescript copy, South Carolina Baptist Historical Society Collection, James B. Duke Library, Furman University, Greenville, South Carolina.

Owens, Loulie Latimer. *Oliver Hart, 1723-1795: A Biography.* Greenville SC: South Carolina Baptist Historical Society, 1966.

Owens, Loulie Latimer. *Saints of Clay.* Columbia: R. L. Bryan and Co., 1971.

Page, William, ed. *Victorian History of the County of Suffolk.* London: Constable, 1907.

Paschal, George W. *History of North Carolina Baptists.* Raleigh: The General Board, North Carolina State Convention, 1930, 1955.

Perry, Richard L., and John C. Cooper, eds. *Sources of Our Liberties.* American Bar Foundation, 1952.

Quincy, Josiah. *Figures from the Past from the Leaves of an Old Scrapbook.* Boston, 1883.

Raboteau, Albert J. *Slave Religion: The "Invisible Institution" in the Antebellum South.* New York: Oxford University Press, 1978.

Ramsey, David. *History of South Carolina from its First Settlement in 1670 to the year 1808.* Charleston: Walker, Evans and Cogswell Co., 1858.

Reid, Alfred Sandlin. *Furman University: Toward a New Identity, 1925-1975.* Durham NC: Duke University Press, 1976.

Reynolds, J. Alvin. "A Critical Study of the Life and Work of Richard Furman." Ph.D. dissertation; American Baptist Historical Society, Rochester, NY, 1962.

Riley, B. F. *History of the Baptists in the Southern States East of the Mississippi River.* Philadelphia: American Baptist Publication Society, 1898.

Rippon, John, ed. *The Baptist Annual Register of the State of Religion among Different Denominations of Good Men at Home and Abroad.* 4 volumes. London: Dilly, Button, and Thomas, 1790-1802. James P. Boyce Library, Southern Baptist Theological Seminary, Louisville, Kentucky.

Robinson, Frederick, and Ruth Robinson Wheeler. *Great Little Watertown, 1630-1930.* Cambridge MA: The Riverside Press, 1930.

Rogers, George C., Jr. *Charleston in the Age of the Pinckneys.* Norman: University of Oklahoma Press, 1969.

Rogers, George C., Jr. *History of Georgetown County.* Columbia: University of South Carolina Press, 1970.

Rogers, James A. *Ebenezer: The Story of a Church.* Columbia: R. L. Bryan and Co., 1978.

Rogers, James A. *Theodosia and Other Pee Dee Sketches*. Columbia: R. L. Bryan and Co., 1978.

Rutman, Darret B. *Winthrop's Boston; Portrait of a Puritan Town, 1630-1649*. Published for the Institute of Early American History and Culture at Williamsburg, Virginia, Chapel Hill: University of North Carolina Press, 1965.

Ryland, Garnett. *The Baptists of Virginia 1699-1926*. Richmond: The Virginia Baptist Board of Missions and Education, 1955.

Salley, Alexander S., Jr., ed. *Warrants for Lands in South Carolina 1692-1711*. Columbia.

Savage, James. *Early Settlers of New England*. Baltimore: Genealogical Publishing Co., 1965.

Savage, James. *Genealogical Dictionary of New England*. Baltimore: Genealogical Publishing Co., 1965.

Semple, Robert B. *A History of the Rise and Progress of the Baptists in Virginia*. Richmond: John O'Lynch, printer, 1810.

Shipp, Albert M. *The History of Methodism in South Carolina*. Nashville: Southern Methodist Publishing House, 1884.

Shurden, Walter B. *The 1980-81 Carver-Barnes Lectures*. Southeastern Baptist Theological Seminary, 1980.

Smith, Henry A. M. "Charleston—The Original Plan and the Earliest Settlers." *South Carolina Historical and Genealogical Magazine* 9 (1908).

Smith, James. *History of the Christian Church*. Nashville, 1835.

Sommers, Charles G. *Memoir of the Rev. John Stanford, D.D.* New York, 1835.

Sprague, William. *Annals of the American Pulpit*. New York: Arno Press and the *New York Times*, 1969.

Staughton, William. *Memoir of the Rev. William Staughton, D.D.* Boston: Lincoln, Edwards and Co., 1843.

Stephen, Sir Leslie, and Sir Sidney Lee, eds. *The Dictionary of National Biography*. Volume 16. Oxford: Oxford University Press, 1967-1968.

Stout, John. *Historical Sketch of the Welsh Neck Baptist Church, 1738-1888, For the 220th Anniversary of the Church*. Greenville SC: Hoyt and Keys, 1889; Columbia: State Printing Co., 1963.

Sylvester, Nathaniel B. *History of Ulster County, New York*. Philadelphia: Everts and Peck, 1880.

Taylor, Ellery K. *The Lion and the Hare, being the Graphic Pedigree of over One Thousand Descendants of John Winthrop 1558-1649*. New England Historic Genealogical Society, Boston.

Taylor, James B. *Memoir of Rev. Luther Rice, One of the First Missionaries to the East*. Baltimore: Armstrong and Berry, 1840.

Tepper, Michael, ed. *Passengers to America*. Baltimore: Genealogical Publishing Co., Inc., 1977.

Thompson, Benjamin Franklin. *History of Long Island*. New York: E. French, 1839.

Thompson, Evelyn Wingo. *Luther Rice: Believer in Tomorrow*. Nashville: Broadman Press, 1967.

Torbet, Robert George. *A History of the Baptists*. 3rd edition. Valley Forge PA: Judson Press, 1950.

Torbet, Robert George. *A Social History of the Philadelphia Baptist Association: 1707-1940*. Philadelphia: Westbrook Publishing Co., 1944.

Townsend, Leah. *History of South Carolina Baptists, 1670-1805*. Florence SC: The Florence Printing Co., 1935.

Tupper, H. A., ed. *Two Centuries of the First Baptist Church of Charleston, 1683-1883*. Baltimore: R. H. Woodward and Co., 1889.

Turner, Frederick Jackson. *The Frontier in American History*. New York: Henry Holt and Co., 1920.

Vail, Albert L. *The Morning Hour of American Missions*. Philadelphia: The American Baptist Publication Society, 1907.

Walker, Williston, ed. *The Creeds and Platforms of Congregationalism*. Boston: Pilgrim Press, 1960.

Wallace, D. D. *The History of South Carolina*. Volumes 1-3. New York: American Historical Society, 1934.

Wallace, D. D. *South Carolina: A Short History, 1522-1948*. Columbia: University of South Carolina Press, 1961.

Wates, Wylma Ann, ed. *Stub Entries to Indents Issued in Payment of Claims against South Carolina Growing out of the Revolution*. Columbia: Printed for the Historical Commission of South Carolina by The State Co., 1910.

Weaver, Rufus W. "The Place of Luther Rice in American Baptist Life." *The Review and Expositor* 33 (April 1936): 135.

Weisberger, Bernard A. *They Gathered at the River: The Story of the Great Revivalists and Their Impact upon Religion in America*. Boston: Little, Brown and Company, 1948; New York: Quadrangle/New York Times Book Co., 1958.

Welsh Neck Church Book. Microfilm copy. South Carolina Baptist Historical Society Collection, James B. Duke Library, Furman University, Greenville, South Carolina.

Wertenbaker, Thomas Jefferson. *The Puritan Oligarchy*. New York: Charles Scribner's Sons, 1947.

Wesley, Edgar Bruce. *Proposed: The University of the United States*. Minneapolis: University of Minnesota Press, 1936.

Wightman, William M. *Life of William Capers, D.D., One of the Bishops of the Methodist Episcopal Church, South, Including an Autobiography*. Nashville: Publishing House of the Methodist Episcopal Church, South, 1858.

Williams, Frances Leigh. *A Founding Family: The Pinckneys of South Carolina*. New York: Harcourt Brace Jovanovich, 1978.

Williams, George W. *St. Michael's, Charleston*. Columbia: University of South Carolina Press, 1951.

Winslow, Ola Elizabeth. *Jonathan Edwards: A Biography*. New York: Farrar, Straus & Giroux, 1973.

Winthrop, John. "History of New England," *Winthrop's Journal*, 1630-1649. New York: Barnes and Noble, 1966.

Winthrop, John. *Life and Letters of John Winthrop*. Boston: Little, Brown and Company, 1869.

Wolfe, John Harold. *Jeffersonian Democracy in South Carolina*. Chapel Hill: University of North Carolina Press, 1940.

Woodmason, Charles. *The Carolina Backcountry on the Eve of the Revolution*. Edited by Richard J. Hooker. Chapel Hill: University of North Carolina Press, 1953.

Woodson, Hortense. *Giant in the Land: A Biography of William Bullein Johnson*. Nashville: Broadman Press, 1950.

Yearbook, City of Charleston, S.C. Charleston: Lucas and Richardson, 1896.

PERIODICALS AND NEWSPAPERS

American Baptist Magazine. Boston, 1822. Volume 5, number 10, October 1825. James P. Boyce Library, Southern Baptist Theological Seminary, Louisville, Kentucky.

American Baptist Missionary Magazine. September 1882.

The Baptist Memorial and Monthly Chronicle. Volume 15, 1856. The Samuel Colgate Baptist Historical Collection, American Baptist Historical Society, Rochester, New York.

Georgia Analytical Repository. November-December 1802. James P. Boyce Library, Southern Baptist Theological Seminary, Louisville, Kentucky.

Massachusetts Baptist Missionary Society Magazine. Volume 3, number 10, May 1813. American Baptist Historical Society, Rochester, New York.

South Carolina Historical Magazine. Volumes 2, 9, 17, 19, 31, 36, 46, 54, 68 (*South Carolina Historical and Genealogical Magazine*, volumes 1–53).

Charleston Courier, 18 September 1804, 19 September 1804, 29 June 1822.

Charleston Mercury and Morning Advertiser, 16 March 1825, 17 March 1825, 1 September 1825, 4 September 1825.

Royal Gazette of South Carolina, 25 September 1781.

South Carolina Gazette, 6 October 1758, 7 January 1765, 27 August 1825.

The (Columbia, S.C.) State, 5 May 1930, 16 April 1933.

MINUTES

Minutes of the Board of Agents of the Triennial Convention. Printed copy, Southern Methodist University, Dallas, Texas; also copies at the American Baptist Historical Society, Rochester, New York. 1814, 6 March 1815, 11 April 1815, 12 September 1815, 1818, 1822, 16 and 17 March 1826.

Minutes of the Charleston Baptist Association. South Carolina Baptist Historical Society Collection, James B. Duke Library, Furman University, Greenville, South Carolina. 1774, 1777, 1786, 1787, 1788, 1790, 1791, 1793, 1797, 1799, 1800, 1802, 1803, 1804, 1813, 1819, 1821, 1822, 1823, 1824, 1825.

Minutes of the Edgefield Baptist Association, September 1907. South Carolina Baptist Historical Society Collection, James B. Duke Library, Furman University, Greenville, South Carolina.

Minutes of the St. David's Society. South Carolina Baptist Historical Society Collection, James B. Duke Library, Furman University, Greenville, South Carolina.

Minutes of the South Carolina State Baptist Convention. South Carolina Baptist Historical Society Collection, James B. Duke Library, Furman University, Greenville, South Carolina. 1821, 1822, 1823, 1824, 1825, 1826, 1828, 1830, 1835, 1840, 1849.

Proceedings of the Baptist Convention for Missionary Purposes (Triennial Convention). Printed copy, Southern Methodist University, Dallas, Texas; also a copy at the American Baptist Historical Society, Rochester, New York. 1814, 1817, 1820.

ARCHIVES

County Records from the Office of the Clerk of Court or Register of Mesne Conveyence, Charleston County, Sumter County, South Carolina.

Journals of the Commons House of the Assembly. South Carolina Department of Archives and History. Columbia, South Carolina.

Journals of the Council. South Carolina Department of Archives and History. Columbia, South Carolina.

SERMONS

Richard Furman

Sermon on the Constitution of the Christian Church, Preached Before The Charleston Association of Baptist Churches, Charleston, 1791.

Humble Submission To Divine Sovereignty The Duty of a Bereaved Nation: A Sermon, Occasioned by the death of His Excellency General George Washington, Charleston, 1800.

An Oration delivered at the Charleston Orphan House before the Intendants and Wardens of the City, the Board of Commissioners and a Large Assemblage of the Benefactors of the Institution, 18 October 1796.

Sermon On the Analogy Between The Dispensations of Grace By The Gospel and A Royal Marriage Feast, Delivered before the Marine Bible Society of Charleston.

The Crown of Life Promised To The Truly Faithful. A Sermon, Sacred To the Memory of the Rev. Edmund Botsford, A.M., Georgetown, 19 March 1820.

Unity and Peace: A Sermon Preached at the High Hills of Santee, 4 November 1793.

A Sermon on the Constitution and Order of the Christian Church, Charleston, 20 November 1790.

America's Deliverance and Duty: A Sermon Preached at the First Baptist Church of Charleston on the Fourth Day of July, 1802, Before the State Society of the Cincinnati, The American Revolution Society and the Congregation. South Carolina Baptist Historical Society Collection, James B. Duke Library, Furman University, Greenville, South Carolina.

Rewards of Grace Conferred on Christ's Faithful People: A Sermon occasioned by the Decease of the Rev. Oliver Hart, A.M., Charleston, 7 February 1796.

Death's Dominion over Man Considered. Cited in J. Alvin Reynolds, "A Critical Study of the Life and Work of Richard Furman." Ph.D. dissertation; American Baptist Historical Society, Rochester, New York.

Joseph B. Cook

The Good and Faithful Servant Approved and Honoured By His Divine Master. A Funeral Sermon, occasioned by the Much-Lamented Death of the Rev. Richard Furman, D.D., 6 December 1825.

William T. Brantly

The Saint's Repose In Death. A Sermon, Delivered On the Death of the Rev. Richard Furman, D.D., Charleston, 1825.

MISCELLANEOUS

Address to the Churches, the State Convention of the Baptist denomination, in South Carolina, to their Constituents, and their Brethren throughout the State, in *Minutes of the South Carolina State Baptist Convention,* 1822.

Edmund M. Botsford Papers and Personal Letters to Richard Furman and Others, South Carolina Baptist Historical Society Collection, James B. Duke Library, Furman University, Greenville, South Carolina.

Congressional Record, 25 June 1980.

Constitutional Principles Agreed Upon by the Baptist State Convention of South Carolina, an appendage to the *Minutes of the South Carolina Baptist State Convention,* 1821.

Furman Papers, South Carolina Baptist Historical Society Collection, James B. Duke Library, Furman University, Greenville, South Carolina.

Richard Furman, John M. Roberts, Joseph B. Cook. *To the Different Associations in the state of South Carolina,* from *The Charleston Association calling for the organization of the State Baptist Convention of South Carolina,* 18 November 1820.

Wood Furman, *Will,* South Carolina Archives, Columbia.

Georgia Baptist Association Circular Letter, 1801.

Hartwell, Jesse E. *A Brief View of the Furman Theological Institution,* included with the *Minutes of the South Carolina Baptist State Convention,* 1830.

Marriage Register of Kingston, New York, 1742, from Furman Papers, South Carolina Baptist Historical Society Collection, James B. Duke Library, Furman University, Greenville, South Carolina.

Memoir of the Rev. Richard Furman, D.D., author unidentified, James P. Boyce Library, Southern Baptist Theological Seminary, Louisville, Kentucky.

Memorial to South Carolina Senate by the Washington Society, original held by the Darlington County Historical Commission.

Rules for the Government of the Board of Trustees and of the Theological and Manual Labor Seminaries, in *Minutes of the South Carolina Baptist State Convention,* December 1836.

Sainsbury Transcripts from the British Record Office. MS, Historical Commission of South Carolina, 32.

Elizabeth Furman Talley Papers, Southern Historical Commission, University of North Carolina, Chapel Hill.

Winthrop Papers, Massachusetts Historical Society, 1931.

INDEX